W9-BLF-520

AMERICAN MYTH, AMERICAN REALITY

AMERICAN MYTH, AMERICAN REALITY

James Oliver Robertson

HILL & WANG · NEW YORK
A division of Farrar, Straus and Giroux

Published simultaneously in Canada by McGraw-Hill Ryerson Ltd., Toronto
First edition, 1980
Printed in the United States of America
Designed by Irving Perkins

Library of Congress Cataloging in Publication Data
Robertson, James Oliver. American myth, American reality.
Bibliography: p. 1. National characteristics, American.
2. Mythology, American. 3. United States—Civilization.
I. Title. E169.1.R7215 1980 973 80-18557

The author gratefully acknowledges permission to reprint excerpts from the following works:

"Daniel Boone," in *A Book of Americans* by Rosemary and Stephen Vincent Benét. Published by Holt, Rinehart & Winston, Inc. Copyright 1933 by Rosemary and Stephen Vincent Benét. Copyright © 1961 by Rosemary Carr Benét. Reprinted by permission of Brandt & Brandt Literary Agents, Inc.

"John Brown's Body," in *Selected Works of Stephen Vincent Benét.* Published by Holt, Rinehart & Winston, Inc. Copyright 1927, 1928 by Stephen Vincent Benét. Copyright © 1955, 1956 by Rosemary Carr Benét. Reprinted by permission of Brandt & Brandt Literary Agents, Inc.

Western Star by Stephen Vincent Benét. Published by Holt, Rinehart & Winston, Inc. Copyright 1943 by Rosemary Carr Benét. Reprinted by permission of Brandt & Brandt Literary Agents, Inc.

"Bernard De Voto: Historian, Critic and Fighter" by Catherine Drinker Bowen. *The Atlantic Monthly,* December 1960. Copyright 1960 by The Atlantic Monthly Company. Reprinted by permission of Harold Ober Associates.

Slouching Towards Bethlehem by Joan Didion. Copyright © 1967 by Joan Didion. Reprinted by permission of Farrar, Straus and Giroux, Inc.

"Population: Back to the Land," *The Economist,* September 22, 1979. Copyright © 1979 by The Economist Newspaper Ltd. Reprinted by permission of The Economist Newspaper Ltd.

Fire in the Lake: The Vietnamese and the Americans in Vietnam by Frances FitzGerald. Copyright © 1972 by Frances FitzGerald. Reprinted by permission of Little, Brown and Company.

Daniel Martin by John Fowles. Copyright © 1977 by J. R. Fowles Ltd. Reprinted by permission of Little, Brown and Company.

Man's World, Woman's Place by Elizabeth Janeway. Copyright © 1971 by Elizabeth Janeway. Reprinted by permission of William Morrow and Co., Inc.

The Culture of Narcissism: American Life in an Age of Diminishing Expectations by Christopher Lasch. Copyright © 1979 by W. W. Norton and Company, Inc. Reprinted by permission of W. W. Norton and Company, Inc.

Main Street by Sinclair Lewis. Copyright 1920, renewed 1948, by Sinclair Lewis. Reprinted by permission of Harcourt Brace Jovanovich Inc.

The Folk Songs of North America by Alan Lomax. Published by Doubleday and Company, Inc. Copyright © 1960 by Alan Lomax. Reprinted by permission of Alan Lomax.

Death of a Salesman by Arthur Miller. Copyright 1949, © renewed 1977 by Arthur Miller. Reprinted by permission of Viking Penguin Inc.

"Chicago," in *Complete Poems* by Carl Sandburg. Copyright 1950 by Carl Sandburg. Reprinted by permission of Harcourt Brace Jovanovich Inc.

The End of the American Future by Peter Schrag. Copyright © 1973 by Peter Schrag. Reprinted by permission of Simon & Schuster, a division of Gulf & Western Corporation.

Radical Chic and Mau-Mauing the Flak Catchers by Tom Wolfe. Copyright © 1970 by Tom Wolfe. Reprinted by permission of Farrar, Straus and Giroux, Inc.

The Right Stuff by Tom Wolfe. Copyright © 1979 by Tom Wolfe. Reprinted by permission of Farrar, Straus and Giroux, Inc.

"Horatio Alger, Andrew Carnegie, Abraham Lincoln and the Cowboy" by James O. Robertson, *The Midwest Quarterly,* April 1979. Copyright © 1979 by Pittsburgh State University. Reprinted by permission of Pittsburgh State University.

TO

James Oliver Robertson and Charles Wallace Hensel,
of Carrington, North Dakota,
who left me an American inheritance

Helen Maud Cam,
of Sevenoaks, Kent, England,
who taught me how to use it

Mary and Tommie D. Harvey,
of Fort Smith, Arkansas,
who helped me understand it,
and who wanted me to tell about it

Acknowledgments

IT HAS TAKEN nine years to write this book, but the process of becoming a historian, which brought up the questions to which the book is addressed, started long before. It started with Edward Gibbon and my grandfather, both of whom told long and fascinating stories of places which were real to them but mythical to me. Those places, as well as the complex stories about them, have become part of my real world.

Two teachers, Professors Helen Maud Cam and Clyde K. M. Kluckhohn, helped me acquire the professional tools necessary to a scholar and teacher. They both in different ways insisted that the use of those tools be accompanied by an effort to understand the subtle complexity of human life and to enjoy that complexity. I hope I have not failed them.

I am indebted, too, to the teaching and guidance of Professors Charles Taylor, Glanville Downey, Erik Erikson, Oscar Handlin, Marcus Cunliffe, Bernard Bailyn, and Frank Freidel, from each of whom I have taken much. Frank Freidel read this book in an earlier form, and I am deeply in his debt for both his suggestions and his constant encouragement.

The University of Connecticut has provided me with students, colleagues, and sabbatical leaves, without which this book could not have been written. Over many years, Robert Lougee, Harry Marks, Marvin Cox, Kent Newmyer, William Hoglund, Edmund Wehrle, James McKelvey, Fred Cazel, Thomas Paterson, Edmund Dickerman, Anita Walker, Ronald Coons, Hugh Hamill, Lawrence Langer, Richard Curry, Bruce Stave, Joel Kupperman, Karen Kupperman, and Nathan Knobler helped me with comments and conversations. Richard D. Brown has been an outstanding source of suggestions and encouragement.

Jonathan Steinberg, of Trinity Hall, Cambridge, spent much time and effort criticizing and encouraging this book, and me. He has provided me with rare opportunities to learn, which have contributed directly to what I have written. And he has tried valiantly to keep me from foolishness and error.

I am also grateful to Alan Stripp and the Extra-Mural Board of Cambridge University for the opportunities they have given me to learn from their students.

There are many people who have patiently read or heard parts of this book in preparation, and who have given freely of their time and knowledge to improve it. I am particularly grateful to: G. Phillip Dolan, Thomas Lambdin, Miranda Marvin, Emily C. Holmes, Michael and Kitty Dukakis, Alexander Lipson, Steven and Ingrid Stadler, William and Frances Ackerly, Walter Plotch, Ethan and Pamela Tolman, Elizabeth M. Gregg, Jack and Lillian Beauvais, David Steinberg, Rad and Leila Ostby, Bonnet and Frank Sornberger, Llewellyn Roberts, Captain Eleftherios Travlos, Victor J. Emmett, Jr., and James W. Rodriguez. Barbara Belanich and the history teachers of Greenwich High School gave me a responsive forum for some of my ideas. And my neighbors in Hampton, Connecticut, have given me remarkable opportunities to learn how an American community works when it works well, and to participate in such a community.

Libraries, large and small, and their librarians have provided me with books, manuscripts, journals, and help, without which it would be impossible to write history. I am particularly indebted to the following: Library of Congress, Manuscript Division; Cambridge University Library; University of Connecticut Library; Fletcher Memorial Library, Hampton, Conn.; Houghton and Widener Libraries of Harvard University; the Boston Public Library; the Santa Fe Public Library, and its Oliver LaFarge Branch; the Rodham Library, Nelson, N.H.; the Public Libraries of Harrisville, Peterborough, and Keene, N.H.

Barbara Fisher typed and retyped early manuscripts, bravely insisting that her pleasure in history was increasing as she went.

The advice and help of Jeremy Tarcher, Israel Shenker, and Edwin Way Teale, and the comments of Eric Foner, have made this a much-improved book. And I thank the fate, and the friend, which brought me to Arthur W. Wang. He has made delightful reality of the myth of the good editor.

Haney and Frances Robertson are ultimately responsible for this book's existence, although not necessarily for its content. That I am grateful to them has, I hope, been often and properly said. And this book would not have been written without the original suggestion—now quite transformed—made by Leonard and Fannie Cohen.

Jonathan and Rachel have encouraged, criticized, and argued with the ideas, the book, and the author. I am very grateful. And without Janet's ears, thoughts, support, understanding, arguments—and much more—there would be no book at all.

J.O.R.

Nelson, New Hampshire
S.S. *Eurylochus,* Piraeus
West Wickham, Cambs.
Santa Fe, New Mexico
Hampton, Connecticut

Contents

Preface

THIS BOOK IS ABOUT some of the myths Americans believe, and the reasons for their believing them.

Myths are stories; they are attitudes extracted from stories; they are "the way things are" as people in a particular society believe them to be; and they are the models people refer to when they try to understand their world and its behavior. Myths are the patterns—of behavior, of belief, and of perception—which people have in common. Myths are not deliberately, or necessarily consciously, fictitious. They provide good, "workable" ways by which the contradictions in a society, the contrasts and conflicts which normally arise among people, among ideals, among the confusing realities, are somehow reconciled, smoothed over, or at least made manageable and tolerable. Everybody likes a good story; most people admire someone heroic: myths are often couched in good stories, very often told of heroes and heroines. But myths are not always narratives, they can be highly abstract; and complex myths, especially in literate societies like ours, are not easily separable from ideologies.

Myths are not rational, at least in the sense that they are not controlled by what we believe to be logic. They are sometimes based on faith, on belief rather than reason, on ideals rather than realities. And they are passed on from one generation to another by an unconscious, non-rational process somewhat similar to the process by which language is transmitted. As language is changeable and adaptable, so are a society's myths; language is conservative and slow to change, so are myths.

All of us are aware of our myths. They are part of the world we live in. But when we study our history, when we try consciously and rationally to understand ourselves and our past, we tend to discount myths. We think of them as fictions, "only stories," "made-up" things which have nothing to do with reason and understanding. We contrast myth and reality; the one is mistaken, unreal, false, a lie; the other is objective, understandable, real, the truth.

But the "truth" about a people, the "truth" about America and Americans, resides *both* in American myths *and* in American realities. The myths are part of the world we live in; so were they part of our grandfathers' world. If we would understand our world, or anyone else's, we must understand its myths as well as—indeed, as part of—its realities.

If all human beings before the modern and civilized world used myths as an essential part of the structure of their understanding of their individual, social, and physical universes, then it is legitimate to assume that we use myths in the same way for the same purposes. Put another way, we believe that nearly all the human beings we know of in the past—from the ancient Egyptians and Sumerians and Chinese through the Greeks and Romans, the medieval and Renaissance Europeans as well as the Indians, the Khmers, the Japanese, the Zulu, the Maya—all these, and all others, used myths and complicated mythologies in order to understand and organize the realities of their worlds. The assumption I have made is that we are not, in our modern civilization, so different. We, too, use myths and mythologies in order to organize and understand our real world.

Since the development of Greek philosophy, humanity has had available to it another mode of thought, another way to organize and understand the real universe: self-conscious, logical rationality. Logical reason is conscious, dialectical, experimental, investigative; it is openly and actively contradictory to myths. Because of the pervasiveness of myths in human experience, the advocates of rationality are in a constant battle posture. Over the past two or three hundred years in Europe, and in the offshoots of European culture throughout the world, modern Europeans have attempted to see human life as an entirely rational affair, and have turned to reason and science to understand the organization of human experience. The result has been an insistence that the modern world is essentially different, that change is more rapid and more important, that our understanding of the universe and of human experience is more real and more true than that of all human beings before us.

The advocacy of reason has led to the denial of the existence of myths, in precisely the same way that the advocacy of one particular body of myths—say the belief in a particular god or set of gods and the accompanying theology and mythologies—has led human beings for millennia to deny the existence (as well as the insight and validity) of all other bodies of myths. It is not impossible, of course, that our belief in reason and science is our myth.

The analogy is tempting—and fruitful. People have, evidently, believed their myths as completely and absolutely as we believe in reason and science. They seem to have felt, in their cultures and in their times, that their myths were as certain, as true, as efficient explanations and organizations of the universe as we believe reason and science to be. If nothing else, we can gain insight into the power of belief in myths by comparing myths to our reason, our science.

My purpose is not to challenge the efficacy or the validity of reason and science. I do challenge, however, the modern assumption that the modern world is without myth, and that modern myths, where they do exist, are either lies, perpetrated in order to manipulate unreasoning, unthinking people, or aesthetic creations, individual and personal, subjective—and therefore untrue and invalid as organizing principles for any significant human experience.

Years ago, Perry Miller, an astute and subtle historian of New England Puritan thought, wrote in *Errand into the Wilderness* that he made the decision to "expound" his America "to the twentieth century" while he was unloading oil drums at Matadi "on the banks of the Congo." I can make no claims to such romantic adventure—although shortly after I began this book I did watch drums of nitroglycerin being off-loaded from a freighter in hundred-degree heat standing in the middle of Manila Bay. I confess that when I watched from the deck of that ship I was concentrating more on the skill of the crane operator and on the tensile strength and possibilities of rust or metal fatigue in the cables than I was on expounding anything to anybody. But I can understand how spending time outside America in close contact with other people can make a historian want—urgently want—to tell what is true and real about Americans. I have had the opportunity on several occasions to explain the modern United States to intelligent and interested foreigners—from European corporate executives to university students abroad. Such experiences convinced me that one could not understand any people without understanding their myths—the non-rational, often irrational, embodiment of their experience as a people, upon which they depend as much for their vision and their motivation as they do on their formal ideologies and their rational analyses and histories.

This is an essay. It is a trial, a foray into relatively uncharted areas. It is an effort to hack a trail, to make a path into the wilderness of contradictory American beliefs. The essay is based almost entirely on the work of historians and analysts of American society. I have put the work of those others together for a single purpose: to chart a path.

The Overture introduces the themes—the existence, the nature, and the functions of myths in American society—which underlie the four parts of the book. Each part then describes a set of closely related American mythologies in some detail. The result is a description, not a judgment; it is written in the hope that Americans might be able more clearly to see and understand the structure and implications of their inherited beliefs and ideals. There seems little question that the myths people share affect their behavior as well as their thought and understanding. And myths do seem to have an important function in social life: they *explain* the world.

OVERTURE

AMERICANS AND MYTHS

1

Where Are We?

THE HUMAN WORLD is a funny messy disorderly illogical nonsequitur sort of place in which most people bumble most of the time, don't see any but their own little bit of logic, and stick to it no matter what the reality around them may be. They often don't see what it is they are trying to do, much less the implications of what they are actually doing. How can you explain that state of affairs to people who function in precisely the same way but who want logical explanations and rational motivations for everybody else?

America is a memory—a memory of the lives and actions, the beliefs and efforts, of millions of human beings who have lived in American spaces, participated in an American social world, and died Americans. The memory is contained in American names—of people, of places, of events and institutions. The memory is contained in stories Americans tell one another—in poems and histories, in speeches and broadcasts, in shows and pictures, in jokes and obituaries. It is contained in the ways Americans behave and in their expectations of behavior; it is contained in the rituals Americans perform and in the games they play; it is contained in American social groupings, and in the political, economic, and religious institutions Americans maintain.

In the American memory are contained many of the truths which are self-evident to Americans, which help them to understand their country, and to explain their lives.

Some of those truths seem to have grown out of American spaces: America is a vast and productive land; it is the most powerful nation on earth; it is a great breadbasket of the world; it is resourceful and wealthy.

Some of the truths seem to have come out of the American past, out of historical experience: Columbus discovered and Europeans settled and civilized America; Americans fought a Revolution for freedom and independence; Americans fought a Civil War over nationalism and slavery; America created a vast industrial world; Americans require automobiles, and energy, and a high standard of living.

Some of those truths seem to be absolute, more like revelation than the remembrance of things past or the consciousness of great space: America is a New World, America is a democracy, America has a special and important destiny in the world, America is some kind of paradise, America is uniquely influential in modern human affairs—for good or for evil.

But we do not live in some abstract land. Where we are is a very real America near the end of the twentieth century. And we make great efforts to understand and to explain to ourselves and to the world what that America is, what we are, and why we do what we do. Our explanations, as we see it, are modern explanations based on our real, modern world—not leftovers from some mythical past.

Michael Herr, in his award-winning book, *Dispatches,* wrote of sitting at a battalion aid station during the fighting in the Vietnamese city of Hue with a Marine "with minor shrapnel wounds in his legs." They were both waiting for a helicopter to take them out, "a long wait with all of the dead and badly wounded going out first, and a couple of sniper rounds snapped across the airstrip, forcing us to move behind some sandbagging. 'I *hate* this movie,' " the Marine said. And Herr thought, "Why not?"

Was the Vietnam War a movie? An American movie? Made in Hollywood? or New York? or Washington? or Saigon? For actors and audience alike, it often seemed to take on characteristics of a movie shown on television, interrupted by commercials, with a rock-music background and a voice-over narration in sharp contrast to the visual images. Was it real? or really a movie?

Both the perception of the war as a movie and the reality of the war itself were part of the peculiarly American realities of the 1960's and early 1970's. Once the war was over, Americans seemed to try to forget that it had happened, but at the same time, they made and watched and even gave awards to movies about it. "The Vietnam War has become accepted as a proper subject for every form of American popular art," Hans Koning wrote in *The New York Times* in 1979: "Now, while entertained, we can purge our doubts and guilts and heal the suppressed divisions of the war years." Or, as Michael Herr put it: "Vietnam Vietnam Vietnam, we've all been there":

> . . . After enough time passed and memory receded and settled, the name itself became a prayer, coded like all prayer to go past the extremes of petition and gratitude: Vietnam Vietnam Vietnam, say again, until the word lost all its old loads of pain, pleasure, horror, guilt, nostalgia.

The social process of explaining and understanding is often very different from the realities of the actual phenomena being explained. The difference is vividly true of wars. "Then and there," in Vietnam, Herr continued:

> . . . everyone was just trying to get through it, existential crunch, no atheists in foxholes like you wouldn't believe. Even bitter refracted faith was better than none at all, like the black Marine I'd heard about during heavy shelling at Con Thien who said, "Don't worry, baby, God'll think of something."

For the individual, "existential crunch" may remain the only explanation, the only way to understand what happened and why; nightmares and the endless retelling of war stories continue throughout a war veteran's lifetime. But for a society, the telling of stories—the construction of social myths—gradually takes on the quality of explanation. The myths create the social illusion that understanding has been achieved.

In an ancient and long-dead society that we think of as simpler, somehow less sophisticated, and more innocent than ours, less scientific and rational, the Trojan War became a proper subject of popular art. The "tellers of tales" of Archaic Greece entertained their society with stories of the war and of the returning veterans; at the same time, they purged and healed. So, too, the modern American tellers of tales with movies, plays, and books about Vietnam. And while there is no guarantee that any great national epic poetry like Homer's will come from the Vietnam War (Homer, after all, did not sing his epics until four or five hundred years had passed—about the distance in time between us and Columbus), still the technique of telling stories in the popular culture and of generating a social mythology about a traumatic war is very much the same.

How are Americans to explain the war in Vietnam? How are they to understand that war? Such questions have disturbed many Americans for nearly two decades. Their answers have been American answers.

"The impulse to escape, the drive to conquest and expansion, was never contradicted in America . . . by physical boundaries or by the persistence of strong traditions," Frances FitzGerald wrote in *Fire in the Lake,* a widely acclaimed book explaining the Vietnam War even before that war had come to an end. Part of FitzGerald's explanation of the Vietnam War was an explanation of Americans. Americans' sense that they are unique in the world, vested with characteristics so peculiarly their own that they cannot be understood without explanation, leads to frequent self-examination. The explanations characteristically appeal to circumstances of the peculiarly American experience and to the mythologies Americans believe, as FitzGerald wrote:

> . . . The national myth is that of creativity and progress, of a steady climbing upward into power and prosperity, both for the individual and for the country as a whole. Americans see history as a straight line and themselves standing at the cutting edge of it as representatives for all mankind . . .

A myth is a story told or an oft-told story referred to by label or allusion which *explains* a problem (for example, "that's his Achilles' heel," or "it was a Trojan horse"). Very often, the problem being "solved" by a myth is a contradiction or a paradox, something which is beyond the power of reason or rational logic to resolve. But the telling of the story, or the re-creation of a vivid and familiar image which is part of a myth, carries with it—for those who are accustomed to the myth, those who believe it—a satisfying sense that the contradiction has been resolved, the elements of the paradox have been reconciled. Dramatic retelling provides catharsis, as Aristotle pointed out about tragedy, which the audience—the participants in the myth—takes to be an explanation, a structured understanding, of the original problem.

Myths often surround, and explain, heroes and heroines. But in modern America, many believe there are no heroes, that we have become either too disillusioned or too rational to participate in the myths that create heroes and heroines or to believe in human efficacy sufficiently to create heroic myths. Yet Americans do have "stars" and "superstars"; there are still national figures in the contemporary world as well as the remnants of traditional heroes and heroic stereotypes from the mythical past. When then Secretary of State Henry Kissinger was asked by an Italian interviewer, Oriana Fallaci, how he explained "the incredible movie-star status" he enjoyed, Kissinger replied that it came from "the fact" that he had always "acted alone." "Americans like that immensely," he said.

> Americans like the cowboy who leads the wagon train by riding ahead alone on his horse, the cowboy who rides all alone into the town . . . with his horse and nothing else. Maybe even without a pistol.
>
> . . . this cowboy doesn't have to be courageous. All he needs is to be alone, to show others that he rides into the town and does everything by himself. . . .

The image of the cowboy riding alone is an image in American heroic mythology. It is available to Americans: it comes to their minds easily, in many variations; it is rich in associated images and ideals; it grows from thousands of tellings and retellings—in stories, movies, television programs, history books, children's play—of cowboy stories which are part of life in America. Almost intuitively, Americans know it explains American loneliness, independence, conviction, and the need for approval, while at the same time it reconciles some of the contradictions among those characteristics.

The cowboy is a heroic type, and even for those who do not believe heroes exist in America, the use of such a mythological image by an American Secretary of State in order to explain his behavior seems natural. Particularly when the explanation is of "movie-star status." Stars and national figures in contemporary America may not fit some scholarly typology of heroes or heroism, but they are part of our social mythology. They exist, and like all other heroes and heroines, they are perceived to be set apart from ordinary human beings and at the same time to be models for and explanations of American social life.

Americans frequently voice the fear that their world is falling apart. The specter of war threatens either imminent atomic holocaust or continuing Vietnams. There is fear that the wealth and productivity of America may decline or cease to exist. There is great ambivalence among Americans, increasingly conscious and obvious, concerning government of all kinds, the Presidency, the military and defense, and the availability and consumption of American resources. There are conscious, public discussions of and ambivalence about the fundamental distinctions to be made among human beings and the propriety of such distinctions in American life—distinctions in regard to caste, race, and sex, as well as distinctions between life and death, and human and animal life.

Many Americans believe that their ambivalence is new in American life, that they are unique in discovering contradictions among ideals or in discerning irreconcilable opposition between what Americans profess and what they do. Many feel that they have of necessity parted company with the past, with traditional ideals as well as with American practice, because the realities they perceive in this world do not coincide with the "traditional" American view of the world and its realities.

The sense that the present world is in increasing crisis, that the wars and weapons, the waste and pollution, the reforms and revolutions, the exhaustion of resources and the economic crises of contemporary life are signs that today's world is very different from the past, has led to a sense that the ideals and perceptions, the interpretations and explanations of reality, upon which Americans seem always to have depended no longer apply. Yesterday's easy solutions do not solve today's complex, sophisticated, relativistic, insoluble problems: so many of us believe. Our world is different; change itself is more rapid, more far-reaching than ever before. Things happen faster.

It is not necessary to deny that there are differences between the contemporary world and the past in order to repeat Frances FitzGerald's "Americans see history as a straight line and themselves standing at the cutting edge of it as representatives for all mankind" as a partial explanation of the way contemporary Americans feel. As a nation, as a society, we may possibly feel the way we do *because* we are connected to our past, *because* we participate in the traditional mythology of America—not because, as many of us feel, we are separated from that past and those myths. Our sense that we live in a new world, with new crises, new problems, new solutions, even new horrors, may stem as much from Columbus's discovery and the enormous human migrations that followed, along with the beliefs that grew in conjunction with the discovery and migrations, as it does from the realities of new crises, problems, and horrors. Does our sense of being at the cutting edge of history come from our ancestors' belief that they were colonizing and settling at the edge of the earth? A belief we have not only not lost, but one we rather fiercely hang on to?

There are no simple answers to the question "Where are we?" We are in a world which we have made *and* inherited; a world which, at the same time, has happened to us. But it is identifiably an *American* world, and such a world is possible only if it is inherited. The inheritance is not genetic—it is a social inheritance: it is not physical parentage and "bloodlines" but rather a matter of the estate and even more importantly the upbringing, training, and education within the family. The American world is a world looked at through American perceptions, explained in American ways, discussed and rationalized in the American language, told about and understood in American stories, peopled by Americans. It is a real world—so was the world of the ancient Greeks—but it is perceived, understood, and explained in ways which are fundamentally American: the myths, the stories, the slogans, the images are socially comprehensible, bundled together with traditions and associations which are pleasing and logical to Americans, which tell satisfying stories and give off "good vibes."

We are Americans in a world we are trying to explain and understand. Our myths, whether they lead us to positive or negative responses—and they can do both—give us a sense that the world is understandable and explicable. They lead us to believe that the manifest contradictions among our ideals, or between our ideals and the realities we see around us, can be reconciled. They keep our ideals for our society and for the world alive in us. And at the same time, they pose the problems and underline the polarities in American society which generate tensions in individuals and give the society its energy.

2

What Holds Us Together?

IT WAS A cold raining miserable November morning in Venice. We had arrived the day before on a ship from Asia, from Bombay. As we had sailed almost into the Piazza San Marco and then up a Venetian canal, and as we had disembarked, we had felt we had come *home:* here was Europe, the West, our world.

We had to buy gloves at least, to keep from freezing. It was too gray and dark to see inside San Marco. So we shopped—bought gloves, looked at lovely glass.

Not once, but several times, as it became obvious to the Venetians that we were Americans, they asked: "What is this holiday you celebrate today? This Thanksgiving?" or they said: "Today is *your* holiday"—dissociating themselves from this incomprehensible practice.

We had always known Thanksgiving was American, but somehow we had also felt that what was Western was American, and vice versa. How do you *explain* Thanksgiving? I don't think it had ever occurred to the Italians we knew to give thanks for the existence of Italy. Or was it really *America* we were thankful for?

America has a calendar, just as most peoples and nations do. It is based on the movement of the sun, but it retains ancient lunar features as well as remnants of pagan and early Christian ritual. It marks days and weeks and seasons, as most calendars do. And it also marks an annual cycle of specifically American secular and religious ritual celebrations, which make the year American and which provide for the annual renewal of American ideals and national myths. In this it functions no differently from the calendars of other peoples, both ancient and modern, although many Americans are not consciously aware of its functioning.

The first national holiday (after New Year's Day marks the beginning of the cycle) is Washington's Birthday, a celebration of the Father of Our Country, of both the establishment of the nation and the Revolution which gave it birth. That celebration is supported in the calendar—and therefore emphasized in American beliefs—by Martin Luther King Day, Lincoln's Birthday, and Robert E. Lee Day (none is completely national). These commemorate the Civil War and celebrate freedom from oppression and slavery, a second revolution, the part played by black Americans in national life. The next nationally celebrated holiday is Mother's Day, with its emphasis on origins, nurturing, and family in the midst of the revolutionary portion of the cycle. Memorial Day follows, a remembrance of all American wars and of the preservation of the nation. Finally, the first portion of the annual cycle culminates, in the summer, with the Fourth of July, Independence Day, a ritual reinforcement of the ideals of revolution, independence, freedom, and nationalism.

The second half of the annual cycle is less concerned with the revolutionary mythology of America, and more with the celebration of the peoples and the land of America. Labor Day, Columbus Day, and Veterans Day all build a pattern of remembrance of the New World, of pathfinders and discoverers, of workers and fighters. This part of the cycle culminates in Thanksgiving, a ritual celebration of family and community in the New World.

The cycle is climaxed by Christmas, an official national holiday, which, if treated in a secular way (ignoring its powerful and important religious significance), is a celebration of hope, of newness, of salvation, and of great bounty and blessings—a combination of many of the dominant elements celebrated in the rest of the annual cycle.

The beginning and end of the year are marked by festivals which are not specifically American: New Year's Day, which is a slightly displaced Saturnalia, a part of Western culture since the Romans; and Christmas, which is an important part of the Christian heritage of the Western world—although both holidays, in America, have characteristics which distinguish them from those of other Western nations. Washington's Birthday marks the beginning and Thanksgiving the end of the specifically American cycle. Both these holidays, along with the other national holidays, are ritual celebrations of American myths. The function of these myths, and the reason for their annual ritual celebration, is to project specifically American ideals as imperatives in all Americans. It is to provide American explanations for American experiences, for the American past, for the existence and continuation of the American people. It is to provide a logic for the reconciliation of the contradictions in important aspects of American life and experience.

How the stories at the core of these myths are told, and with what elaborations and variations, is not important to the functioning of the myths—so long as they are told to and listened to by Americans. The historical veracity and accuracy of the stories is also unimportant to the functioning of the myths. It does not matter whether George Washington actually cut down a cherry tree, so long as Americans "know" that he did—so long as there is in that story a structure of ideals and understanding, a "logic" which answers important American questions.

In 1800, Mason Weems set out to write a pamphlet biography of George Washington, who had died the year before, and who was already being revered as the Father of His Country. Weems intended to emphasize Washington's great virtues, in order to provide examples to the new and self-conscious nation. Not the most dependable of men, Weems claimed to have been the minister of the (nonexistent) parish of Mount Vernon and in later years was almost always referred to as "Parson" Weems. His pamphlet grew into a book, which ultimately went through eighty editions. Some of his stories about Washington were incorporated into McGuffey's *Readers* and were thus imprinted on the minds of generations of Americans throughout the nineteenth and early twentieth centuries. The most famous of all was Weems's parable of the cherry tree.

Seen without the benefit of his early-nineteenth-century inspirational prose, the story Weems told was a simple one. George Washington, as a little boy, was given a hatchet for his birthday. Tempted by his shiny new tool, George went out and practiced chopping on one of his father's cherry trees. When the tree was found dead (Weems did not actually write that George chopped it down), George was asked by his father if he had done it.

" 'I can't tell a lie, Pa; you know I can't tell a lie. I did cut it with my hatchet.'

" 'Run to my arms, you dearest boy,' cried his father in transports."

This is the one story almost all Americans know about George Washington. It is still told, particularly in schools, in connection with the celebration of Washington's Birthday. Clearly the story has something about it which has made it survive. On the face of it, it is merely a child's moral tale, quite as forgettable as most such tales. Yet, for some reason, Americans have found it a peculiarly memorable myth—one of the things that hold us together.

First of all, the story implies the challenge and the thrill of a child deliberately disobeying what must have been parental injunction, or deliberately destroying something the parent presumably treasures. It is a truism of modern American psychology that defying parents, challenging parental authority and parental limits, is a universal phenomenon indulged in for a variety of strong psychic reasons. The tale of George Washington and the cherry tree appeals to that psychology; the myth calls upon the energies of the child challenging the parent.

The story also describes—and by describing in a strongly favorable light encourages—the projection of the boy-child into the world through chopping with his new tool. Again generally recognized and generally available psychic energy is called upon by the story. But it is not called upon in some vague and general way; rather, it is placed clearly in an American context, and in a context intended to symbolize both America and Americans.

The child involved in this act of defiance and destruction was the "Father of His Country"—a man who was "first in war, first in peace and first in the hearts of his countrymen." There is no way to miss that this act on the part of this child is symbolic, as Washington himself is a symbol. It is a deliberate signal that what might in other circumstances be an innocent parable is much stronger and more important.

The child set out to disobey, or defy, or destroy something valuable to his father. Is that father God? or the King? or Europe, with its older, more tired, more decadent ways? or fathers and parents and families in general? Any or all of these are possible, and the unconscious of an American listener to the tale can slide easily through all of them. America will defy the old ways, the established authorities, whatever they are. So will Americans, and so they do; as George Washington did. (In Weems's original tale, the tree, significantly, was an "English cherry-tree," and although the "English" is usually not mentioned in modern tellings, the meaning seems to remain.)

Every American (except those entirely descended from native Americans) had and has, in personal or ancestral background, a "break" with family—a defiance. The immigrant to America had to defy the family and the familiar, in fact "destroy" the treasured possessions of place and family tree and community in order to leave them and venture into the New World. Those who came as slaves had those treasured possessions cut off involuntarily. It was a "chopping down" of the older trees of life, a "cutting off" of oneself from family tree and father's tree. Americans remain fascinated by family trees. And with that break, that cutting off, came a venturing into the unknown, the forbidden, certainly the terrifying—a venturing to a New World and a frontier.

In the story, no reason for George's act is given, only that he had been given a hatchet for his birthday. Very rarely does it occur to an American to ask, "Why did he chop a tree with that hatchet?" The answer seems obvious to all of us. He *could* chop a tree because he had a tool for chopping trees: so he did chop a tree. Tools and the knowledge of how to use them are, for Americans, imperatives to action. So the defiance or disobedience becomes "necessary" because there is a way to carry it out. The cherry tree becomes a temptation, a dare to George, because he has a tree-cutting tool in his hand. The New World is, by its existence, a defiance to the Old; it is a way out, a new beginning, a new experience. Those who came to it defy those who are left behind. They "dare" because they are in a New World.

We insist on believing that the child cut down a tree—the one central act all Americans know as the act of civilizing the wilderness. The trees had to be cut, the great forests leveled, in order to make civilized land out of the wilderness; in order to clear the land and plant it and make it grow; in order to build log cabins for civilized shelter; in order to get fuel for warmth and cooking; in order to split rails for fences to make boundaries and keep animals and other uncivilized things in their place; in order to build stockades against the Indians; and, in a more modern world, in order to have lumber for houses and paper to read from. The backwoodsman, the tree-cutting harbinger of civilization, the hardy pioneer, rail-splitting honest Abe, lumberjack Paul Bunyan can all be summoned up by the vision of an eighteenth-century Virginia boy in silk breeches with a hatchet in his hand—when that boy is Father of His Country.

The hatchet, the tree-cutting implement, is the essential tool for civilizing the wilderness. It is wholly appropriate, indeed necessary, that it be put into the hands of the Father of Our Country at an early age and on a significant day, his *birth*day. In the symbolism of the wilderness, and perhaps often in fact, the hatchet could also become a tomahawk—the man-killing weapon of the native inhabitant and symbol of the wilderness, the Indian. In the hands of a white American it could be a killer of Indians, and an implement for civilizing the wilderness. To use a tomahawk to kill a man was, however, an Indian skill, a wilderness skill which required learning from the Indian, in a sense becoming an Indian and part of the wilderness. The symbiotic relationship of Americans and the wilderness is in the hands of little George Washington as a hatchet which could turn into a tomahawk.

The tree the child cut was a cherry tree. It was a domestic tree, a thing of gardens and orchards, which belonged to his father. To cut it, then, was to cut down tame and domestic things, established and old things, in favor of youth and tools, of wilderness and newness. George Washington, the leader of the Revolution, chopped down the cherry tree of the fertility of the old civilization, the Old Country, the "old man" and his civilization; he cut America away from the protection and richness of King George's England.

The cherry, too, is an ancient symbol of fertility and of virginity. To cut into the virgin land, the fecundity of the wilderness, is to cut down a cherry tree. The boy becomes, symbolically, the Father of His Country by cutting down a cherry tree. The tool-hatchet carries the energy of a phallic symbol.

The child-father refuses to hide his act from the father-god. He is honest. He *intended* the act, intended to cut England away, intended to tame the wilderness, intended to break the virgin land, clear the forest, and civilize the New World. Not for him the dark evil of untamed wilderness. Like the wilderness, he is innocent, but his is not a hidden, malevolent innocence; rather, he is openly and honestly innocent. And the father approved of that honest innocence *despite* the destructiveness of the act. The honesty, in fact, redeemed the child in the father's eye and sent the father into "transports."

George Washington cutting and killing the cherry tree is a paradigm of the young revolutionary, of the American entrusted with the Revolution. The act of revolution is the destruction of the father's treasure, but for us it is significant that the act is done innocently and honestly. Only by innocent, honest destruction is independence gained or acted out. Independence is both individual and national when the story is told of the child who is father of the nation, leader of the Revolution, progenitor of independence.

"Run to my arms, you dearest boy," the father had cried, and the Revolution was validated by the love and approval of the father. The story fulfills the wish of every rebellious child that rebellion and independence will be met with approval and will result in being once again enfolded in the arms of the father.

The tale is told onWashington's Birthday, which emphasizes its connection to birth and beginnings and newness and innocence; the deep significance of the cherries is ritually established by eating them in sweet pies. The way the story is told matters little; it can be elaborated; it can be dramatized; it can be made a parable of Oedipal feelings. So long as the elements of George Washington, hatchet, cherry tree, honesty, and redemption remain, the mythic power remains.

The cherry-tree myth is, for Americans, a clear statement of a logical and moral proposition. It is as obvious as the self-evident truth that all men are created equal. Americans can do what they wish to improve their lot, to defy ancient authority or restraint, so long as they are open and honest about what they do; honesty of purpose can replace whatever purity and innocence might be destroyed. America is redeemed because she is transmuted into the wilderness that has been destroyed and civilized. The innocence of the wilderness is ours, because we *are* the wilderness. Americans have found a new innocence—the innocence of honesty—in the New World. When aroused, they will even try to impeach a President, not because he did evil things, but because he lied and persisted in lying, because he refused to be open—and therefore refused to be innocent and redeemed.

The logic is, of course, not rational at all. It is a function of myths, in any society, that they can—and do—by their juxtaposition of images and metaphors and ideals make logic out of the rationally illogical. They provide, thereby, a tension which seems necessary to human thought and necessary, too, to maintain dynamic human societies.

Myths carry with them the implication that they have resolved the paradoxes and contradictions they contain. Do you want destruction of the wilderness reconciled with admiration of the wilderness? shame at its destruction reconciled to a vision of a virtuous people? Tell the cherry-tree story. The mythical logic is something we seek out and make every effort to maintain; we appeal to it in the face of reason because reason often does not produce resolutions but rather gaping holes in what we urgently hoped was logic. The myths create frustration, because they do not do what they promise, but their near-fulfillment of their promise is powerfully satisfying. Parson Weems's tale has been told for more than 175 years and it shows little sign of decay.

Embedded in the cherry-tree story are allusions to many of the elements in the complex of American mythology. Most of the mythology of a people will spiral in and out of the telling of any single myth. But the cherry-tree story, and George Washington, are quite specifically connected to Thanksgiving by the annual cycle of American festival and ritual. The mythology of the New World and of the wilderness, which Washington's Birthday introduces each year, are elaborated and ritually celebrated in Thanksgiving at the end of the year. The connections between them, for Americans, are inescapable.

Modern celebration of Thanksgiving Day is a ritual affirmation of what Americans believe was the Pilgrim experience, the particularly American experience of confronting, settling, adapting to, and civilizing the New World. Turkey is consumed at Thanksgiving feasts because it was native to America, and because it is a symbol of the bounteous richness of the wilderness and of the sustenance Americans have taken from the wilderness. It is a symbol of the peculiar combination of wildness and civilization which is America. Pumpkins, cranberries, squash, and corn—all native, some cultivated, all plentiful—reinforce the symbolism of the feast. (So, of course, do tomatoes and potatoes—also natives of the New World—although Americans are less conscious of those facts and less likely to see these common foods as part of the ritual.) In the feasting as well as in the family reunions of Thanksgiving, Americans affirm the survival of civilized people and their culture in the New World through the use of the plenty which was native to the wilderness and through the ingestion of the wilderness itself.

Like the cherry-tree story, the myth of the First Thanksgiving is a simple one: The Pilgrims, persecuted in England and unhappy in Holland, took the ship *Mayflower* and sailed ultimately to a place they called Plymouth, near Cape Cod. They met with harsh times and starvation through the winter, while they struggled to build log cabins to live in and hunted to get food. In the spring, the Indians taught them how to plant corn (maize) and fertilize it with fish, and how to plant other Indian foods. When the harvest was in, the Pilgrims had a feast of thanksgiving to which the Indians came. At the feast, they ate the corn, beans, squash, and pumpkins which they had learned to grow from the Indians, and they ate wild turkeys and other game the Indians had taught them to hunt. And they gave thanks to God for the new land, for their new life in it, and for all the bountiful things He had given to them.

The myth of the First Thanksgiving, which is associated with the holiday, contains reminders of the violence and dangers of the New World wilderness. Children are taught in school that during the first winter the Pilgrims starved and that many died, the victims of disease, storms, cold, hunger, and despair. But eventually (according to the familiar story it was the next spring) they learned the ways of this New World and they survived and prospered. The "savage" Indians terrified the new settlers, appearing out of the desolate forests, shooting them with arrows, killing them with tomahawks. But the Indians also taught the Pilgrims how to grow corn. The violence was mitigated by the bounty. The Indians taught the settlers what to hunt in the forests, and what fruits and berries to eat.

So, the myth has it, the Indians (who were, to the European immigrants, the powerful symbols of the violence of the New World) were invited to the First Thanksgiving. They were thus taken in and made part of the Pilgrims' lives, they and their skills and their bounty (and their violence?)—the Pilgrims were not, therefore, in the logic of the myth, taken in by the Indians. And the thanks were, of course, given to God (whom the Pilgrims brought with them)—not to the Indians—for the bounty of the wilderness and for survival in it.

The connection of Thanksgiving to God and to Christianity is overt: thanks are given to God for all the bounty of the New World, for home and family and the good things of American life. The Pilgrims came to the New World bringing a religion and intending to find a home for that religion. So did the Puritans, and so have many of the millions of people who have migrated to America since. The religion brought by the Pilgrims was a form of Protestant Christianity which they consciously intended to establish in the New World and spread, free of the persecution it faced in the Old. Thanksgiving celebrates freedom of religion (as a freedom of protest) in America today, and it reinforces the strong American belief that settlers came to the New World seeking such freedom and that they found it.

Thanksgiving is celebrated almost exactly a month before Christmas, and the myth of the First Thanksgiving is strongly reminiscent of the First Noel: the First Thanksgiving is myth and symbol of a new world, of hope, of salvation, and of a new dispensation. Men—of exotic color—brought gifts to the First Thanksgiving, as others had to the First Noel: gifts of life and survival, treasures of the New World. There were no inns in this wilderness—something William Bradford mentions in his account of the Pilgrims' trials, *Of Plymouth Plantation, 1620-1647.* The native Americans who resided in the Plymouth area, like the shepherds of old, surrounded the First Thanksgiving.

The First Thanksgiving was a birth ceremony much more than it was a harvest feast—which ties it to the First Noel, as well as to Washington's Birthday. It was a harvest feast as well, but the time of year for such a feast is wrong, a fact many Americans have noticed. The holiday celebrates the birth of a people, of a nation, of a new Christian civilization in a New World—a secular, national Christmas. Americans have long been wary of associating specifically religious festivals with national festivals. The logic of the Thanksgiving myth and its juxtaposition with Christmas in the national calendar make the association of Thanksgiving and Christmas very close for Americans; the sympathetic vibrations between the First Thanksgiving and the First Noel are part of the imagery of Thanksgiving.

Thanksgiving affirms adaptability as the essential element of survival—in the New World, in America, in Americans. The assumption of the Thanksgiving story—reinforced by the ritual foods—is that all right-minded, sensible human beings will seek out and accept and use those things in their environment which will contribute to their physical and social survival, and that they will take up such things immediately and make them part of their lives—whether foodstuffs, techniques of building shelter, fuel, clothing, plants, animals, or trails through the woods. Log cabins, corn, turkeys, canoes—all these are symbols of the settlers' adaptability. The model of behavior which underlies the story was first introduced to literature by Daniel Defoe in *Robinson Crusoe* in 1719. That model of adaptability has become so ingrained in Americans that all Americans assume such behavior to be human nature, not something conditioned by their own culture. The Thanksgiving story and celebration affirms the myth that all Americans, since the Pilgrims, are, have been, and ought to be people who survive in a hazardous, violent world by protest, ingenuity, and adaptability.

No human society is a rational construct. All societies depend for their continuation, for their very existence, on common assumptions, common forms of communication, common referents for thoughts and ideas, common patterns of behavior and ritual, and a common inheritance. The stories of the cherry tree and the First Thanksgiving, accompanied by their repeated ritual celebrations (and in these cases, ritual foods), are among the myths Americans use to maintain common ideals, common images and referents, common behaviors.

These myths function to preserve and to inculcate belief in innocence, in honesty, in freedom, in the use of wilderness, in adaptability, in the right of the individual to act freely without restraint—they even preserve and project guilt for destruction and ravages—by their continued existence in our minds. Like all myths, their function is to say this is the way it was with Americans, this is the way it is, and this is the way it ought to be.

Myths, like King Arthur, are once and future things: descriptions of the past and imperatives for present and future. The myths of a people carry what uniquely belongs to that people from one generation to the next. What is unique is not always what is good. Any body of mythology—the Bible,

Homer's epics, the Norse sagas, or the stories of King Arthur and Camelot—clearly demonstrates that. And while the explicit moral of a myth-story often emphasizes what is good, the energy of the myth is unselective.

These two myths—George Washington and the Cherry Tree, and the First Thanksgiving—along with all the images and ideals associated with them, *and* the annual calendrical cycle which happens to connect them to each other as well as to a great many other American myths, are examples of the kinds of stories we tell ourselves and of the functions those stories have in our collective social lives. They are not unique: Americans have a rich store of living, functioning myths. They make us Americans, those myths, able to identify one another because important elements in the identity of each of us are the same, and able, by the same tokens, to distinguish ourselves from the rest of humanity.

The store of American myths is available to all Americans, but not all Americans participate in the same myths. And not all use the same myth in the same ways. While the George Washington stories, for example, are available to all Americans, black Americans rarely use those stories or refer to them. On the other hand, many black Americans use the stories and myths of Abraham Lincoln more frequently than other Americans and very often in order to provide explanations similar to those the George Washington stories provide for others. Southerners use the mythologies of the planter aristocracy to explain their attitudes and behavior more frequently than other Americans. The myths and rituals of Thanksgiving, on the other hand, seem both available and universally used. Even the Pueblo Indians of the Rio Grande valley region, who tend to be highly conscious of their cultural differences, use the myths of American Thanksgiving. The mythologies, stories, and songs which are part of "soul" are available to white Americans, and sometimes used, but not so frequently as by black Americans. The regional, cultural, and group variations in the use of American myths are legion: it's a big country with a lotta people. But those myths are American. They are available to Americans. Their existence and their availability are what make us, *all* of us, Americans.

3

Facts and Fantasies

PEOPLE LIVE OUT OF the past into the present. They cannot see, and for all their efforts, they cannot predict the future. They depend, therefore, on their knowledge of the past to create a rational pattern which leads from present to future. Their working knowledge of the past is based on the myths they have inherited.

Myths are self-justifying. Because they often carry social ideals, the people who use them and participate in them assume that the ideals justify the past out of which these ideals came. It is, rationally, as unwise to try to justify the American past on the basis of American myths as it is to try to justify the past of others on a similar basis. While it is true that modern Americans have not participated in organized atrocities on the scale of those that took place in the German Empire of the 1930's and 1940's, or on the scale of those in the Soviet Gulag Archipelago since the 1920's, yet American efforts to get rid of the American Indian tribes, to enslave millions of blacks, to change the nature of Vietnamese society do not support an argument that Americans have been more virtuous and less vicious than other people.

It is important that American myths be examined by Americans, because only those who participate in them can comprehend their power and their imagery. It is, however, of great value to be aware of the insights of others, because outsiders see things we often don't. Alexis de Tocqueville, Frances Trollope, Lord Bryce, even Charles Dickens with his snobbery, and more recently Sir Denis Brogan, J.-J. Servan-Schreiber, and Alistair Cooke have perceived us, distortedly, through *their* myths and thus made it possible for us to see ourselves and our myths more clearly. "One must remember," Luigi Barzini, an Italian journalist, wrote, "that Americans, like the Chinese, when observed long enough separately at close quarters, no longer look alike." The shock of such a perception, of seeing ourselves as others see us, can often make it possible for us to look at ourselves more clearly. But what a person not brought up in America sees is not the whole truth, because no one can see our world through our myths. It is necessary to see our world through our own eyes, and to see our myths at the same time, if we are to understand ourselves.

Myths are not accurate descriptions of events which actually took place at some definable time in the past, involving people who were alive at that time. George Washington did not, so far as any evidence shows, mischievously cut down a cherry tree in his youth. Parson Weems seems to have made the story up out of whole cloth. The people at Plymouth did, according to William Bradford's account, have a harvest feast with some Indians participating. However, Bradford did not mention turkeys being eaten. The people at Plymouth did not live in log cabins—in fact, log cabins were not used until more than a century after the Plymouth settlement. And Plymouth was neither the first nor even the first permanent settlement in North America.

Most of us are shocked to discover that these good stories are false—and the shock goes from one generation to the next as students are taught "the facts" in history courses. We immediately seek to find the perpetrators of these myths and to discover what vile—and perhaps conspiratorial—motives they might have had, or might have, for telling such lies. Or we seek the fault in ourselves and beat our breasts in repentance for our ancestors and for these lies we have all unconsciously accepted. These attitudes—the attack on the conspiracies of "them" and the sense of guilt at what "we have done"—are reactions to the perception that what we thought was real and true has turned false, has become myth, before our very eyes.

Many of the books historians have written about American myths reflect these attitudes. Some histories are elaborate efforts to debunk myths through logic or research. But the debunked myths seem to pop up again; the stories continue to be told and the rituals re-enacted. The vivid imagery of the myths continues to appeal to Americans.

Some historians have given up debunking and instead have attempted to describe the complexity and the meanings of some American myths or of whole mythologies. Yet even in such a complex, well-written book as Richard Slotkin's *Regeneration Through Violence: The Mythology of the American Frontier, 1600-1860,* the author beats his breast (and ours) for the guilt of Americans in having sought innocence and redemption through violence. He concludes that American innocence has led, inevitably, to the exaltation of "warfare between man and nature, between race and race" as an American heroic ideal, and that "our passage through the land" is signified by "piles of wrecked and rusted cars, heaped like Tartar pyramids of death-cracked, weather-browned, rain-rotted skulls." Yet despite widespread guilt among Americans today about violence and about the war in Vietnam, the ideal of innocence, the possibility of redemption, and the connection with violence remain part of our realities.

Myths are by their nature vague. A myth is often a vivid story, but sometimes its characters are abstractions. Myths bundle together images and symbols, metaphors and models, and complex ideas. They are, as G. S. Kirk wrote, "a cultural storehouse of adjustive responses for individuals" in a particular society, and they are carriers of social ideals. Myths are "strongly reminiscent of dreams"; they make use of fantasy, they suspend or distort "normal reasoning and normal relationships," and they produce a "special kind of logic."

No people's myths are static; there is no canonical version of a mythic story. Myths are accretions of many stories and many images which transform themselves in new circumstances and differing realities. Myths always represent the past—the tradition, the social ideals, the imperatives of explanation and behavior—to the present. In each of them there is a specific core of logic. And they die, they become meaningless, they become "myths" (in a pejorative sense), instead of logical explanations, when they cease to provide imperatives.

But what has this to do with American society today? Myths, Claude Lévi-Strauss wrote in *Structural Anthropology,* have been replaced by politics in modern societies. Modern and "modernized" societies do not need myths, so we believe; they have been replaced by rational sciences and logical ideologies, by sociological analysis, psychological experiment, and scientific explanation. Yet the insights and explanations of Freud and Jung—and much of modern psychology—and even Lévi-Strauss's own efforts to create a science of mythology, all lead to the conclusion that mythical thinking or "mythopoeic thought"—myths, in short—are still part of the human individual psyche and therefore undoubtedly part of the shared structure of beliefs even in a modern, complex, industrialized, scientific society.

Mythopoeic thought in modernized societies is overlaid by rationality, logic, and scientific thought; nevertheless it continues to function. As we shall see, the myths in modern American society provide available images by which we, perhaps unconsciously but nevertheless consistently and continuously, attempt to resolve the contradictions and paradoxes in our lives, measure the world we live in, judge it, explain it to ourselves and others, define our reality and act upon it.

The stories we Americans tell arrange themselves logically (the logic is derived from our myths) around several questions. The questions seem very important to us—a reflection of the power of our mythic imperatives. I have selected four of these questions as the basis for the four parts of the book which follow.

The questions are: What is the purpose of America? What is the place of the individual? What is the nature of community? And what is power for? I believe that most American myths can be understood as answers to these questions. Our myths are logical explanations of an American world in which those four questions have been asked again and again over the past five hundred years by increasing numbers of people who have called themselves—and call themselves—Americans.

I

MISSION AND DESTINY

1

Crusader, Fortress, Policeman, Peacemaker

MOST AMERICANS AGREE that the United States is among the most powerful nations on earth. They would also agree that that power ought to be "good for something." They believe America has a mission and that its destiny is not simply to be rich and powerful and big, but to be so for some God-given purpose. Few believe that America arrived at its present state of wealth and power by accident. Most would and do argue about what the mission ought to be, or about what America's destiny really is, but few would disagree that America is uniquely effective in the world. Americans may be beginning to doubt the effectiveness of American power for the good, but they show little sign of giving up the belief—whether the "good" is defined as assuring a supply of petroleum, destroying oppressive dictatorships, preventing pollution, bringing "all power to the people" at home and abroad, solving the energy crisis, creating world government, or colonizing the moon. Even those Americans who have argued that the United States is the cause of the continuing oppression of blacks in South Africa, or is the cause of the success of Communism in China, or is the cause of war or peace in the Middle East believe America is uniquely effective and that there is some peculiarly American mission and destiny in human affairs. Whether rebels or reactionaries, hard hats, blue collars, middle Americans, liberals, blacks, establishment, native Americans, or power elitists, most Americans believe America can do *something* about the state of the world: America has a responsibility.

Modern nationalism, with its religious sense of destiny and its missionary-like zeal for re-forming the world in the image of a nation and its people, is not unique to America. It seems to have its origins in the Protestant Reformation, the Counter-Reformation, and the religious wars of Europe which coincided with the European colonization of the Western Hemisphere. Nationalism grew and was nurtured, too, by the *philosophes* of the eighteenth-century Enlightenment, as well as by the development of absolute monarchies, *l'État,* and romanticism. It is a phenomenon of the development and spread of modern European civilization, of which America was a part and to which American revolution and nationalism have contributed.

What is specifically American in American nationalism is the widespread belief in the unique origins of the nation. Americans are a *new* people, formed out of a migration of people seeking freedom in a *new world.* The nation was founded in a revolution which was both the first war of liberation and the first lasting overthrow of an *ancien régime.* That revolution created a *new* nation dedicated to the spread of freedom and democracy and equality. The history of that people and nation has been the struggle, physically and geographically as well as morally and ideally, to spread freedom across the continent and throughout the world.

The American sense of uniqueness has come also from the belief that the mission of its people was to create a nation where a nation did not exist. Nationalism included expansion, but it was expansion into the wilderness—into a wilderness which was *part* of the nation and at the same time *had to become* part of the nation. So Americans were crusaders, bringing civilization and freedom to the wilderness. The crusade was unique; it took place in a New World, and it created one.

The imagery of uniqueness, mission, and of the efficacy of power is still widespread in the stories Americans tell. There are Americans who can remember Woodrow Wilson's efforts to fortify the United States and Theodore Roosevelt's urging of "preparedness" in the years before America entered World War I. There are many who remember President Franklin Roosevelt proclaiming America the "Arsenal of Democracy," and who conjure up visions of a mighty industrial fortress pouring forth arms for the democracies in World War II against the powers of darkness and tyranny. There are those who remember arguing for "America First," for the creation of a great Fortress America to protect and preserve the nation as a refuge in a world at war.

The image of the nation as an arsenal-fortress, busy, productive, filled with mountains of the best-wrought weapons, self-sufficient, isolated, impregnable, in the midst of a threatening world is still an important part of the available mythic imagery. It is the modern image of the New World, a fortress filled with crusaders eager to bring the benefits of their arsenal to the rest of humanity (who live in the wilderness).

Dwight D. Eisenhower wrote of his and America's *Crusade in Europe* in World War II. America joined with and took leadership of the Allied Cause, which was a crusade to bring the "Four Freedoms" (of the New World, of America)—Freedom from Want, Freedom from Fear, Freedom of Religion, and Freedom of Speech—to a world oppressed by tyranny and fear, living in the wilderness of militarism, Nazism, fascism. The "cause" was the creation, in Wendell Willkie's words, of *One World* (an echo of the American

Pledge of Allegiance's "one nation, indivisible . . .") by the *United* Nations led by the *United* States: the New World would unite the Old. America, the crusader, was the champion of the people, guardian of the fundamental rights of life, liberty, and the pursuit of happiness, defender of the free world and of human rights.

Many Americans self-consciously perceive these images to be fantasies and are scornful of them. Yet even for them, the images provide explanations ("Others believe them, act upon them, and as a result have gotten America into the mess it's in today"), a logic by which one can reconcile some of the apparent contradictions.

In the world of the 1950's, 1960's, and 1970's, the United States has been, for its citizens, a World Power, the Leader of the Free World, the Most Powerful Nation on Earth, a Peace Keeper and a Peacemaker, a World Policeman, a Cold Warrior and a Hot Warrior, a Nation Maker, a Defender of Human Rights, and a Capitalist Warmonger. The vision of Crusader, of Fortress, of Champion, of the freedom and democracy and happiness (the unique qualities) of the New World, is still the controlling vision, still the primary explanation Americans can find—the logic they find most reasonable—for their sense of mission and destiny. Even the involvement in wars in Korea and in Vietnam, in the Cold War with the Soviet Union, in the "loss" of China and the "opening up" of China, have reinforced the American belief—inherited from the days of San Juan Hill, World War I, and World War II—in the imagery of the nation as crusader, peacemaker (sheriff-marshal of the world), and fortress. Americans have long been ambivalent toward these images, arguing violently among themselves over the good or evil implied by them and created by their real effect. But they are recognizably images of America.

The sense of uniqueness and responsibility, and the isolationist "fortress mentality," are modern aspects of complex myths. They grew out of clusters of stories and images, explanations and traditional understandings, which have developed over the centuries since the discovery of the New World and the birth of the nation. Even the annual calendar, with the celebrations of freedom, revolution, and independence in the first half of the year tied logically to the celebrations of discovery, adaptation, and hope in the fall and winter, reinforces the connections.

The visions of discovery, the New World, of El Dorado and Paradise still make Americans try to shape the real world according to their mythical explanations of it. The logic of the myths combines the ideals and the rhetoric of many American heroes:

Christopher Columbus reporting "banners raised on the towers of the Alhambra," Thomas Jefferson holding "these truths to be self-evident" and all humanity "endowed by their Creator with certain inalienable rights, among which are life, liberty, and the pursuit of happiness," Abraham Lincoln recalling that "our Fathers brought forth upon this continent a new nation, conceived in liberty and dedicated to the proposition that all men are created equal," and even "Black Jack" Pershing proclaiming, "Lafayette, we are here!"

The ideals of crusade and mission, of a national destiny of liberty and equality and the pursuit of happiness, are inextricably part of the mythology of a unique nation in a New World.

2

Banners on the Towers

AMERICAN DESTINY WAS INFORMED, in myth, by one central principle: America is a fresh place, a new beginning, an opportunity; it *is* the New World. True, the crusading nation in its Fortress Independence was born in the Revolution, and acquired its expanding mission, its high ideals and moral purpose, from its Founding Fathers and from its mother country, as we shall see. But the myths of the New World are basic to the imagery and the understanding of Americans; they are the foundations upon which subsequent mythology is erected.

The vision of a New World was first seen through the eyes of Europeans. They were conscious of the brightness of the new as contrasted with the shadows of the old: "I called the new world into existence to redress the balance of the old," said George Canning, British Foreign Secretary in 1826.

Christopher Columbus first brought this New World into the ken of the old (although he may not have been the first European to visit these shores). "Most Christian, most exalted, most excellent and powerful Princes, King and Queen of the Spains and of the islands of the sea," he began his report to Ferdinand and Isabella:

> In the present year I saw the banners of your Highnesses raised on the towers of the Alhambra in the great city of Granada, and I saw the Moorish king go out to the gates of the city and kiss the hands of your Highnesses. . . . In the same month your Highnesses told me about a prince called the Grand Khan, which means in our Spanish tongue the King of Kings, who many times had sent to Rome for teachers of our religion but the Holy Father had never sent any to him, wherefore many cities were lost through idolatry and belief in hellish sects. Therefore your Highnesses, as Catholic Christian Princes and propagators of the Holy Faith and as enemies of the sect of Mohammed and of all other idolatries and heresies, determined to send me, Christopher Columbus, to the countries of India, so that I might see what they were like, the lands and the people, and might seek out and know the nature of everything that is there. And you ordered me not to travel to the East, not to journey to the Indies by the land route that everyone had taken before me, but instead to take a route to the West, which so far as anyone knows no man had ever attempted. . . .

> Therefore you granted me great favors and bestowed noble rank on me. . . . You named me High Admiral of the Ocean Sea, and Viceroy and Governor of all the islands and continents which I might discover and conquer . . . in the Ocean Sea.
>
> So on Saturday the twelfth of May 1492 I set out from Granada, and I traveled to the seaport of Palos. There I fitted out three vessels and got crews for them and supplied them well with provisions. And on the third of August that same year, a Friday, I left Palos and stood out to sea, half an hour before sunrise. . . .

So began one of humanity's great adventures.

Like all those who, before him, had set out to find new worlds to conquer (Alexander, Mohammed, Genghis Khan), Columbus helped create a great myth which was both story and justification of his actions, and which provided metaphors, images, and a logic around which explanations were generated and the actions of many others justified. The germ of what would become this myth was in Columbus's first report to Ferdinand and Isabella.

There was, first of all, the imagery of the towers and palaces of a great city whose ruler went out of the gates to kiss the hands of the conqueror. We call the vision romantic today, and unreal. Yet that vision forms a powerful reality for thousands who see themselves, as Columbus did, in the place of the King and Queen of the Spains receiving the homage of strange rulers of fabulous places—whether those places are El Dorado, Mexico, Cibola, Oregon, Hollywood, or any of the fabled palaces of the East. The echoing image of Alhambra's towers is part of the lasting vision of the New World, from the time when "stout Cortez . . . with eagle eyes"

> . . . stared at the Pacific—and all his men
> Look'd at each other with a wild surmise—
> Silent, upon a peak in Darien

to the present day.

From the surrender of Granada, Columbus's imagery moved easily to the Grand Khan, the King of Kings, ruler of "many cities"—like Granada—all fabulous, all inviting discovery and conquest by Christian Europeans. From the Khan, Columbus moved to the countries of India, and from the Indies in the East to a voyage to the West. He was to seek the rising sun and find the dawn of a New World by traveling into the setting sun.

Columbus undertook his voyage of discovery and conquest at the invitation of those who were to be discovered and conquered: "the Grand Khan . . . many times had sent to Rome for teachers of our religion." Conquest and conversion, as any crusader knew, go well together. The East—which became the New World West—was crying out for the only true religion, and it was a European's Christian duty to see that "teachers of our religion" went forth. The theme of religious invitation would remain a constant. "Religion stands on tiptoe in our land / Ready to pass to the American strand," according to a seventeenth-century English Puritan poet, George Herbert. The story told in the 1820's, of the four Flathead Indians who walked two thousand miles to find William Clark in St. Louis in order to get a Bible, would call forth the formation of missionary societies all over the United States, and would lead to the settling of the Oregon country. The invitation to go to the New World came from the New World itself.

The invitation also came from within, from the demands of faith and the responsibility to proselytize. Faith cried out at the horror of many cities "lost through idolatry and belief in hellish sects." Even should those who dwelt in the New World not wish to be enlightened, not desire true Christian faith, it was still the responsibility of every Christian, of every crusader, to do what was necessary to destroy idolatries, heresies, and heathen sects. One could focus either on invitation or on Christian responsibility, or on both, as Columbus did, but the logic was that the proper conclusion of a voyage to the New World was the destruction of idolatry and the salvation of souls through their allegiance to Christian rulers—Christian banners would fly over the towers and palaces and great cities of that world.

Discovery and exploration of worlds no one ever knew existed were part of the magic attraction across the Ocean Sea. But there was a contradiction in that magic. It was hidden and easy to ignore: if the lands being discovered were peopled, then they weren't really being discovered: people knew about them. But not the *right* people. The theme of "discovery" required a contrast with an Old World, the world known to Europeans, in order to be comprehensible; it required constant reference to European knowledge, European belief, and patterns of a European past. However dim and distorted the European background might become in the minds of the descendants of those who came after Columbus, it was a permanent and necessary part of the myth of the New World. The reality is, however, that for native Americans, the Western Hemisphere is the Old Country. Only for those who came—or whose ancestors came—from Europe, or Africa, or Asia after Columbus was this a New World.

The image of discovery remains valid, however, if the people who lived in the "discovered" lands are made nonexistent by the power of the myth: "the land vaguely realizing westward, / But still unstoried, artless, unenhanced . . ." as Robert Frost put it. It was an empty land, unenhanced because unpopulated. The New World can become, in the twinkling of a metaphor, empty of people, filled with trackless forests, deserts, grasslands, and mountains "vaguely realizing westward," and waiting for the first human footprint. European ignorance and European maps reinforce the image of vast lands stretching westward, empty, the stuff of dreams.

If the presence of people in the New World impinged on the consciousness of discoverers, if those people could not be ignored, they could be made less than human (and moved or destroyed). They were savages in the wilderness, possibly noble, but lacking the essential characteristics of the civilized. They were primitive, benighted peoples, possibly struggling upward toward the light, but not yet arrived. They were idolators, believers in hellish sects. They were innocents, searching for a truth which could only be provided once they were "discovered" by the Old World. There might be people but they were only "natives," and the reality of discovery was thereby unmarred.

Even if this world was not new, the *process* of its discovery was new. Columbus did not journey by the "route that everyone had taken" before. He went a new way, found a new path—and quite logically found a New World. He became the first of a long, long line of "pathfinders." Exploring and pathfinding would, in the centuries after Columbus, become great rituals by which the myth was re-enacted and reconfirmed, and the logic of the connection between new way and New World reaffirmed.

Part of the myth Columbus created was the image of great odds against a few puny men—unknown distances, elemental forces, and unpredictable hazards. Columbus set out to become "Viceroy and Governor of all the islands and continents" he might discover and conquer in all the Ocean Sea, clearly a vast undertaking. He took a route "which so far as anyone knows no man had ever attempted." He set out in three small vessels to travel thousands of miles over unknown waters. He sailed in the dark. And he arrived. Even 450 years later, as Stephen Vincent Benét wrote in *Western Star,* in 1943, the myth was still filled

With something of the wonder and the awe
Those mutinous sailors saw,
Dogs of the sea and sweepings of the dock,
When the Italian devil drove them on
Past all known land, into the utter seas,
Into the whirlpool, into nothingness,
And, after all the travail and the stress,
The mortal struggle and the mortal fear,
They tumbled up at dawn,
Sleepy and cursing, damning drink and bread,
To see before them there,
Neither the kraken nor the loadstone rock,
But, thin with distance, thin but dead ahead,
The line of unimaginable coasts.

The fifteenth-century European world from which Columbus sailed was already becoming a "new" world in which the explanations and logics of old myths were being replaced. The intellectual, cultural, social, and political patterns that had held medieval European civilization together were crumbling before the onslaughts of plagues, internecine wars, "barbarian" attacks, changing economics, and intellectual challenges. New patterns of political organization (the nation state, and "absolute" sovereignties), of social groupings (bourgeoisies, professions, armies, and companies of "adventurers"), of intellectual interests (secular law, humanism, the classical world, astronomy, geography, physics), and of culture (shifts in family institutions and educational norms, Protestantism in religion and politics) were developing. The New World myths became central to the Old World's explanations of these changes.

The New World was a dream and could be made into any fantasy. Its discovery was due to visionary madness. It was also hard reality, more fabulous than any dream. Its discovery was due to superior knowledge, genius in navigation, a high level of technology, proof of the inadequacy of outmoded minds and ideas, of tired myths that had held men back for centuries. The discovery was due to God's favor; it was part of His plan for a fresh beginning for mankind. The New World myth did not ignore older myths; it took Paradise, the Garden of Eden, the Golden Age, empire, barbarians, and even religion itself, and transformed them into "something rich and strange."

MYTH AND REALITY

Hundreds, then thousands, ultimately millions of people came to the New World from Europe. They brought with them, among other things, two essential elements of the vision of the New World. (And their coming was, for each of them, an unconscious ritual enactment of discovery—a literal rite of passage into a new life.) Each person who came, whether in the sixteenth or the twentieth century, whether from Europe—whence came the majority—or from Africa or Asia, brought a consciousness of a world left behind. The Old World stood in contrast, for better or worse, to the New World they came to. The contrast lived and grew in the images the immigrants created and their descendants have maintained. These images started with Columbus and the *Niña,* the *Pinta,* and the *Santa Maria* sailing across dangerous oceans to an unknown, unimaginable world. The second element was inseparable from the first: the *newness* of the Western Hemisphere.

The contrast to the Old World—dim and mythical—is central and unavoidable to Americans. It is almost impossible for us to imagine ourselves on the shores of the Americas watching Columbus's ships come at us over the horizon. We are *on* those ships. We are descendants of the *Mayflower*'s passengers, or of the men and women in the holds of slave ships, or of steerage passengers; we are not Squanto or Powhatan watching unknown ships full of unknown people sail in. It is that which makes the American world perennially new: we see it with eyes "made in Europe" or "made in Africa."

There had been contact with the Western Hemisphere by Europeans before Columbus. While we know that now, we ignore it. Such knowledge makes no difference to the myth of the New World we hold; it does not alter the images around which we organize our thought (we don't want to "know" it). The major recorded contact between Europeans and the Americas was that of the Norse in the eleventh century. That contact was brief, and, as Samuel Eliot Morison and Henry Steele Commager put it in the fifth edition of their eminent textbook, *The Growth of the American Republic,* "The significance of this discovery as the key to a brave New World never seems to have occurred to the Norsemen, or to anyone else." Whatever the impetus which had moved the Norse, and the Irish before them, into the North Atlantic to Iceland, Greenland, Labrador, and beyond, it generated its sagas and it died. Medieval Europe, evidently, did not want a new world to conquer, and our myth makes it clear that we came from a more modern Europe. Our newness has a specific beginning in time: "In fourteen hundred ninety-two, Columbus sailed the ocean blue." It wasn't Leif Erikson. We insist that the New World was discovered by Columbus; and the New World, which provides essential logic for our understanding and explanation of ourselves and our national life, *was* discovered by Columbus.

There are three imperative elements in the myth of the New World: that Columbus discovered it, that it was new and empty, that those who lived here were uncivilized, primitive, and "lower" than those who came here from elsewhere. It is possible to debunk each of those elements, and indeed contradictions are built into the myth itself. But the effect of the myth is that we do not want to know the contrary evidence—indeed, we generally refuse to accept it—and no matter how effectively debunked the myth may be, we continue to believe it to be true.

The New World had long been inhabited when Columbus came:

> O, wonder!
> How many goodly creatures are there here!
> How beauteous mankind is! O brave new world,
> That has such people in't!

There is, however, no evidence that *Homo sapiens* developed in the Americas; the evidence is quite contrary. Humanity has always migrated to the Western Hemisphere. The greatest number of migrants before Columbus, the ancestors of the millions of people Columbus found here, probably came via Siberia and island-hopping to Alaska. Whether there was a dry-land bridge over what is now the Bering Strait must await further knowledge about the Arctic, the effects of glaciation and of plate tectonics. People found their way across, and they lived on Arctic Ocean beaches that are no longer beaches. They found their way southward, along the coast and through breaks in the glaciers. They probably favored a high-protein diet, and some of the oldest archaeological finds indicate a highly developed flint technology, at least among some of them. Although the standard story has it that people trickled down the Americas following food, pushed by other groups or by the elements, there is no reason to believe that these human beings, like all others, did not generate their Alexanders and Columbuses, who led some of their number off to find new worlds to conquer. Human beings had inhabited the Western Hemisphere for thirty thousand years or more before Columbus "left Palos and stood out to sea."

The first peoples of the Americas—we call them Indians—had been as inventive as most others on earth. They had developed extensive networks of trade. They moved from one place to another, concentrated in some places, avoided others, and pushed weaker peoples into peripheral backwaters. They built cities and destroyed them; created great art and forgot it. They spoke complex languages, and developed elaborate myths, rituals, and religions. They lived their daily lives as most human beings do, eager to fulfill themselves, convinced of the singularities of their ways of doing things, and annoyed when the world outside forced itself upon them. Geniuses among them invented tools and technologies, devised ways to build with stone and wood and mud, invented games, calendars, techniques of record keeping, agriculture, textiles, baskets, pots, metallurgy, boats. They had elaborate pharmacopeia, laws, medicine, and they speculated about the nature of the universe and man's place in it. They were self-centered, kind, cruel, humanitarian, generous, proud, arrogant, humble, and frightened in about the same proportion as others are, and they expressed themselves and their emotions in ways conditioned by their own beliefs, languages, and cultures.

Our view of these peoples, and of their thousands of years of life in the Americas, is nicely summarized in Morison and Commager's textbook: "The primitive American" got on, they wrote, "but very slowly." Still, in the millennium between 500 B.C. and A.D. 500, " 'progress' hit the inhabitants of America. They learned agriculture, basketry, and pottery." Some of them began to weave, to build with stone, to make metal alloys. "The entire race moved upward."

All such "put-downs" are generated by the imperatives of our New World myths. They are ways of insisting that America was a New World, if not empty then inhabited by primitives who were far behind the Old World, who could make progress and move upward, who could learn—presumably from older and wiser peoples who were higher and had devised superior things. The people in the Americas did not learn agriculture, any more than the ancient inhabitants of the Iranian plateau learned it. Someone among them invented it—without any reference to or contact with any other human being who had done it before. Based on the agriculture invented in America, some American peoples devised complex political, military, and religious systems supporting concentrated populations; they thereby created civilizations.

The technologies of the Americas were, like their civilizations, perhaps less elaborate and specialized than those of the "older" worlds. While they had no wheat, barley, rye, or rice, the peoples of the Americas had developed and hybridized varieties of corn (maize), tobacco, potatoes, and chocolate—to name a few which did not exist outside the Americas—into fairly high producers of proteins, vitamins, carbohydrates, or pleasure. Cotton was domesticated and used for textiles, as it was in Africa and Asia. The llama had been domesticated as a beast of burden; the dog was both beast of burden and food animal. The proto-horse had long been extinct in the Western Hemisphere; there were no horses and no asses. Nor were there cows. Someone in the Americas had invented the wheel; it provided movement for some toys, but it was not used to do work in any American society. No American had invented the arch, but monumental building using flat lintels, the cantilever, and corbeling had proved versatile and highly satisfactory. Americans had performed a feat of maritime engineering in the development of the birchbark canoe, which, like the kayak and the outrigger canoe, was an elegantly fit answer to their needs.

The Western Hemisphere was not an empty piece of geography when Columbus led Europeans to it. The countryside was inhabited, explored, and crisscrossed with roadways; it was familiar to human beings—just as, of course, the steppes of Siberia, the Himalayan plateau, and even the "trackless wastes" of the Pacific were. But our assessment of that world, the peoples in it and their accomplishments, is still controlled by a vision which insists that it was strange and new—fabulous perhaps, but less civilized, less developed, more romantic, and more primitive than what was brought to it and created in it by the peoples of the Old World.

The European civilization which was grafted onto the New World was superior to the cultures and the human civilizations which existed in the Western Hemisphere—those cultures were inferior: that is the assumption which controls our perception of a world we often label "pre-Columbian." We see the New World as Columbus and his men saw it—never as it was seen by its earliest inhabitants. It is a distant, romantic, unknown land, full of wonders and miracles, inhabited only by "natives" whom we can blithely misname. "It was like the enchantments told about in the book of Amadis," Bernal Diaz wrote; "some of our soldiers asked if what we saw was not a dream. It is not to be wondered at . . . since we were seeing things that had never before been heard of, or seen, or even dreamed about"—except, of course, by the millions of human beings who had built and who lived in all those "enchantments." No amount of evidence or debunking seems able to change the logic of our belief in a pre-Columbian, empty New World, inhabited by small numbers of primitive (virtually invisible) natives.

CRUSADE

The Europeans who came to the New World were united by a fundamental ideology: a powerful vision of the New World and an equally powerful myth of Christian crusade. As crusaders, they could and did assure themselves that what they brought to the New World, imposed upon it, and transformed it with was the highest, best possible achievement of humanity: Christianity.

The differences between Spaniard, Frenchman, and Englishman, between Protestant and Catholic, between Baptist and Congregationalist and Quaker, were often mortal, but all assumed the superiority of Christian civilization over all others and all dreamed of making their civilization even more superior with the riches, opportunities, resources, utopias, and new beginnings available in the Americas. The Europeans were not united, but their perceptions of the New World and the uses they saw for it and its peoples were fundamentally the same. What they wrought was, armed or not, a Christian crusade (as each group of them understood it).

Christian Europeans differed, and we, as inheritors of their differences, are more conscious of them than we are of their similarities. Yet the similarities were important in their vision of the New World. Aside from their basic belief in the same deity, their similarities—so far as the New World is concerned—were not theological.

Being "Christian," to Europeans, meant in the first place being fully human and civilized. It was possible to be Christian and still be a heretic, but it did not put one in the subhuman category of "heathen" or "pagan." There were certain essential signs of being Christian which were universally recognized and which did not have to do with the particular brand of Christian theology a person or group espoused. Those signs were so essential that one who did not have them, however conversant with Christian theology, belief, and practice such a person might be, was suspect.

In the first place, it was necessary that a person wear clothes of the proper kind. Native Americans were easy to recognize by their pagan dress (or lack of it) and their hair fashions. (Color and race as a category of recognition developed very slowly—as did the mythology of racism.) A native American who adopted Christian dress (however it was defined by the European in his locality) had gone a long way to being accepted as Christian. "They wore cotton shirts like jackets, and narrow breechcloths," Bernal Diaz wrote of a group of Americans, "so that we thought they were superior to the Cubans, who go about naked, except the women." Clothes could make them "superior," but the breechcloths prevented entry into the Christian category. Diaz wrote about another group "dressed in good cotton robes, so that they looked like chiefs." Clothes were often given to native Americans who granted favors to Europeans, or helped them, so that they might appear to be the superior sort of persons their acts proved them to be. The Pilgrims gave Squanto "a suit of clothes and a horseman's coat," according to Bradford, when he was going to guide Pilgrim missionaries to native villages, so that he could look a proper Christian's guide.

It was also necessary that Christians live in houses—or at least acceptable huts—and till the soil. The livelihood of all properly human, Christian societies came from agriculture, and from the active participation of a great part of the people in it. Christian life, therefore, required living in permanent villages and cities, or at least in permanent residences. It required, too, long-term tenure of fixed plots of ground. Any other practice, or way of life, was clearly un-Christian, if not worse.

A Christian was expected to attend a church—not a mosque or a synagogue, and certainly not a pagan temple or heathen grove. Being properly Christian also meant participating in and abiding by the sacraments, the liturgy, the covenants of the Church. It meant regulating one's life and the cycles of months and seasons and years by the calendar of the saints or of the Church. It meant participation in and proper reverence for the correct Christian rites of passage into life, into adulthood and marriage, and into death and the afterlife. Other rites, other calendars, other liturgies were pagan, heathen, savage abominations. Few Europeans who came to the New World disagreed with Columbus that here were "many cities" or peoples "lost through idolatry and belief in hellish sects." The idea of being "lost," the contempt for "idolatry," and the concept of "hellish sects," were foreign to many native Americans, but they were an essential element in a European's Christianity, and therefore the European understanding of the New World.

The behavior of a Christian was also recognizable in the work assigned to each sex, in the household, in public, and in play. It was recognizable in sexual practices and in the relationship of the sexes. It was clear in the way children were brought up and educated. Wherever one looked in the New World and among its peoples, it was obvious to any European that it was not a Christian world and that it needed to be.

The Christianity brought to the New World was perceived to be both an all-encompassing ideology and a complete prescription for proper human behavior. The belief and practice of Christianity in this very general sense was held by all Europeans to be the *only* true, accurate, scientific way to perceive and interpret all the phenomena—human, natural, and supernatural—in the universe.

In the New World, the European Christian interpreted his own acts as "right" and "good," and those of the native Americans as "barbaric," "idolatrous," or "evil." The essential unity and vision this Christianity gave to all Europeans made the conquest of the diverse cultures and the differing beliefs of the native American peoples possible.

Columbus and his men were the first scouting party of what swiftly became a crusading, military invasion, an invasion followed by a mass migration. The invaders made use of the accessible coastlines of North and Central America and of the Caribbean Islands which the native Americans had used primarily for fishing and for some local communication. The coastlines provided excellent havens for European ships and so enabled the Europeans to maintain communication with Europe and with each other—links essential to their survival. Had all the eastern coasts of the Americas been like those of most of South America—narrow beaches backed by high bluffs with few indentations and contrary winds—the history of the European invasion of the Americas would have been very different.

The Europeans had open supply and communication lines to their home bases and with each other, lines which were never endangered by the native Americans. As a result, the European invasion forces had mobility and the possibility of concentrating out of the reach of the enemy. They had internal communications (by ships at sea) which were not in danger of enemy attack. The initial advantage for an amphibious invading force of unchallenged control of the sea proved enormous for the Europeans.

Once beachheads were established, the Europeans had other advantages over native Americans. Their weapons were iron and steel, whereas they were met, initially, with weapons of copper, stone, and wood. Native Americans slowly adapted to European weapons. Guns and iron goods had become universal trade items over native American trade routes long before the Europeans themselves discovered those routes. Guns provided superiority for the Europeans, based primarily on their continued monopoly of manufacture. Improvements in firearms over the centuries increased the European edge in wars against the native Americans, because the improvements were always available earlier to the Europeans.

Armor and horses gave the initial invaders advantages which, in more recent years, have gone to invaders with tanks who were opposed by forces without them (as in the Italian invasion of Ethiopia in 1935, or the German invasion of Poland in 1939). Improved guns ultimately made European body armor obsolete. The horse, introduced by the Spanish, quickly adapted to the Western Hemisphere. By the seventeenth century, some native

Americans had adopted the horse. But the successful beachheads were established early in the European invasions because of the advantages gained by armor and by horses.

The draft horse, the mule, the ass, and the ox provided more lasting, and probably more important, advantages to the European than did the military horse. These animals did work and carried burdens, enormously increasing the efficiency of the invaders. In combination with the wheel and the plow, they made possible a more intensive agriculture than the native American could manage, and more concentrated populations in areas which the native Americans were unable to use or farm. Supplies and equipment could be moved and carried more easily and quickly by these animals. And they were, of course, walking and controllable food supplies as well.

The mineral resources of the Western Hemisphere, particularly gold, silver, and gemstones, were of much more value to the European than to the native American. Europeans lived in money economies, based on the powerful myth of the intrinsic value of gold; native Americans did not. A European, in *his* world, could buy things with these precious metals and stones, and acquire power by the use of them. The native American could not. Gold, precious stones, and silver were, in native American societies, sometimes the trappings of status or power, but one could not acquire power or status by possessing them. The availability of precious metals and stones in the Western Hemisphere combined with the "naïve innocence" of the native peoples in regard to the value of such riches to create the mythical visions of the cities of gold, the streets paved with gold, which have remained such an important part of the mythology of the New World. It was by Old World norms that the opportunities of the New were continually measured.

The resource which drew millions of migrants from Europe was land. "Land for the taking" was the dream of peasant and gentleman alike in the Old World. Land meant agriculture, crops, surpluses, rents, food in the belly, and riches; it meant place and position, status and power, security and continuity. Land was something for which a European was willing to kill or be killed if necessary, because it was that which gave him identity and purpose: A true Christian had place and status because of the possession of land. It was a resource which the New World offered in limitless abundance, so it seemed. Native American beliefs about land and the possession of land were diverse, but only a few had that compulsion to hold particular plots of ground. That compulsion, backed by the technology available to the European, made the invader a persistent and formidable competitor.

The native Americans adapted some of the tools, technologies, and attitudes of the Europeans, sometimes under coercion and sometimes according to the felt needs of their own cultures. Only slowly did most of them become aware that they were threatened by no less than extinction; and even when that awareness came, it did not necessarily bring with it a willingness to adapt to the ways of the Europeans. Very often it led to a determination to fight the Europeans, whatever the odds and whatever the cost.

The invasion and conquest of the Americas took four hundred years. The wars that accompanied the conquest were rarely fought simply between Europeans on one side and Americans on the other, but rather between specific groups of each. One group of native Americans might join one group of Europeans to fight another group of Americans—as some of the peoples of Mexico joined the Spaniards to fight the Aztecs. Or native Americans might join one group of Europeans to fight another group of Europeans—as the Huron joined the French to fight the British in the mid-eighteenth century. Neither the Europeans nor the Americans were, in fact, one nation or one people; both were divided by language and culture. Only much later did those who lived in the United States of America try to realize a dream of one people and one nation.

Yet it was a formidable combination of visions and images, "hardware," ideals, and desires that first appeared on the horizon of the Americas with those three small ships in the autumn of 1492. That combination made Spain, a recently united set of little kingdoms on the periphery of Europe, the envy of all Europe. Later, vast, imperial sixteenth-century Spain, sprawled over half the globe, possessing riches and glory, became yet another of the powerful images contained in the myth of the New World: America was an imperial paradise.

The elements in the mythology of the New World are, when looked at separately, a chaotic jumble of visions and images, ideals, metaphors, hopes, and dreams. Their repeated association with one another, in endless tellings and retellings over the hundreds of years since Columbus, have given them the active, imperative effect of being logically connected with one another in reasonable and necessary ways. Through our stories, histories, novels, poems, dramas, we *know* the New World is fresh, innocent, wild, and empty in contrast to the decadent, sinful, teeming civilizations of the Old World. The New World is Paradise regained and refurbished; it is Utopia, El Dorado, Atlantis, Eden. The Old World, by contrast, is Paradise lost, the tower of Babel, and the fleshpots of Rome. The Old World has the great responsibility to carry to the New proper Christian faith, and to give the New World civilization, humane values, and decent ways of behaving. The New World invites the beneficent faith and high culture of the Old, and fiercely clings to its barbarous ways, its heathen beliefs, and its savage innocence. The New World is populated, traveled, and inhabited, yet it invites discovery, exploration, and migration because it is untrammeled, available, and rich.

The magic of the myth, the force which holds people to belief and drives them to act on it, comes from all the contradictory images bound up in it: puny little men on tiny ships making their way by uncharted routes across vast and furious oceans to continents never before dreamed of; strange peoples and fabled cities, in great forests, among sparkling mountains, on rich prairies, invite *and* defy the efforts of men from the Old World to find them, understand them, and conquer them. The myth is an imperial vision of paradise, of the kingdom of heaven on earth *and* made earthly. It gives permission to break with an Old World and its ways, to break the chains of the past and to seek something new, something better. In the New World of pagan peoples and un-Christian, uncivilized lands, there was—and is—and will be—more opportunity for better ends.

People could come to and live in the New World legitimately seeking to break with the Old because it was the New World, because it was America. They could come and break restraints, as they saw them, on ideas or on greed, on religion or politics. They could come and perfect institutions they saw as corrupt or decayed or imperfect. They could break the restrictions of birth and class imposed by an old order, an *ancien régime.* They would always compare and contrast the New World to the Old, and many would come to the New World only to improve themselves in the eyes of the Old.

Thus, in reality, Columbus discovered a new world of the mind. By his discovery, and the swift growth of the myth, a world was created in which the human mind did not need to be limited by the barriers of geography, a world in which human knowledge, human past, and the memory of all human experience and inventiveness could be available to any human being. Such a world was as new to Europeans as it was to Incas or Aztecs or Chinese. The barriers between groups were not only geographical, however, and the potentialities of such a new world would be realized only by the destruction of myriads of old worlds—safe, human, predictable worlds found and destroyed by the Europeans. It was Europeans who created the vision of the New World, and it was their vision which would gradually and painfully be imposed on the natives of the Western Hemisphere—as it has been and is still being, equally gradually and equally painfully, imposed upon the rest of the human world.

The myth of the New World is a glittering vision still. It is part of the world of Americans because they believe America to be the New World. The grandeur and the potentialities of the mythology are still obvious to Americans. As Frances FitzGerald wrote in *Fire in the Lake* about the national myth, Americans have always had before them

> . . .a seemingly unlimited physical space—a view of mountains, deserts, and prairies into which a man might move (or imagine moving) to escape the old society and create a new world for himself. The impulse to escape, the drive to conquest and expansion, was never contradicted in America. . . . Ameri-

> cans ignore history, for to them everything has always seemed new under the sun. . . . Americans . . . believe in the future as if it were a religion; they believe that there is nothing they cannot accomplish, that solutions wait somewhere for all problems, like brides.

The original "bride" that awaited was the New World itself. However blinding the vision it presented and presents, it drew millions of human beings from Europe, from Asia, and from Africa, who, with Columbus, "stood out to sea, half an hour before sunrise . . ." and who are now Americans.

3

No Friends to Welcome Them

THE ARMED CRUSADE to create a Christian empire and the expansion of civilized people into the limitless wilderness are both images central to American mythology. The "drive to conquest and expansion" *and* the national mission to spread liberty, democracy, and the pursuit of happiness through the world are supported by those images. But America is a new nation in a New World, so Americans believe. If the Christian crusade to civilizc the wilderness of the New World succeeded, then logically both "new" world and wilderness must have disappeared, must have become "old" and civilized. Yet in American myths they did not: America still has a mission into the wilderness; America *is* a New World and will redress the balance of the old. What is the mythic logic which reconciles this great contradiction, the simultaneous existence of American civilization and New World wilderness?

The logic, as we have seen, is ritually celebrated every Thanksgiving. Wilderness and civilization are reconciled in the peculiarly adaptable American. Out of the crusade Columbus began, and out of the Protestant, Puritan mission into the wilderness, has come a new kind of human being: the American. The American has, does, will *adapt* civilization and wilderness to each other. In the mythic process of adaptation, the wilderness can be civilized, civilization can be improved, and the wilderness can be preserved; thus neither civilization nor wilderness is destroyed. All that is required are Americans who "believe that there is nothing they cannot accomplish, that solutions wait somewhere for all problems, like brides."

Myths are attractive because they offer, and really seem to deliver, the possibility of eating one's cake and having it, too. As E. M. Forster wrote in *A Passage to India:* "Nonsense of this type is more difficult to combat than a solid lie. It hides in rubbish heaps and moves when no one is looking." But myths are not perceived as nonsense by the people to whom they belong. "The images in which" myths live, according to philosopher Ernst Cassirer in *The Myth of the State,* "are not *known* as images. They are not regarded as symbols but as realities. This reality cannot be rejected or criticized; it has to be accepted in a passive way." We accept the myths which affirm our belief that by adaptability we can reconcile civilization and wilderness—and we annually reaffirm them at Thanksgiving.

Yet were all the people who came to the New World so adaptable? Had they come intending to give up their accustomed ways, the food they knew how to grow and eat, the ideas they held about life and work, the sense they had of being civilized people? They knew they were coming to a New World, but how different did they expect it to be from the world they left behind? What *was* this wilderness?

The process of discovering the wilderness and somehow reconciling it to civilized life began, in American mythology, when the first settlers faced the new land. William Bradford, ten years after he and the other *Mayflower* passengers landed, described what they faced and how they felt:

> They had now no friends to welcome them nor inns to entertain or refresh their weatherbeaten bodies; no houses or much less towns to repair to, to seek for succour. . . . Savage barbarians, when they met with them . . . were readier to fill their sides full of arrows than otherwise.

There was no recognizable human life, no communities, no refreshment, welcome, or help in this New World. Nature itself was unfriendly:

> . . . It was winter, and they that know the winters of that country know them to be sharp and violent, and subject to cruel and fierce storms, dangerous to travel to known places, much more to search an unknown coast.

And the country they expected to live in was horrifying:

> . . . What could they see but a hideous and desolate wilderness, full of wild beasts and wild men—and what multitudes there might be of them they knew not. Neither could they, as it were, go up to the top of Pisgah to view from this wilderness a more goodly country to feed their hopes; for which way soever they turned their eyes . . . they could have little solace or content in respect of any outward objects. . . . The whole country, full of woods and thickets, represented a wild and savage hue.

The settlers had cut themselves off from their old, familiar world. "If they looked behind them, there was the mighty ocean which they had passed," and the ocean, along with the difficult, dangerous journey across it, was "a main bar and gulf to separate them from all the civil parts of the world." They had little hope of supply or help from the Old World. They were isolated and alone in the wilderness.

They could look only to God for help: "What could now sustain them but the Spirit of God and His grace?" Bradford asked. But they also looked to their children, and those who came after them, to reaffirm and carry out the "errand into the wilderness" that God had sent them on. "May not and ought not," Bradford concluded, "the children of these fathers rightly say:

> "Our fathers were Englishmen which came over this great ocean, and were ready to perish in this wilderness; but they cried to the Lord, and He heard their voice and looked on their adversity."

It is possible for us now, more than 350 years later, to look at the situation of these and the many other immigrants to America as a set of rational problems and to sift the evidence they left behind in order to discover the solutions they devised. But they had no such opportunity. The problems they had and their implications were only gradually unfolded over generations, and the solutions, too, were developed very slowly with considerable physical and spiritual anguish.

Bradford stated the central problems. First, there were "no friends to welcome them." Second, there was cruel and violent nature in a "hideous and desolate wilderness" to confront and civilize. They were, furthermore, cut off from "the civil parts of the world," separated from all that was familiar and good. They were also unable to explain their circumstances or find any rationale for what happened to them except by appealing to God and depending on posterity to fulfill their mission. Each of these problems was complicated by the realities of existence and the frequent conflict of those realities with the expectations and beliefs the immigrants brought from their Old World. And none of the problems was separable from the others.

There were not only no welcoming friends, but many of the friends who sailed with them did not survive. Five thousand immigrants came to Virginia between 1606 and 1623 to establish the first successful English colony in North America. The Virginia Company began to send women and children to the colony after 1619 in order to increase the population and provide some stability in the lives of the predominantly male colonists. One hundred and forty unmarried women were sent in the Company's ships by 1622. Three years later 105 of those women were dead, and the population of the colony, out of the five thousand immigrants who had come, was *one thousand* souls.

More than half the *Mayflower*'s passengers were dead within seven months of their arrival. In the first winter (1629–30) of the great Puritan migration to Massachusetts Bay, there was "not a house," as Samuel Sewall wrote in his *Diary,* "where there is not one dead." Infant mortality was high; there were many widows and widowers; remarriages and recombinations of pieces of families were commonplace.

As a result, families in the New World could not be relied on to give a sense of security or permanence to the colonist or to the later pioneer. Families were small and the work of settlement was harsh. Young people tended to leave home as soon as they could. Servants and laborers, when they could be obtained, lived as part of the family, but they were in great demand and the availability of land constantly lured them away. They contributed to the crowding of the household, and their comings and goings to the impermanence of the family. Houses were tiny, poorly constructed, crowded, and dirty. In the early stages of any settlement, the houses themselves were impermanent, generally slapped together to provide the minimum necessary protection while the work of getting food proceeded.

Part of the welcome all immigrants expected in the New World included the familiar patterns and institutions that had always surrounded their everyday lives. Few were conscious of those patterns; all simply assumed they existed. Most immigrants came to America intending to better themselves and some of their institutions. They may have wanted to become rich and rise in the world, but they also expected that there would be an existing upper class which behaved in known ways. They may have intended to purify a Church, but this postulated the continuous existence of a Church to purify. They may have come because they wanted land, but "land" meant to them fields and hedgerows, cottages among neighboring cottages, villages with people about, mills, markets, and churches. Even if such things did not exist in their expectations of the New World (and it took a considerable act of imagination for them *not* to), they expected to be able to build them and then have them function as those things did in the familiar world. Yet they found nothing. Everything was chaotic, disordered, unstable.

Most of the people who came to the New World were young, unmarried, and landless; their ambition was to reconstitute a familiar village and community life, but with each one owning land. As young people, they had to add to the chaotic experience they faced their own lack of experience with the full content and operation of the patterns of the community life they wanted to rebuild. They had few of the specialized skills necessary to produce the material life of communities. And they ordinarily lacked the older relatives, servants, and apprentices who were a normal part of Old World family life, at the same time that there were more tasks to perform. "Civilized" patterns of education, training, and apprenticeship fell apart in America because there were no specialists to attend to them, and because the migrants themselves imperfectly understood those patterns.

Many of the settlers became acutely aware that they failed somehow, at each stage of their efforts, to reconstruct a proper, civilized life. This sense of failure drove them to seek explanations: despite all their efforts and intentions, their lives seemed to be falling apart. Why? Because this New World was a wilderness, a desert; an empty terrifying place, which, while empty, was at the same time filled with demons and dangers and destruction. Out of their frustrations they created the myth of the New World wilderness, and the necessity of violence against it and all it contained.

Most of the migrants (at least until late in the nineteenth century) sought land, intending to settle on it. There was a great deal of land in the wilderness, yet it was anything but "settling." Rather than the stability and civilized organization they believed it would bring, the land itself was the cause of great anxiety. They had never seen anything like it. It was uncultivated and covered with trees (west of the Mississippi it was covered with grass). None of the things which meant "land" to them were to be found anywhere. Yet it continued to lure them, and their children, and streams of newcomers. Land was a continual temptation to people who thought of "real" property, "real" security, and "real" status almost solely as "real" estate. The vast lands available provided the possibility of escape from difficult or intolerable circumstances (although the escape was often fantasy, especially for people who did not have the capital or the skills to clear and exploit the land). Thus the land itself was a constant threat to the stability of family and community.

Social life could not be stable when it was postulated on the inheritance and husbanding of particular pieces of land while there was all that land available. Sons did not wait for inheritance, nor did they have to; laborers were not tied to landowners, because there was so much unowned land that could be worked and possessed. Even the rich who owned land could assure their wealth and increase it only by possessing more land.

The lack of friends, houses, inns, towns, and all that those things meant, was not limited to the very earliest colonists. Every time a new area was opened to settlement, every time someone went into the wilderness to carve out a farm, every time a new immigrant arrived even in an older settlement, the experience was repeated. The problem Bradford perceived, that they had "no friends to welcome them," remained a problem of American life so long as there was a frontier or new immigrants. It was a problem the myth of wilderness helped them understand and explain.

The Americans did not solve the problem without confronting the "hideous and desolate wilderness, full of wild beasts and wild men." A wilderness, to seventeenth-century Englishmen, was a "desert," and both terms were used to describe a place which was unusable by civilized human beings (the Great Plains would be called "the Great American Desert" through much of the nineteenth century for the same reasons).

Wilderness had to be actively civilized before it could be used, and the settlers turned themselves to that task reluctantly. The wilderness was threatening. Its violence could destroy them utterly. It could defeat their efforts to civilize it. It might, somehow, turn them into savage barbarians in the image of its own native inhabitants. But they wanted the land, with the sustenance and wealth only land could produce, and they could get it only by attacking the wilderness.

"The whole country, full of woods and thickets," was forested. There were some natural clearings and some which the Indians had made, but generally there were forests of "wild and savage hue." For most Europeans, forests were mysterious places, dark and suggestive of evil, the dwelling places of strange and frightening beings. In them dwelt witches, cannibals, savages, and ferocious animals. The fairy tales Americans still tell their children are full of mysterious (but identifiably European) forests. In reality, European forests usually belonged to kings and nobles, and woe to those who hunted in them or took wood without permission. Even for those few Europeans familiar with forests, they were fairly clear and kept-up places through which people could ride or walk and in which they could hunt (or poach) familiar animals. American forests were impenetrable, except by the fearsome Indians. And they covered most of the land.

As the European myths the settlers brought with them predicted, the forests were inhabited with savage and incomprehensible beings who could appear and disappear by means unknown to civilized people. These beings lived in strange places and did mysterious things. And they might attack at any moment. Yet they were, at the same time, often kind and curious, generous with their food and their shelter. They were wonderfully skilled at finding food, at making what they needed, and at finding their way. They seemed, at times, innocent and even noble. The early settlers called their leaders "kings" (later Americans would call them "chiefs"), called their settlements "cities" or "villages," and tried thereby to make them comprehensible. If Pocahontas was a "princess," an immigrant from Europe knew how to think about her. If "King Philip" waged war against the New England colonies, the colonists knew how to deal with an aggressive foreign king. The idea that a social structure might be completely different from the European model was almost as intolerable as the idea that there was a true religion other than Christianity: the Devil himself ruled a hellish kingdom structured as were all other kingdoms.

America, according to the myth, was wild, desolate, impenetrable, savage desert. Civilization and Christian life were utterly incompatible with it. Proper Christian people had literally to "carve out" a place for themselves; singly they could plunge into the wilderness, hacking out trails and roads where there were none, discovering rivers and streams, mountains and valleys, searching for the wealth concealed by the wilderness; in groups they could "hack out" and "plow up" places to farm and to live, cutting down the trees, killing the animal life, buying or driving out any native inhabitants—

and building and marking boundaries between civilization and the wilderness, frontiers to keep the savage wilderness and its denizens from encroaching. In this early image—and it is a lasting part of the mythology—there was no reconciliation of wilderness and civilization. If civilization was to prevail, it was by the destruction of the wilderness. If wilderness survived, then it had destroyed and defeated civilization.

The stories of contact between the Europeans and the Indian natives mark the contrast, the necessity not for adaptation but for destruction. The Indians of the North American coast—like the rest of the North American tribes in turn—were decimated by European diseases. Pocahontas saved John Smith, became a princess in the eyes of Virginians, married a Virginia colonist, and moved to London—a quaint, native American, dusky, Christian princess. Squanto and his friends taught the Pilgrims to grow corn because they had run out of proper Christian grain—and having grown Indian corn, the Pilgrims invited the Indians to a Thanksgiving feast but thanked the Christian, European God. The Indians appeared out of the forests and savagely massacred the settlers; the Europeans just as savagely surrounded, trapped, tricked, and massacred the Indians. There was no reconciliation of civilization and wilderness.

The shock of contact with "savage barbarians" was a lasting one for Americans. The Indians were fascinating and attractive in their naked, pagan innocence—and contact with them made the wilderness in which they dwelt more attractive. They were highly skilled in wilderness life, and Americans (very slowly) came to see a need for those skills. But they were alien, foreign, and fearsome.

The shock of contact with the settlers was as powerful for the Indian peoples. Settlers were greedy. Once they took possession of a place, they did not tolerate others—especially savages—wandering about in it. Settlers destroyed the game and tore up its habitats. They cut down forests. They plowed the earth. Their numbers increased and the destruction spread. The Indians were driven back. Their economic life was disrupted by the introduction of new trade goods—implements, textiles, guns, and rum. Their social life and their communities, their relationships with each other, were disturbed.

Some North American Indians gave way to "culture shock" and despair and, like many of the peoples of the Caribbean, simply died, unable to comprehend or survive the destruction of the patterns of life they had inherited from their fathers. Others rebelled at the destruction and fought back with every means at their command. Several hundred of the four thousand settlers who died in Virginia before 1623 were killed in 1622, when the Indians tried to drive all the Virginia settlers away. Fear bred violence, and violence fear, for both the Indians and the settlers.

The problems posed by the wilderness and its inhabitants could not be avoided by the migrants to America because they had made a break with the past. The journey of migration, enacted by millions of people in the history of the United States, was a great ritual unconsciously performed. The ocean was a womb which ensured rebirth in America, a crossing of a Red Sea into the wilderness which barred the way to the past, separated the chosen people from their ancient enemies, and gave hope of a promised land. The ritual of ocean passage and the immigrants' "parturition" was enacted by millions of human beings individually, and provides all Americans a basis for the private confirmation of the myth of the New World, and of the myths of American wilderness and civilization.

"Being thus passed the vast ocean," there was nothing left of the womb. There were no friends there and only the "hideous and desolate wilderness" to face. Such circumstances could well justify and explain whatever changes American immigrants found themselves making in their civilized lives. Yet it was difficult. To learn to hunt *and* eat what grew in America did not come easily to peasants, farmers, and artisans who had little of the aristocratic experience of hunting and who could determine the edibility of a plant only by trying it. A Christian knew what was Christian food and how a Christian was supposed to get food—as God had ordained. It was not laziness and putting on aristocratic airs that brought the "gentlemen adventurers" in Jamestown to starvation; they simply could not imagine how to live off the land. American settlers and immigrants continued to import foods, tools, and materials in order to get what was familiar and "right" (to some extent they still do). It would only be over many generations that the idea of surviving and living in the new land on its own terms, conforming to its requirements—that the myth of American adaptability would become widespread. That myth grew as part of the slow development of an "American character." It would be "this American, this new man," who was able to bridge the irreconcilable conflict between wilderness and civilization (as we shall see). Out of the early and fundamental postulation of the wilderness as American myth came not adaptation to the wilderness but mission: the civilization of the wilderness.

It appears to us today that the pressures of the circumstances of life in the New World both caused and justified the changes early settlers made in their lives. They did not see things as mechanistically as we do; they did not possess our mythology of adaptability. If extraordinary changes were required of them, then, as they saw it, there was some extraordinary *purpose*—God-given—underlying those changes. Why, after all, had the Puritans been allowed to come to Massachusetts Bay in such great numbers to establish a "city on a hill" for all the world to see? Why had the Virginia colonists, despairing of their economic survival, discovered that they could grow and sell tobacco? Why were the pagan Indians, who were so clearly the agents of the Devil, always seeking to subvert or destroy the Christians? Why did so many, even the innocent, die?

God, in the Christian world, out of which the pattern of American mythology grew, was the mover of all human events. He, or the Devil, underlay all that happened. And the omniscient Providence always had a plan. If the ordinary paths of nature and of society, which God Himself had ordained, were being set aside, it was because God had some particular plan for the New World. Special, unusual things happened. "Going to Cambridge-Lecture," Samuel Sewall wrote in 1686, "I saw a Rainbow to the North, being just about Noon. . . . Cloud rose suddenly very black and hail'd afterward. Ministers pray together at Boston this day." The only explanation that justified all the hardships and terror of life was that God had some extraordinary purpose in creating the New World and bringing them to it.

Why had they come to this harsh world at all? They believed, in part, that they were forced to come, and it is an explanation favored by many Americans still. Persecution of their religious or political beliefs drove them to America. The disruption of traditional patterns of agriculture, manufacture and trade, unemployment, and poverty forced them out of the Old World. Increase of population and the insufficiency of older agricultural methods drove them to the New World. But they, much more than their descendants and later historians, were also conscious of the question: Why me? There were people in the Old World in exactly the same circumstances—persecuted, impoverished, unemployed, crowded, and starving—who did not leave home to brave the unknown.

It was only those who *chose* to do so who came to the New World. They had decided; they had volunteered to participate in God's plan. They had been chosen—even driven, it was true—but they had also chosen. They were, as a result, set apart, not merely physically, but apart in destiny as well. Samuel Sewall had his young son baptized Joseph "in hopes of the accomplishment of the Prophesy, Ezek. 37th and such like." The prophesy was: "I will take the children of Israel from among the heathen . . . and will gather them on every side, and bring them into their own land. . . ."

If God's plan for America was to make a new land in the desolate wilderness, a better land than the world had yet seen, and the new children of Israel had chosen to carry out God's plan, then those children had to become a new kind of people. How else could they survive in the wilderness, civilize it, and make it a Christian world? The children who would one day remember their fathers who had crossed the great ocean and who had been ready to perish in this wilderness, except that the Lord had heard their cries, had to bridge the great chasm between wilderness and civilization.

They had a mission, a mission which grew out of the very nature of the

New World (as they understood it in their myths). They were to become one people—gathered in their own land from among the heathen—and they were to make that land the Promised Land. They were to create an Eden, a paradise, by adapting that world and its ways to proper civilization, as God would have them do. Out of all the peoples God had created and put on earth, they were chosen. They *were* the New World. And, as the New Revelation had been brought to the world by Christ and replaced the old, so the chosen people had their mission. In William Bradford's account of the Plymouth settlement, the imagery of Christ was widespread and pervasive in his descriptions of the sufferings and mission of the Pilgrims. So it remains in the mythology of the New World, hidden in the mythic perceptions of the wilderness and of the American mission.

4

The Birth of the Nation

THE REVOLUTION

On July 4, 1776, a new star, a Western Star, was born into the firmament of nations, according to American myth. The star was a nova, exploding into dazzling brilliance from obscure origins and burning ever brighter since. It was the United States of America, the hero of American myth.

July 4, 1776, is the birthday of the nation, and the date of the Declaration of Independence from the mother country. (The infant nation is simultaneously an adult—or at least an adolescent—establishing its independence of the parent.) It is the beginning of the American Revolution. July 4, 1776, is the Beginning, in the belief of most Americans: the real date of the real beginning, celebrated each year; splendidly and nationally reaffirmed in a centennial celebration in 1876 and a bicentennial celebration in 1976.

The myth that the nation was born on one day has had a long-term and obvious effect on Americans, who mark the beginning of American history at the birth of the nation. Everything before that day is "mythical," *pre*historic, vague, and dreamlike: there were *pre*-Columbian Indians, mound builders, cliff dwellers, "lost" civilizations; there were Columbus and the explorers, who wore funny clothes and came from Spain; there were Pilgrims and Puritans, who wore different funny clothes, were very grim, and started Thanksgiving. Then came the Fourth of July—and reality.

In all the standard texts of American history, the centuries of time and generations of people before 1776 are treated as prelude to the Revolution and what comes after. Although the years between 1492 and 1776 exceed by several decades the years *since* 1776, Americans and the writers of American history devote far less time, space, and energy to the years before 1776 than to those since. The Indians are all but ignored—and their history is almost never considered American history.

The myth of the birth of the nation provides the structure through which Americans understand their history. The years before the Revolution were not important: there was no nation before the Americans rejected England and the Old World, before the truths upon which all governments and all nations are legitimately based had become self-evident. Such times cannot, by their very nature, according to this mythology, be as important as the years of independent nationhood. The myth of the birth of the nation includes an imperative ignorance of the irrelevant past.

The Revolutionary War was at the beginning, then. The war itself began with a shout, "The Redcoats are coming!" and a "shot heard 'round the world" (since celebrated in history and poetry that was, until very recently, part of the imagery effortlessly available to all Americans). It was a *war* as well as a revolution, and the memory of it would give both war and revolution a special place in American myth as well as American reality. The war (as revolution) transformed frontiersmen, backwoodsmen, and pioneers into "minutemen," who brought all their skill with guns and at survival, all their ingenuity and industry, to the service of the nation, to the cause of independence and democracy. In endless stories, the war brought Ethan Allen and his Green Mountain boys, Francis Marion (the "Swamp Fox") and his followers, George Rogers Clark and the men of the West, together with pioneers, "Yankee Doodles," militiamen, volunteers, irregulars, Continentals, and minutemen; together they made a revolution and a new nation.

The war was also the story of the agony of the nation's birth, and of the victory finally wrung out of that agony. From Lexington and Concord the war went, in mythical perception, from defeat to defeat until it reached its symbolic nadir at Valley Forge. After the Americans had faced the "desolate wilderness" and cried out to the Lord (and by hard work and ingenuity put together an army), the war proceeded inevitably to Yorktown and victory.

The logic of the myth leads Americans to certain "inevitable" conclusions: that war makes men, willy-nilly, into nationals and patriots; that war creates nations; that fear and desolation along with hard work and ingenuity are elements necessary to the victory which American war produces; and that war fought for the nation brings victory. The logic of the myth is based on people who actually existed, on events which actually took place, and even on rational interpretations of those events and people. The particular relationships and associated stories, images, and ideals are what give the myth its quality. The myth of the birth of the nation does not merely describe the course of the war for independence, it explains the inevitable outcome of the American Revolution.

Within the war, part of it, indeed the whole reason for it, was the Revolution. The Revolution, first of all, created the nation. It united people who had been divided into colonies: it made them Americans. It affirmed the commonality of their experiences in the New World, it gave them a common background and a shared past, and it created a common "body politic." The

Revolution created a civilized, Christian, modern nation which intended to take its proper place among the nations of the world (that is, of the Old World).

Historical time may be telescoped in myths, and events that actually took place years apart are often juxtaposed and given an association in the mythic logic, which then operates to distort rational perception of time. In the mythology of the birth of the nation, the Revolution includes the war for independence, the creation of the political nation, the formation of the federal government, and even the Presidencies of most, if not all, of the "Virginia dynasty." The deaths of John Adams and Thomas Jefferson on the same day, *July 4,* 1826, exactly fifty years after the nation's actual birthday, mark the temporal end of the mythical Revolution. The discovery of the coincidences of their deaths on that date and year, and rational consideration of the great extent of fifty years in a human life, brings to many Americans a sudden awareness of the nature of their mythical perception of the Revolution.

The Revolution, according to the myth, created a lasting American political system which established justice, ensured domestic tranquillity, provided for the common defense, promoted the general welfare, and secured the blessings of liberty to the revolutionaries and their posterity, including, of course, ourselves. The Revolution made explicit the self-evident truth that all men are created equal and endowed by their creator with the inalienable rights of life, liberty, and the pursuit of happiness. The Revolution established a nation in which government rested on the consent of the governed, in which the people were sovereign. It established the rights all people must have in order to live freely. And it established the independence of the United States of America from the entangling affairs of all other nations.

THE FOUNDING FATHERS

The myth of the Revolution is the "charter myth" of the United States, and as is the case with the similar myths of other peoples, there are Lawgivers and Founding Fathers associated with the beginning of the nation. The stories of Moses, of the Seven Philosophers, of Solon, and of Romulus and Remus have much the same intent—and content—as the stories of the Founding Fathers. The purpose of the stories is the same: to explain the origin of the nation, to provide a logic and proper models for the maintenance of the nation, its character, and the cohesiveness of its people. And the heroes and stories remain part of American popular culture: the stories quite literally sung in the recent popular musical *1776* and still evocative of powerful, affirmative responses from Americans.

The stories of the Founding Fathers provide a mythic summary of

American experience up to the Revolution, and establish a *cursus honorum* which forms a basic pattern and model for the lives and behavior of the people in the nation the Fathers founded. Three of those Fathers are towering heroes of the Revolution and of American life: Benjamin Franklin, George Washington, and Thomas Jefferson.

Each was real. In the story of the Revolution, each represents one of the generations living in America in the last half of the eighteenth century (between the beginning of the French and Indian War in 1754 and the inauguration of Jefferson as the third President in 1801). Each man is also representative of characteristics, attitudes, and life patterns which form both the basis of the mythology of the Revolution and the mythic models for American behavior. Franklin embodies civilized colonial life, pragmatism, and the virtues of the industrious individual. Washington is the symbol of the Revolution itself, and the father of the new country. Jefferson represents the democratic idealism of the young nation, the powerful implications of independence. These three heroes, along with the three documents of the Revolution associated with them—the Declaration of Independence, the Constitution, and the Bill of Rights—make up the fundamental trinities of the mythology of the birth of the nation.

The realities of Franklin's life and work are inextricably part of the mythical Founding Father. Franklin was, first of all, a "common" man. He came of no particularly distinguished parentage, he was apprenticed as a boy and ran away, he educated himself, and he went into business for himself. He rose, in short, by his own hard work and self-education. He became a printer and an editor, an inventor and a scientist, devoted throughout his life to finding out how things worked and to applying his knowledge to useful ends: his own pleasure and profit, and the betterment of the conditions of men (he was the living embodiment of the useful "pursuit of happiness"). He had virtues, skills, and background similar to those of frontier Americans, but he was a town dweller and his skills were those of civilization—printing, writing, seeking knowledge, and making "experiments," inventing and manufacturing complicated "machines," like stoves, rocking chairs, and clocks. The "Doctor" Franklin of the Parisian salons, the Franklin of the mistresses and the bastard children, the Franklin who founded schools and libraries, the shrewd propagandist and practical politician, the Franklin who was an imperial civil servant, the intellectual Franklin, was a man of cities and of courts, a familiar of the "real" civilization of Europe.

But Franklin was primarily the embodiment of American practical adaptability. The stories about him celebrate the rise of the common man as an individual, with his practical skills, his shrewd, commonsensical morality, and his native ability to use and improve his surroundings. His *Poor Richard's Almanack,* which became an important mythological guide for Americans, combined Enlightenment epistemology with the frontier experience to provide an ethical and moral base for adaptability, "making do," and inventiveness: in Franklin's hands, it was all eminently practical and moral "common sense."

Franklin was not a frontiersman or a pioneer but a participant in the society of cities, schools, newspapers, and culture. Yet he brought frontier values, American values, to settled American towns, to European courts, and to the creation of the new nation. In the Revolution, he was the incarnation of all that was good in the colonial past, the summary of the American experience and all that had been created in the years of colonial life.

Two years before Benjamin Franklin died in 1789, he participated in the Constitutional Convention. At the end of the Convention, he said about the painting of the sun on the back of George Washington's chair (Washington had presided over the Convention) that he was happy "to know that it is a rising and not a setting sun." For the real Benjamin Franklin, for his generation, and for the colonial past, however, it was a sunset.

George Washington, in the triumvirate of Revolutionary heroes, is the most heroic—and the least subject to human foibles so far as myth is concerned. While Franklin's mistresses and bastards, and Jefferson's slaves (and possible mistress), are always somewhere present in the stories told of them, Washington was so faithful and true that our memory of his slaveholding is virtually lost. The children's stories of his honesty and strength, and of the cherry tree, have no widely known counterparts in the stories of Franklin and Jefferson. While they were acknowledged to be politicians, courtiers, political manipulators, and shrewd ambassadors to decadent European nations, Washington was above politics. Only about Washington was there ever serious rumor that he was offered a crown—and that he refused one. Only Washington was a military commander, with dashing and romantic young heroes like Lafayette in attendance on him. No one ever accused Washington of being an intellectual, much less a philosopher; no one chuckled over or was infuriated by his wit or charm. Even the cherry-tree story adds to his mythical quality, whether it is believed literally or not.

Unlike Franklin or Jefferson, Washington was never associated with cities or European courts, the powerful symbols of established civilization for most Americans. Washington was a farmer and surveyor; he was a pioneer made civilized by his "nobility." The myth of Washington reconciles what seems irreconcilable. Washington was an aristocratic military leader, yet he was an amateur soldier, the American Cincinnatus, the noble farmer who left his lands to take up the sword for his country. He was also the apotheosis of the minuteman, the far-from-aristocratic farmer who kept his rifle close at hand so that the plowing would not be unduly interrupted by shooting, and whose shooting was in defense of his land and home. Washington was an aristocrat, yet he was a common man. His plantation, his business dealings, his land speculations were no more than other men aspired to. His mansion-like house at Mount Vernon, still a major shrine to Americans, is a big, comfortable farmhouse—better decorated than most, and magnificently situated, but not beyond the aspirations of ordinary people.

Washington was a great general who shared the privations and hardships of his men—the preservation of the camp at Valley Forge enshrines that part of the myth. He chaired the Convention at Philadelphia and was the first President of the United States; yet he was above politics, the embodiment of Jefferson's later plea: "We are all Federalists, all Republicans." John Adams was laughed at in Congress when he proposed that the President of the United States be addressed as "His Highness," yet Washington the President stood, in his black velvet suit and dress sword, before his drawing-room mantel at his weekly levees as stiff and uncondescending as any European prince. But, of course, those levees were open to any who wished to come off the street to see the President. He retired to his farm after the war was over, and again after he was President, dying peacefully, again the true Cincinnatus, in his own home on his own land. So powerful is the mythology of Washington that even his most recent and rational biographer, James T. Flexner, calls him *The Indispensable Man.*

Thomas Jefferson belonged to the younger generation, the men in their twenties and thirties, like Adams, Madison, and Hamilton, who provided the sinews of the Revolution and the continuity of leadership for the new nation. In the end, Jefferson towered above them all as a politician, a philosopher, and an idealist. Like Washington, he was a Virginia planter, land speculator, and slaveowner. He was an inventor, a tinkerer, and a profound observer of natural phenomena, like Franklin. He was also an architect and a writer. Yet it was Jefferson more than any of the other heroes who *was* the Revolution. He is the embodiment of the peculiarly American revolutionary spirit.

While the reality is that the idea of independence grew gradually, and political independence was, for most Americans, a last desperate resort, the myth of the Revolution has Independence springing full-blown from the colonists' reaction to tyranny. The heroic colonists, in the myth of the birth of the nation, were aware that they were Americans, not Englishmen, and they fought for clearly formulated ideas about government, representation, and democracy. It was the hero, Thomas Jefferson, who gave final form to those ideas associated with revolution and independence that a whole people believed were self-evident.

Jefferson stands as the spokesman for all the people, giving voice to their thoughts and making their feelings and aspirations articulate. He is, in myth, the Great Representative, and embodies what all Americans want to believe about representatives. He both represents and embodies the common man.

The operation of the Jefferson myth is exceedingly powerful; even historians, trying to be objective, are unable to break it. Jefferson is always representative: he is made into an "ism" which includes him, his political followers, and very often his political enemies as well. He characterizes an age, and is not merely the spokesman for, or the founder of, American liberalism; he is the personification of it, without reference to time, circumstances, or events.

In reality, Jefferson was himself a great American mythmaker. He was intensely conscious, as are many revolutionary leaders, of the need to create vivid images to explain patterns of behavior necessary to the survival of the nation, the people, and the new form of government. The Revolutionary generation committed itself, its fortunes, and its honor to the independence of the newly formed nation. Success was not obvious to them, and the dangers seemed immediate: Would the government survive until tomorrow? Could it defend itself? Would periodic elections work? Would the defeated leave office? Would rebellious and increasingly independent people acquiesce in government? Could the debts of the war be paid? Each such question opened an abyss of potential danger. Each move might be the last in the new nation—or it might establish a form or an institution which would shape the thought, the behavior, and the potentialities of generations to come.

Jefferson was aware, as were many of his generation, of the need for specifically and identifiably American patterns in language and in ideas, as well as in behavior and institutions. Noah Webster set to work on a dictionary of the American language, in order to distinguish it from English. Parson Weems wrote his fables of Washington in order to provide American models for American children. Jefferson, in his work on the Land Ordinance of 1785 and the Northwest Ordinance of 1787, revised the language as well as the concept of American empire: the United States would thenceforth possess territories, never colonies; and such territories would, by a regular and established process, be in due course integrated with the metropolitan center: never would there be a mother country separate from the colonies she spawned. Jefferson changed the title of the President from "His Excellency" to "Mister," not, as the story would have it, as a reflection of his simple (few men have been as complicated as he) modesty, but rather as a deliberate and conscious effort to shape the Presidency and to give direction and point to his democratic ideals. That change contributed as much to the myth of Jefferson as it did to the Presidency (which might not have displeased him), but it accomplished the end intended: the Presidency was made less elaborate and the attitude that the President was the simple executor of the people's will was maintained in Jeffersonian form for more than a century and, transformed considerably, still exists.

While Jefferson's laws and precedents, Webster's American dictionary, and even Weems's moral tales were not deliberately intended to create myths, they became, because of their closeness to the Revolution and their vivid imagery, parts of the mythology of the birth of the nation. Jefferson was the source of much of that mythology because of his codification of American attitudes and images in his writings and because he deliberately and closely attached those attitudes and images to the new nation.

The yeoman farmer became, in Jefferson's hands, the embodiment of American equality, and the protector and rightful inheritor of the inalienable rights to life, liberty, and the pursuit of happiness. "Those who labor in the earth are the chosen people of God, if ever He had a chosen people, whose breasts He has made His peculiar deposit for substantial and genuine virtue," Jefferson wrote in his *Notes on Virginia.*

Those who dwelt in towns, or engaged in trade or manufacture away from the land, were, by contrast, without virtue. Corruption of morals was, Jefferson wrote, "the mark set on those who, not looking up to heaven, to their own soil and industry, as does the husbandman, for their subsistence, depend for it on casualties and caprice of customers." Such people became not only corrupt, they became the means for the establishment of tyranny. "Dependence begets subservience and venality, suffocates the germ of virtue, and prepares fit tools for the designs of ambition." Dependence was the cardinal sin of the town dweller, the merchant, and the artisan. Independence, to Jefferson, was the prime characteristic of the American yeoman farmer. There was about this yeoman an aura of buckskins, of hewing trees and clearing land, of industrious adaptability to the wilderness. Jefferson did not create the sturdy, independent yeoman, but by giving him independence, he tied him inextricably to the new American nation.

"Independence" had a rich variety of connotations in the eighteenth century which we, in the twentieth century, no longer associate with it. In the first place, in "normal" society, being dependent was considered natural. Everyone in the social structure depended on the King, who was the font of sovereign power, the sole possessor of the right to govern, and the anointed of God who dispensed the goods of this world. If a person sought place or position in the society, access to wealth or land, or desired to join with others to govern themselves in the conduct of their joint affairs—as, for instance, in a commercial company or in a club—it was necessary to seek access to the King, or to people close to the King, in order to be granted place, position, wealth, or self-government. Only the most powerful, the people who "counted," had direct access to the King. For others, it was necessary to attach themselves to someone who counted in order to gain place or favor or power. To be the dependent of some powerful patron was perceived to be both honorable and prestigious, and had been so at least since Roman times.

To serve a patron, however humble one's station, was to have a place in the dependent social scheme of things.

By contrast, to be independent, to have independent means or an independent position was to be in a most enviable state, hardly attainable for most. What we consider the quaint forms of eighteenth-century address, both the high-blown salutations and dedications that introduce most literary works and most letters, as well as the inevitable "your humble, obedient servant" with which letters end, were the constant and important indicators of the dependence of people in proper society. The colonies, and the colonists, had also been dependents, one of England and her King, the other of the King in the social structure. To declare themselves independent was to rend the fabric of society and social relationships, and much of the effort of the Founding Fathers (it is clear in the Declaration of Independence) was to make such a revolutionary step seem legitimate in the eyes both of the rest of the world and of the people at home. "Dependence begets subservience and venality," Jefferson wrote as part of that effort. The American was to be, henceforth, as individual and as a nation, independent; and the sturdy husbandman, his independence his outstanding characteristic, was to be the embodiment of the nation.

Jefferson obviously did not create the idea of independence, just as he had not created the yeoman or agrarianism. A great mythmaker takes the characters and situations that are available to him and by his combinations of them and his great voice imparts new meaning and further life—in the generations to come—to ideals and to the visions of his world. Homer, for example, dealt with old themes and legends; he told a story that had undoubtedly been told and told again for centuries before his time. In that sense, probably nothing he said was new. Yet his experience, his travels from court to court and from island to island, his trained bard's mind, his slowly acquired intuitions about the desires of his audiences and the problems of his world—the very distance from his world created by his blindness—combined with his genius to formulate an epic which provided images and ideas, patterns of thought, and logical explanations to generations of Greeks who lived after him. Jefferson's mythic characters were almost entirely abstractions—like the Yeoman, the People, Rights, and Truths—and he, too, created a body of myth out of his observations: his years of developing political intuitions in Virginia, in diplomacy, and in national politics, out of his correspondence with men of other nations and his years in France, seeing his world through the eyes of others, and out of his own genius.

All three of these heroes, Franklin, Washington, and Jefferson, had not only their Revolutionary experience in common, they also, in different ways, embodied the American idea of the practical man. George Washington was both a skilled technician—he was a land surveyor at a time when surveying was the technical basis for the creation of communities; the surveyor was to early American society what the engineer is to modern society—and a practical man of affairs who built a bankrupt plantation into a going business. That Washington was also a successful general was a result not of military training and expertise, in popular belief, but of his practical ability to see the problems the war presented and to solve them. Jefferson was an inventor, like Franklin, as well as an outstanding architect, philosopher, scientist, and businessman. All three men speculated in land.

There was, in their practicality, a kind of hedonism (a pursuit of physical happiness) which has remained part of the fundamental American mythology, which includes the consumerism of modern America. Franklin is most often remembered as the inventor of the lightning rod, the Franklin stove, and the rocking chair: all designed to make life more comfortable and cozy. Washington is remembered for planning townsites with convenient layouts in salubrious places. Jefferson is remembered for his architecture as well as for all kinds of gadgetry—chairs, beds, pens, clocks; verging sometimes on the ridiculous—designed, in what has become the great tradition of American gadgets, to make the life of the individual easier and more comfortable by the manipulation of material things. As heroic tinkerers, each of these men would conceivably find himself at home at the console of a computerized American home, factory, or spaceship.

The list of Founding Fathers does not end with Franklin, Washington, and Jefferson. Together, they tower above the others as symbols of the synthesis which is the fundamental myth of the Revolution. They put together in one package, or bundle of beliefs, the colonial experience with its "bridge" of adaptability between wilderness and civilization, the image of the New World, and the ideas of independence and revolution (which include equality, democracy, and the pursuit of happiness). The stories about them make logical—for Americans—connections among all those beliefs.

They do not stand alone, however. There are other heroes and anti-heroes whose stories add rich texture and almost inexhaustible variation to the significance of the Revolution for all Americans. Each has become a symbol, a mythical being. There was Patrick Henry ("Give me liberty or give me death!" "If this be treason, make the most of it!"), a great orator, the voice of popular anarchy, symbol of extreme democracy and of outspoken confrontation. There was Samuel Adams, the radical revolutionary who devised political techniques, propaganda, and organization—the Sons of Liberty, the Boston Tea Party, the Committees of Correspondence—in order to bring down tyrannical government and create a government responsive to the people's desires. There was Benedict Arnold, the arch-traitor, who was worse by far than Loyalists, who were merely blind to the good: he betrayed the cause he supported, the cause of liberty and democracy. His name has become anathema. There was John Adams, the complicated, conservative revolutionary, mythic symbol of the overeducated, overcivilized New England Easterner, who was committed to the decadent ways of Europe but redeemed by his recognition and support of the right and the good in the Revolution. There was the Marquis de Lafayette, representative of all that was romantic and youthful in the European aristocratic tradition, who was lionized by nineteenth-century Americans because he carried the word of equality, democracy, and the pursuit of happiness back to France. There was James Madison, the shadow and heir of Jefferson, who always argued for the right, and who created the intricate and delicate system which permitted democratic government to work and prevented its becoming tyrannical.

Of all the lesser lights of the Revolution, Alexander Hamilton stands out in American myth as the man who embodied the alternative to Jefferson and who has come to be the symbol of what there is of an American conservative tradition. Hamilton is a reject, the supporter of rejected causes, the prime symbol of the ambivalence of the Revolutionary generation. He was a romantic figure: dashing military aide to Washington, handsome social climber who married wealth, brilliant political organizer equaled only by Jefferson and Madison, and governmental policy-maker without peer; he was a West Indian adventurer (from tropical islands redolent of wealth, ease, and slaves) who rose by his wits and skill and who was a charmer of the ladies; but he was illegitimate. He tried to form an aristocratic order (the Order of the Cincinnati) in a new democratic society. He offered George Washington a crown. He tried to make the American government a parliamentary government and himself the Prime Minister, in a nation which had just rejected Parliament and its ministers. He tried to base a political party on established wealth and social position in a country becoming increasingly democratic. He proposed an active and powerful central government heavily involved in the economic development of the country at a time when Americans insisted on weak, decentralized government and economic individualism. He proposed large-scale industry and manufacturing to a predominantly agricultural nation. He proposed reviving the close economic and commercial ties with Great Britain in an increasingly Anglophobic nation. And he lost his life in a duel with Aaron Burr.

The power of the Hamilton myth lies in the constant contrast of Hamilton with Jefferson. Many of the contradictions and paradoxes in Revolutionary idealism and American nationalism are reconciled, explained, and justified by contrasting Hamilton with Jefferson.

Hamilton was the parvenu. (But who was more parvenu than the sturdy pioneer who has hewn his land out of the forest?) Hamilton was devoted to the protection of new-made wealth. He wanted to secure and stabilize what men had fought to get. He wanted to make legitimate, by retracing the patterns of the old society, the power and acquisitions of the new nation.

Jefferson's yeoman was concerned with securing the opportunity for acquiring wealth, while Hamilton's best men were concerned with the opportunities for using and increasing wealth. Jefferson saw all virtue in the breasts of those who tilled the soil, while Hamilton found the greatest virtue in the men of substance who were merchants and manufacturers, the denizens of towns and cities. Jefferson trusted the people and was distrustful of individual men of power and ambition, so he sought to limit the powers of government and play influence and interests against each other within the structure of government. Hamilton distrusted the people in the mass and put his trust in individual men of power and influence, so he sought to tie such men to the government, give them control over it, and make government the instrument of social stability and economic growth.

In the mythology of the birth of the nation, the struggle between Jeffersonianism and Hamiltonianism, two aspects of political nationalism, has been given vivid images, even personification, by the two heroes. "All American history has since run along the lines marked out by the antagonism of Jefferson and Hamilton," the great American historian John Fiske wrote late in the nineteenth century. "The struggle of these two giants surpasses in importance any other waged in America," Claude Bowers wrote in his *Jefferson and Hamilton* in 1925. And the 1970 edition of Morison and Commager's famous textbook said that "the secret of Jefferson's power lay in the fact that he appealed to and expressed America's better self: her idealism, simplicity, youthful mind, and hopeful outlook, rather than the material and imperial ambitions which Hamilton represented." Despite the efforts of careful historians to demonstrate that American history is not essentially a conflict between Jeffersonianism and Hamiltonianism, the myth that American political life is dominated by choices between democracy and elitism, economic freedom and economic control, majority rule and minority rights remains alive and operative, and is still personified, even for historians, by those Revolutionary heroes.

THE HOLY WRIT

As the nation was created in the Revolution by the Founding Fathers, so it was given ideals and structure by those Founding Fathers in a permanent body of writ—the Declaration of Independence, the Constitution, and the Bill of Rights. That body of writ is very nearly viewed as revelation.

Americans had inherited the radical Protestant tradition of the sixteenth and seventeenth centuries, and along with it the idea that a people chosen by God possessed a body of Holy Writ which was a contract between God and that people, a revelation of God's intent, and the ultimate source of morality, social structure, law, and government. It was impossible that a people could exist or hope to flourish without such Holy Writ. In secular practice and on a less significant scale, the writ was supplemented by various "covenants" between rulers and people, like the Magna Charta, the English Bill of Rights, and the various colonial charters. These lesser versions of writ served people in their ordinary relationships as Holy Writ served on a grander and more fundamental scale.

Americans had also inherited from their English forebears the Whig distrust of kings and other consecrated people who could too easily become despotic and tyrannical. They had developed, in the years of deepening Revolutionary crisis, a growing conviction that it was inevitable that power led to corruption of men, and power and corruption together led to conspiracies to destroy life and liberty.

The story of the creation of American democracy, which is included in the mythology of the birth of the nation, has long been told by Americans (including historians). Like all mythical tales, there is considerable truth mixed into the story:

People came to America to escape the oppressions of government and rulers in Europe. They found—the *Mayflower* and the Jamestown experiences are the common examples, but the assumption is that the experiences were repeated on every frontier—that they could not do without government. So they made formal compacts, usually in a written, contractual form, to create governments in which they participated and which they controlled. The British government was rather lackadaisical ("salutary neglect" was the epithet created by one of the professional bards of the myth) and did not interfere with the growth of such self-government in the colonies. Attempts by ambitious royal governors to control the nascent democratic institutions of the colonies merely toughened the determination of the American people to govern themselves and gave strength to representative institutions.

The Revolution came as the result of a British conspiracy to tighten imperial control over the colonies and destroy their self-government. The British effort to tax the colonists made obvious the democratic principle that governments which do not directly represent the people are tyrannical. "No taxation without representation" became a rallying cry of the Americans.

The Declaration of Independence made explicit what was already clear to the colonists: that the people were sovereign and whatever governments the people created were legitimate. The rights of the people, particularly as those rights were related to government, were the primary concern of the Declaration: "That to secure these rights, Governments are instituted . . ." "That whenever any form of government becomes destructive of these ends, it is the right of the people to alter or abolish it. . . ." Life and liberty are mentioned only indirectly after the first time, since they are accepted as fundamental. But the right to pursue happiness is revolutionary: it is the end and goal of the state of independence. The right was underscored, so that its importance could not be missed: the people have the right to "institute new Government, laying its foundation on such principles and organizing its powers in such form, as to them shall seem most likely to effect their Safety and Happiness." "Happiness" is immediately coupled with "prudence" ("Prudence, indeed, will dictate . . ."), but the meaning has been made doubly clear: the purpose of independent government is to produce the happiness of independent people.

The phrases of the Declaration concerning equality and happiness became fundamental to all American thought and mythology. "We hold these truths to be sacred and undeniable" was the beginning of Jefferson's draft of the Declaration of Independence. He changed the words, and continued:

> We hold these truths to be self-evident; that all men are created equal and independent; that from that equal creation they derive rights inherent and inalienable, among which are the preservation of life, and liberty, and the pursuit of happiness.

The final wording was changed, by Jefferson, his committee, and the Congress, so that the Declaration was not diffused with political prose, but read with the succinctness of the poet:

> We hold these truths to be self-evident, that all men are created equal, that they are endowed by their Creator with certain unalienable Rights, that among these are Life, Liberty, and the pursuit of Happiness.

"That . . . that . . . that . . ." raps out the rhythm and signals the important phrases like a tap on a drum. The epithets are sharp and clear: "self-evident" truths, "inalienable" rights—they are as powerfully evocative for the generations of Americans that followed as those of the King James Bible had been for their forefathers. Self-evident truths did not require argument, they were "revealed." The bald statement of the equality of all men was not simply a high ideal, it was the reality on which the American nation was, is (in the present, whatever the year), and ought to be, based. It is this Declaration which is the imperative for all of American writ, and for the American practice and reality which followed the establishment of the writ.

Because of their unfortunate experience with British government, the story goes on, the Revolutionary Americans at first created an extremely weak central government under the Articles of Confederation. That government, in the mythical explanation, failed because it was not created by the people but rather by the governments of the states. The political ineffectiveness of the Confederation permitted economic and commercial anarchy which, Americans have long told themselves, became a threat to the very existence of the American people. The mythical lesson of the Confederation is that weak government can endanger the nation.

To meet the threat of national dissolution, a convention of Founding Fathers (a *Miracle in Philadelphia,* according to Catherine Drinker Bowen's title) then wrote a Constitution which established a strong (but federal) government. That government was representative of all the people and limited in its powers—but the powers it was given were strong and effective (the mythical logic makes it strong, effective, popular, weak, limited, and possibly tyrannical all at the same time). In it, the interests of the people, the interests of the states, the corruptibility of men in politics, the desires of the majority, and the need for internal stability and protection from external threat were all carefully balanced. The federal system, the division of powers and the checks and balances now assured a strong American government which could act, but only when a majority of the interests, ambitions, and desires of the people coincided.

Immediately they had created the federal government, Americans felt that such a strong government, however balanced and representative, would become oppressive, because it would always be operated by men who would use it, whenever they could, to serve their own selfish interests. The people, and the individuals who made up the people, had therefore to be protected from the newly created federal government. The Bill of Rights enshrined the liberties of the armed individual pursuing his own happiness in order to protect him from the potential incursions of government, both in detail and in principle.

The establishment of the trinity of American writ created (mythically speaking) a single American people with common ideals, rights, and government. The writ provided for the chosen people the ultimate bases of morality, society, law, and government, and guaranteed the immediate control of ambition, corruption, and conspiracy. The Declaration of Independence established the fundamental principles of American society: equality, liberty, the pursuit of happiness, the sovereignty of the people, and the right of revolution. The Constitution established the federal form of government, the separation of powers, the right of participation, the majoritarian ideal, the principle of checks and balances, the protection of minorities, and the assurance that government could act only when a clear majority desired action. The Bill of Rights enshrined the rights of individual Americans and made emphatic the sovereign omnipotence of the people as opposed to the people's agent, the government.

Two principles are clear in the American writ. On the one hand there is the principle, grudgingly accepted, that there must be government. If it is necessary, it must at the same time be carefully controlled. Government at any level is untrustworthy, but the higher, the more distant, the more centralized and potentially powerful it is, the more it must be limited, because the more removed it is from those governed, the more liable it is to conspiracy, corruption, and abuse of its powers. On the other hand, the fundamental basis of society is the free and independent individual. The individual must control all government, and must be protected from tyranny and abuse. Yet the individual human being is greedy, ambitious, and corruptible. It is individual greed and ambition which make government necessary, while those same qualities are what give government its energy. The intricate balances created between these polarities in the three enshrined documents are central to the myth that American democracy, American nationalism, logically resolve the problems of man-the-sovereign and man-the-governed.

American government, once so established, the story continues, has to be operated by two political parties: one party based on essentially Jeffersonian principles ("liberal" ideals) and the other on essentially Hamiltonian principles ("conservative" ideals). These two parties form the *yin* and *yang* of American democracy, and the mythology is that the nation cannot survive without both. In practice, one party is in control of the government—that control obtained by coordinating the interests and desires of a majority of the voters—and it uses the powers of the government to fulfill the desires of its supporters, the majority. The other party attempts to organize a majority of voters from among those dissatisfied with the government in order to take control of it to satisfy the interests of *its* supporters; by mythical definition, it represents the minority. Based entirely on the states and the people within each state as the primary political units, both in the Congress and in the Electoral College, political majorities in the federal government are informal and relatively impermanent. Such majorities are difficult to bring together because of the diversity of their interests, and they are almost impossible to satisfy for long.

THE DESTINY

The dominating image in this story, as it is in the whole mythology of the birth of the nation, is of individuals and small communities that fiercely desire to control their own affairs, shape their own destinies, and pursue their own versions of happiness, but who at the same time want to be one people and one nation. (The language of myth is the present tense: *is* encompasses *was* and *will be.*) Out of the agonies of birth came a nation—with a destiny to fulfill, a mission to accomplish. The mission and the destiny were inherent in the Revolution: democratic government, equality, and individual pursuit of happiness were the legitimate inheritance of all mankind (if the Revolution was legitimate), and Americans (the people who came to the New World for these rights and made the Revolution to ensure them) were charged by God (as His chosen people) to represent all mankind and to bring the blessings of His inheritance to the world.

The American writ was made in order to make the Revolution legitimate—both in American eyes and in the eyes of the rest of the world. "A decent respect to the opinions of mankind requires," the Declaration says clearly, "that they should declare the causes which impel them to the separation." The birth of the nation was a conscious, obvious break with all that to which Americans had professed allegiance, and with much that they held dear and familiar. They who had protested rather loudly that they were "Englishmen" had chosen to be Englishmen no longer. They replaced their sovereign of long-standing and unquestioned legitimacy with themselves. No usurpation could have been greater, no break with the past more obvious. They had migrated to America and adapted themselves to its life in order to improve upon the world as they knew it. Now, by declaring their independence, they broke with the known world and usurped legitimate sovereignty. Nothing, in their eyes as well as in the eyes of the rest of mankind, could have been more revolutionary. The justification was made clear by the principles, practices, and rights made explicit in the writ.

The real social, economic, and political world in which Americans lived changed very little as a result of the Revolution, as historians have delighted in pointing out. The social and political structures of the former colonies were not enormously altered; very much the same people, and certainly the same *kind* of people, continued to lead the society, run the governments, and control the wealth. Trade, commerce, and the patterns of landowning continued on much the same lines as before. Industry developed slowly and agriculture continued to expand.

Why did Americans insist that the birth of the nation was a revolution? And why do they continue to see it as a revolution when the French, the Russian, the Chinese, and many more recent revolutions have demonstrated what revolutions, as many now believe, can or should be? Such questions have forced historians into interesting, and sometimes very strained, arguments. "Make no mistake," Morison and Commager said to young American rebels in the 1960's:

> . . . the American Revolution was not fought to *obtain* freedom, but to *preserve* the freedom that the colonies already had. Independence was no conscious goal, carefully nurtured in cafés, cellars, or jungles by bearded conspirators; but a last resort, reluctantly adopted, to preserve life, liberty, and the pursuit of happiness.

But in January 1776, Thomas Paine did not see the Revolutionary struggle as merely an effort to preserve freedom. In *Common Sense,* written and published to convince the colonists that independence was the only way to gain freedom, Paine cried out:

> Freedom hath been hunted round the globe. Asia and Africa have long expelled her—Europe regards her like a stranger and England hath given her

> warning to depart. O! receive the fugitive and prepare in time an asylum for mankind.

The Revolutionary mission of the nation was not merely to be a passive asylum for all the virtues associated with freedom but actively to espouse the cause and expand the base for freedom in the world.

Not until the American Revolution was the individual pursuit of happiness made an explicit goal of a nation. Not until the Revolution was the sovereignty of a people composed of free and equal individuals made the basis for the formation of a state and nation. And not until the Revolution was the idea of independence for the individuals in a society made the goal of a whole nation. While freedom, or as they would have said, "liberty," may well have been already part of the lives of most eighteenth-century colonists, independence, equality, and a political life based upon the sovereignty of the people were not. These became conscious goals, and they were carefully nurtured by the mythical heroes, the Founding Fathers—very often in taverns, coffeehouses, and in illegal, conspiratorial meetings.

The British military bands at Yorktown after Cornwallis surrendered played a popular tune, "The World Turned Upside Down," as they marched out. The American Revolution had turned the old, familiar world of the British, of Europeans, and of the Americans upside down. The elaborate social pyramid of the Old World, in which people depended on the King and the levels of society above them, was inverted and squashed: in the new nation all men, equally, were the sovereign, and they were all independent. A complex governmental structure was devised to carry out the ends of the new nation, based on liberties that evolved out of the freedoms and practices of Englishmen.

But most important, the tune played by the bands at Yorktown heralded the birth of a new nation and a new people destined, so they swiftly came to believe, to represent freedom, equality, independence, and democracy in the world, and chosen to spread those great gifts over the globe, to all of humankind. The mythology of the birth of that nation, the myths of the Revolution, of the Founding Fathers, and of the Holy Writ, however imperfectly realized, are still fundamental to the beliefs, ideals, and practices of the American people.

5

Nationalism Made Manifest

"SIR, OUR NATURAL BOUNDARY is the Pacific ocean," Massachusetts Congressman Francis Baylies said in 1823:

> The swelling tide of our population must and will roll on until that mighty ocean interposes its waters, and limits our territorial empire. . . . To diffuse the arts of life, the light of science, and the blessings of the Gospel over a wilderness, is no violation of the laws of God; it is no invasion of the rights of man to occupy a territory over which the savage roams, but which he never cultivates. . . . The stream of bounty which perpetually flows from the throne of the Almighty ought not to be obstructed in its course.

Americans were that "stream of bounty" flowing westward toward the Pacific.

"Alas! for the moving generation of the day," Timothy Flint wrote in his *Recollections* three years later, "when the tide of advancing backwoodsmen shall have met the surge of the Pacific. They may then set themselves down and weep for other worlds." They would, in fact, not let the Pacific stop them, but for the first generation of Americans after the Revolution the continent marked the most immediate challenge to their destiny.

The rising tide covered the land. Their destiny was manifest: they were driven westward by the hand of God, and they carried with them all that was best of civilization, education, improvement, republican government, and democratic ideals. They filled a vast and "empty" continent with the virtues and institutions of the freest people on earth. That is the myth and the dream. For more than a century, it permeated every story Americans told, it created the world every American inhabited, and it dominated every explanation Americans made of their world—its influence, although less obvious, remains as powerful today.

The purpose of the nation, in American myth after the Revolution, was to make one people out of many diverse individuals and groups, a people focused on their own uniqueness and unity. America was integrative and exclusive. It was also expansive. Nationalism promises freedom, individual and collective: freedom from outside oppression and interference; freedom to expand, move, and find happiness; freedom to determine a common course, common ways, and common purposes, and to follow them.

THE DREAM OF EXPANSION

The dream of expansion has never been exclusively American. Other nations have sought empire, and some have achieved it. This nation was born out of an empire, and Americans since the Revolution have been intensely conscious of the empires of others. The modern preoccupation with Russian expansion and empire, or the even more recent concern about the Chinese, are not new patterns of concern.

Most post-Revolutionary Americans knew of the Roman Empire, and considered its experience both lesson and example: the concern with Rome was reflected in early national architecture, oratory, statuary, art, and some literature. Americans generally were very conscious of the Spanish empire, and jubilant when, as they saw it, the ideas of their Revolution spread southward and the peoples of the Spanish empire broke away from Spain. The Spanish-American War of 1898 finally destroyed the last vestiges of Spanish imperialism and gave the United States—as most Americans thought only proper—hegemony over those parts of that decadent, Old World empire (Puerto Rico, the Philippines) whose peoples were yet incapable of freedom and self-government (as Americans perceived them). The revolutionary empire of France, the expansion of the Russian empire, the growth of the German empire, the modernization of the Japanese empire, as well as the colonial empires that grew in the nineteenth and twentieth centuries, have all provided living and consciously perceived models of empire and expansion to Americans—who saw America's mission as expansion. Throughout most of their history—from the founding of the colony at Jamestown in 1607 until the end of World War II in 1945—Americans were most concerned with and most conscious of the British Empire: it was, above all others, the prime pattern of expanding nationalism *and* the prime warning of the errors of imperialism.

The British Empire had established no policy for expansion, no equitable rules for empire. The British government had made only haphazard provision for the distribution of land and the establishment of government in the empire, while at the same time it had manipulated and controlled the economic opportunities empire offered to Britons. It had made no provision for the inclusion of the peoples of the empire in the sovereignty and government of the empire. For such gross errors, the British suffered the outcome of the American Revolution—and, of course, the loss of its empire in the twentieth century.

The British were imperialists rather than nationalists in their expansion—

a careful distinction made in the mythology of American nationalism and expansion. The motives underlying British expansion had been ignoble and unworthy, as Americans perceive them, doomed from the start to invasion, decay, and revolution. All expansion not American was undertaken because kings, or governments, or great men, or parties wanted conquest, riches, resources, aggrandizement, or imperial control of the lives and fortunes of other peoples.

Perhaps by accident, but more probably by the design of God, in American mythic belief, the people who had come to America under the aegis of the British desire for empire had come seeking *freedom,* the seed of "proper" nationalism, and the basis for righteous expansion. That seed had flourished in the rich soil of the New World, and blossomed into a new nation.

That nation, conscious of its uniqueness and exemplary purpose, had to expand, not because kings and famous men wanted glory, but because the people and democracy and freedom could not be stopped; as Francis Scott Key sang:

> . . . Blest with victory and peace, may the heav'n-rescued land,
> Praise the power that hath made and preserved us a nation.
> Then conquer we must, for our cause it is just.
> And this be our motto—"In God is our trust" . . .

The destiny of the nation had become clear in the Revolution, and the mythology of expansion is inextricably tied to the mythology of its founding. The Founding Fathers not only sired the nation, gave it its high ideals, associated it with the liberty, independence, and pursuit of happiness of the agrarian yeoman, they also defined the parameters of the nation's mission. They tied the nation and its nationalism to an expanding western dream, and to the independence of isolation. American independence and expansion (America as fortress and as crusader) became in the mythology of manifest destiny logically inseparable ideals and concepts, connected intimately with the creation of the American nation. In short, independence, nationalism, and expansion are *mutually* causative, as well as the logical and inevitable results of each other, in American myth.

The Founding Fathers, led by Thomas Jefferson, first connected independence and expansion and nationalism. In the course of the Revolution, the unoccupied land in the former colonies was turned over to the government of the United States. The Land Ordinance of 1785, which Jefferson helped write, and its many successors, including the Homestead Act of 1862, provided for the orderly distribution of the public lands to Americans from their national government. The nation, not the individual states or local governments, owned the land; it was to the nation, then, that individual Americans who wanted new land had to turn. The national land laws established American colonial policy.

The Founding Fathers were ex-colonials. They had known and felt acutely the snobbery and slights of Englishmen who treated them as colonials or provincials. They did not intend to perpetuate such treatment in the new nation. Neither did they desire to preserve any of the social, political, or economic ideas they associated with colonialism or imperialism.

Jefferson helped create a new vocabulary which distinguished American expansion from older and odious systems of empire. He was neither cynical in this, nor did he attempt to delude himself. The Founding Fathers were creating new institutions: there would be "territories," not colonies, as that nation expanded. They were determined that the whole nation would expand and carry all its benefits as it did so. They did not call their American empire an empire because it was a single nation. It was not imperialism which drove them to expand, it was the destiny of the United States made manifest. The words and ideas which applied to empires of old did not apply to the nation of the New World. The Northwest Ordinance of 1787, along with all the instruments which accepted new states into the "union" of America, provided for the government and integration not of an empire but of an expanding, single nation.

Jefferson and the Founding Fathers were tied even more completely to the mythology of expansion by Jefferson's purchase of Louisiana. Jefferson the President felt that the purchase of the huge territory of Louisiana was unconstitutional. Jefferson the Founding Father stretched the powers of the federal government far beyond the limits he believed were rightly set in order to expand American territory and to accommodate the American dream. And even before he acquired the land, he had prepared to send Meriwether Lewis and William Clark to explore it and to find a way to the Pacific Ocean. The Louisiana Purchase and the Lewis and Clark Expedition provided vivid and fundamental images, stories, slogans, easily available to all Americans.

Jefferson the Founding Father argued that if the Louisiana Purchase was an error, then a sovereign people could revoke it. If, on the other hand, it was not an error, the new territory would provide the sturdy, independent yeoman and his descendants—the people, in short—with all the land they could ever need for a thousand years, stretching in time all the way to the Western Ocean. It would be land they could use and inhabit, and to which they would bring all the blessings of independence and democracy. The mythic logic of Jefferson's argument lay in the tying together of the sovereign people, democracy, the responsibility of government to pursue the happiness of the people, and the vision that the way West was the way to happiness, liberty, and independence.

THE DREAM OF ISOLATION

The way West was protected from outside interference, and so was a guarantee of the independence of America and Americans. The oceans, and her own people, were proof against foreign invasion: such was the myth which developed after independence had been won. (The War of 1812, with its British invasions, gave Americans some pause about that protection. The myth that the great oceans, combined with an aroused citizenry, afforded all the protection the United States needed suffered some damage with the British invasion of Virginia and the capture and burning of the capitol at Washington. But Perry's victory at Put-in-Bay and Jackson's at New Orleans after the war was over restored confidence that Americans could defend themselves if an enemy were again to land significant forces on American shores, confidence that:

> . . . the star-spangled banner in triumph shall wave
> O'er the land of the free, and the home of the brave.

A poem written in the only war since the Revolution in which the United States was invaded became, in the twentieth century, the National Anthem of the United States—an affirmation of isolation and independence.)

Americans were and are sensible of the origins of their culture. By American definition, Europe is old and decadent and corrupt; yet it is seductive. Americans trade in European markets, seek European capital and investment, and for centuries freely borrowed European industrial ideas, machinery, and technology. The greatest threat to independence, as Americans have long believed, is to be tied to Europe, economically or politically, just as the greatest threat to an individual's independence is to be tied to the authority and community of one's parents.

To be isolated from Europe was as vital in mythology to the freedom and independence of the nation as the break with family is to the freedom and independence of the adolescent. It was, in theory, possible for the United States, after the Revolution, to make open and unembarrassed ties with European nations, and indeed it did develop economic and diplomatic ties. But political or military ties with European nations, implying involvement in the European system of alliances and balances, were rejected by most Americans. Those who advocated, or seemed to advocate, such ties were perceived (at least until the twentieth century) by most as subversive of the very existence of the nation.

American isolation, as it was stated by George Washington (and elaborated since), is couched in the most positive terms:

> . . . The great rule of conduct for us in regard to foreign nations, is, in extending our commercial relations to have with them as little political connection as possible. . . .

> Our detached and distant situation invites and enables us . . . [to] defy material injury from external annoyance. . . . we may take such an attitude as will cause the neutrality we may at any time resolve upon to be scrupulously respected. . . . Belligerent nations . . . will not lightly hazard the giving us provocation. . . . We may choose peace or war, as our interest, guided by justice, shall counsel.

America's prime responsibility is to herself, to her mission and her destiny. She cannot fulfill that responsibility tied to others. Isolation from "entangling alliances," from the "toils of European ambition, rivalship, interest, humor, or caprice," would leave the United States free to choose how much it desired and how much it was willing to pay for commercial or political support or cooperation at any particular time. As American isolation gradually developed into government policy and powerful myth, its intent and its effect—from Washington's neutrality to Jefferson's embargo to Madison's war to Monroe's doctrine and far beyond—were not to prevent American commercial, political, or military involvement anywhere in the world; its intent and its effect were to leave the United States free to make its own decisions based on its own interest, without long-term political or military commitments to any European nation.

Isolationism created and reinforced (and was created and reinforced by) the image of a virtuous, free America, set apart from the entanglements and the seductions of the rest of the world. America, like her waving banner, "mid the rockets' red glare, the bombs bursting in air," would stand separate, alone, and ultimately triumphant. Her isolation gave her room to find her way in relationships with other nations, without compromising American ideals or limiting American freedom. Early in the nineteenth century, William Cullen Bryant portrayed the image of the virtuous and isolated America most Americans believed in:

> O mother of a mighty race
> Yet lovely in thy youthful grace!
> The elder dames, thy haughty peers,
> Admire and hate thy blooming years . . .
>
> . . . Power, at thy bounds,
> Stops and calls back his baffled hounds.

OUT OF MANY . . .

Simultaneous expansion and isolation required the creation of a single people out of the many individual, independent Americans who came from so many places and who were part of so many different localities and societies.

"Every engine should be employed to render the people of this country national . . . and to inspire them with the pride of national character," Noah Webster wrote in 1789. The Founding Fathers had self-consciously set about the task of creating a single nation out of thirteen separate political entities. They had chosen *E pluribus unum* as the motto of the nation, and they had achieved a measure of success. The Constitution had established a potentially strong federal government, but its federal nature also preserved great elements of fragmentation. The individual states carried the primary loyalties of their people, and the system of federalism assumed the continuation of that state of affairs. *E pluribus unum* was the motto of a nation intended to last a long time.

The task of making one nation was a continuing task, not one which would end with the replacement of one set of loyalties by another, but rather one which postulated at least two sets of loyalties. "In all things," Webster wrote, "we should be federal; be national. . . ." But the terms were not synonymous, and the focus of political loyalties and social identities was on states and localities first, and on the nation only when it was a matter of the "respect due to the opinions of other nations," or a matter of expansion. Eighty years after the Revolution, it was still possible for a great American soldier, Robert E. Lee, who had served all his life in the United States Army, to say that Virginia was his "country," and that he would follow Virginia, not the United States of America, "with my sword, and if need be, with my life."

Fragmentation of loyalties was actively furthered by the expansion of the United States and the American population. The migration to new land, the advent of numbers of immigrants, the establishment of new communities, territories, and states, all tended to confuse the sense of national identity. The act of settlement encouraged people to identify themselves with the actual ground they were on and the actual communities they helped form. Migration encouraged nostalgia for, and a sense of identification with, the communities they had left behind. The political activism and interest required for the creation of territorial governments, and for the creation and admission of states, powerfully focused identities on the locale of those activities.

But the same tendencies which contributed to the fragmentation of loyalties also provided possibilities for the development of nationalism. Breaking away from the native community, migrating westward, and building new communities were terrible wrenches to individuals, leading them to seek a set of values and an identification which was unchangeable in the midst of change. The necessity of meeting, living with, and being dependent upon "strangers in a strange land" brought a powerful urge to find common values and common beliefs. The whole thrust of education in the schools and the tenor of the mass media was to sing the praises of the nation, and to identify, extol, and teach the peculiarly American virtues of the American people. Being an American in Texas, or California, or Oregon could bring a sense of community with other Americans wherever they came from, a sense of shared purpose and shared identity.

Local loyalties and identities bounded by state lines were the primary means Americans had for identification with their society. Beyond local identity, and closely intertwined with national identity, was the possibility of identification with a region. Regions do not have fixed geographical boundaries. They depend for their existence on local history, current problems, and a perception by the people who dwell in them that they are peculiarly American in those characteristics which distinguish them from other regions. Regionalism, like nationalism, is a way of providing large groups of people with a basis for social cohesiveness and for distinguishing themselves from other peoples.

EAST AND WEST

The oldest American regional division is that between East and West. Underlying it is the mythic imagery of the contrast between frontier and settlement, between wilderness and civilization. Even before the Revolution, each colony had, in fact, an eastern and a western region. The East was more settled, possessing established towns and churches, better dwellings, more goods, closer trade connections with other colonies and with the world, functioning centers of government, operating courts, and sometimes centers of higher learning. Eastern counties or towns had large representation in colonial assemblies, power and patronage in the colonial government, access to the governor and to the seat of ultimate authority in London. The eastern part of each colony was the "establishment," more self-assured, more literate, more cultured, and generally more powerful than the western part. The western part of the colony was usually more recently settled, less well organized, with cruder buildings, poorer roads, less "refinement," sporadic courts and weak government, fluctuating and uncertain trade, and much less political power. The "crude" Western settler was a "rube" to the Easterner long before the term was used, and the Western perception of the Easterner was as a "dude."

The larger concept of "the West," without reference to colonial or state boundaries, as the vague area on the edges of, and beyond, permanent settlements, had also formed before the Revolution. The rapid migration into the West during and after the Revolution brought an equally vague definition of "the East." The lack of political boundaries outside the established states—both on maps and on the ground—contributed to the growth of these regional perceptions. The only identity possible for the first settlers in most frontier areas, when it was necessary for them to compare themselves to people in more established areas, was that they were Westerners. As new localities and new states began to form in significant numbers, it was generally simpler to accept regional identification. The terms of identity were always relative: to a Kentuckian in the 1820's, for example, a person from the Shenandoah Valley was an Easterner, while to a Tidewater Virginian the same person was a Westerner. For those who moved from one place to another, there was the conscious choice which had to be made concerning the acquisition, and the active construction, of a local and regional identity.

Peculiarities of speech, dress, and behavior were often seized upon and emphasized by people in new areas to distinguish themselves from those left behind and those who came later. The process of forming new local and regional identities was accompanied by the process of trying to fit those identities into a national, American form, and to win acceptance of the new variations from those in more established areas. The social process of integration and the process of creating the myths of local and regional identity were accompanied by the political process of establishing territorial governments, winning admission as states, and the development of political parties and government in the new states.

Daniel Boone, George Rogers Clark, Ethan Allen, John Calhoun, and Henry Clay were among the earliest Western heroes, joined ultimately by a wide-ranging pantheon of immortal Westerners. But the outstanding Western hero of the early nineteenth century, and the symbol of the acceptance of the West and its mythology by the entire nation, was Andrew Jackson.

"Old Hickory" was the embodiment of the virtues and the vices of the West as they were perceived and made into myth by both Westerners and Easterners. He was a rough-and-tumble backwoodsman, a fierce Indian fighter, a tenacious—and victorious—general against both Indians and British; he was a hard-working farmer, a wily and underhanded politician, a gambler, a defender of women, and at the same time a plantation owner and aristocrat; he was a leader of the common herd, a convinced democrat, a brilliant political leader; yet he was ostentatious in dress and household, incredibly touchy about his honor, modest, a hard bargainer, generous, optimistic, handsome, tough-minded, and naïve. He was a sturdy, independent American success, or a dirty, ill-mannered demagogue, depending on your politics and your regional identity. He remains a national mythic hero of Westernness—of "logically" combined violence, innocence, and democracy.

Jackson's election to the Presidency signaled a change in American attitudes as well as a political change, a change so important in the perceptions of later Americans that Jackson is the only American President whose name, in American historiography, is attached to an age. Many Americans in

Jackson's day were conscious of the change, which friends and opponents alike saw as the full-fledged integration and participation of the West and of Western Americans—with their muddy boots on the White House's elegant furniture, and their boisterous habits of dress, manner, speech, and drink—in the life of the nation. Beyond that, later historians have argued that Jackson symbolized the "rise of the common man," the active participation of voters qualified only by age, sex, color, and citizenship, not by property, in all American political affairs.

These perceptions, whether statistically true or not, are based on Andrew Jackson as a symbol of what the West came to represent. The West, as symbolized by Jackson, was not merely an acceptable adjunct of the United States but a permanent and essential part of the nation, of its society, and its politics. There is an element of triumph on the part of Jacksonians that Americans had, by the acceptance of the West, successfully integrated colonies into the mother country in a way that Britain had been unable to do. The West was boisterous and rough and new; so was all of America when compared to the rest of the world (i.e., Europe), and in that respect it was uniquely American. The West, in the symbol of Jackson, represented "democracy"; in it, the democratic ideals of the Revolution were more completely realized than anywhere else, and its integration into the nation was the triumph of those ideals over the residue of Old World behavior in other parts of America. The democratic West represented the "lasting hopes of the American nation," and with Andrew Jackson as President, those hopes were permanently part of the nation. The integration of the West "proved," in the logic of mythology, that expansion was necessary to the health of the nation and its ideals, and that it was morally good—beneficial to the liberty, equality, and pursuit of happiness (as well as the democracy) of all humanity.

The image of the East contained two elements. There was, first, the mythology and the regional identity of that only true—in the sense of having fixed geographical boundaries—American province: New England. New England was populated with Yankees, who had their own distinctive accents, and their own long moral and political traditions. There was, on the other hand, the much more vaguely defined "East," which included New England and most of the rest of the original thirteen states. Identity in the East was strongly fragmented and its boundaries were only very slowly broken by immigration and the exodus of more established people as the nation grew and movement became easier. Except for New England, the East was very often a Western state of mind.

Comparisons both to Europe and to other American regions were essential to the development and maintenance of local and regional identities. The comparisons were frequent. A poem of Fitz-Green Halleck's, "Connecticut," written in Jackson's day, is an example of the qualities Americans saw in their regional identities, and the humor with which at least some of them regarded those identities:

> . . . 'Tis a rough land of earth, and stone, and tree,
> Where breathes no castled lord or cabined slave;
> Where thoughts, and tongues, and hands are bold and free,
> And friends will find a welcome, foes a grave;
> And where none kneel, save when to Heaven they pray
> Nor even then, unless in their own way.
>
> . . . They love their land, because it is their own,
> And scorn to give aught other reason why;
> Would shake hands with a king upon his throne,
> And think it kindness to his majesty;
> A stubborn race, fearing and flattering none.
> Such are they nurtured, such they live and die:
> All—but a few apostates, who are meddling
> With merchandise, pounds, shillings, pence and peddling;
>
> Or wandering through the southern countries teaching
> The A B C from Webster's spelling book;
> Gallant and godly, making love and preaching,
> And gaining, by what they call "hook and crook,"
> And what the moralists call over-reaching,
> A decent living. The Virginians look
> Upon them with as favorable eyes
> As Gabriel on the devil in Paradise.

Very early, Easterners, especially intellectual Easterners, were contemptuous of the West and those who went West. Timothy Dwight, the president of Yale, in 1821 wrote, in his *Travels in New-England and New York,* that those who had left the settled New England states to establish themselves in the West, in Vermont, were men who "cannot live in regular society. They are too idle, too talkative, too passionate, too prodigal, and too shiftless to acquire either property or character." They were people "who had rather talk than work," and Dwight was happy they had left New England. He was contemptuous of their delight "with innovation," and he thought it unlikely that the West would ever develop "energetic government" or possess the "high sense of religion and morals" necessary for civilized society. Timothy Flint, commenting on Easterners like Dwight, wrote in his *Recollections* in 1826 that "the people in the Atlantic states have not yet recovered from the horror inspired by the term 'backwoodsman.' This prejudice is particularly strong in New England," he wrote, but it was felt from "Maine to Georgia."

The formation of these mythic stereotypes, which still exist, was very early.

Some Easterners believed that the superior experience and civilization of the East ought to be used to improve the West. Edward Everett, the great New England orator, proposed, in 1833, to extend the "New England system" of public education to Ohio. "If ever there was a region where it was peculiarly expedient that this should be done," he wrote, "most assuredly the western part of America . . . is that region." The West possessed everything material: "The soil is fertile, the climate salubrious; it is settled by as truehearted and substantial a race as ever founded a republic," Everett wrote. But the West needed education, religion, and the institutions to support them. Only the East could provide them, and it was the East's obligation to carry "the soul's food" to their brethren in the West. The West was admitted to be part of America, and the superior East had to see that it became civilized, to the greater glory of the whole nation. The mission of the East—to send "missionaries" to civilize the West—was the same as the mission of America to the world.

THE "PECULIAR" REGION

The self-conscious intensity of regional mythology is most visible in the South. It was in the South that conflict with national mythologies became real. In the South ("*at* the South," as Southerners used to put it), the existence of the "peculiar institution" of slavery provided an obvious and important difference, around which Southern identity was made explicit. Slavery had existed in the colonies almost from the beginning, and it was built into the Constitution at the Philadelphia Convention. It was, therefore, an identifiably American institution, but because many states had abolished or prohibited it, it was at the same time peculiarly Southern. Institutional differences between regions had ordinarily been eroded by westward expansion, population growth, and improved transportation in the first half of the nineteenth century, but slavery was maintained in the South, and where that institution spread, so did "the South." Around slavery, other institutions and characteristics were defined as peculiarly Southern: the plantation, an aristocratic vision, the recognized dominance of an elite, and the ideal of a cash crop.

The image of the sturdy, independent yeoman, self-sufficient on his own land, was, as we have seen, a powerful part of American nationalism. Southern planters, with their self-sufficient plantations and their "natural aristocracy," saw themselves as the true expression of independent yeomanry. At the same time, the existence of Southern planters, with their "high-falutin' airs" and their dependence on slavery, strengthened the self-image of the independent, democratic yeomen in other regions.

The Southern cash crops, tobacco and cotton, were particularly visible in the mythology of the agrarian yeoman because neither were foodstuffs. Such crops had to be sold in the marketplace, and it was obvious that they were grown solely as sources of cash. Dependence on the marketplace was something the independent yeoman was supposed to avoid.

In reality, of course, American agriculture had, from its colonial beginnings, been based on the production of marketable cash crops in order to create the capital necessary for economic growth and development. The Southern planter could, in his production of cash crops, certainly consider himself one of the normal American agricultural capitalists and, when he was successful, could and did feel himself an outstanding representative of American farmers.

Farmers in other regions could, conversely, reinforce their own myth of independence of the marketplace by pointing to the "decadent" Southerner as the exemplar of dependence, and could insist that, because they grew food crops primarily, they were somehow less dependent on the marketplace in which they sold their crops than the planter was.

Slavery remained, however, the primary basis for Southern identity and for regional comparisons. The Southerner justified slavery as a solution to the labor shortage, a problem endemic in American agriculture. The slave was no different from the children or the servants or the hired hands of other farmers, the Southerner argued. The slave was in the traditional position of a servant in a family, and the master was *in loco parentis* economically, socially, and politically, as masters always had been. Nor, they said, were slaves in any worse position as laborers than the "operatives" of factories "at the North"; indeed, Southerners argued, slaves were better cared for and their masters more responsive to all their needs than were the employers in industry. In defense of slavery, the Southerner appealed to his own vision of an aristocracy with control and tutelage of the blacks, and at the same time appealed to the general American desire for a homogeneous society (another form of the vision of "one nation") which the slaveowner "protected" by keeping black Americans enslaved.

Regional identity, like national identity or indeed individual identity, does not depend entirely on economic or physical or political reality for its existence. It is characterized, as Wilbur J. Cash wrote in *The Mind of the South,* by "a fairly definite mental pattern, associated with a fairly definite social pattern—a complex of established relationships and habits of thought, sentiments, prejudices, standards and values, and associations of ideas." It is based on a mythology which provides the logical explanations and understandings of beliefs and behavior.

Central to Southern patterns and mythology was slavery. Ownership of slaves was not essential to identity because the class and racial superiority of all whites to all blacks, which the mythology of the South created and maintained, was believed by all to require the existence of slavery. A threat to slavery, then, was a threat to Southern identity. The Southern myths implied (as all regional myths do) that Southerners were peculiarly and intensely American. To stop the expansion of slavery, then, was to stop the expansion of the South; since the dream of expansion was a national dream, the effect was to brand Southerners un-American: either the South was not part of America, or American expansion was unnecessary or wrong. The abolitionist effort to destroy slavery could be seen by Southerners—using the logic of American regionalism—only as an effort to destroy both the South *and* the nation. On the issue of Southern identity, with its basis in slavery, the rational contradictions between regionalism and nationalism came into the open, and led Americans to war.

WAR AND THE NATION

"A house divided against itself cannot stand," Abraham Lincoln said in 1858:

> I believe this government cannot endure, permanently half *slave* and half *free*.
>
> I do not expect the Union to be *dissolved*—I do not expect the house to *fall*—but I *do* expect it will cease to be divided.
>
> It will become *all* one thing, or *all* the other.

Lincoln's voice was the voice of American nationalism. The vision was that the individuals in the nation would be, or become, "all one thing." The promises of concerted action and of freedom which were inherent were postulated on that premise. Regionalism was a variant of nationalism which allowed people to differentiate themselves within the nation, which provided an alternative to purely local loyalties and identities, and at the same time encouraged identification with national purposes. But when regional differences are perceived to be fundamental and intractable—seen to be "differences" rather than "variations"—both by the people in a region and those outside, then the force, the logic of nationalism is that either those differences must be reconciled, or they must be removed.

Slavery was a "real difference," a "peculiar institution," and efforts to reconcile it and Southern regionalism were extensive, complex, and took place over generations. In the end, reconciliation failed. The final attempt to remove the difference—by the withdrawal of ten Southern states from the nation and the formation of a new nation based on Southern regionalism as full-fledged nationalism—was rejected by the rest of the nation. The Civil War was the result.

Modern war is a creature of nationalism. Its aim is the destruction of those things, and the people who maintain them, which are believed to threaten the existence of a nation. Since a nation is composed not only of land and the people who dwell on it but also of the complex patterns of thought, belief, behavior, and promise which provide people with their national identity, a threat to any of those things is a threat to the existence of a nation.

Americans fought a Civil War because they believed (Southerners as well as others) with Lincoln that a nation had to be "all one thing, or all the other." The nation had been created in the Revolutionary War, and the Civil War was the test of "whether any nation so conceived and so dedicated can long endure." The nation and its destiny, its independence and its expansion, its mission to the world were challenged and tested in the Civil War. And out of that war came many of the fundamental myths which have supported and directed American nationalism since.

The Civil War has demanded explanation, and the explanations have been various. Two perceptions, however, condition the ways in which all Americans see that war. First, that a great and fundamental cause was at stake, over which both sides fought passionately and honorably. "The generation that carried on the war has been set apart by its experience," Oliver Wendell Holmes, Jr., said to a group of Keene, New Hampshire, veterans on Memorial Day, 1884. "Through our great good fortune," he said, "in our youth our hearts were touched with fire. It was given to us to learn at the outset that life is a profound and passionate thing."

The second universal perception of the Civil War is that the result of the war was a stronger, greater nation. Stephen Vincent Benét's epic of the Civil War, *John Brown's Body,* concludes:

> Out of his body grows revolving steel,
> Out of his body grows the spinning wheel
> Made up of wheels, the new, mechanic birth,
> No longer bound by toil
> To the unsparing soil
> Or the old furrow-line,
> The great, metallic beast
> Expanding West and East,
> His heart a spinning coil,
> His juices burning oil,
> His body serpentine.
> Out of John Brown's strong sinews the tall skyscrapers grow,
> Out of his heart the chanting buildings rise,
> Rivet and girder, motor and dynamo,
> Pillar of smoke by day and fire by night,
> The steel-faced cities reaching at the skies,

The whole enormous and rotating cage
Hung with hard jewels of electric light,
Smoky with sorrow, black with splendor, dyed
Whiter than damask for a crystal bride
With metal suns, the engine-handed Age,
The genie we have raised to rule the earth.

If both sides fought for a great cause, then how was it possible to reconcile the Southern loss and the continuation of the South as a part of the United States? The transformations required of the myths of the Civil War in order to make it possible for Southerners to find solace in their "lost cause" and at the same time to participate in American nationalism are remarkable. If the North fought to destroy slavery, then surely the North was fighting in an "idealistically right" and "morally good" cause: the war was, indeed, a "Civil War." But if the South sought to preserve her agrarian society and her gracious way of life, then surely the South fought in an idealistically right and morally good cause: the War was "the War between the States." On the other hand, while the North's battle against slavery was right and good, its destruction of an agrarian way of life was wrong and bad. The South, fighting to preserve its way of life, was right and good, but in trying to preserve slavery, it was wrong and bad.

But if, in this mythical vision, the sides are separated, then *both* can be right. The North fought to preserve the nation and to destroy slavery. The South fought for its independence and to preserve its agrarian way of life. So, in the myth, while the South lost the war, its *cause* was good; furthermore, it did not destroy the nation, nor did slavery survive. The South could find in its lost cause solace for having fought, and the nation could find reconciliation between North and South.

It was in warfare that the mythical reasons for Southern loss and Northern victory could be found. The Southern myth maintains that the South had the better-trained, more brilliant, more honorable and dashing generals, and a more efficient fighting army, sustained primarily by eager volunteers. (Both sides, in fact, had to resort to conscription.) The North had poor generals or, when good ones were found, brutal generals, and its army was large and chaotic. The North won the war only because it had more of everything—men, machinery, guns, railroads—and it was willing to spend its material wealth and the blood of its men prodigiously. Most Americans accept that myth. The South was the underdog, overwhelmed by superior numbers and equipment thrown ruthlessly into battle. The source of the North's power, however, lay in its industrial might and great resources. The South, while it could have, therefore, all the sympathy (and nostalgia) that Americans give to the underdog, *had* to lose to the wave of the industrial future of

America. The outcome was inevitable, and the North won because it embodied the nation that was to be.

The Civil War myths provided for heroism, romance, and nostalgia. The antebellum South can safely be revered and romanticized by generation after generation of Americans because it is *ante*bellum. It is destroyed and dead. Single-minded pursuit of victory, even if it entails brutal waste of lives, does not keep Grant or Sherman from the ranks of American heroes, because they succeeded. The unsuccessful Northern generals, like Burnside or McClellan, who wasted lives, are not heroes to Americans. Robert E. Lee, on the other hand, lost but is still a hero. He was a brilliant general, and a gentleman. The Civil War made gentlemen losers: they were not suited to nationalism or its spawn, modern industrial war. The aristocratic-gentleman ideal suffered total destruction in the myths of the Civil War (see the most popular modern telling of the myth, Margaret Mitchell's *Gone With the Wind*). Even in the Southern variants of the stories, the great planters, the aristocrats and gentlemen, however dashing and romantic, were defeated. The leaders of the new nation, and the leaders of the "New South" along with them, had more of Grant and Sherman in them than they had of Lee. Southern throats might tighten and eyes water at thoughts of old "Marse Robert," but later Southerners often followed Tom Watson or Huey Long or George Wallace.

Americans believe that the hell of Civil War was required of the nation because the nation had failed. In the mythic parable of the "necessary" war, there had grown in the midst of America, part of her history from the very beginning, an institution which had prevented law-abiding, good Americans from fulfilling the national promise of liberty and equality for all. That institution, slavery, had also perverted the dream of independent yeomanry by supporting a monstrous aristocracy. As the slave could not be the equal of any free person, so the common free man could not be the equal of the slavemaster aristocrat. Jefferson, the spokesman of equality, had prophesied that God's justice could not sleep forever, and the Civil War was the justice of God visited on a nation that had accepted slavery too long. The only arguments that Americans could bring to counteract the notion of God's justice were the arguments made by Southerners, and acquiesced in by Northerners, that slavery benefited, protected, and improved the "inferior" blacks. Those arguments were tenacious, and they remained an underlying part of the treatment of black Americans after the Civil War. But the fact of slavery, and the need to destroy it, is at the heart of the belief that the Civil War was a necessary war.

The aim of destroying slavery, in fact, had only gradually infused the North after the Civil War started. The preservation of the Union had been the initial and official aim of the war. But it became increasingly obvious that slavery was fundamental to Southern identity, and as long as it was not attacked, so long would the North implicitly support Southern independence. Lincoln's decision to issue the Emancipation Proclamation was not merely a shrewd propaganda move on the part of that shrewd man. It gave renewed energy to the Northern war effort, because the Proclamation acknowledged that in order to preserve the American nation, Southern "peculiarity" had to be destroyed. It did not free any slaves at the time it was issued (1863), but it gave a moral purpose to the ghastly business of brother killing brother, and it made the war necessary to the preservation of the national ideals.

Lincoln's reluctance to take the step of emancipation, given his awareness of the regional feelings of Americans and his felt responsibility to preserve nationalism and unity (even in the South), is understandable. More than most Americans of his time, he realized the implications and the enormous difficulties of black equality. He also realized the pain the destruction of slavery would bring to Southerners, and the difficulty it would cause in reuniting the South with the rest of the country. Yet he took the step because the war would destroy the essential difference which stood in the way of a common nationalism. Without slavery, North and South could reunite. With it, they could not.

In the myth of the Civil War, there is no doubt that the war was an irrepressible conflict. It generated powerful myth because it is seen as the inevitable result of contradictory elements in American life. Americans do not believe that a conflict of interests, or even of ideologies, must always result in bloodshed. Quite the contrary, they attempt ordinarily to avoid confrontation and conflict, even when beliefs are involved. But the conflict which brought on the Civil War was basic to the very existence of the nation. The conflict, in the myth, was between freedom and slavery, between the national ideals and a perversion of those ideals, between the agrarianism of the past and the industrialism of the future, between God's design for American progress and man's attempt to prevent progress. The conflict was fundamental: the war was inevitable.

The Civil War was the visitation of God's wrath on the land, but the hell and destruction had a useful purpose. Out of it, in the myth, came national growth, expansion, progress, and "reconstruction." Although Reconstruction failed in the sense that the black Americans were left to the tender mercies of the Southern whites, it also succeeded in the sense that slavery was destroyed and the South was integrated into a modern, industrializing nation. Out of the war had come freedom and unity, at least for the whites.

War, in the myth, then, was the means of organizing and unifying Americans and their resources to accomplish the great ideals of the nation. Out of the Revolutionary War had come the American nation, "conceived in liberty and dedicated to the proposition that all men are created equal." Out of the Civil War had come the vast, effective, irresistible organization of the people, the strength, and the agricultural and industrial production of the nation in order to bring to fruition the extension of freedom and equality, the destruction of odious institutions, and the reconstruction of that better society which was the promise of the American nation. War had brought out all that is best in America, and the Civil War established that best permanently.

American unity in war, and the high purposes for which that unity was created, were expressed by Abraham Lincoln, and Lincoln came to symbolize for many Americans all the good, important things which came from the Civil War. "We here highly resolve," Lincoln said at Gettysburg, "that these dead shall not have died in vain—that this nation, under God, shall have a new birth of freedom—and that government of the people, by the people, for the people, shall not perish from the earth." The Gettysburg Address was planted in the memories of millions of American schoolchildren: a new birth of freedom and imperishable democracy were, as Americans came to believe, the results of the Civil War.

Out of the memories and explanations of the Civil War, war became, in the imagery and metaphors of American myth, the ultimate defense of the nation and the ultimate expression of nationalism. In Lincoln the emancipator, war leader, frontier hero, and spokesman of charity, freedom, and democracy, is the image of the great and good uses to which American war is put. That vision makes war not an extension of foreign policy, because in her isolation and with her democracy America eschews the diplomatic, dynastic, imperial, policy wars of other nations. American war is an affirmation of American independence. American war, like the nation, is democratic: it is fought by the whole nation for the morally righteous ideals upon which the whole nation is founded. It is total war. It is defensive and protective of that which is clearly American: democracy, freedom, manifest destiny, and the independent pursuit of happiness. From American war come organized, national efforts to extend freedom and democracy, and all the institutions which are necessary to them.

Hail, Columbia, happy land!
Hail, ye heroes! heav'n-born band!
Who fought and bled in Freedom's cause,
Who fought and bled in Freedom's cause,
And when the storm of war was gone,
Enjoyed the peace your valor won.
Let independence be our boast,
Ever mindful what it cost;

Ever grateful for the prize,
Let its altar reach the skies.
Firm, united, let us be,
Rallying round our liberty;
As a band of brothers joined,
Peace and safety we shall find.

6

Frontiers and Other Dreams

FRONTIERS AND LINES are powerful symbols for Americans. The moving frontier was never only a geographical line; it was a palpable barrier which separated the wilderness from civilization. It distinguished Americans, with their beliefs and their ideals, from savages and strangers, those "others" who could not be predicted or trusted. It divided the American nation from other nations, and marked its independence. People who crossed frontiers did it with aggressive, expansive intent, as did Americans moving westward; or they did it on invitation, voluntarily giving up what they left behind, as immigrants to America did.

When Americans felt themselves or their beliefs threatened, they drew a line and dared their enemies to cross it. Children and adults drew lines, on the ground or in their imaginations, to separate themselves from danger. They gathered their friends behind the line; by definition, those on the other side of the frontier were enemies. The expected response to the drawing of a line was a violent effort to cross it; a line was a "dare," a challenge which had to be accepted. The expected response to a violation of such a frontier line was violent defense: the American was not fighting merely for a boundary or for a piece of territory but for the primary distinction between Americans and others. What was at stake in the drawing of lines and the establishment of frontiers was *identity,* personal, communal, and national. Inside that line, the American *belonged*—everything inside the frontier belonged. Inside the line was the community of the American nation.

The metaphorical image of the frontier separates Americans from other peoples. Behind that frontier, inside the community, all Americans are one, ideally. The ideal of national homogeneity, the ideal of the "melting pot," was one of America's Revolutionary, radically democratic ideals. Anyone who volunteered was promised assimilation into a democratic, egalitarian, libertarian nation the like of which the world had never seen. Background, birth, wealth, inheritance, social position, and class did not count. In fact, the immigrant was required to give up national and class identity and culture and language; that was the dare, the challenge of crossing the frontier: to become an American!

MYTHS OF COLOR AND RACE

Within the nation, however—inside the American frontiers—other lines were drawn. The most obvious, the most powerful, the most long-lasting of those internal lines were the frontier lines of color and race.

Color and race had gradually replaced class and birth as primary determinants of belonging in the course of the colonial period. The differences which had seemed innate to Europeans—birth, inheritance, social class—at first led colonial Americans to the logical conclusion (based on their inherited vision of society as a predetermined, class-structured pyramid of mutual dependence) that such innate differences made people either superior or inferior. But since class differences based on birth and inheritance were difficult to sustain, the logic of differentiating among people dealt with the differences which were most obvious *in America.* The American Indians, the natives, with whom conflict over territory and frontiers was almost constant, were clearly different from the European settlers and their descendants. So were the blacks, who had come to America involuntarily, who were pagans, and who were enslaved. By the time of the American Revolution, Indians and blacks, who had initially been identified by Europeans by their peculiarities of dress, speech, hairstyle, and behavior, had come to be perceived not only as pagan and savage but as ignorant, inferior, and, most importantly, *colored.* Lines were drawn around these peoples of color, frontiers to separate white Americans from others. The legal boundaries of slavery created to bind the blacks served the same purpose of separation and distinction that reservations and "permanent" frontiers did for the Indians.

After the Revolution, most (white) Americans believed that primitive and native peoples of color like the Indians and the blacks could not possibly be included in the melting pot. They could not lose their color. And even if they could, there was little hope of their assimilation until they spent generations being educated, trained, and polished by white Americans, under controlled conditions, and with the possibility of their living in their own cultures completely removed. It was, after all, not possible to make Americans even of white Europeans unless they were in America, controlled by Americans, and trying to live as Americans.

The logic of race and color led many white Americans to see blacks and Indians as fundamentally similar. In the first place, neither was in America by choice. The qualities which made Americans, in their own estimation, superior to all other peoples on earth depended on freedom, and the outstanding symbol of freedom, buried deeply in the myths of Americans of European descent, was the act of voluntary migration. "Real" Americans had chosen to come—or their ancestors had. But the Indians had not chosen to come: they were indigenous. They were the "natives," with no choice at all about their place of residence.

And black Americans had been slaves. Their ancestors had been brought to America in violence and chains; there was nothing voluntary about their being here. They had come from darkest Africa, and were strange, wild, and unpredictable. They had been kept in bondage and treated brutally, in a country which based its existence on equality and freedom: there was no reason they should love America or want to be part of it. They had learned how to survive the violence and inhumanity of slavery: how to be docile, smiling "Sambos," or sullen, blank-faced, and seemingly unmoved by callous brutality; how to communicate among themselves without the white man knowing; how to keep their own violence and rebellion internal, or reveal it only to their own kind.

"Natives" is a term used to refer to lower orders of persons who are indigenous to "uncivilized" portions of the globe—Asia, Africa, the Pacific. American Indians were natives. Black Africans were natives; black Americans were their descendants and were "tarred with the same brush," as the popular saying went.

The color of natives, as of all peoples, is—in the logic of American myth—a racial characteristic, connected to a cluster of mental, physical, cultural, and moral traits. Color is the distinguishing characteristic of race, from which all other traits follow. Color, in this logic, includes visible skin pigmentation, facial characteristics, and hair; it is by a combination of these that an American determines race. (It is worth noting that other peoples and other nations do not make determinations of color and race on the same basis; for many "foreigners," for example, all Americans look alike—regardless of race, creed, national origin, or color.)

In the confused American myths of race, the world is divided into white, yellow, red, brown, and black. White races are superior, and the others are inferior in degrees, according to how "primitive" (low) or "civilized" (high) they are considered by whites. In the Alice-in-Wonderland mythic logic, the colors are moral polarities: "pure white" is the most superior, and "pure black" or "pure red" the most inferior. In between are half breeds, mixed breeds, quadroons, octoroons, "high yallers." A white person with some black ancestry ("a touch of the tar brush") is polluted and inferior. A black or an Indian with some white ancestry is improved and more civilized. Even among contemporary Americans who have given up much of the traditional logic of race and color, the belief remains strong that color is *always* identifiable; the power of the myth is measurable by the extremely subtle characteristics which Americans (of all colors) continue to believe betray nonwhite ancestry.

The ideal of national homogeneity has long implied a high value for purity (oneness, unity)—of ideology, of religion, of color and race. That value is made clear because only those whom Americans believe to be pure white are considered to be white at all: mixtures are identified with the non-white race, whatever it is assumed to be. American Indians, black Americans, Chicanos, Puerto Ricans, Oriental Americans are identified with those "races" by most Americans, whatever their mixture of white blood. People who don't look as if they have non-white ancestry are able to pass for whites; it was only thus that blacks and Indians and others of colored ancestry were, until very recently, able to participate fully in American society. The taboos against whites mixing with them were powerful and, in many states, a matter of law. The impact, for example, of William Faulkner's 1936 novel, *Absalom, Absalom!,* depends on the emotional power of that taboo. Otherwise, the destruction of generations of a family because one member of the family had mixed blood, which is central to the novel, is incomprehensible—and without emotional impact.

There have been millions of immigrants to the United States who, because they were of Latin or Slavic origin, or because they were Jewish, were categorized by others as part of colored races. However, their participation in voluntary migration along with their belonging to white although inferior races gave them a way into society. They, after all, had chosen to come to America; their desire to become Americans made them in the mythic logic "almost white men," however strange their appearance, dress, language, and customs. As they became Americanized and shed those manifestations of strangeness, at least in public or in American-born generations, they were able to pass into the society of whites. Jews, because their religion was associated with their presumed racial characteristics, found the process slow but not, finally, one which barred them from the American inheritance.

"I always thought," the wife of a college president said to a young Jewish faculty wife in the early 1960's, "that Jews were like white people." Anti-Semitism remains, as do anti-Catholicism and other prejudices, but they no longer keep Jews, Catholics, and many others from full participation in American life.

AMERICAN "RACISM"

It has always been easy for Americans to confuse national identity with the imperative for homogeneous communities. *E pluribus unum,* the national motto, meant one nation out of many states, and it meant as well one people and one society out of many peoples. When confronted with Indians, Mexicans, or any other foreigners, Americans discover a strong sense of national identity. New immigrants since the 1840's have contributed to a sense of nationality in Americans. The fearful, sometimes xenophobic reaction of some

Americans to immigrants has been an affirmation of Americanism, of an American "race." Anti-Catholicism, anti-Mormonism, anti-Masonry, anti-Semitism all have the same source and imperative: the enforcement of unity and homogeneity in the American nation. Closed, apparently self-sufficient, mutually reinforcing communities of foreigners or religious groups, with their strange practices, languages, and beliefs, have often caused Americans to succumb to extreme affirmations of nationality. The existence of "foreign" communities challenges the logic of homogeneity and reveals the insecurity of American national identity.

This mythology of race was strongly influenced by nineteenth-century Darwinism, which encouraged Anglo-Saxons and Anglo-Americans to believe in the innate superiority of their race and in the impossibility of the peaceful coexistence of any two races in proximity. The logic of innate superiority—whether arrived at by Darwinian evolution or by some other process—was carried to a "logical" and horrifying conclusion by the Nazis and the German government in the Holocaust of the 1930's and 1940's. As a result, the mythology of race in America has recently changed, and many Americans have consciously and rationally tried to destroy the power of the myths.

Race, in America, has been primarily linked to color. It is something involuntary and *internal* to America: blacks and Indians are Americans. Their color is the *line,* the frontier, which defines their race in the logic of American myths. But the frontier definition ties them, with their color, to America, because only America is a frontier nation.

Three frontiers have enclosed the blacks: slavery, the South, and color. Without some recognition of the peculiar historical experience of the Old South and of slavery, American racism (as differentiated from the racism of others) is incomprehensible.

Slavery became an institution peculiar to the South. It was hedged about with the laws of Southern states, federal Fugitive Slave acts, the federal immigration acts, and ultimately, in the Dred Scott decision, with the Constitution itself. The slave society was like a distant foreign country to white Americans, within which slaves lived obviously poor and benighted lives. It was incomprehensible to most Americans how slaves could tolerate their conditions unless they were culturally, morally, and racially deficient. Yet slavery was not really distant; it was inside America. It became a challenge to some Americans, who sought its destruction and found the blacks in need of enlightenment and the benefits of American freedom and democracy.

The slavery frontier was broken, violently, by the Civil War. The laws and Constitutional amendments of Reconstruction permanently destroyed the institution of slavery (although they accomplished little else) and erased the enclave of blacks. Blacks legally became Americans, all of them, and with the frontier between them and the white Americans destroyed, they were in the melting pot. They were candidates for assimilation, by the logic of American myths of community.

The Southern defenders of slavery had erected the boundaries of the Confederacy and tried to make both slavery and the South inviolable. They had drawn a line. But the North broke the line and violently destroyed both slavery and the Confederacy. The blacks were invited to cross over, as they assumed, into the promised land.

But the South had not been destroyed, and neither had the color line. Even those white Americans who had worked and fought to destroy slavery did not regard the color line as broken, or violable. H. R. Helper, a vigorous and longtime abolitionist, wrote, in 1868, after the Civil War and after the ratification of the Thirteenth and Fourteenth Amendments to the Constitution, that no American should make "the gross error of inferring or supposing that color is the only difference . . . between the whites and the blacks!" There were, he said, "numerous other defects, physical, mental, and moral," which combined with his "black and baneful color" to mark the black American "when compared to the white man, as a very different and inferior creature."

Helper made a catalogue of the "defects" of black color which illustrates the stereotype of the myth of color. When "we behold the crime-stained blackness of the negro," he wrote, "let us, also, at the same time, take cognizance of":

> His low and compressed Forehead; His hard, thick Skull; His small, backward-thrown Brain; His short, crisp Hair; His flat Nose; His thick lips. . . . The Malodorous Exhalations from his Person; His Puerility of Mind; His Inertia and Sleepy-headedness; His proverbial Dishonesty; His predisposition to fabricate Falsehoods; and His Apathetic Indifference to all Propositions and Enterprises of Solid Merit.

With minor variations for different colors, Helper's catalogue expressed the mythical characteristics of all colored Americans—black, red, brown, or yellow.

THE DREAM OF EMANCIPATION

Many blacks had assumed that the myths of freedom and equality, of individual independence and the pursuit of happiness, would prove stronger—once slavery was destroyed—than the myths of race and color. At a convention in Syracuse, New York, before the Civil War had ended, black leaders announced that "the chief values and ideals in American culture" should be the basis for black progress after emancipation. They urged freed blacks to "shape their course toward frugality" and the "accumulation of property," traditional prerequisites for the successful pursuit of happiness. "Above all," they urged all blacks "to leave untried no amount of effort and self-denial to acquire knowledge, and to secure a vigorous moral and religious growth." The image of the native, the slave—ignorant, reckless, and immoral—had to be counteracted as soon as the slaves were free. The struggle, as these black leaders saw it, "for integration into American society," required the elimination of all the differences that separated blacks from other Americans. They did not see color—and race—as uncrossable lines. They saw themselves and their fellow blacks as fully capable of traditional individualism, a vision of equality more inclusive than the vision of most whites.

Emancipation—becoming free of strictures on body and mind, on movement and ambition—was, and remains, a powerful image, ideal, and imperative for black Americans. It is not the same image, although it has some of the same qualities, as the image of freedom for white Americans. For whites freedom—the ability to move about (movement and mobility), the ability to seek and seize on opportunity—*exists* in America. Immigrants come to America to find freedom; and ultimately, they do find it. But for blacks freedom did not exist in America. The dream of being freed from slavery and restriction in the midst of freedom was the myth of emancipation. It was release! It was being able to cross an invisible Jordan into a promised land which blacks were able to see but for generations not enter. It was taking up an inheritance long promised. It was integration into American society, freely, equally. The cry of Martin Luther King, Jr., in Washington in 1963—"Free at last! Free at last! Thank God Almighty, free at last!"—revealed to many white Americans the power and the imperative of the black myth of emancipation.

Emancipation has come and been snatched away again and again in the black American experience. It came with Abraham Lincoln and the Union armies and it was snatched away by the Black Codes. It had come with the Reconstruction governments in the South and the Freedmen's Bureau; and it was snatched away by the refusal of Congress to confiscate plantation lands or appropriate money for the Freedmen's Bureau. It disappeared altogether as home rule returned to the South.

Emancipation came as some of the freed blacks found land to work. But the price of land was high. Debt, foreclosure, and failure snatched it away. Former field hands became what they had been under slavery: agricultural laborers. Many became sharecroppers—a peonage which was almost, but not quite, slavery. Once again, emancipation was snatched away and a kind of slavery visited on another generation.

The intense desire for land, to work if not to own, was an affirmation of black freedom; a search for a way to be American. Black Americans, like other Americans, were workers of the soil. As slaves, they had been the hard-working and utterly indispensable base of a lavish society. To a people born and raised on Southern plantations—as to Americans everywhere—the ownership of land was the mark of a free man. Even to work land one did not own was to be more sturdily independent—emancipated, for the black.

But the dream of emancipation remained a dream. It was still in 1963, when Martin Luther King, Jr., repeated: "I have a dream!" Some blacks after the Civil War found the capital to go west and homestead. Some migrated out of the South to become railroad hands, cowboys, farmhands, miners. In increasing numbers in the twentieth century, they migrated northward to the great cities, assuming that machines and factories would provide the emancipation which Lincoln, Reconstruction, Populists, and all the American myths of individual freedom had failed to provide. Blacks dreamed of redeeming America from violating the promise of the Declaration of Independence. But the color line remained. And the result of violating that line, of trying to cross it, was violence.

COLOR AND VIOLENCE

Much of the violence was not directly physical. It was violence to the soul and spirit; the violence of ostracism and enforced deference; the violence of openly voiced contempt, of deliberately limited opportunity, of being the public butt of scorn and jokes. Americans, black and white, were trained from their earliest youth to be sensitive to such things, to resent them fiercely, and to respond to them violently.

There was the violence of economic exploitation, backed by white authorities. Laborers were forced to hire themselves out at low wages. Stores and commissaries extended credit, used only tickets and chits, charged high prices, and manufactured debts. The black was helpless to challenge them: "No one of us would have dared to dispute a white man's word." Courts were used to force blacks into bondage, and prisoners on chain gangs were hired out by state and local authorities. Wages for free blacks remained much lower than wages for whites in comparable jobs.

The black Americans were all but helpless in the face of white physical violence. Beatings, whippings, rapes, burnings, hangings, shootings, tortures, and mutilations, accompanied by all the available symbols of fear and terror and death, were used by whites against the blacks—as they were against Indians, and sometimes against Chinese "coolies" and other immigrants—in order to defend or draw the color line.

Paramilitary organizations, like the Knights of the White Camellia and the Ku Klux Klan, grew in the South after the Civil War and revived throughout America after World War I in order to terrorize blacks and defend the color line. Their activities drew both on the memories of military paternalism and action in war and on the need for voluntary associations in American society, to make them acceptable to whites. (The same traditions, ironically, gave acceptability to black organizations in the 1960's.) The near-chaos and instability of economic conditions in postwar periods, the available imagery of posses and outlaws, Cavalry and Indians, gave added strength to the temptation to use organized violence in order to protect the stability of "basic American values," i.e., the frontier, the *line,* the color line.

One of the outstanding excuses for violence on the part of whites, one with continuing and powerful appeal, was the excuse of black "violation." In the Victorian nineteenth century, the extreme symbol of violation was sexual violation, rape. The South had been "violated"—raped—by the North in the Civil War. Slaves had violated the status of free people. Any black who violated the color line symbolically violated the whites, white homogeneity, white purity. That violation *became* the rape of a white woman, the symbol of the purity of the white race. The interpretation was made even more logical by the sexual ambivalence of whites toward blacks: if white men found black women sexually attractive because of their blackness, then it followed that black men desired white women. It also followed that all such desires were morally as well as racially evil. Any violation of the color line became sexual violation. And such violation was an invitation to further violence.

SEGREGATION

The function of the myths of race and color in America after the destruction of slavery has been to maintain a vision of black Americans as outsiders in American society, as people beyond the frontier (and thus savage, uncivilized natives). The myths were physically and legally reinforced by the development of segregation. At the same time, the general American myths and institutions of independent individualism, voluntary association, community service, and community life were regenerated and reinforced in the black communities, rural and urban, because they were American communities.

In segregated black communities, black churches and schools were built, black fraternal organizations and businesses established. Restricted to activities and behavior which did not challenge white dominance, or appear to violate the color line, black leaders until the 1950's and after operated in exclusively black contexts. The survival techniques of secrecy, impassivity, and mutual aid—developed in the long centuries of slavery—continued to be useful to them in the face of the deliberately alien and often violent whites.

Blacks seized upon the ideals of self-help, voluntary association, and education as part of their inheritance as Americans, and used them to demonstrate—to themselves as to others—their assimilation into American society. The black schools which appeared throughout the South during Reconstruction—aided in some cases by the Freedmen's Bureau, missionary "school marms" from the North, and philanthropists like George Peabody—were built by blacks. The same forces and motives which press other Americans to build schools and hire teachers and tax the community to pay for them—in frontier towns, in growing cities, in spreading suburbs, even in foreign countries—raised money, built schools, and hired teachers in black communities. *All* Americans agree that education is an important part of building a homogeneous and egalitarian culture and of transmitting essential values and morality.

Just before the beginning of the twentieth century, in 1896, the Supreme Court, in the case of *Plessy v. Ferguson,* admitted segregation as "a valid exercise of the legislative power" and established the doctrine of "separate but equal" as the fundamental Constitutional principle governing the color line in American law. The effect of the decision was to remove any Constitutional (and for Americans, believers in the fundamental revelation of their writ, any God-given or moral) basis for crossing or violating the color line.

The Supreme Court said that "in the nature of things" the Fourteenth Amendment to the Constitution "could not have been intended to abolish distinctions based upon color, or to enforce social, as distinguished from political equality, or a commingling of the two races upon terms unsatisfactory to either." It also said that "the assumption that the enforced separation of the two races stamps the colored race with a badge of inferiority" was "solely because the colored race chooses to put that construction upon it." Were the situation reversed, the Court said, "we imagine that the white race, at least, would not acquiesce in this assumption."

The Court rejected any argument that "equal rights can not be secured to the negro except by an enforced commingling of the two races." If blacks and whites were "to meet on terms of social equality," the Court concluded, "it must be the result of natural affinities, a mutual appreciation of each other's merits and a voluntary consent of individuals." The purpose of the Court was to legalize segregation. By making it constitutional, the myths of race and color became, for many Americans, almost immutable.

The only dissenter, Justice John Marshall Harlan, predicted that the Court's decision would prove as "pernicious" as the Dred Scott decision. "The destinies of the two races in this country are indissolubly linked together," Harlan wrote, "and the interests of both require that the common government of all shall not permit the seeds of race hate to be planted under the sanction of law." Nothing could "more certainly arouse race hate," he argued, than a decision "that colored citizens are so inferior and degraded that they cannot be allowed to sit in public coaches occupied by white citizens." He concluded that "the thin disguise of 'equal' accommodations . . . will not mislead anyone." The decision, Harlan warned, left all black Americans in "a condition of legal inferiority."

"God may forgive this corps of unjust judges," H. M. Turner, a black minister wrote in 1883, when the Supreme Court overturned the Civil Rights Act of 1875, "but I never can, their very memories will also be detested by my children's children."

The decision of the Court in *Plessy v. Ferguson* was not replaced until the *Brown v. Board of Education* decision in 1954, when a unanimous Court decided that "separate was inherently unequal," that the entire mythology of race and color implied the inferiority of those Americans who were considered to be on the other side of the line. In the years since *Brown v. Board,* the American mythology of race and color has begun to be transformed because it is no longer unconstitutional to cross the color line.

Segregation, with its emphasis on the metaphor of the line, and its clear reinforcement of the image of superiority on one side of the frontier (the "moral," "civilized" side), generated a powerful logic. It reconciled for many white Americans the myths of color and of equality. It made it possible for blacks in American society to be "invisible," as Ralph Ellison put it. Blacks could be ignored. The logic of segregation made it possible for whites to assume that separation brought equality: blacks had their own communities, their own schools, churches, and businesses, and within their own society they were able to rise, develop individually, seize opportunities, pursue happiness, and gain success. If whites felt qualms or doubts about black equality, then appeals to the inferiority of the black race (and the need for a period of civilizing tutelage) reinforced the necessity for segregation.

The myths never completely reconciled segregation with equality for Americans. But few could see any alternative to the solution the myths contained. "I am a firm believer in the democratic solution of the negro problem," William Allen White, the Emporia, Kansas, editor, wrote to Oswald Garrison Villard, New York liberal editor, in 1919. "But I don't see how it can be worked out geographically in this country," White continued.

> You can't put two kinds of people in the same territory. . . . The white race seems to be determined that the black race shall exist as an inferior race, economically, and do the inferior work, under an inferior standard of living, as expressed in the inferior social plane upon which we are putting them. . . . And so long as we are in a majority, and as we are brutal in our majority, we white people, I do not see how there is any fair solution, or even fair compromise, and I cannot be hopeful. I shudder to think what I would do if I had a black skin.

The image of the frontier was so strong, and the logic of the myths of the frontier so convincing, that a geographical solution seemed improbable, even to whites of good will.

"What a curse some old black mother in Africa, two hundred years ago, must have put upon the South when they took her child to the slave ship," White wrote to Villard nine years later, in 1928. "And how the curse has bitten its terrible way into the destiny . . . not only of the South, but of America as well."

BLACK AMERICAN MORALITY

Many black Americans accepted segregation. They, too, participated in the available mythologies. Blacks more than whites wanted to explain and understand segregation, but they could not escape their American heritage. The two men who have come to represent alternative logics for black American behavior in the face of segregation are Booker T. Washington and William E. B. Du Bois. Both men attempted to provide the black community with leadership within the context of the beliefs and images and myths available to all Americans. Washington was an ex-slave who rose to prominence among the first generation of freed black Americans (he died in 1915); Du Bois was the highly educated child of free parents, who helped provide direction for generations of blacks in this century (he died, aged ninety-five, in 1963).

Booker T. Washington, in his most famous pronouncement on segregation, his Atlanta Exposition address in 1895, implied that blacks would accept segregation if they could participate in American economic progress:

> In all things that are purely social we can be as separate as the fingers, yet one as the hand in all things essential to mutual progress.

Throughout his career, Washington appealed to the logic of individual success and community progress. His vision was based on images generated by rags-to-riches stories, the successes of the robber barons, Horatio Alger's tales, and the innumerable stories of the *nouveaux riches* breaking into society. "No race," he said, "that has anything to contribute to the markets of the world is long in any degree ostracized." He expected that eventually the American mythical imperatives of success and equality would outweigh the imperatives created by frontiers, color, and segregation.

Washington's stance was perceived by some blacks as a new way of being sold down the river, a new way of losing their emancipation. His acceptance of separatism and the building of specifically black institutions was a denial of the struggle for integration into American society which many blacks felt was *the* essential. In his willingness to accept segregation, he seemed to many to accept disinheritance at the hands of the whites.

Washington was a powerful leader. He was the head of the exclusively black Tuskegee Institute. As black institutions developed, and more and more blacks became leaders in segregated black communities, black vested interest in segregation developed. Black institutions and black communities—forced into separate existence by white pressure and white terrorism—tended, like all human organizations, to become self-perpetuating. They provided jobs, status, importance in the community, leadership positions and prestige, and economic as well as social opportunity.

Many blacks, committed to their own communities and institutions, and under severe—and often terrifying—pressure from outside to stick to their own kind, were loath to give up what they had to seek integration. Integration could mean leaving one's community, working and seeking opportunities in strange places, alone and exposed to the callousness, and the possible brutality, of another world. That "mankind are more disposed to suffer, while evils are sufferable, than to right themselves by abolishing the forms to which they are accustomed" became as true for black Americans in their segregated world as it had been true for white Americans in 1776.

By no means all blacks found segregation sufferable. And W. E. B. Du Bois seemed to offer a clear alternative. Du Bois insisted that black Americans had to struggle, directly and immediately, to achieve their legal and political rights, and to gain complete social integration into American life. While Washington appealed to the myth of American progress, Du Bois appealed to the equally powerful myth of freedom and equality. Du Bois helped found the National Association for the Advancement of Colored People in 1909, an integrated organization of whites and blacks. The purpose of the organization was to work, through publicity, to educate all Americans about the evils of segregation and race prejudice, and through the courts actively to challenge all the practices and institutions of segregation.

In rejecting segregation, Du Bois appealed to black pride and black ideas in *Black Reconstruction* (1935):

> . . . Of all human development . . . not the least singular and significant is the philosophy of life and action which slavery bred in the souls of black folk. In most respects its expression was stilted and confused; the rolling periods of Hebrew prophecy and biblical legend furnished inaccurate but splendid words. The subtle folk-lore of Africa, with whimsy and parable, veiled wish and wisdom; and above all fell the anointing chrism of the slave music, the only gift of pure art in America.

Blacks had not only music and art to give to America. Above all, they had their moral character to contribute. The victim was superior to the tormentor. Blacks were superior to the whites who forced them to live separately and tried every means to degrade them. The black American was patient, industrious, long-suffering, loyal, and law-abiding. It was the white who preferred the company of law-breaking, cruel, boisterous, slovenly "trash." "Trash" was white, by definition. It was the "white man in starched shirt setten in de shade" who was the "laziest man God ever made." It was the white who broke the law, ignored the Constitution, and disenfranchised, lynched, terrorized, and segregated the black.

In the logic of black morality, black American culture and moral character was superior to the culture and character of white America. Black mothers tried to teach their children that, no matter what was done to them, *they* were the ones who were moral, Christian, and civilized.

"I am not the one that is being degraded on account of this treatment," Frederick Douglass said when he was forced to ride in the baggage car of a train, "but those who are inflicting it upon me." It was Pharaoh who was execrated by mankind, and who was destroyed by God, not the ex-slaves who were the Chosen People. It was the Romans who were remembered with hatred and whose empire collapsed, not the supposed "criminal" they crucified, or the religion He founded. Br'er Rabbit always got away, always proved smarter and morally superior to Br'er Fox. A briar patch held no horrors for one born and bred in one.

The logic of black morality drew heavily on the traditional Protestant Christianity and on the fundamentalism which has spread so widely among twentieth-century Americans, white and black. The stories of suffering in captivity in Egypt, of wandering in the wilderness, the visions of the Chosen People and the promised land; the wisdom, morality, suffering, and resurrection of Christ—all are taken as prophesies of the black experience and descriptions of its reality. The blacks were the Chosen People of America, sent to this land and suffering in it, in order to bring it redemption by making it truly free and by bringing its great promise of equality to fruition. The "rolling periods" and "splendid words" of the Jews and the Christians were part of the metaphors and imagery blacks used to understand their own experience.

But the logic of innate black strength, of the extraordinary morality of the black, of the ultimate superiority of the black experience, participates in the logic of *American* strength, morality, and superiority. The Christianity upon which black Americans drew for mythic sustenance and hope was a much-Americanized Christianity, common to blacks and whites—much as the words and rhythms of black spirituals are now to both. Finally, even the arguments Du Bois made for the superiority of blacks over whites drew heavily on the logic and assumptions and metaphors of American racism.

"In the character of the Negro race is the best and greatest hope" for the world, Du Bois wrote. "For in its normal condition it is at once the strongest and the gentlest of the races of men." That strength and that gentleness came from evolution in Africa. In Africa, blacks had proved to be "the only race which has held at bay the life destroying forces of the tropics." If further proof of their strength was required, it had only to be remembered that blacks had been the one race "to look the white man in the face and live."

It was in this fertile mythology that Marcus Garvey's slogan "Black is Beautiful" took root, that black nationalism, black Muslims, and Black Panthers ultimately grew. It was the imagery of the blacks as the redeemers of America which underlay Martin Luther King, Jr.'s "I have a dream." The imperatives of that black mythology have eroded away the constitutional base for segregation, and the myths of moral superiority have provided the logic for the activities of the Southern Christian Leadership Conference, the Congress of Racial Equality, and the Student Nonviolent Coordinating Committee in the 1950's and 1960's, as they had much earlier for the efforts of the National Association for the Advancement of Colored People. Such is the power and the continuity of those myths. And they are American myths. They make blacks Americans, and at the same time keep them separate from other Americans.

AMERICAN INDIAN SEPARATION

Black Americans have become the present-day paradigm of otherness. They are the model to which all contemporary minorities turn; they provide, for all who are outside the mainstream of American social life, a pattern for behavior, attitudes, and action. But they were not always the model. Until the twentieth century, the American Indians were the paradigm.

The Indians have been part of American history and life since the beginning. They were the original Americans, although the contemporary effort to use the term "native American" instead of "Indian" seems to be meeting with little success, because "native" suggests as much overt prejudice to thinking white Americans as "Indian" does to many native Americans. To the Indians, even more powerfully and immediately than to the blacks, the imagery and logic of the frontier have applied. And with the frontier came the full mythology of race and color.

"As our borders have been extended, and civilization with its attendant blessings has taken possession of the once unbroken wilderness-home of the Indians," the Commissioner of Indian Affairs wrote in 1864, treaties had been negotiated with the Indians which recognized them as "a separate and distinct people, possessing in a restricted sense the peculiarities and characteristics of distinct nations." The Commissioner believed—as did most white Americans—that "it was perhaps inevitable, owing to the peculiar character of the Indians, that they should retire as their country became occupied by the whites." The segregation of Indians from the rest of American life, their separation from the whites, long seemed to the whites to have been of the Indians' choosing. The Indians, after all, retreated as their country was occupied. They refused to be incorporated into white civilization. They "pertinaciously" adhered to their own ways of life and to their own institutions and societies.

Bewildered by the whites, and often terrified of them, the Indians indeed had tried to retreat before the advance of civilization. "We were like deer," Young Joseph, chief of the Nez Percé, said late in the nineteenth century:

> They were like grizzly bears. We had a small country. Their country was large. We were contented to let things remain as the Great Spirit Chief made them. They were not; and would change the rivers and mountains if they did not suit them.

By the end of the nineteenth century, the country of the whites was so large it included all the countries of the Indians. There was no longer any place to retreat.

The mythology of the frontier had developed a line between wilderness and civilization, a line between the savage Indians and the civilized settlers. "The tribes of Indians inhabiting the country," Chief Justice John Marshall had written in Johnson and Graham's *Lessee v. William McIntosh* (1823):

> were fierce savages, whose occupation was war, and whose subsistence was drawn chiefly from the forests. To leave them in the possession of their country was to leave the country a wilderness; to govern them as a distinct people was impossible, because they were as brave and high-spirited as they were fierce, and were ready to repel by arms every attack on their independence.

The Indians were therefore pushed back behind ever-retreating frontiers. "Permanent" boundaries were established between the United States and the Indians, tribes were moved out of the United States and established beyond those boundaries. Again and again the boundaries were violated by the whites. As the whites advanced, lines were drawn around tribes of Indians and the land within the lines reserved for the Indians. On reservations, islands of Indians in an increasing sea of whites, the land was owned by the tribe and was theoretically as inviolate as any other private property. On reservations, the federal government acted as guardian of the Indians and undertook to civilize its wards.

The generic concept "Indian" had meaning—until quite recently—only for whites. Indians were initially defined by the frontier. Gradually the mythology of color and race combined with white perceptions of frontier and Indians: all those natives looked alike, and very "other" to the whites. To each other, Indian peoples certainly did not look alike. They spoke different languages, lived in different ways, believed in different gods, and generally felt their Indian neighbors to be as different from themselves as were the whites.

For the whites, the nomadic life of many of the Indian peoples was the primary characteristic of the savage independence of all Indians—just as mobility was the primary characteristic of the American. But the Indians were savages, they were colored, they were on the wrong side of the frontier (or they violated it from the wrong direction), and they were uncivilized, un-Christian. So *they* were nomads and savages in *their* mobility. And if they could all be fixed in a particular place, and given land to work (like proper Christians, proper rural, agrarian Americans), the first step toward civilizing them would have been taken. Indians by the latter part of the nineteenth century were deprived of "any tracts, portions, or parcels of land, not actually occupied or used by them" as a matter of policy, and lines were drawn around "such pieces of vacant land as they occupy with their villages and other improvements." (Whites still considered all land not occupied by whites vacant land—and the lines drawn around such land tempting.)

The mark of civilization in white eyes was farming. Native Indians who did not farm had no claim to land. Even those who did farm had to be forced to give up their savage ways. Indian agents on Oregon reservations in 1867, for example, recommended that the Indians on their reservations be deprived of their fishing rights, and that they be paid for those rights "a moderate sum in necessary agricultural implements or other useful articles." "Upon the consummation of this arrangement," the agents wrote, "and the restriction of the Indians to the cultivation of the soil, their condition will be greatly improved." The model of improvement was and remains white American society.

The myth of the savage native made it impossible for most whites, even concerned whites, to believe Indians were other than inferior human beings, subject to less-than-human motives. "What qualities . . . does this American Indian lack, that he is so little impressed by the efforts which have been put forth for his amelioration?" Elwell S. Otis, an Army colonel, well acquainted with and admiring of the Plains Indians, asked in 1878.

Otis's catalogue of the missing qualities paralleled that of H. R. Helper about blacks. According to Otis's *The Indian Question,* the Indian lacked:

> the faculty of abstraction, and consequently his imagination, reason and understanding are of a very low order. He is almost entirely destitute of the moral qualities. . . . His Divinity has none of the attributes of goodness, for he, in his utter ignorance of virtues, is unable to imagine their existence. . . . Like all savage people, the Indian has not the slightest conception of definite law as a rule of action. He is guided by his animal desires. . . . He takes little thought except for the present, knows nothing of property in the abstract, and

has not therefore any incentive to labor further than to supply immediate wants. . . . These deficiencies, together with that spirit of communism which is prevalent among all tribes . . . make the reception and understanding of our American civilization very improbable.

In the extreme circumstances of frontier life—and the real, physical frontier did not disappear until the last decade of the nineteenth century—the Indian, for most whites, was an incomprehensible devil. If Indians lived peacefully on reservations, they were considered lazy, drunken, thieving, and untrustworthy. If they were still free, in their own territories, they were murderous savages. It was so difficult to find law officers who would arrest, or juries which would convict, whites accused of crimes against Indians that such rarities were reported to the Commissioner of Indian Affairs. My grandfather, who had migrated to the end of the railroad line in North Dakota in the early 1890's, told me that the entire male population of his small homesteading community sat up all one night, armed, with the houses shuttered and the oil lamps burning, because a group of Sioux, under Army guard, were camped near the town on their way from one reservation to another. My great-aunt told of her speechless terror when an Indian appeared at her homestead kitchen door, evidently asking for food, walked in and took a loaf of bread, and walked out again. The ghost of such frontier terror remains in the continuing white American belief in the otherness of the American Indian.

The massacre at Wounded Knee, in 1890, ended the last major Indian attempt to break out of reservation life—which, for the panicky Indians, was simply running away, but which, for the whites, was a rejection of settlement and civilization, a return to savagery, and thus a betrayal. There was no place left for Indians to escape to. Their worlds were utterly destroyed. They have become Americans, whether they wish to or not. They have been forced to live in ways they have found incomprehensible, in the midst of a nation which promised to care for them, but whose care has proven inadequate and also incomprehensible. "I cannot understand," Young Joseph of the Nez Percé said in 1879:

> why so many chiefs are allowed to talk so many different ways, and promise so many different things. . . . They all say they are my friends, and that I shall have justice, but while their mouths all talk right I do not understand why nothing is done for my people. . . . Words do not pay for my dead people. They do not pay for my country, now overrun by white men. They do not protect my father's grave. They do not pay for my horses and cattle. Good words will not give me back my children. . . . Good words will not give my people good health and stop them from dying. Good words will not get my people a home where they can live in peace and take care of themselves. I am tired of talk that comes to nothing. . . .

The policy of the federal government toward the Indians has clearly reflected the myths and metaphors of all white Americans. From the late nineteenth century until the 1930's, that policy was to make farmers of the Indians, to distribute all tribal lands to individuals (under the Dawes Allotment Act of 1887) and so remove the "un-American" communal ownership of land, to encourage missionaries on the reservations to Christianize the pagans, and, through missionaries, teachers, and agents, to destroy tribal organization and obliterate the languages and customs of the tribes. The Indians needed schools, as the whites saw it, to put them "on the highway towards the goal of civilization." Once properly educated, Indians would, according to the white Indian agents in New Mexico in 1864, "gradually become merged in the general population of the country, forget their distinctive customs and laws, and require no further special care from the government." Since the 1930's, government policy has been to encourage the Indians who live on reservations to maintain something of their tribal cultures and to develop institutions of local self-government—on the model of American democracies, not on tribal models. The American Indians, in the twentieth century, have finally been made citizens of the United States. But the benefits of these changes are not clear to the Indians, who remain among "the others" in their native America.

The mythology of the frontier and the powerful imperatives of color and race still apply. The alternatives which the myths offer to the Indians create such tension that choice seems impossible. Indians are tempted to merge in the general population by the imperatives and ideals of American belief. But such merging requires ceasing to be Indian, a difficult choice at best. At the same time, the mythology of color tends to prevent that choice. The alternative is to be segregated, or self-segregated, outside the mainstream, and thus to live as Indians. But the logic of segregation is that separateness is inferior, un-American, and possibly uncivilized. It is contrary to the imperatives of the myths of equality and democracy and individual independence, the logic of which belongs to the Indians as other Americans. Full participation in American life—which was the goal of the nineteenth-century whites who wanted to Christianize the Indians—seems as difficult of achievement today as it did in 1881, when Helen Hunt Jackson wrote in *A Century of Dishonor* that "time, statesmanship, philanthropy, and Christianity" were required in order to bring the Indians "slowly and surely" to full civilization. Is that civilization to be American, or is there some separate Indian civilization?

TRANSFORMATION

Because Indians were on reservations separated from the rest of society, and because the frontier with which they were associated disappeared, they have until very recently vanished from the consciousness of most urban, industrial, modern Americans. They have ceased in the twentieth-century to be the paradigm of otherness for Americans, and ceased to define the mythic boundaries of American community. Black Americans—who have obviously and in great numbers participated in the urbanization, industrialization, and modernization of America—have become the paradigm. The complex myths of the modern black experience provide the logic and the models of modern American otherness, and of modern community boundaries.

The traditional logic of color and race—that people of some colors are superior and those of others inferior—has kept blacks and Indians from full participation in American life. That logic has prevented white Americans from accepting blacks or Indians as equal human beings. Against that logic, and the realities it has helped create and sustain in America, blacks and Indians for a long time could only plead. "These parting words are in behalf of an outraged, heart-broken, bruised, and bleeding, but God-fearing people," Congressman George H. White, black Populist from North Carolina, said in his valedictory address to the United States House of Representatives in 1901. (White was called, in a book published in 1970, "the last Black Southern Congressman"; a description which no longer applies.) White ended his speech quoting Sir Walter Raleigh defending Bacon: "Sir, I am pleading for the life of a human being."

Young Joseph also pleaded:

> I know that my race must change. We cannot hold our own with the white man as we are. We only ask an even chance to live as other men live. We ask to be recognized as men.

At the beginning of the twentieth century, the power of the frontier, the image of the great line between civilization and the wilderness, between the American white and the savage black or Indian, was very strong indeed. The reality of the frontier is today just barely beyond the memory of living Americans. The myths of the frontier were, at least as they applied to the matters of race and color in America, overwhelming. "Let me be a free man," Young Joseph said:

> . . . free to travel, free to stop, free to work, free to trade where I choose, free to choose my own teachers, free to follow the religion of my fathers, free to think and talk and act for myself—and I will obey every law, or submit to the penalty.

But no American, when Joseph spoke those words, was willing to allow these ideals to overcome the careful definitions of community boundaries which were embodied in the beliefs about color and race. The distinction between Americans and others was clearly more important, *inside* America, than questions of individualism or equality.

Today, the strength of the frontier (reality, image, and metaphor) as the community boundary has lessened. Modern Americans still believe, however, that color is a line and a definition of otherness, as the treatment of Indians, blacks, Mexicans, and Puerto Ricans indicates. But, using the model of black Americans since the 1950's, more and more Americans believe that ethnic Americans with their ethnicity are American minorities: and the logic of that belief requires emphasis on American ("we are *all* Americans") and it requires protection of the rights of the minority. The myths of color and race are, it seems clear, undergoing transformation. What those myths may become, or what their logic will be, is not yet clear. But all Americans believe that Thurgood Marshall is a Justice of the Supreme Court of the United States, and that Andrew Young was the United States Ambassador to the United Nations and an outspoken American. They are *also* black Americans. But in that "also" is the beginning of a recognition Young Joseph pleaded for: the recognition of a free American human being without a boundary defined by color or race.

7

Transformation of the Wilderness

"THIS NATION WAS SPAWNED in wilderness, and from the beginning of settlement it has obtained sustenance from the boundless forests on every hand" is the opening line of a United States Department of Agriculture Forest Service pamphlet published in 1970, entitled *Search for Solitude: Our Wilderness Heritage.* "Viewed with awe and misgivings by early settlers of the New World," the pamphlet continues, "the American wilderness has been interwoven into the Nation's folklore, history, art, and literature. Even today, these wide expanses of forested mountains help shape the character of our youth."

Much of the original wilderness has been tamed, the pamphlet relates, but there are some "untamed lands, majestic reminders of primeval America" which are part of the National Forests of the United States: "Here, as wild and as free as ever," are over nine million acres of wilderness "for the use, enjoyment, and spiritual enrichment of the American people."

"Wilderness shaped our national character as our forefathers met and conquered its early challenge," the Forest Service pamphlet goes on. "The National Wilderness Preservation System will assure all future Americans of a continuing opportunity to test their pioneering skills." Of course, the pamphlet admits, "man's actions now must be disciplined so that Nature may be free." It is no longer possible for Americans to exercise "freedom with native materials" in the wilderness as Daniel Boone and Jim Bridger did. The Forest Service today manages "wilderness as a *resource,* in which naturalness is perpetuated" so that "the elemental simplicities of wilderness travel" which so thrilled our forefathers and which gave them "complete freedom" remain part "of the heritage, of the progress, of the expression of America."

While Forest Service prose, at least in this pamphlet, tends toward purple, it nevertheless expresses most of the essential elements in contemporary American perceptions of the wilderness.Those perceptions are rather different from those of our forefathers, who believed they had a mission into the wilderness. The contemporary wilderness exists (like its former inhabitants, the Indians) on "reservations"—islands of anachronism in the modern sea of progress. Wilderness is an "area," part of the National Wilderness Preservation System, which is part of the Forest Service, which is part of the Department of Agriculture, which is a large, but by no means the largest, bureaucracy in America today. The Forest Service manages the Wilderness System (resources in the contemporary world must be *managed*) in order to perpetuate the naturalness of the wilderness. The nature which is thus protected is "wild and free," while the people who travel in that nature "must be disciplined." (And while there are still faint echoes of the ideas of training, education, and adaptation in the contemporary use of "discipline," its principal meanings imply regimentation—suitable to bureaucracies—and punishment.)

A trip into the wilderness today is made by individuals or small groups of specially equipped people, not to seek out resources and use them or to change and civilize the wilderness, but to test their own skills, adaptability, survival, and individual psychological and physical endurance. The purpose is to test while leaving the wilderness untouched. Like Thoreau's sojourn at Walden, the contemporary American sees "in wildness the preservation of the world"; the wilderness is always compared to civilization, its use is measured by departure from *and* return to the civilized world.

"Out of his wilderness, out of the freedom of his opportunities," the Forest Service pamphlet quotes the great historian of the frontier, Frederick Jackson Turner, as saying, "the American fashioned a formula for social regeneration." Today, wilderness is equated with freedom and individual regeneration. The contemporary American in a wilderness area is a pathfinder and a pioneer (the ritual is powerful because it is not consciously re-enacted), is simultaneously an immigrant, a settler, a frontiersman, and an Indian who learns from the wilderness—learns the independence and isolation, the liberty and equality and pursuit of happiness, as well as the power, bounty, and beauty of nature, which are the American's rightful inheritance. The American emerges from the wilderness eager to carry the lessons learned to those who do not know them—the American is, from the name of one wilderness program, "outward bound," carrying regeneration to the world. "The character of our youth" (and thus of our society), according to the Forest Service pamphlet, is shaped by the "continuing opportunity to test their pioneering skills."

The wilderness in our century is outside our everyday urban, industrial, and civilized world. It is natural and scenic, something to be looked at, traveled through, and enjoyed for its beauty and contrast to the works of humanity. It is wild and therefore full of dangers. It is also resources, which require proper management so that they can be used to support the growth and progress of the civilized world. Those resources, some fear, are, like the wilderness itself, in danger of disappearing—as the frontier disappeared—from America. Modern conservationists and ecologists have widely publicized the equation of wilderness and resources and have tried to make *The Pursuit of Wilderness* (the title of a 1971 book by Paul Brooks) an important part of reform.

The direct and immediate connection between wilderness and mission, which was so obvious to early Americans on their errands into the wilderness, is no longer obvious or immediate. The myths which shaped American perceptions of the wilderness have been transformed over the past two centuries, and have slowly diverged from the myths of America's mission and destiny with which they were previously so intimately connected. Wilderness today is a symbol of, and provides an unconscious ritual for, the American mission; it is a metaphorical stage for a historical pageant, no longer the real world.

The transformation of the wilderness that began in the early colonial mission to Christianize and civilize it gradually achieved increasing success as the British, French, Spanish, and others penetrated America. The Revolution, the establishment of the United States, and the expansion of the nation—and nationalism—increased the tempo of the process. An important part of the creation of wilderness myths was the development of a typology of American "characters," as we shall see. Succeeding waves of backwoodsmen, frontiersmen, and pioneers adapted to life in the wilderness, became almost like Indians, and brought civilization to more and more of the New World with their axes, their guns, their plows, and their willingness to make the ways of the wilderness their own. In their characteristics as typical Americans, they reconciled the conflict between civilization and wilderness; their myths implied that America could somehow *have* the wilderness, *be* the wilderness, and civilize it, too.

As the wilderness was civilized, it became the frontier in myth—a place that was constantly moving westward, a place where most Americans did *not* live. For those who were not "out West," the mythical wilderness became a beneficent nature from which Americans could learn valuable lessons and in which they could lead improved lives. Henry David Thoreau, in his very influential *Walden; or, Life in the Woods,* published in 1854, became the leading bard of that transformed wilderness.

WILDERNESS BECOMES NATURE

"When one man has reduced a fact of the imagination to be a fact to his understanding," Thoreau wrote in *Walden,* "I foresee that all men will at length establish their lives on that basis." Thoreau was consciously creating myth in *Walden.* Based on his perception that "the mass of men lead lives of quiet desperation" and that "one generation abandons the enterprises of another like stranded vessels," he attempted to create a view of the wilderness (and therefore of American purpose and mission) which was perceptibly different from that of the generations preceding him, and which would offer hope of some sort of peace and salvation to those who lived in the burgeoning cities and actively participated in industrial civilization. Yet it was to Americans that Thoreau sang of the wilderness; it was Americans who could understand, because they were part of this wild New World, that "in wildness is the preservation of the world."

"I lived alone, in the woods, a mile from any neighbor," Thoreau proudly wrote at the beginning of *Walden,* "in a house which I had built myself . . . and earned my living by the labor of my hands only." Ruefully, he admitted at the end of the paragraph that "at present, I am a sojourner in civilized life again." The contrast of civilized life to life alone in the wilderness is ever-present in *Walden*—as it was ever present in American belief. Thoreau admitted the necessity of civilized life, but, instead of adhering to traditional American belief that it was civilized life which produced morality and virtue, that civilization would in the end overcome the wilderness, he insisted that it was the *wilderness* which produced morality and virtue. Only in the wilderness could one acquire the true isolation and independence which was the birthright of every American. Only there, as his opening paragraph implied, could an American really be a sturdy, independent yeoman. Only in the wilderness could one find the liberty, the equality, the democracy peculiar to America, and the independence to pursue true happiness which was the goal of every American.

Wilderness, for Thoreau as for many of his Romantic and Transcendentalist American contemporaries, had become Nature. "At the same time that we are earnest to explore and learn all things," he wrote in a passage from *Walden* quoted at the opening of Paul Brooks's *The Pursuit of Wilderness:*

> we require that all things be mysterious and unexplorable. . . . We can never have enough of nature. We must be refreshed by . . . the wilderness with its living and its decaying trees. . . . We need to witness our own limits transgressed, and some life pasturing freely where we never wander.

Nature was refreshing, something to be looked at, where life was somehow free.

It was only by living in nature and becoming part of it that Americans could learn its romantic, innocent, noble secrets. Thoreau thus emphasized the necessity that Americans adapt to the wilderness, which was already part of the mythology, but the purpose of the adaptation was different in the myth he was creating. It was only by living in the wilderness, and learning the hazards, the powers, the bounty, and the beauty of nature, that Americans could become proper Americans; it was the wilderness that made them so, rather than they who should make the wilderness American.

Thoreau's vision was that the American errand into the wilderness was not primarily to acquire the skills necessary to survive long enough to civilize it but rather to learn the peculiarly American virtues of freedom, independence, isolation, equality, democracy, and true happiness *from* the wilderness and bring them to civilization. His vision became an increasingly important part of the imagery of the myths available to Americans, in great measure because Thoreau appealed to images and myths which already belonged to Americans. He did not reject the mythology he inherited; rather, he told a "good story," as Americans judged it, of his life at Walden, a story which appealed to much of American mythical belief. He made nature and the wilderness, as he defined them, the central operators in the creation of Americans. After Thoreau, more and more Americans came to believe that it was the wilderness which made them American.

USEFUL NATURE

In 1864, ten years after *Walden* appeared, in the midst of the Civil War, George Perkins Marsh, a Vermont scholar, entrepreneur, politician, ambassador, and naturalist, published a book entitled *Man and Nature; or, Physical Geography As Modified by Human Action.* Many now attribute the beginning of the American conservation movement, as well as the beginning of modern American forest management, to Marsh's book. Marsh wrote that

> Man, the domestic animals that serve him, the field and garden plants the products of which supply him with food and clothing, cannot subsist and rise to the full development of their higher properties, unless brute and unconscious nature be effectually combatted, and, in a great degree, vanquished by human art. Hence, a certain measure of transformation of terrestrial surface, of suppression of natural, and stimulation of artificially modified productivity becomes necessary. This measure man has unfortunately exceeded.

Marsh proceeded to catalogue the destruction of forests (and the resulting erosion), the destruction of watersheds (and the resulting deserts), the plowing up of grasses (and the resulting blowing away of topsoil), and the uprooting of coastal plants (and the resulting spread of dunes). "The destructive agency of man becomes more and more energetic and unsparing as he advances in civilization," Marsh continued. He made a distinction between "the wandering savage," whose life does not destroy his surroundings and man in "the pastoral state" who "commences an almost indiscriminate warfare upon all the forms of animal and vegetable existence around him" and who "gradually eradicates or transforms every spontaneous product of the soil he occupies."

Marsh assumed, in the traditional logic of earlier American wilderness myths, that civilization was superior to wilderness and that humanity, at least civilized humanity, was separate from the ecology of nature. The wilderness, in Marsh's view, however, did not exist simply to be civilized. Marsh believed, as did Thoreau, that the wilderness had contributions to make to civilization. Wilderness was *useful.* It supplied resources essential to civilized life, and humanity's task was to nurture those resources.

The essential difference between "brute" (in nature) and "human" (civilized), according to Marsh, is that humans are capable of the reasonable management and progressive use of the resources of nature. Nature, the wilderness, must be understood, the complicated interrelationships of its natural production of resources comprehended, and its resources then managed so as to provide supplies for the progress of civilized humanity. Wilderness was, in the view Marsh fostered, no longer an enemy to be conquered, a state of natural chaos to be eradicated and replaced by civilized people; it was rather a complex set of delicately interrelated forces, processes, and resources which humanity could reasonably learn *about* (not necessarily *from*) and then carefully use to its own advantage.

The conservation movement did not spring full-blown from Marsh's book. It was more than a decade after its publication that the Yellowstone area of Wyoming was set aside as a park for the American people, and several decades before the "use" of the wilderness came generally to mean its management and possible preservation to Americans.

Many Americans were aware that their world, and its wilderness, was changing by the time the Civil War ended. But "the old Crusading spirit lives," an article in *The Atlantic Monthly* in 1867 assured its readers. This issue of the magazine is remarkable in that it contains several articles directly concerned with the wilderness. *The Atlantic,* published in Boston, supported and contributed to by some of America's leading literary figures, was probably the most influential magazine in the United States in the post-Civil War era. In 1867, when Reconstruction was reaching its height, when the Civil Rights Act and the Fourteenth Amendment were being debated all over America, when President Andrew Johnson seemed to be heading for direct confrontation with Congress (and, as it happened, the only presidential impeachment so far in American history), several writers in *The Atlantic* devoted themselves to the question of what was happening to the wilderness.

The poet Bayard Taylor, in an article entitled "Travel in the United States," seriously looked forward to the demise of the wilderness, and with it "the rude pioneer phase, which accommodates itself to everything." Taylor was disgusted with American adaptation to the wilderness, and he sought that "happy day" when *all* of American territory would be "at least thinly settled from ocean to ocean" and "the work of consolidation" could commence. He was eager to see "a convenient, well-regulated life" established, in which the wilderness no longer obtruded its chaos, its violence, its natural disorder. He wanted America to be, finally, "settled."

Taylor was a modern tourist who traveled for pleasure—a phenomenon made possible by railroads, industry, and cities. He was dependent upon accommodations and his primary interest was in scenery. The Eastern part of the United States, as he saw it, was drab and unsightly, full of stumps, undrained swamps, and "spindling trees left here and there as forlorn monuments of the original forests." West of the Missouri, however, the "ragged, shabby character" of Eastern scenery disappeared and nature displayed some perfection:

> The fields have the smoothness of a long-settled country; the trees grow up, taking their perfect characteristic forms; and the young forests which issue from the earth . . . will rise in walls and mounts of exuberant foliage. . . .
>
> From that meridian line where the peaks of the Rocky Mountains first rise above the horizon of the Plains, to the shore of the Pacific, there is no region without its beauties and its wonders. . . . They combine the highest elements of beauty and sublimity, in new forms. Within ten years . . . all those sources of enjoyment, of inspiration, of native growth and development, will be opened to us.

Taylor combined the old mythic image of a New World in which greater perfection was possible with the newer vision (which Marsh had expressed) of the usefulness of the wilderness. He was self-consciously part of a productive, organized, industrial society in which nature was intended to serve people and which could provide leisure for all:

> Even our farmers are beginning to have their little after-harvest trips to the sea-shore, the Hudson, Niagara, or the West. The old men, whose boast it was that their lives had been spent within a radius of twenty or thirty miles, are going unhonored into their graves.

Nature was a source of "growth and development" and therefore useful. Leisure was a very different kind of use of nature—requiring that it be convenient and well-regulated—than the management George Marsh had contemplated, but the usefulness Taylor espoused was much closer to Marsh's "nature" than it was to the old mythic American wilderness.

Like many of his contemporaries and many Americans since, Taylor was eager for the closing of the frontier and the spread of industrial civilization.

He believed, as did Americans traditionally, in the incompatibility of wilderness and civilization, and yearned for the day when America would learn "the important truth that it is better off without any more" wilderness, without any more frontiers and frontiersmen. For him, as for many others who continued to see the wilderness as the Pilgrims saw it, wilderness was valuable only when it was being *used*, when it was civilized and therefore no longer wilderness.

In the later part of the nineteenth century, and throughout the twentieth century, Americans have eagerly built an empire of progress across Nature. Nature was arranged, and carefully regulated, by Frederick Law Olmsted in Central Park, in Brooklyn, in metropolitan Boston, in the suburbs of Chicago. It was crisscrossed by railroads, and again by highways; it was stripped by lumberjacks (who created Paul Bunyan), and managed by Forest Rangers (symbolized by Smokey the Bear); sodbusters plowed it up and agribusiness made it a breadbasket; Buffalo Bill shot its buffalo to feed railroad construction gangs, and buffalo bones lay in piles twenty feet high and miles long to be shipped to fertilizer factories.

The disappearance of the American wilderness into a nature which was entirely for human use and manipulation was not something most Americans regretted. From small-town "boomers" to men of sober reflection, for the past century the progress of urban, industrial American civilization has been something to be excited about. "Life is action, the use of one's powers," Oliver Wendell Holmes, Jr., said in a 1900 speech:

> The chief worth of civilization is just that it makes the means of living more complex; that it calls for great and combined intellectual efforts, instead of simple, uncoordinated ones, in order that the crowd may be fed and clothed and housed and moved from place to place. Because more complex and intense intellectual efforts mean a fuller and richer life.

The city replaced the natural wilderness in American belief as the prime *locus* of opportunity, adventure, and success, just as industry replaced agriculture as the primary means to success. Nature had become merely the accumulation of the "variety and quantity of what man needs for the sustenance and the decoration of his life." It was in cities that the accumulations of nature were put to proper use by the systematic organization of the human resources which are available only in cities.

Quite prophetically, James Parton wrote a paean to the city of Chicago in the 1867 volume of *The Atlantic Monthly.* In it, he rhapsodized over the exciting possibilities which accompanied the commerce, large populations, and creative abilities of the human intellect in cities. In Chicago, the outstanding example of urban opportunities well used, according to Parton, was the stockyards:

> Nothing is more simple and easy than the working of the system. . . . While the tired and hungry animals are enjoying respite from the torture of their ride, their owner or his agent finds comfort in . . . a handsome hotel . . . built solely for the accommodation of the "cattlemen." . . . A few steps from the hotel is the Cattle Exchange, another spacious and elegant edifice. . . . The cattlemen leave this fine Exchange and go forth to view the cattle. . . . They move about in the midst of those prodigious herds, and inspect the occupants of any particular pen, with as much ease as a lady examines pictures in a window. . . . The men return to the Exchange, where the money is paid, all the cattle business being done for cash; after which they conclude the affair by dining together at the hotel, or at an excellent restaurant in the Exchange itself.

The Cattle Exchange, he wrote, lifted "a repulsive and barbarizing business" (one which partook thereby of all the negative characteristics of the mythic wilderness) "out of the mire," and rendered it "clean, easy, respectable and pleasant." In such a complex, urban, and industrial organization as the Chicago stockyards, the wilderness and its resources were made useful.

The stockyards were but one example of the civilized use of the resources of a modern city, whose resources included "these grain mountains, these miles of timber, this entanglement of railroads, this mighty host of newcomers." For Parton and for increasing numbers of Americans, the resources of nature were no longer separate from those of civilization: such resources were *part* of the cities, and by right belonged to the cities. The benefits of urban life, set amid such resources (as opposed to life on the frontier or in the wilderness), were many: Beautiful "temples," excellent schools, local "benevolences," "innocent" social life, ceaseless "battlings with vice," an "instinct" for decoration, a "conscientiously conducted" press, libraries, and bookstores. Cities like Chicago were the locations *and* the resources for American progress, for the continued growth of civilization.

All that the wilderness had come to represent of opportunity, of riches, of equality and democracy, innocence and paradise, and all the virtues of the American frontier (as well as its vices) slowly became part of the mythology of American cities. Cities, for modern Americans, became glittering symbols of opportunity; they also became jungles inhabited by savages, dangerous to civilized life. Like Carl Sandburg's "Chicago," they replaced the wilderness as the symbols of American progress and the self-conscious creation of civilization:

> Laughing the stormy, husky, brawling laughter of Youth, half-naked,
> sweating, proud to be Hog Butcher, Tool Maker, Stacker of Wheat,
> Player with Railroads and Freight Handler to the Nation.

THE MISSION BEYOND

As the mythic American wilderness disappeared into the cities, into managed nature and its resources, and into reservations in the course of the late nineteenth and early twentieth centuries the mission of America—which is so intimately attached in mythic symbiosis to the American wilderness—also underwent transformation. As a westward movement, an errand into the wilderness, the mythic *and* the real accomplishments of the American mission had been great. The westward movement had, according to Frederick Merk, one of the most eminent of its recent historians,

> . . . created a nation. . . . It gave the nation many of its fundamental democratic institutions. . . . It imparted emotional and spiritual values to successive generations. To them the open West was the land of promise, the Utopia of their dreams. . . . Conquest, speculation, exploitation, and violence were all part of this crusade into the wilderness.

The historical reality of civilizing a real wilderness has long given Americans—including contemporary Americans—a focus for the energies generated by contradictions and paradoxes contained in the mythology of mission.

But the real wilderness was fast disappearing by the twentieth century. And there were great temptations generated by the increasing national wealth. There was a growing fascination with power, which the actual conquest of the real West helped produce. There were possibilities for expansion beyond the disappearing wilderness, beyond America. The growth of great American cities with their human resources, the exciting and rapid development of huge and productive industrial organizations, and the crusading possibilities which the experience of the Civil War opened to Americans—all these real and mythic changes in America produced new possibilities for the American mission.

The essential structure of the myth of the New World remained: America is the New World. It is a nation which is the refuge and light of freedom, democracy, equality, and opportunity. The Americans are a Chosen People, part of a new plan for Creation, specially endowed by their Creator as representatives of the possibilities and potentialities of the Brave New World. They are on the cutting edge of history, pathfinding, discovering, and settling the chaotic wilderness which is just beyond—over the next hill, across the next desert, over the next ocean, on the next satellite or planet. But the possibilities for the realization of the American mission are transformed, and that has produced, as Americans very gradually have come to perceive it, a whole new ball game.

"The old Crusading spirit lives," W. Winwoode Reade wrote in that 1867 volume of *The Atlantic Monthly,* but "the Holy Land of the present day," he told his American readers, was Central Africa. And even that was "all so romantic and medieval" a wilderness that he feared it would not last. The real wilderness was moving to places outside America, beyond the urban and industrial world, and any errand into the wilderness, as the author saw it, would be made in order to use the wilderness for personal ends:

> It is a glorious and awful thing to be alone in the desert—a speck in that mighty solitude,—a spark in the abyss. . . . Every step is a novelty, a sensation; the summit of every eminence may disclose to him a prodigy; and all the while his mind is caressing this one idea: —"I am the first white man who has trodden on this land, who breathes this air. I can call that mountain after anybody I choose: it belongs to me. The Geographical Society will give me a gold medal; I shall have to make a speech; my name will be printed on all the maps."

The phrase "I am the first white man . . ." makes clear that wilderness is *beyond* civilization, not necessarily something which is part of it.

The dwellers in such non-American wildernesses were, like the land itself, only there to be used. "The natives of the country" the modern explorer regarded "simply as savage or domestic animals." They were dishonest, "ignorant of the value of time," and they were even offended by the contemptuousness which explorers did not care to hide. Not surprisingly, a bad feeling would often spring up between natives and such explorers, but only, according to *The Atlantic*'s author, because natives were "the most vain and sensitive creatures in the world." There was nothing to be learned from such peoples. They obviously needed to be taught—by the crusader, the explorer, the missionary.

Only missionaries would think of living among such people. The missionary acquired their language, understood "their methods of thought," became "habituated to their constant duplicity," learned "how to handle their stubborn, suspicious natures," and sometimes even learned "how to win their poor little childish hearts." The wilderness and its inhabitants had become, in this *Atlantic* article, a problem in exploration and in resource management and use, *conducted outside America,* for American benefit, and in order to bring the blessings of civilization to a world without them.

Whether it was "taking up the white man's burden," providing "oil for the lamps of China," freeing Cuba from Spain, "making the world safe for democracy," bringing the Four Freedoms to the world, "saving the Western Democracies," or "nation-building" in Vietnam, America's mission, her errand into the wilderness, has become—with the disappearance of the American wilderness—something to be carried out in the larger wilderness which is not-America. In the myths of nationalism, of the manifest destiny of America, the wilderness has become a metaphor. Those places and peoples and nations on earth which Americans perceive to be without democracy, without liberty, without independence, without the possibility of the individual pursuit of happiness, *are* wildernesses. It is the mission of America and Americans to civilize such wildernesses.

It is also the case, and part of the imperative of American mythology, that Americans must pursue real—as distinguished from metaphorical—wilderness. But the contemporary effort is no longer to civilize the threatened, disappearing real wildernesses. Americans want to be able to enter the wilderness, survive in it (through the instrumentalities and the equipment of modern industrial science and technology), use its resources, and accomplish some mission in it without disturbing, more than necessary, the delicate balance of forces in it, the ecology of it. In this sense as well, there is still the challenge of mission into the wilderness, but the goal is no longer to transform the wilderness into something civilized; it is rather to *use* the wilderness and the resources it possesses *as wilderness.*

The sense of the existence of wilderness, the powerful imagery of contrast between civilization and wilderness, must be maintained if the logic of New World mythology is to be maintained. American myths tell us still that there is no New World without wilderness. If we are to be true Americans (and thus part of that New World and its destiny), there *must* be wilderness. The symbol is an imperative for our real world.

The wilderness as symbol and as metaphor, as well as the wilderness as creator of Americans, keeps its strength and its presence in American belief through the constant, paradigmatic excursions of individual Americans into the available natural wildernesses. Today, most Americans read Thoreau, especially *Walden.* And large tracts of American countryside are deliberately maintained to provide the wildernesses necessary to preserve the reality of the wilderness contradiction of civilization.

Since its birth, the American nation has tied itself to a dream of expansion into the wilderness. The destiny of the New World and the mission of America have been the interchangeable focuses of powerful, still-living American myth. The actual demise of a New World to conquer—the American West, the American wilderness—has not destroyed the power of the myth to generate energy in Americans, to provide a dynamic for American society, to make a logical explanation of the American universe. The imperative of the mission myth requires new worlds (new wildernesses) to conquer. Americans—pathfinders, discoverers, pioneers, explorers, crusaders, reformers—have not ceased to seek the liberty, democracy, equality, independence, and happiness those new worlds offer, *in new worlds.*

II

THE PURSUIT OF HAPPINESS

1
Sex and Self

"SCRUPLES," BY JUDITH KRANTZ, was one of the best-selling novels in America in 1979. In the novel, "Scruples" is the name of a boutique, not a characterization of moral principles or behavior. A book club advertising the novel warned that it was "sexually explicit." One of the principal attractions of the book, which it shares with many contemporary popular novels, is a persistent combination of name brands, money, the consumption of goods and services, and sex—its fictitious Beverly Hills boutique is symbol and focus of many modern American fantasies.

The book opens in Beverly Hills, and the first paragraph includes a "stately, nearsighted retired banker" who is making an illegal turn in "his Dino Ferrari," a "teen-ager speeding to a tennis lesson in a fifty-five-thousand-dollar Rolls-Royce Corniche," and a "matronly civic leader" illegally parking "her bright red Jaguar." The combination of California, fast illegal traffic, name-brand automobiles, and three important contemporary social types—banker, civic leader, and athletic teenager—makes the first paragraph sound almost like satire. But the combination of popular fantasy, social status, and the vague sexuality evoked by fast traffic and California reflects much of the content of contemporary beliefs about individuality.

The remaining two or three opening pages of *Scruples* describe the heroine of the novel and her boutique interchangeably. Heroine and store are combined in a pastiche of sex, money (in dollar amounts), names (of exotic people and places), and consumer goods, which has the cumulative effect of a very new, very complex and luxurious, very elaborate and extensive American shopping mall:

> Billy . . . brought her vintage Bentley to a stop . . . in front of Scruples, the world's most lavish specialty store. . . . She was thirty-five, sole mistress of a fortune estimated at between two hundred and two hundred fifty million dollars. . . .
>
> Billy's tawny wool cape was lined in golden sable. . . . Billy . . . always wore her signature jewels, the great eleven-karat diamonds known as the Kimber-

ley Twins, which had been her wedding present from her first husband. . . .
She strode rapidly . . . threw open her cape and exposed her long, powerful throat. . . . A female of rampant sexual vitality combined with an ultimate and totally authoritative sense of personal style. . . .
She . . . ran a flourishing retail business, the most successful luxury shop in the world. . . . The fact that Scruples represented the smallest part of her fortune didn't make it any less important to her. . . . It was at once her passion and her plaything, a cherished secret come to life, tailored on a human scale that she could see, smell, touch, possess, change and make perfect and ever more perfect.

Popular novels like *Scruples* (which sell millions of copies as hardcovers, paperbacks, and book-club selections in their normal year or so of popularity) are, with television (and they are often televised), contemporary purveyors of myths. Such books do not necessarily *create* myths. Generally they accept and convey, in story form, the ideals and explanations, the images and metaphors, the attitudes and stereotypes which are already widespread and easily available in the culture. Their popularity rests on their being perceived as good stories—with the implication always present that they are "stories," not realities; yet if they are good stories they suspend the disbelief of those who read them and thereby become, at least momentarily, real descriptions of real people living real lives. Their "goodness" also rests on their familiarity, their fitting into patterns of belief and expectation which already exist in the minds of those who read them.

Individual freedom and the pursuit of individual happiness are, with life itself, the inalienable rights of Americans. These are articles of faith generated and sustained by all American myths. A novel like *Scruples* uses the symbols of individual freedom and the pursuit of happiness (particularly the *successful* pursuit), and the myths which sustain American individualism and consumer orientation, in order to assure the appeal of the story. The book opens, for example, with symbolic people (not characters in the story but simply symbols of social position) driving cars, and often driving them in violation of traffic laws. Freedom in contemporary society finds its most powerful (because most ubiquitous) symbol in the automobile, its operation by individual Americans (thereby assuring them of both freedom and mobility) and its operation in defiance of visibly established laws and authority (a *proof* of individual liberty). The addition of the names of particular brands of very expensive, "exclusive" cars adds the stamp of success, clearly understood by all, to the pursuit of happiness. (The foreign manufacture of the automobiles named makes them apt symbols, because contemporary American success is measured by the accessibility and control of the goods of the rest of the world.)

A free American in pursuit of happiness—and all Americans not in physical and legal duress are assumed to be such—is *mobile,* is, has been, will be, in motion, *and* is defying authority, pathmaking (trailblazing), is in fact a revolutionary. Moving, trailblazing revolution in defiance of establishment is the *way* of the proper American individual. That is the ideal, the symbolism, the myth, the imperative which is reinforced and appealed to, easily and casually, in the opening of *Scruples.*

The mythology of modern American individualism is, like all mythologies, complex. No single element, image, or symbol is an adequate description of the complexity (which is why "good" stories about American individuals, successful or not, are not simple stories). The heroine of *Scruples* (whose name, Billy, like the description of most of her personal characteristics, is androgynous) is not merely a moving, pathbreaking, successful, rich American; she is also part of a corporate, highly bureaucratized, carefully status-structured world. Her very individualism and success are corporate and bureaucratic, having to do with government agencies (the IRS), tax-free municipal bonds, Wall Street, as well as a flourishing retail business (which represents "the smallest part of her fortune"), employees of carefully defined status—even uniforms ("his black Scruples tunic")—and the intricate and arcane practical knowledge of how to succeed in *haute couture,* the boutique business, the movie business.

"The best of all the books on our industry," Bud Knight, "a Dallas retailer and co-author of *The Store,"* is quoted as saying about *Scruples* inside the cover of its paperback edition. That a novel about a contemporary American heroine can be a book about an industry is not surprising to Americans; indeed, many Americans find pleasure in "how to" books which do not distinguish between individual persons and the industries which they create or in which they rise to success. *Scruples* is, by its title, a novel about a store—"the world's most lavish specialty store, a virtual club for the floating principality of the very, very rich and the truly famous"—and from the very beginning of the book, the store and the heroine are inextricably connected. The contemporary mythology of American individualism does not distinguish between an individual and corporate, bureaucratic entities: the implication is that they are the same.

Part of the identification of individual with corporate entity is simply personification: the President *is* the government, Stalin *was* Russia, Hitler *was* Germany, Hoover *was* the FBI, Thomas Watson *was* IBM, John D. Rockefeller *was* Standard Oil. Yet most of this personification does not involve abstractions, nor does it personify by the use of mythical figures; real individuals are identified with real corporate entities, and the "growth," the "behavior," the "lives" of those entities are identified with the characteristics and lifetimes of the individuals. Russia was "de-Stalinized" after Stalin died; Howard Hughes's "empire" has been broken up since his death.

"Rugged individualism" has come to be identified with corporate capitalism for most Americans. Ironically, vast regimented corporate bureaucracies are believed to be the apotheosis of the traditional rights of life, liberty, and the pursuit of happiness. Critics of American society believe that traditional American individualism has brought violence, exploitation, inequality, and regimentation to modern America, that individualism has been incorporated into giant industrial, commercial, and governmental entities, and that the result is a military-industrial complex which behaves like a gunman-outlaw-robber baron-"traditional" American. But very nearly all Americans have come to believe that the big companies and even the big agencies behave—*as corporate entities*—in exactly the same ruthless, selfish, greedy, exploitative manner that the robber barons of old behaved. No one believes that the head of a giant corporation is exactly like Carnegie or Rockefeller or Vanderbilt were; in fact, few even know who the head of any giant corporation is. But most Americans believe that corporate giants behave like those men are supposed to have behaved; are in the world today *the* exemplars of American rugged individualism. The result of that belief is that twentieth-century Americans have long searched for symbols of individual freedom and the individual pursuit of happiness which are easier to live with, more consonant with the American ideals of equality and democracy and freedom than regimented, powerful, and exploitative corporate bureaucracies.

Energetic sexual activity has become the most available contemporary American symbol of individual expression and freedom (as well as implied movement!). But Americans have not given up their fascination with more traditional symbols. The result is a frequent combination, in the tales told by modern mythmakers, of sexual activity, corporate enterprise, and individual freedom. *Scruples'* heroine is described as possessing "rampant sexual vitality combined with an ultimate and totally authoritative sense of personal style," the words "ultimate," "totally," and "authoritative" evoking government, regimentation, corporate behavior, and bureaucracy. *Scruples'* author, like most contemporary bards of individualism, combines such images with sexual expression in the same individual character. The mythic logic is that they are interchangeable; therefore they share the same virtues, the same traditions, and are the rightful inheritors of the value Americans have always put on free individualism. There is no rational connection between sexuality, individual freedom, and corporate activity: but widely held American belief associates them; the association is evidently satisfying to great numbers of Americans (they buy the books and watch the shows in which they are associated), and they are thus logically connected in American myth.

Billy, the heroine of *Scruples,* is a formidable consumer of all the available goods and services of the world—as well as, through her "most successful luxury shop in the world," a purveyor of goods and services (in this she is not unlike a great corporation or government agency, although American stories rarely carry the mythic logic so far). In the patterns of her life as a consumer, there is an important, and very common, American parable. The paperback blurb for the book summarizes it: "the rise of a fascinating woman from fat, unhappy 'poor relative' of an aristocratic Boston family to a unique position among the super-beautiful and super-rich."

Billy ate a lot and got fat. She was unhappy and poor. She was part of an aristocratic family. She was, in short, a parasite in American society, waxing fat by consuming food, but obviously unproductive (because poor, because unhappy, because aristocratic). Then she became a proper American: she shed her connections to aristocracy, she "worked" at getting thin and at learning a trade, she pursued happiness—through sexual activity, marriage (which provided both sex and wealth), and the consumption of goods other than food (except exotic, brand-name food and wines)—and she moved (from place to place, and up the scales of beauty and wealth in fast cars and planes). Again she waxed fat, not physically, but on corporate wealth originally acquired by others. And she became an entrepreneur (but only on a small part of her fortune; she was not a "throwback," merely a unique but full-fledged member of a *corporate,* not an entrepreneurial, society). By such activity, she became a contributing, properly consuming member of society. In her—as in many heroes and heroines of modern American tales—fat, consumption, and wealth, poverty and aristocracy, as well as sex, individual freedom, and corporate activity are joined in a mythic resolution of the problems and contradictions their real presence in America has created.

In American belief, the individual has always been the primary economic unit of the society. Columbus discovered America, frontiersmen and pioneers led the way across the continent, the sturdy American yeoman tilled the soil and created the wealth, entrepreneurs started the businesses and made them thrive, and behind these rugged individuals had come civilization, government, and organized, cultivated society based on the wealth they discovered, created and manufactured. The frontiers, the settlements, the businesses and industries, the cities and towns had all been made and made to grow by the industrious, productive economic activity of single individuals. That is the historical vision, the ideal, and the myth which Americans believe to be—or to have been—the reality of the economic aspect of individualism. The individual is the engine of progress and wealth.

So, too, is the contemporary individual. The *pattern* of the myth has not significantly changed, but some of the *content* has been transformed over the past century. Today, the American individual is expected to go out there and generate money, consume as much as possible of the goods available in the world, provide for the distribution of goods to others, and thus fuel the growth of wealth and prosperity. "Consumer" is the modern label for the American individual in economic clothing. The consumer is the engine of contemporary American progress. The intricacies of money and consumption are as fascinating to Americans today as the nature of machinery and production were half a century ago.

The contemporary mythic image of the mobile, corporate, consuming American has led many critics of contemporary society to the conclusion that American individualism has disappeared in modern bureaucratic life, a casualty of its own logic. According to Christopher Lasch, in *The Culture of Narcissism: American Life in an Age of Diminishing Expectations,* the contemporary American has "surrendered most of his technical skills to the corporation," can no longer even bring up children "without the help of certified experts," and has so allowed the traditions of self-help and individual competence to erode that he is entirely "dependent on the state, the corporation, and other bureaucracies." What Lasch called "the culture of competitive individualism" is, he wrote, "a way of life that is dying," and "in its decadence" in contemporary America, it "has carried the logic of individualism to the extreme of a war of all against all, the pursuit of happiness to the dead end of a narcissistic preoccupation with the self."

The contemporary American narcissist is, however, according to Lasch, not isolated or alone. He "depends on others to validate his self-esteem." While he is apparently free "from family ties and institutional constraints," yet that freedom does not allow him "to stand alone or to glory in his individuality"; rather, it makes him so insecure that he requires "reflections" of himself "in the attentions of others," or he is driven to attach himself "to those who radiate celebrity, power, and charisma." This contemporary narcissist has no connection to the traditions, the myths, or the realities of American individualism, according to Lasch, because, for the narcissist, "the world is a mirror, whereas the rugged individualist saw it as an empty wilderness to be shaped to his own design."

Such narcissism is an obvious part of the appeal of stories like *Scruples.* But the "teller of tales," the novelist or the scriptwriter, keeps the contradictory elements of any mythic story in a state of tension, implying resolution by reiterated association. The ardent social critic, like Christopher Lasch, on the other hand, pushes the logic of the myth to rational conclusions. The sharp contrasts of ideals with realities, of logic with hope, which the critic sees and relishes, are softened and blended by the storyteller because the purpose of myths—indeed, their *function* in human life—is to reconcile those contrasts and make it possible for people to live with them. It is unclear, ultimately, whether the logic of the critic is closer to reality than the good story of the novelist.

Narcissism, as Lasch contended, is indeed part of the mythology of American individualism, but it is not the sole content of the mythic stories of American individuals today or in the past. The loner, the rugged individual, the sturdy yeoman, the pioneer, and the cowboy are all bundled together in the mythology of American individualism. All of these are arguably "narcissists," all are associated with mythic wildernesses of various kinds, but all are also simultaneously and inextricably associated with civilization, with society, with family, with group work and cooperation, and with community. So the narcissism inherent in American individualism is continually tempered by a pursuit of happiness which has as its aim a happiness beyond the self.

Individual isolation and the "mirror" of the world have also long been part of the logic of American individualism. The independence of the individual—from other individuals, from society, from government and regimentation especially—has been the long-stated aim of all American individuals. As individuals, Americans are therefore revolutionary, and opposed to, in conflict with, and contradictory to government, established authority, social imperatives.

The logic of independence in American myth requires the protection of the individual from government. Its central premise is that individual rights are *in contrast to* the rights of society and state (but the presence of a society and a state to be independent of is necessary to the dynamic of the myth). Governmental, legal, social, and economic institutions are, in the logic of individual independence, always threatening to overwhelm individual life, liberty, and the pursuit of happiness. Any perceived increase in such threats brings increased concern for individual freedom, individual privacy, individual rights.

The mobile, corporate, consuming contemporary American individual is concerned about problems of privacy. He or she is also concerned about the rights of those individuals who—in the real, urban, industrialized, highly technological, impersonal world of late-twentieth-century America—most come in conflict with the bureaucracies of governments and corporations: consumers, criminals, workers, students, clients, the poor, the old, the young, and perceived minorities. Today, the independence of the individual is often associated with membership in an identifiable group—yet another example of the mythic logic which reconciles contradictions. The contemporary association of individual rights with privacy is a further assertion of the necessary relationship Americans perceive in the contrast of independence to society: the individual is by definition beleaguered by the public and publicity, and must be protected and self-protective. The present-day definition of "privacy" includes personal liberty to move and to associate with others in groups, personal health, and personal sexual practices and preferences.

Novels, like the social criticism, of contemporary America therefore focus on the contemporary content of the mythology of individualism. The popular American storyteller appeals to contemporary tastes and concerns and, whether telling a story of the past, the present, or the future, focuses on corporate life, individual and collective power, money and consumption, and sex. The past is either portrayed as a variation on the present, as in E. L. Doctorow's popular *Ragtime,* in which people behave just as they do now, with the same motives and imperatives but in different costumes, or it is described in sharp contrast to the present, an unbridgeable gulf separating it from modern life and contemporary concerns, as in Lasch's comparison of the narcissist of today with the rugged individualist of the past. In neither case is there any consciousness of the structure of the mythologies being assumed or of the transformations those myths may have undergone in the course of time.

For more than two centuries at least, Americans have been centrally concerned with the creation and preservation of individualism. In the context of a New World and then of their new nation, past Americans developed a complex mythology which stated ideals, established a logic, provided imagery, metaphors, symbols, and rituals, and created a dynamic imperative for specifically American individualism. The concerns of many of those who participated in the creation of that mythology were not concerns about corporate life or consumption or sexual styles and practices. The realities of their lives evidently did not require those concerns. Yet with the passage of time and the changing realities of the American world, those concerns have become contained in, have become central to, the myths those earlier Americans created.

To state the problem another way: individualism has long been recognized as a quality, a set of attitudes, which is very important to Americans and which has been very important for a very long time. What is the relationship of the individualism the Americans in the Revolution were worried about, say, to the individualism which Americans today believe they have, or have lost, or has been corrupted? Is there such a gulf between the American who today sees the world as a mirror and some past American who was a rugged individualist shaping an empty wilderness to his own design? Is Billy, the heroine of *Scruples,* recognizably American because her story follows a pattern, has some structure of myth which is the same structure as in the stories of Daniel Boone and Annie Oakley and all the other American individualists?

2

Prototypes

THE SHARP CONTRAST in the New World between wilderness and civilization is the original contradiction which gave rise to the mythology of the American individual. The Founding Fathers later codified individualism, but it was the trauma of the clash between Old World and New, between barbarism and civilization, between a missionary errand into the wilderness and the splendid savagery of the wilderness itself that generated the prototypical American individuals.

That contrast is given its essential symbolic form (ignoring the variations, permutations, and accretions which are the realities of such mythic symbols) in the towering figure of a great, gray Puritan on the one hand and the equally imposing, bronzed, buckskinned Frontiersman on the other. The associations immediately evoked by such symbols, although variable, are almost universal. These forms are fundamental representations of what the modern American theologian Reinhold Niebuhr has called "the children of light and the children of darkness." (Which is which has become a matter of contemporary American debate.)

The great, gray Puritan is Christian civilization on its mission to the New World, its errand into the wilderness. That Puritan works (labors mightily) because work is virtuous, is necessary to the preservation and spread of civilization, is productive of works, is the travail which is the sign of the proper Christian. The Puritan battles against barbarity and wilderness, fights the wilderness for the sake of Christianity, civilization, and the salvation of his or her own soul. Only by the improvement of one's soul, through work, works, faith, crusading, and self-conscious self-examination can the model of the Puritan be lived up to. The Puritan is the protester who confronts barbarism, the Protestant who brings Christianity, the revolutionary who would make paradise in the New World, the re-former of worlds and societies and individuals, the organizer, the master craftsman.

The bronzed, buckskinned Frontiersman is the New World and its wildness. The Frontiersman is the discoverer, the pathfinder, who adapts to whatever he finds and who lives in the wilderness. The Frontiersman is the survivor, skilled in natural life, who knows the wilderness and its ways, loves it, and is part of its wild, pagan, sensual chaos. The Frontiersman uses barbarity and wildness, and lives in it and of it, for the sake of its richness and for the pursuit of happiness, individual happiness. The Frontiersman is the heroic survivor, the adapter, the ambitious and greedy hedonist, the jack-of-all-trades, who bestrides his wild world like a colossus and (such contradictions are always possible in myths) slides unseen through the wilderness, using its fruits and leaving no trace of his passage.

These two figures are archetypes of experience, celebrated in American myth and ritual, widely available to Americans as models, explanations, and rationales of themselves and their universe. And the contrasts between them, while great, are not absolute. Both are American characters; both inhabit the New World; both have survived. Within each of these archetypal symbols an imperative is carried and transmitted from one generation of Americans to the next: adapt! Wilderness and civilization must adapt to each other, Old World and New must be joined and adapted: that *is, must be, has been* the essence of an American!

The idea of adapting to entirely new and strange circumstances, of creating peculiar combinations of the known and familiar with the new and wild, did not come easily. Somehow a bridge—of adaptability—between the wilderness and civilization had to be built. But that is an imperative we recognize: it was not so visible nor so obviously imperative to early migrants to the New World. Therefore, it is possible to catch glimpses of the process by which the myths of the frontier individuals who were the bridge to adaptability were formed.

People who adapted to the wilderness did not simply appear during the first winter in Plymouth or the early years in Jamestown. They developed slowly. It was two hundred years before James Fenimore Cooper, in *The Pioneers,* created a standard American character out of the accumulated tales and experiences of Americans who tried to domesticate the wilderness and who became part wild men in the process. The character was Leather Stocking, the American frontiersman, and his type had only gradually grown out of the lives of the colonists in North America.

"By 1763, the type was well fixed," Allan Nevins wrote in *The American Heritage Book of the Pioneer Spirit.* "From the Mohawk Valley to the Georgia Uplands were hunters, Indian fighters, fur traders, and primitive farmers" who were "inured to the perils" of the wilderness, who could find their way through the forests, and who could "clear the trees, rear log huts, and scratch crops into the soil between the stumps." They and their families faced hardship stoically in "an environment full of roughness, sink-or-swim emergencies, and bitter deprivations." They were recognizably Americans; adapted to the wilderness and working hard to make it into something else, something more "civilized."

We have a great many labels to describe these people; they are "settlers," "pioneers," "backwoodsmen," "frontiersmen," "sodbusters," sometimes even "cowboys." We rarely distinguish among these labels; for most of us, they seem equally applicable to the Americans who settled the country. But in order to describe the myths as they developed, and make the adaptive function of the many stories clear, three of the common labels—"backwoodsman," "frontiersman," and "pioneer"—will be used to characterize three different, overlapping sets of wilderness experiences. "Backwoodsmen" are the Leatherstocking types who explored the physical wilderness and acquired survival skills from the Indians. "Frontiersmen" are those who began to clear the wilderness and make it accessible to civilized society. "Pioneers" are those who established permanent communities and provided for their continued growth. (In the mythical stories, many heroes and heroines combined the characteristics of all three.)

BACKWOODSMEN

One hundred years before Cooper created Leather Stocking, a Virginia plantation owner, William Byrd, was sent by his colony on an expedition to determine the border between Virginia and North Carolina. Surveyors and surveys were a crucial part of the process of civilizing the wilderness, for only they could establish the lines, boundaries, and maps which were the basis of landed property and of all the rights and privileges that went with it, and of the political boundaries which were essential to civilized government. Byrd was a member of the Virginia government, an educated man, one of the pioneers who contributed heavily to the permanent settlement and improvement of Virginia. His surveying party was accompanied, however, by woodsmen (as Byrd called them) and by Indians, who hunted to provide extra food and who broke trails for the party. Byrd's descriptions of these men, and of his relationship to them, provide an early glimpse of the myths of the backwoodsmen and the frontiersmen in the making, before they had acquired all the characteristics which would later make them familiar to Americans.

Byrd's woodsmen could build shelters when the party's tents weren't available. One night they "made a Circular Hedge" of cedar branches "Wrought so close together as to fence us against the Cold Winds." Inside the roofless shelter, they "kindled a rouseing fire" and all "lay round it, like so many Knights Templars." The "True Woodsman," according to Byrd, slept in the raw between his blankets, "believing it much more refreshing to ly so, than in his cloaths," and he placed himself so the smoke would blow over him and keep off the "cold Dews."

The woodsmen were constantly alert on the trail for "any track or other token" of those "insidious foresters," the Indians. Such a task took skill, and it was easy for a young woodsman to mistake a bear track for a human one. When one of the party got lost, two woodsmen were sent "to beat all the adjacent woods in quest of him." He found his way to camp when the woodsmen fired guns as they searched for him.

Byrd himself was full of suggestions to improve the woodsmen's lot. He wrote down recipes (borrowed from the Indians) for concentrated, lightweight food (like pemmican) for foresters to carry. And he argued that they should give up riding horses. Horses, he said, took too much worry and care, and too much time. If men were "light and disengaged from every thing but their Guns" in the wilderness, they could go anywhere with ease. Without horses "men would . . . be able to travel safely over hills and dales, nor wou'd the steepest mountains obstruct their progress." "So long as Woodsmen continue to range on Horseback," Byrd warned, "we shall be Strangers to our own Country."

While the woodsmen were undoubtedly useful, they were far from heroes in Byrd's estimation. "Woodsmen are certainly good Christians in one respect, at least," Byrd wrote of a day when his woodsmen left their provisions behind and found nothing to eat in the woods: "they always leave the Morrow to care for itself; tho' for that very reason," he said, "they ought to pray more fervently for their Dayly Bread than most of them remember to do."

The backwoodsmen of Byrd's day, the early eighteenth century, had already acquired the ability to hunt and make shelters. They could read "sign" in the forests. They were not so cautious as they would later become, as shown by their random firing of guns when searching. And they had not yet shed civilized transport—the horse—in favor of the easier movement and the greater adaptability to the wilderness that came with going on foot, as the Indians did. (Byrd pointed out that the French *"Couriers de Bois"* traveled on foot, and knew more of the continent than the English as a result.) The backwoodsman's Christianity (i.e., his adherence to the standards of civilized conduct) was suspect: he slept in the raw, he was not very industrious, and around him there were already accumulating boastful, ribald stories which smacked of pagan ways.

The woodsmen of Byrd's party frequently shot bear, which Byrd himself relished, for food.

> Certainly no Tartar ever lov'd horse-flesh, or Hottentot Guts and Garbage, better than Woodsmen do Bear. The truth of it is, it may be proper food perhaps for such as Work or Ride it off, but, with our Chaplain's Leave, who lov'd it much, I think it not a very proper dyet for saints, because 'tis apt to make them a little too rampant. . . .
>
> And thus I am able to say, besides, for the Reputation of the Bear Dyet, that all the Marryed men of our Company were joyful Fathers within forty weeks after they got Home, and most of the Single men had children sworn to

them within the same time, our chaplain always excepted, who, with much ado, made a shift to cast out that importunate kind of Devil, by Dint of Fasting and Prayer.

From Byrd's day, the frontiers of settlement moved slowly westward to the Appalachians, crossed the mountains (by a road suggested by Byrd and developed by Daniel Boone), and moved still farther west. Kentucky—"O my dear honeys, heaven is a Kentucky of a place" (according to *The Christian Traveler* in 1828)—became the frontier, and the backwoodsmen became the myths of Daniel Boone, Davy Crockett, and scores of others. By the time James Fenimore Cooper apotheosized the backwoodsman in the character of Leather Stocking, the frontier had moved far beyond Kentucky.

The fictional backwoodsman Leather Stocking was, first of all, a white man, the child of settled Americans who were farmers or even townspeople. He was, thus, always identified with civilized, organized society. He was, under his rough exterior, kind and gentle and courteous. Through tragedy or choice, he was forced to leave his civilized background (separate himself from "all the civil parts of the world" just as the Pilgrims had) and take to the wilderness. The circumstances of his departure varied from one tale to another—he was captured by Indians, his parents died and he wandered into the forest, he was self-exiled because of unrequited love, he was driven there by conflict with religious, political, or military authorities—but all echoed the many and various reasons there were for coming to the New World or for repeating the pattern of that coming by seeking out the frontier. The Leather Stocking ontogeny continually recapitulated the philogeny of the immigrant experience.

Once in the wilderness, the backwoodsman became like an Indian and learned Indian ways. Sometimes the Leather Stocking hero would have compunctions about taking to Indian ways, but the inexorable forces of the wilderness (often in the shape of the Indians themselves) would make it necessary for him to kill or be killed, to become a savage or to be savaged. The wilderness did not permit passivity: it was too seductive, too full of elemental forces. Often the hero was adopted by Indians; sometimes he adopted an Indian companion, who became his mentor and guide. The backwoodsman learned and used both the "noble" ways of survival in the wilderness, of living close to nature and making use of all the resources and animals of the forest and stream, and also the "savage" ways of uncouth, dirty, barbaric living. He wore leather stockings and buckskins, ate strange, raw foods, and sometimes even became a "squaw man" and married into an Indian people. One enduring message for Americans in his story was that if the beauty and the bounty of the wilderness were to be enjoyed, one must "go native."

Because he was both civilized and savage, the backwoodsman hero was a loner without a proper place in *any* society. Civilized society was uneasy with him. He had his uses: he could lead people into the wilderness and find good places to settle; he could teach people how to survive and help them do so; he could make trade, treaties, and war with the Indians, and train settlers to do the same. Leather Stocking became a "pathfinder," reincarnating Columbus in the forests and reconciling civilization with the wilderness by being an intermediary between the two. For himself, however, there was no place in civilized society: it threatened his very soul as a backwoodsman. To settle down in society was to cease to be a child of the wilderness (just as for an Indian to become "civilized" was to cease to be an Indian). If he remained a backwoodsman, then he constantly moved on, following the wilderness as it retreated before the settlers he had led into it. He moved ever westward. "He shrank from men, even of his nation," Byron wrote of "General Boon, back-woodsman of Kentucky," in *Don Juan:*

> . . . When they built up unto his darling trees,
> —He moved some hundred miles off, for a station
> Where there were fewer houses and more ease.

Settled society had no place for uncouth savages in its midst, so it rejected backwoodsmen, however valuable they might be on the frontier. They left behind them a haunting vision of wilderness adventure, the loneliness of man in nature, the attractiveness of Indian life, the savagery of man and beast, and the magnificent self-sufficiency of the skilled, adaptive individual.

The singularity and loneliness of the backwoodsman was a symbol of the experience of the whole of American society as it settled and formed. The stories of the backwoodsman made a towering virtue of what was, in the real experience, a dubious circumstance.

Yet almost unconsciously the backwoodsman was tied to civilized society. He led settlers and other adventurous spirits from civilization to the wilderness's resources. He depended for his wilderness life on the gun, a product of civilized life. The gun was a demonstration of the superiority of the white man ("civilization"), who could manufacture it, over the Indian ("wilderness"), who only used it. The rifle, made by skilled, specialized gunsmiths (or later by industrial machines) gradually became inseparable from the Kentucky backwoodsman and his successors. Even when Jim Bowie invented a savage knife, it would be produced from "civilized" steel by expert smiths. For all his self-sufficiency and skills, the backwoodsman was ultimately dependent for his very life and survival on the production of a complex, civilized society.

The backwoodsman was an intermediary between the wilderness and the settlers. But it was not he who cleared the trees, reared the log huts, and scratched the "crops into the soil between the stumps"—at least, not if he could avoid it. The frontiersman—to make a distinction not made in normal usage—followed the backwoodsman, and was a step closer to civilization.

FRONTIERSMEN

The frontiersman had some of the backwoodsman's abilities: he could hunt in the forest, survive in the wilderness, and fight the Indian. But he was also intent on *using* the wilderness and scratching a living out of it for himself and his family. He lived with his family and he farmed, two acts symbolic of strong ties to civilized society. He cleared forests in order to use the land. He used lumber to build houses and barns and fences, and he was willing to sell lumber or cut trees wherever he could find a market, but what he could not use or sell, he destroyed. His aim was not simply survival in the wilderness, it was to make a living. He saw the wilderness as a vast resource. There was plenty more where that came from. What was not useful to his purposes he tried to destroy or push out of the way.

For William Byrd, these frontiersmen were "primitive farmers." "His Habitation was a Bower, cover'd with Bark after the Indian Fashion," Byrd wrote of one frontiersman. He lived off the land, and for clothes "he depended mostly upon his Length of Beard, and She upon her Length of Hair" just like "one of Herodotus's East Indian Pigmies." Such "Wretches" as these lived "in a dirty State of Nature, and were mere Adamites, Innocence only excepted." The frontier lacked not only innocence but religion as well: "They do not know Sunday from any other day, any more than Robinson Crusoe did, which would give them a great Advantage were they given to be industrious."

But they were not industrious. "The Men, for their Parts, just like the Indians, impose all the Work upon the poor Women," Byrd went on. "They make their Wives rise out of their Beds early in the Morning, at the same time that they lye and Snore till the Sun has run one third of his course." The frontier farmers, in short, "loiter away their Lives, like Solomon's Sluggard, with their Arms across . . ."

Byrd's frontier was a Garden of Eden without innocence; it was a castaway's island, sunny, fertile, and enervating; and the frontiersmen who inhabited it became exotics, sluggards, inventive castaways, and just like the Indians. These people had, to some degree, adapted to the wilderness; they knew some of its ways and were able to reap some of its riches, unhindered by the religion, laws, social status, codes and behavior of civilized people. They, along with the backwoodsmen were useful to Byrd's society: they explored, opened roads for trade and further settlement, cleared fields, found the lost, fed the hungry, and discovered the rich resources of the wilderness.

The frontiersman used the animals of the wilderness just as he used the trees. They were supplements to his diet, they could be marketed where markets could be found, and they were "varmints" to be destroyed—particularly any which, on foot or wing, invaded the civilized realm of fields, pastures, or farmyards. He saw them, too, as grossly overabundant, their supply inexhaustible, and once he carved his own place out of the wilderness, they had no place in it. As he hunted and shot, the game moved away or was killed off, and as with the trees, he successfully cleared an area for settlement.

The frontiersman was a loner (like the backwoodsman), but *with* his family. The family was there to meet the more diverse needs of the civilized task of farming. Frontierswomen and children were expected to do much the same work as the frontiersman, although when there was a separation of tasks, women and children were given the more obviously civilized things to do—plowing, fence making, woodcutting, cooking, cleaning, clothes making—while the man more closely emulated the backwoodsman as hunter and shelter builder. The stories of Abraham Lincoln's childhood in Indiana and his youth in Illinois are typical of the functioning frontiersman's family.

The frontier family as a unit was isolated, far removed from roads, settlements, schools, churches, and all the other amenities and complexities of society. But the frontiersmen perceived themselves as harbingers of civilization. They *intended* to lead the way for permanent and extensive settlement; they were the first Pilgrims, the first adventurers at Jamestown; they believed that others would join them, and that successful settlement would result. Yet, as more settlers came to their area and communities began to be built, they were torn and threatened: they could not remain frontiersmen in booming, settled towns; they ceased to live a frontier life when the frontier moved beyond them. Very often, like Tom Lincoln and his family, they sold out and moved on. The Lincoln pattern of movement from Kentucky to Indiana to Illinois was typical of the frontiersman. They—like the backwoodsmen—went farther west, looking for a new place to begin, a new frontier to clear and prepare for civilization. They often found themselves rejected or ostracized by the communities that grew up around them, their language and behavior too uncouth, too dirty, too uneducated, too primitive for the people who brought "the civil parts of the world" to their doorsteps. They were forced to choose, and some chose to keep moving on. Others, like Abraham Lincoln, would follow another pattern, from self-education to school to storekeeping to the law to the political life of settled, complex communities. They chose civilization, and so rejected the possibility of remaining frontiersmen.

As the backwoodsman brought the gun into the wilderness, so the frontiersman brought the ax, the plow, and the family. Both the backwoodsman and the frontiersman showed an adaptability in sharp contrast to the expectations and assumptions that most early immigrants to the New World had brought with them.

An extensive array of skills, along with the processes by which people are educated in those skills, are essential to the maintenance of any civilized society. In the societies from which immigrants came to America, there was an enormous degree of specialization of skills. In the frontier societies, however, there were too few craftsmen and specialists to fill the demands. The result was not that the settlers and pioneers eagerly embraced the attitude of "making do," but rather that they were confused and distressed because the skills they needed were not available and the processes of acquiring the skills were not easy to establish.

Specialization and status in Old World societies were closely connected. A person's work and his place were physically and emotionally the same. (This connection between work and position in the community is still part of the American work ethic.)

At first it did not occur to immigrants to try to produce products or services which were not of their own work, their own specialty. To have attempted to do so would make a person appear a fool, it would be demeaning, and it would be distasteful. People *could* not, and *would* not make or do the things which to us seem obvious and necessary, even for their survival, because they did not have the skills or the training, because such things were above or beneath or simply not part of their station in life, and because it would shatter all the laws and patterns and certitudes of their lives.

Unlike those early immigrants, the backwoodsman and the frontiersman borrowed and learned skills from the Indian and from each other. As the skills they learned were often savage, so their place in society was with the savages. But their skills were very useful to frontier society—indeed, they were sometimes essential—and so there was considerable ambivalence both about them and about their abilities. Skills and adaptability in the same person were not easily accepted by people who believed that structure and specialization were the only civilized ways. The backwoodsmen and frontiersmen were jacks-of-all-trades, skilled, adaptable, survivors; they were also masters of none, in the view of the Puritan representatives of older, established societies—and therefore they were indolent, presumptuous, and outcasts.

PIONEERS

The third and final stage of the mythical bridge between wilderness and civilization was formed by the pioneer. He was not clearly distinguished from the frontiersman, as the frontiersman was not from the backwoodsman, but he was closer to being civilized and he was the last postulate in the logic by which Americans reconciled their wilderness with their civilization.

The pioneer was sturdy, like the English yeoman: he was the yeoman, transformed by the experience of the wilderness. The pioneer brought oxen and other draft animals to the frontier, pulling wagons and carts full of civilized goods. Later, the covered wagon would become the primary mythic image of the moving pioneer. He came to the frontier expecting to build a house and barn, to farm, and to help his neighbors and get their help. He sometimes bought out the frontiersman and began on land already cleared. On the prairie, he was the sodbuster, the homesteader. He expected to find or build a community, and join with others to raise churches, meetinghouses, and schools as the physical and institutional symbols of the properly Christian community he wanted. He was ambitious for himself, his family, and his community. He would—or his wife would—have some conscious culture and be able to read. If he did not, he expected his children to. He carried with him and sought what he knew to be the skills and educational processes of civilized society. He wanted stores and merchants, ministers, teachers, and lawyers, roads and traders, artisans and their products in his community. He was *settling,* and he intended to put himself down and stay put.

He was idealized by Thomas Jefferson as the sturdy, independent yeoman American, and he had important characteristics of his predecessors on the frontier. He admired, and possessed, some of the abilities of the backwoodsman in hunting, trailblazing, and Indian fighting. He was a "minuteman" if danger threatened. Like the backwoodsman and the frontiersman, he found himself restless, and he sometimes became an outcast as new generations grew in his community and new settlers came in after him. He was not immune to the seductions and compulsions of greener pastures, more fertile soil, and newer worlds to settle. Above all, he was convinced that diversified, non-specialized, jack-of-all-trades adaptability was a positive virtue, the only possible way to be in an American community. The pioneer turned his back on specialization as an ideal. He held in great contempt the person who only knew how to do a single job or perform a single service. The pioneer would turn his hand to whatever work needed to be done.

The efforts required to make communities in the wilderness were many. To be a jack-of-all-trades meant higher status in the community because such a person brought greater success to farming, to housekeeping, to marketing, to the survival of all.

Robert Beverly (William Byrd's brother-in-law) observed, in 1705, that Indians lived "without the curse of industry," that is to say, they did no work. The Indians' necessities, Beverly wrote in his *History of Virginia,* were supplied by "their diversion alone and not their labor." It was play that brought the Indians their food, clothing, and shelter, not what a proper and civilized person saw as specialized, trained work. As the backwoodsmen and frontiersmen borrowed the non-specialized adaptability and skills of the Indian, they were also often seen by their more civilized or more Puritan contemporaries as "lazy," "slothful," "indolent"—as Byrd had seen them—because they, too, gained their necessities without recognizable work. The pioneer made work out of the non-specialized skills of the frontier by cultivating those skills industriously, and he raised them above the pagan practices of the Indians by identifying them with his own Christian duty. He brought the Puritan work ethic to the frontier ideal of adaptability.

Implicit in all Protestantism (and for two hundred years, the great majority of those who came to British America were Protestants much affected by Puritanism) was the belief that as a person's relationship to God was direct and immediate, requiring constant wakeful attention, self-discipline, and training, so a person's relationship to Christian labor in the circumstances created by God on this earth also required constant attention and the constant application of physical and mental energies. If the fruits of one's labors were the outward sign of God's infinite grace, as many Protestants believed, then one must labor mightily, with discipline and constancy, at whatever tasks Providence has set. God had imposed a multiplicity of tasks on every individual in the wilderness, and disciplined labor at *all those tasks* was moral, virtuous, and required of all. By these beliefs, the frontiersman was not considered lazy because he did no work; he was lazy because he did not work *industriously* at all the tasks required of him. The pioneer, on the other hand, did work industriously (William Byrd saw himself this way), and he accomplished thereby the miracle of creating a Christian society in the wilderness.

By the time of the birth of the nation, American prototypical heroes and heroines were emerging from the stories and the experiences of six or seven generations of immigrants and settlers. They were creatures of the New World, attracted by the wild beauty and the overwhelming abundance of America. They could find their way in the wilderness and they thrived on its produce, for which they thanked their Puritan God. Yet they also feared the wilderness and peopled it with barbaric devils, fearsome beasts, and hissing, rattling serpents. They lived in that wilderness and destroyed it in order to civilize it.

In their own myths, Americans had become Indians, "native," "innocent," "noble," and perhaps even "savage." Yet they were not Indians but frontiersmen (bronze as Indians were copper or red) who learned from the Indians how to live in, see, and use the wilderness. They invited Indians to join them in giving thanks to God, yet they fought, tricked, and even scalped Indians. "There is but one way of converting these poor infidels, and reclaiming them from barbarity," William Byrd had written, "and that is, charitably to intermarry with them." Few Americans took such advice literally, because such marriage as Byrd proposed would represent capitulation to the wilderness. Yet the Americans had figuratively "married" the Indians by adapting themselves to the Indians' New World wilderness.

Americans still tell stories of Indians, of the wilderness, of pioneers and frontiersmen, and of Thanksgiving. The imagery of the backwoods and the frontier, the metaphors of wilderness and settlement, the phrases of the Bible and the Common Law, of *Pilgrim's Progress* and *Robinson Crusoe,* are bundled together (with Yankee twangs and Southern drawls, with Leatherstocking and Daniel Boone) in those stories in endless, shifting series that mark out the American bridge of adaptation, the mythic, logical reconciliation of paganism and Christianity, work and survival, Indians and Puritans, frontier and settlement. The myths of American individualism still celebrate those fathers who, in William Bradford's words, "were Englishmen which came over this great ocean, and were ready to perish in this wilderness," but who, instead, adapted, survived, and created the civilization of New World America.

3

Independent Individualism

THE REVOLUTION NOT ONLY made a nation, it individualized Americans. Americans were people who came here and committed themselves to America, or they were people who were born here and belonged here. They were not Creoles or colonials, or provincials; they were not exiles, not English or Scots or Irish or German; nor were they "natives." The Revolution made them free of all such identities.

The American individual was and is, thus, by definition, free and independent (today, it would be called "being autonomous" or "doing your own thing"). An American pursues his/her own happiness, develops his/her own abilities, makes his/her own fortune, and establishes his/her own family. The generations of Americans who grew up after the Revolution were and are impatient with the remnants or existence of dependence, inequality, and restrictions on individual freedom which they found and find in their lives. Since the Revolution, Americans have not known the oppression of colonial life, but they intended and intend to destroy any structures within their society which try to teach people their place and keep them there. Americans do not believe that individuals ought to stay in one place. And they do not intend that their nation keep to its place, either; for individuals and for the nation, there is a manifest destiny to fulfill.

MIGRATION AND MOBILITY

Americans had been on the move long before the Revolution. But with the Revolution, with the possibility of independence, that movement became "American"; it became part of the hopes and expectations, the freedom and imperative, which belonged to every American. Heaven became a "Kentucky of a place," and thousands crossed the Appalachians or floated down the Ohio to heaven. Heaven kept moving on, and so folklore tells us did the Americans:

Come all ye Yankee farmers who wish to change your lot,
Who've spunk enough to travel beyond your native spot,
And leave behind the village where Pa and Ma do stay,
Come follow me and settle in Michigan-i-ay.

It was the "Yankee farmers" and their like who moved toward the frontier, wherever it was. They were young men and women, very often leaving "Pa and Ma" behind, who sold what land they had or who had enough family support to provide a stake to cover the expenses of the journey and the capital to get started in a new place. The frontier had some room for those who had no money—as laborers, as explorers and trappers, and always as adventurers with a sharp eye for an opportunity to exploit new resources or their fellow men—but the primary need of all new settlements was for capital, for people with the money to buy land, tools, supplies, and transportation.

There were new immigrants, too, who went West. Those who had capital, either from their own—sometimes pooled—resources, or from land speculators and railroad companies who lent it to them, made it to the frontier. The rest of the immigrants stayed near the ports where they landed, or replaced the Yankee farmers who moved West. It was the American, native perhaps by only a single generation, who wanted to change his/her lot, who formed the backbone of those who sought heaven in Kentucky and all the way to the Pacific. It was particularly the American who responded to the challenge of having "spunk enough to travel beyond your native spot."

The image of the ideal individual took its lasting form in the expanding American "empire." That empire expanded not only by the westward movement of the frontier but also by the increasing population and the constant expansion of settlement within the frontier. And the first requisite of individualism was the "wish to change your lot." The American was not fixed in his or her lot by class, location, or inheritance, or by family, education, or even, necessarily, by ability. The pursuit of happiness required a change of lot, and those who did not change theirs were objects of pity or, more commonly, of contempt.

The roots of this powerful attitude lie in migration to the New World. The regeneration of the attitude in every new generation of Americans both explains and justifies migration. From the very beginning, immigrants came to America to change and improve their lot in life. The act of migration had indeed changed their lot, and it is generally portrayed, in all the American myths and stories, as having improved it.

Americans were and are intensely conscious of migration; it is part of everyone's background. Migration meant a break with the past, and that break required justification. The justification was and is, quite simply, improvement of one's lot. The society immigrants left behind was corrupt, decadent, tyrannical, or at least inferior. American society is new and superior.

The Revolution is a national symbol of the break with the past, and of the improvement which accompanied that break: freedom, independence, and democracy. Immigrants and their descendants, who came to America after the Revolution, found little difficulty identifying with the Revolution, making it part of their past, and making the Founding Fathers their Fathers, because the Revolution and immigration are thus tied together. To every generation of Americans the "need" and desire to "change your lot" became a justification, a ritual of reaffirmation and explanation of the acts of its forefathers and of the Founding Fathers who had changed theirs.

The significant outward sign of the process of changing one's lot, increasingly its most powerful symbol, was to move beyond one's native spot, leaving behind "the village where Pa and Ma do stay." Both village and parents became symbols of origins, nativity, stability, and civilization; in a wider context, they were the Old World as contrasted with the New World of youth, of the frontier, of somewhere else; in the political context, they were the colonial world as contrasted with the Revolution and the new nation. The geographical or physical move became and is the essential step in the formation of the American individual, so the mythical logic of the move bundles together immigration and Revolution and visions of childhood, adulthood, and the family.

The move away from Pa and Ma was the first step in the establishment of adulthood. Americans today accept that break as normal and normative, but it was not part of social development in the societies from which Americans had immigrated. Families in old societies were nuclear and children were expected to stay in or near the family as they grew to adulthood and married. The traditional pyramid of society was reflected within each family, and the father had paramount authority. In American families, as Alexis de Tocqueville pointed out in his *Democracy in America* in the 1830's, children quickly became the equals of their parents. They were treated as separate individuals rather than as subordinate parts of the family, they were encouraged to exceed their father's social, educational, and material position in life, and they were encouraged to depart physically from the circle of the family in order to make their own way in the world.

Adulthood in the American family is marked by independence. Initiation into adult life does not take place within the family, and it does not mark acceptance into a stable order in a fixed community. Rather, the rite of passage into adult life is a "declaration of independence" on the part of the child, accompanied very often by physical departure from both family and community. American folklore—whether traditional or contemporary—reflects the continuing idea that the child's declaration of independence and departure requires spunk. The act of rebellion—the paradigm of which is the American Revolution—is seen as a courageous act in which dependence, security, and familiar ways are rejected. The ritual American act of courage is the declaration of independence-rebellion-migration of the American adolescent.

Stress on the equality of all members of the family, including the children, which foreign travelers early pointed out as a peculiarity of American families, made the break with family more important because in a circle of equals there was little way to make the step from childhood to the adult state clear except by departure. During the time of the Revolution and the forming of the nation, the men who created the new laws and constitutions of the states, and of the United States, devoted considerable effort to the questions of primogeniture, entail, and the division of the property of people who died without wills. In almost all such cases, primogeniture and entail were prohibited, and provisions were made for the equal division of property among all the children. These were efforts to ensure equality. They were directed at property, which was considered fundamental—with life and liberty—to all societies, and which was also believed to be the foundation of family life. These formal, statutory, and constitutional provisions were to ensure an equality necessary if the assertion of equality in the Declaration of Independence was to be guaranteed. With the equality of family members guaranteed in law, and the practices of families already reinforcing the new guarantees, independence for a family member was the final step—as it had been for the nation—in the logic of equality.

(The present-day movement for women's liberation pursues the same logic as it applies the imagery of the myths of the independent individual to wives and mothers in American families. The effort is both to gain formal, statutory, and constitutional provisions for equality, and to assert the potential independence of wives and mothers through "declarations of independence" and the rebellions/revolutions which, in the logic, must follow.)

The importance of mobility to individualism has long been striking, both to Americans and to foreign observers. Physical mobility and social mobility are closely related, so closely that they are often indistinguishable. Going West, seeking greener pastures, leaving home, and moving on are not only physical moves which demonstrate and guarantee independence; they also carry the implication that they lead to better, higher social and economic status.

For example, in the myth of Abraham Lincoln, the moves the Lincoln family made from the Kentucky birthplace to two different places in Indiana and thence to three in Illinois are part of the inexorable progress, growth, and improvement of Lincoln the hero, culminating in the Presidency and the adoration of the American people. Each move was a step toward better land and more profit from it for the Lincoln family; better education and therefore a better economic and social status for the hero; better political opportunities, and therefore higher office, higher standing with more people, or, in times of political setback, more wisdom, more patience and understanding on the part of the hero. The physical moves—like the final move to Washington, and even the funeral train home—are an essential part of the process: without them, the progress of the hero would have been impossible. The distinction between cause and effect, between symbol and reality, is blurred and lost in the myth. The objective reality is that the Lincoln family *moved* (quite probably because the family believed that moving would bring improvement); the myth makes the movement *necessary,* and the improvement a *result* of the movement.

"Mobility"—physical, social, economic, tied together by belief and practice—for Americans is both symbol and reality of the free, independent individual. The lives Americans actually lead are often immobile and frustrating. Physical and economic mobility are not, and have not actually been, very great. But the reality is not so important to Americans as the symbols and logic with which they perceive the reality. They *believe* they are mobile so strongly that mobility has been a constant in descriptions of American life by Americans and by foreigners. And the belief has, for two hundred years or more, been reinforced by stories, histories, and statistics of Americans on the move.

The underlying logic for this perception was that if the immigrant was the uprooted, the Americans, who were the children of immigrants, were rootless. They were not committed by ancestry, tradition, or community, to a particular place. Furthermore, the immigrant's nostalgia for his roots, for the Old Country and all it signified of stability and ancestral past, made his children and their descendants conscious of their different circumstances and their lack of such roots. Home, for them, became the symbolic "village where Pa and Ma do stay," a place to which one could never really return, and their nostalgia for it was reflection, and re-creation. The pattern in American children of tearing up one's roots and leaving home justified the actions of the immigrant by repeating the pattern of that immigrant's mobility.

The break from the parents and the move that was symbolic of that break started the individual on the way to change and improvement, to opportunity and success, and to the active pursuit of happiness. Life was given by parents and family; liberty was obtained by breaking away from home. The pursuit of happiness would bring individual fulfillment and ultimate improvement to American society.

THE CIVILIZATION OF THE RUGGED INDIVIDUAL

The individual was believed to be free to develop himself and his potentialities without fetter, but the success of his efforts would be judged by the whole of his society. Individual development and improvement were useful to American society, and encouraged by it—provided they followed the proper pattern. For there was a pattern which, if followed, led to a socially useful and happy individual. The individual was free, but there were limits to his freedom.

The pattern of those limits was made visible in the self-consciously American, independent, and democratic post-Revolutionary generations, the generations that took Andrew Jackson as their hero and symbol. One educated young American, Francis Lieber, began in 1830 to publish a chart for Americans who wished to make their country truly democratic, and themselves truly free and independent: the *Encyclopaedia Americana.* And in the biographies contained in the *Americana,* the pattern for the free individual in a democratic society was clearly delineated.

Daniel Boone, dead only eight years when the *Americana* was published, was already legendary. He was, according to the *Americana,* "one of the first adventurers who penetrated into the wilds of Kentucky." He had been, "almost from his infancy, addicted to hunting in the woods." "Having determined to cross the wilderness bordering on the Cumberland mountains, in quest of the region of Kentucky, then little known," Boone spent years exploring, adventuring, fighting Indians, and hunting. He was adopted by Indians, captured by others, and escaped from them all. In 1798, after years of adventure, he moved to "upper Louisiana," with his children, friends, and followers. He settled at Charette, on the Missouri River, "some distance beyond the inhabited parts of the country, where he followed his usual course of life—hunting and trapping for bears—until Sept., 1822, when he died, at the residence of his son, Major A. Boone, in Montgomery county, in the 85th year of his age."

Zebulon Pike, a later frontier hero, was born in New Jersey in 1779. His father was a "respectable officer" in the Army. According to the *Americana,* Pike joined the Army "while yet a boy, and served for some time" in his father's outfit, "which was then stationed on the western frontiers of the U. States." "By a life of constant activity and exposure," the young Pike "invigorated his constitution, and prepared himself for deeds of hardihood and adventure." Before he went into the Army, he had learned only "reading, writing and a little arithmetic." Thereafter, "by his own exertions," he learned several languages, and "all the ordinary practical applications" of mathematics. He was full of curiosity, "no kind of knowledge was without interest" to him, he read avidly "every book which fell in his way," and over time, "without any regular plan of study," he "acquired a considerable stock of various information."

In 1805, Pike was given charge of an expedition—parallel to the famous expedition of Lewis and Clark—to explore the sources of the Mississippi. "For eight months and twenty days," Pike and his men "were continually exposed to hardship and peril, depending for provisions upon the chase, and enduring the most piercing cold." They went without food, and frequently had to sleep without shelter on the ground or on the snow. It was Zebulon Pike alone who brought them through:

> During this voyage, Pike had no intelligent companion upon whom he could rely for advice or aid, and he literally performed the duties of astronomer, surveyor, commanding officer, clerk, spy, guide and hunter, frequently preceding the party for many miles, in order to reconnoitre, or rambling for whole days in search of deer, or other game, for provision, and then returning to his men in the evening, hungry and fatigued, he would sit down in the open air, to copy, by the light of a fire, the notes of his journey, and to plan the course of the next day.

Pike successfully completed that expedition. He led another, equally successfully, to the Rockies in 1806. And he died a hero's death in Canada during the War of 1812.

Unlike many others in the *Americana* biographies, Richard Henry Lee was born into the upper classes, in 1732, in Virginia. "After a course of private tuition in his father's house," Lee was sent to England to school. He returned to America when he was nineteen, and, "his fortune rendering it unnecessary for him to devote himself to any profession," he spent his time, "most usefully," improving his mind. At twenty-five, he entered politics, "for which he was peculiarly fitted both by his natural disposition and talents, and the studies in which he was versed." He had studied law, history, and philosophy, as well as "the more elegant departments of polite literature" on his own. He soon became a distinguished politician, who always supported "republican or anti-aristocratic" principles. He was a signer of the Declaration of Independence, and died in 1794, after a long and distinguished public career.

A more recent hero, for the *Americana,* was John Paul Jones. Jones "was a man of signal talent and courage; he conducted all his operations with the most daring boldness, combined with the keenest sagacity in calculating the chances of success and the consequences of defeat." Jones's virtues were, however, balanced by faults:

> He was . . . of an irritable, impetuous disposition, which rendered him impatient of the authority of his superiors, while he was, at the same time, harsh in the exercise of his own; and he was deficient in that modesty which adorns great qualities and distinguished actions, while it disarms envy and conciliates jealousy.

As with other heroes, Jones's "early education was of a very limited kind," and it ended when he went to sea at age twelve. However, "he supplied its defects by subsequent study" and learned "to write with fluency, strength and clearness." Even more important, he learned "to sustain his part respectably in the polished society into which he was thrown."

The patterns of the lives of these four individuals, and of many others, are very similar. Each man possessed, first of all, qualities in his character which would make him famous. Boone was, "almost from his infancy, addicted to hunting in the woods." Pike joined the Army "while yet a boy" and "by a life of constant activity and exposure" prepared for later "deeds of hardihood and adventure." Lee overcame "private tuition in his father's house," schooling in England, and a private fortune, by spending his time "most usefully . . . in the improvement of his mind." Jones, from the beginning, was "a man of signal talent and courage." Whatever the background of the man, whatever the circumstances of his birth or upbringing, it was his own character and his use of it which produced a noteworthy person.

Class, position, family, and even inherited fortune were mere background, as Lee's career demonstrated. The background provided no more than raw materials for individual development. Like the land, the woods, the natural resources of the nation, they were there to be developed and improved, to create something which would enrich both the man and his society.

Education in its broadest sense was essential to development and perfection. It was, as it were, the process by which the individual adapted to the wilderness of personal circumstances and opportunities, and by which that wilderness was "civilized." Education was, for each individual, a repetition of the process of settling the frontier. Formal schooling, on the other hand, was an entirely different matter: it might add polish, but it was of little consequence. Boone was a rough-and-tumble woodsman; the education he needed he acquired from the Indians and from his experience in the wilderness. Pike and Jones both had little schooling, but they supplied the "defects" by subsequent study on their own, acquiring in Pike's case an astonishing variety of knowledge "almost without the aid of a master." Lee had an extensive formal education, but it was subjects not taught in schools which occupied "the principal share of his time" as a young adult studying on his own, and it was that self-education which enabled him to attain "distinction in debate" and to follow a long career of service.

The chance advantages (or disadvantages) of schooling which were the result of birth, location, family, or inherited wealth were immaterial. What provided advantage was the acquisition, through the individual's own efforts, of a broad range of knowledge. It was not possible to predict precisely what information would be valuable, so the most impressive and successful self-education came from having "a general curiosity, to which no kind of knowledge was without interest." The jack-of-all-trades American was self-educated and, as Zebulon Pike's biography showed, "without any regular plan of study." The vision underlying this attitude was anarchistic: institutions and authority were unnecessary to the education of the individual; indeed, they usually impeded individual progress.

While a certain amount of anarchy is contained in the ideal of American individualism reflected in the *Americana* articles, unrestrained egotism is not part of it. While the individual developed his capabilities in the pursuit of his own happiness, success for the individual came only if he served his society. Daniel Boone is given short shrift precisely because his accomplishments were only briefly useful. After he settled himself "some distance beyond the inhabited parts of the country" and went back to "his usual course of life—hunting and trapping for bears," the article ends, significantly, with a story about the coffin he made for himself. Boone's success lay in opening Kentucky and establishing settlements there, not in pursuing his own private happy hunting grounds. In fact, such pursuit of exclusively private happiness—even by a heroic backwoodsman—was tantamount to killing and burying himself.

Overweening personal ambition, too, was not useful to American society, and it could damage an otherwise admirable individual. John Paul Jones was daring, talented, courageous, and calculating—all qualities which made him an American hero. His impatience "of the authority of his superiors" was admirable, but his harshness "in the exercise of his own" authority was not forgivable in a society of burgeoning individualism. Service to the new society was the ultimate goal of American individualism, and its highest glory. Jones in the Revolutionary Navy had so served, and became a hero. But Jones the poseur in Parisian society and the admiral in the Russian Navy was merely an ambitious egoist, overweening and immodest. He was irritable, impetuous, and "deficient in . . . modesty." He was not, as later Americans would put it, "well liked."

The control on individual ambition which American society used to turn rampant egotism to socially useful ends was the necessity to be liked, to have the expressed approval and friendship of other Americans. Without approval, the striving individual was not successful; indeed, such a person was a failure. Approval provided the roots and security that the individual lacked. There was no place, no class, no family, or position which of right, or by schooling, belonged to an American. He or she was alone, self-educated, and dependent only on his or her own abilities for fame and fortune—later generations would call such a person "self-made." Only in the eyes of other Americans could the friendship and approval be found which gave the individual a place and position in society. "First in the hearts of his countrymen" was both capstone and control to the ambitions of the American individual.

TRAITOR TO THE CAUSE

The treatment of Benedict Arnold in the *Encyclopaedia Americana* illuminates the ideal of individualism. The editor devotes nineteen columns to Arnold—half a column more than is devoted to George Washington. Arnold was a lesson not to be lost, because his life portrayed both the despicableness of treason to the nation and the ultimate result of individualism uncontrolled by service to the society.

The opening of the article tells much of the story:

> This man, one of the most distinguished generals in the American army during the earlier part of the contest of the colonies with Great Britain, and subsequently infamous as a traitor to his country, was born in Connecticut, of obscure parentage, and received an education suitable to an humble condition. The occupations of his youth were not fitted to prepare him for the functions which he was called upon to exercise in the sequel. At first a dealer in horses, he sustained losses in his trade. Eager for renown, greedy of money, the troubles of his country inspired him with the hope of acquiring fame and fortune by the profession of arms: accordingly, on the breaking out of the revolutionary war, he embraced the cause of his countrymen with enthusiasm, and took the command of a company of volunteers at New Haven. He soon won a high military reputation.

As Arnold rose in command, his exploits won him admiration, and put him in "the first class of American officers." His expedition against Quebec was outstanding, and he went on from that to further successes:

> The boldness of Arnold was so great, that he was accused of a disposition to entangle himself rashly in perilous situations; but it could not be denied, that his rapid discernment supplied him, in the midst of danger, with the surest expedients, and that success always justified his daring. The admiration of his fellow-citizens kept pace with his services. His love of glory was accompanied with an equally strong love of pleasure and dissipation, and he was very unscrupulous about the mode of obtaining the means of gratifying it.

George Washington, according to the *Americana,* detested Arnold's vices, but insisted upon using Arnold because he was a good general. But Arnold so misused his authority to make himself rich that Washington finally forced him to resign. Arnold, "thenceforth, nourished an implacable hatred towards the cause which he had so brilliantly defended." In deep financial trouble, Arnold, in a complicated plot, sold out to the British.

"He survived the war," the article concludes:

> . . . but to drag on, in perpetual banishment from his native country, a dishonorable life. . . . He transmitted to his children a name of hateful celebrity. He obtained only a part of the debasing stipend of an abortive treason. . . . He

> enjoyed, however, the rank of brigadier-general; but the officers of the British army manifested a strong repugnance to serve with him. He possessed their esteem while he fought against them; they loaded him with contempt when treason brought him over to their side. . . .

The *Americana* makes it clear that excessive greed and a youth misspent were the seeds of Arnold's downfall. A young man who educated himself badly at horse trading would hardly be inspired by his country's troubles; Arnold took up arms only to acquire fame and fortune. Both followed, but he dissipated both. He was a self-made man (i.e., an American), but so badly made that the detestation of his countrymen was followed by the scorn of even the British.

Arnold's was the outstanding example for all Americans of the disaster that comes when the free and independent individual is not controlled by the desire to earn the approbation of his countrymen. Arnold's greatest punishment was to live "in perpetual banishment" from America. A "man without a country" was a specter of horror to the American. Sir Walter Scott's *The Lay of the Last Minstrel* became widely popular in America because it expressed American horror of the man who did not wish to serve his country and so could not win the approval of his countrymen:

> Breathes there the man, with soul so dead,
> Who never to himself hath said,
> This is my own, my native land! . . .
> If such there breathe, go, mark him well;
> For him no Minstrel raptures swell;
> High though his titles, proud his name,
> Boundless his wealth as wish can claim,
> Despite those titles, power, and pelf,
> The wretch, concentered all in self,
> Living, shall forfeit fair renown,
> And, doubly dying, shall go down
> To the vile dust, from whence he sprung,
> Unwept, unhonor'd, and unsung.

The ambivalence between the desire for freedom and independence and the desire for social approval, between individual ambition and community cohesion, creates the tension which controls American individualism. As the Revolution overturned and rejected the old, established society, so must the individual American: that is the imperative of the mythology of American individualism. But, as the Revolution established a new nation based on freedom, so must the individual American—free, independent, equal, democratic, mobile—establish and serve an American community, American society. *That* is equally imperative in the myths of American individuals.

4

The Employee

"When Daniel Boone goes by, at night," the twentieth-century American poet Stephen Vincent Benét wrote,

> The phantom deer arise
> And all lost, wild America
> Is burning in their eyes.

Daniel Boone had already become an American hero, a paradigm of American adaptation to the wilderness, when the deer were not phantoms but venison on the hoof and when Americans still felt themselves surrounded by real wilderness. Boone finally went far out into his "wild America" and died. He lived in American myth, but more and more recognizably as a "phantom."

Boone was overlapped and replaced as a living American hero by the fiercely independent American yeomen and pioneers, politicians and Indian fighters, Revolutionaries and reformers who were celebrated by the *Encyclopædia Americana* and apotheosized by Andrew Jackson. These were men and women who accepted adaptation to the wilderness, who accepted frontier life as a matter of course. They dreamed of the conquest of that "wild America" and the transformation of the frontier into settlement. They told their children and their grandchildren stories of Daniel Boone, they read the tales of Leather Stocking, and they enjoyed the adventures of Kit Carson, Davy Crockett, Jim Bridger, of Andy Jackson and Henry Clay and Daniel Webster. And to keep their independence, to keep the nation expanding, to build a true America in the wilderness, they fought the Civil War.

Shortly before the Civil War, the American economy had started to "take off" toward a modern industrial economy. Settlements became towns, towns became cities, cities grew larger, and new cities were built. A national market was created by railroads and the telegraph. After the Civil War, the giant factories, the armies of workers, and the sprawling sales forces of big business grew. The value of industrial goods produced in America exceeded by ever-increasing percentages the value of the produce of agriculture. Within little more than the single generation between the end of the Civil War in 1865 and the turn of the century in 1900, the United States changed from an essentially rural and agricultural nation into a rapidly modernizing urban and industrial nation.

Most of America's first industrial generation after the Civil War had grown up, as we have seen, believing that America's mission was to civilize the wilderness by bringing freedom, democracy, and *farms* to the forests and plains of America. Their heroes were pathfinders, frontiersmen, and pioneers who found their way into the wilderness and there created rural towns and producing farms. Their ideal of proper behavior, of a true American life, was expressed in stories and images of the sturdy independence of yeoman farmers who fought off the Indians, tilled their own hard-won land, sold their crops, and made some profit, got along with their fellows in cooperatively built communities, and sometimes rose to fame and fortune with the approbation, votes, or help of their fellows. The myths which shaped the beliefs and behavior of the first industrial generations were not, however, those of an industrial or urban world.

POST–CIVIL WAR HEROES

There were new storytellers and new heroes after the Civil War. But the new wore the same clothes as the old, and possessed the same virtues. They, too, achieved success and democratic popularity. Buffalo Bill (1846–1917) dressed in buckskins; he fought Indians and hunted the wild game of the wilderness like Daniel Boone. Abe Lincoln worked hard and educated himself; he rose to fame and the Presidency just as Andy Jackson had. General Custer was the greatest Indian fighter of them all. The new industrial world did not lack for heroes in the traditional mold. Yet the myths were being transformed.

Generations of Americans after the Civil War were brought up on stories of Abraham Lincoln, the war President, the Great Emancipator. The same generations who learned of Lincoln's youth and his rise to the Presidency were also told stories of cowboys in the Wild West, of Custer and the Cavalry, of John D. Rockefeller and Andrew Carnegie, and millions of them read the fictional tales of Horatio Alger, whose heroes rose from rags to success in the modern American world. The stories about Lincoln, however, along with those about the cowboys, bridged the gap between the old wilderness world, the rural, frontier world of America and the new industrial, urban world.

Abraham Lincoln (1809–65) was born when Daniel Boone was an old man, in the same year that Thomas Jefferson left the Presidency. The Lincoln story began in the wilderness and moved to the pioneering, farming world of the Illinois prairie. The story of his early years followed the pattern of older American heroes. But, unlike those earlier heroes, Lincoln was taken away from his agrarian world by a railroad train, the potent symbol of the new industrial world. And he found success in a city.

It was the railroad, the locomotive with its giant machinery, its hissing steam and its piercing whistle, which took Lincoln out of the prairie to the city, with all its busy-ness, took him to the midst of a great war fought with guns, railroads, telegraphs, and millions of men, and then brought him back again dead, assassinated, as that war ended. The railroad was both the symbol and the reality of the industrial age, an age of steel and machinery and organized, machine-like masses of human beings. The railroad marked the death of the wilderness, as it marked the death of Lincoln. "I hear the whistle of the locomotive in the woods," Emerson had written in his journal in 1842; "Wherever that music comes it has its sequel. It is the voice of . . . the Nineteenth Century saying, 'Here I am.' "

Lincoln's assassination was the symbolic death of all that Lincoln came to represent to Americans after the Civil War: the frontiersman, the pioneer farmer, and the agrarian world created out of the wilderness. The railroad took him out of that world into a city, and it brought him back dead.

The railroad created its own heroes—Casey Jones, the "brave engineer" of the Illinois Central; John Henry, the "steel-drivin' man" of the Appalachian railroads. They were new heroes of an industrial world, which, with the railroads, was spanning the continent and destroying the wilderness as it went. Wilderness America and the frontier life did not simply retreat before the railroads as they had before the backwoodsmen and the old wilderness roads; they were penetrated by the railroads and overrun; they finally disappeared.

By the late nineteenth century, there were few frontiersmen left in America. Like Lincoln, most of them were dead. No longer were stories of the frontier about the present, the here-and-now, for Americans; they were about the past. The only living men who resembled the frontiersmen were cowboys, and the stories being told about them were legion.

In June 1860, a few months before Lincoln was elected President, the first "dime novel," an adventure story based in the Wild West, was published. By 1865, when Lincoln was shot, nearly five million dime novels had been sold. The protagonist of most dime novels (and the dominating hero of the Wild West ever since) was the cowboy.

The cowboy was the direct descendant of the backwoodsman, through Daniel Boone, who crossed the Mississippi in his old age and settled there, and Kit Carson, who, as a mountain man and a pathfinder, became one of the earliest popular heroes of the Wild West. Carson, at some point in his mythical career, had mounted a horse—the backwoodsmen had been trackers in leggings and moccasins (like Leather Stocking and Daniel Boone). Kit Carson became, on that horse, in legend at least, one of the first cowboys.

The plains and mountains of the Wild West were a new wilderness, and the cowboy—like the frontiersman in the forests—was the harbinger of civilization who learned the skills necessary for survival in the Wild West, led others, more civilized than himself, into the wilderness and showed them how to survive.

While the cowboy, like the backwoodsman, was often a loner, he was also found in bunches, in the round-up, in the outlaw's gang, and in the sheriff's posse. The cowboy was often rowdy, like Mike Fink had been, and Davy Crockett and Jim Bowie. He was uneducated (or, if heroic, he hid his education like Leather Stocking), rough, "low," and usually dirty. His clothes were no longer the already romanticized buckskins—although cowboy heroes like Buffalo Bill and General Custer often affected buckskins of extreme design, both in reality and in legend—but, rather, dirty jeans or Levi's, which only much later generations would make as romantic as buckskins. And the rifle of the backwoodsman and the trapper became, in the hands of the cowboy (thanks to Samuel Colt, the Texas Rangers, and the Civil War), the "six-gun," the revolving, man-killing modern pistol.

The cowboy hero of legend and story was usually not a rancher, a farmer, or a miner, all of whom were his real contemporaries in the opening and settlement of the trans-Mississippi West. The few cowboy heroes of Wild West stories who were ranchers did not work their ranches. The cowboy was not the descendant of the sturdy pioneer, carving out his own place on the plains. He was not an entrepreneur, either, in the sense that most prospectors, ranchers, and farmers were. Ordinarily, in story and reality, the cowboy worked for someone else.

The cowboy was an employee. He herded or "punched" cattle for a rancher, or, as was frequently the case, for a ranch corporation. He might be a trail boss or a herd boss or a straw boss or a foreman; but whatever position he held, he was a hired hand. Kit Carson worked for a fur company. Buffalo Bill gained his reputation as a supplier of meat for the Union Pacific Railroad. And the real cowboy, or cowpoke, was a skilled technician hired to do the boring, and often dangerous, business of working cows.

The people who read cowboy stories—the same ones who would read Horatio Alger's stories—probably did not notice that cowboys were employees. Most of the readers in industrial America were employees. The cowboy showed how an employee could be an American hero.

The cowboy hero was a gunman. In the traditional stories of the pioneers, the rifle had become symbolic of civilization. And, of course, possession and use of a gun were symbols of the armed, and therefore independent, citizenry of the United States. In the years after the Civil War, the gun also became symbolic of the battle against evil men who opposed progress and destroyed freedom. So the revolver (which was more specifically a man killer than the rifle had been), like the horse and employee status, became an inseparable part of the imagery of the cowboy.

Cowboys-and-Indians became—and remains—a favorite game of American children, and a favorite story for books and films. It is a ritual re-enactment of the winning of the West. On one side are "the good guys"—the cowboys, the settlers with their covered wagons, the Cavalry, and miscellaneous miners, ranchers, farmers, railroads, stage lines, pony-express riders, and towns and damsels in distress; on the other side are "the bad guys"—the Indians, outlaws, renegades, evil agents, and rustlers. In the stories and games, the conflicts between good and evil are battles: ritualistic duels between two men or pitched battles between numbers of people. They are American competition. And they are military contests, in which, with triumphant trumpets blaring, the U.S. Cavalry very often comes charging to the rescue.

The cowboy was, perhaps, the most important good guy in the Wild West, but the Cavalry was a close second. In the logic of Wild West mythology, cowboy and Cavalry are often interchangeable. Both represent good, both fight ritualistic battles, and both are necessary to the winning of the West. The Cavalry is the cowboy, organized, regimented, and therefore, as the Civil War had demonstrated, more effective in bringing about the great ends of progress and reconstruction than an individual. Together, the Cavalry and the cowboy brought law and order, modern civilization and progress, to the West.

On June 25, 1876, just a few days before America's centennial Fourth of July, George Armstrong Custer and elements of the Seventh Cavalry Regiment fought their "Last Stand." They died with their boots on near the Little Bighorn River in what is now southern Montana. One of the largest fighting forces of Indians ever assembled in the West defeated, and killed to the last man, 262 officers and men of the U.S. Cavalry. Within a month of the publication of the reports of Custer's last stand, Custer was an American hero—and he remained so for nearly a century.

Custer's defeat did not lose General Terry's campaign against the Sioux, nor did it lose the war against the Plains Indians. Both, in the end, succeeded. Custer and his men had given up their lives, much as the cowboy hero sometimes did, in order to save civilization. It was the military way of "riding off into the sunset"—to die with your boots on, fighting the Indians. (The imagery of "dying with your boots on" in the Wild West is a cowboy image: those boots are high-heeled and pointed-toed.)

A contemporary biographer of Custer (quoted by Bruce Rosenberg in

Custer and the Epic of Defeat) described him as "the kind of fighter produced only by the bone and sinew of new worlds." He was "tall, lean and rugged, long-haired, dominating and courageous to the point of recklessness," the kind of man who "would have no place in a long-established civilization." Custer and all those like him were not needed by the civilization of railroads, cities, and industry, which had finally triumphed over the wilderness of the New World.

Although Custer was killed, the Indians were defeated; civilization was saved, progress was inevitable and there was no further need for Custer, the Cavalry, or the cowboy. Custer was not, like that other great hero Robert E. Lee, the defender of a lost cause. Custer became the symbol of the victory of civilization and progress over the wilderness and all its heathen denizens. At the same time, he was the symbol of the demise of the backwoodsmen, the frontiersmen, the mountain men, the cowboys; of all pioneers.

Fourteen years after Custer died at the Little Bighorn, the United States Bureau of the Census announced that the frontier had disappeared from America. In the same year, the Army, at the "battle" of Wounded Knee, fired at a large group of Indians for the last time. Three years later, in 1893, a perceptive young historian, Frederick Jackson Turner, made a name for himself with a paper entitled "The Significance of the Frontier in American History." The frontier was history. Like Lincoln, the cowboys, Custer, and the Indians they had fought all belonged to the ages. They were part of the past, not part of the booming, progressing new industrial world of cities and factories, railroads and electricity. The stories of the wilderness and of the men and women who pioneered and fought in the wilderness were told over and over again. The stories became ritualistic, formulaic, little-changing; the cowboy always rode off into the sunset, the Cavalry died with its boots on, the frontiersman moved on to greener pastures. They became the endlessly repeated charter myths of an America which had conquered its storied wilderness.

MYTHS TRANSFORMING

The cowboy, Lincoln, Custer, and all the other mythical heroes and heroines of post-Civil War, industrial, urban America were for most Americans indistinguishable from earlier heroes. But the stories of the new heroes, the new models for the individual pursuit of happiness, included elements of that modern industrial world which helped transform the older myths. The cowboy (as we have seen) was an employee.

The forces the cowboy hero opposed were not merely primitive wilderness (with its savages), or chaos; they, too, were organized, and often as determined to progress in their way as the good institutions that employed the cowboy were. The cowboy was, as Henry Nash Smith put it in *Virgin Land,* a "self-reliant two-gun man who behaved in almost exactly the same fashion whether he were outlaw or peace officer." It is as difficult to distinguish between the institutions being served by the outlaw and by the lawman as it is to distinguish between the heroes.

The lawman served progress, symbolized by operating governments, the safe and regular passage of stagecoaches, the construction and operation of railroads, the predictable use of the open range, and the safe operation of banks. The outlaw was sometimes part of a gang, but he, too, could serve towns, corporations, ranches, and companies. The difference between the lawman hero and the villainous gunman was that the heroic cowboy put the service of progress and society above his personal ambition and greed; he served an openly social and virtuous end. The villain, like Benedict Arnold—this was true even of romantic villains like Jesse James and Butch Cassidy—allowed greed and ambition to outweigh all other considerations. But villain or hero, the cowboy's world, like the new American world, was one of corporations, companies, and organizations.

Whether villain or hero, the cowboy was usually without a future, just as the backwoodsman and the frontiersman had been. They had had two choices once they had performed their services for civilization: they could join civilized society and settle down, or they could move on. They could, in short, continue to be what they were and thereby reject society, or they could join society and reject what they were.

Ordinarily the cowboy in story rode off into the sunset. The implication was strong that he would meet other adventures similar to ones already met, in which he would preserve or create law and order, save the town, wipe out the outlaws, or otherwise protect progress and save civilization. Then he would once again reject society and ride off into another sunset. More modern Westerns carried the story one step further: sooner or later, the hero's eyes got bad or his gun hand shaky or he lost his nerve, and he got shot in turn; obliterated finally, after what seemed endless repetitions of the same adventure.

The cowboy hero never integrated himself with his society. He was a social being, in the sense that he served society and often operated among groups of his peers. Yet he did not enter into full participation in the society as a mature adult; he did not settle down, marry, produce a family, and fulfill himself in a useful vocation. Like the wilderness, the Indians, and the outlaws, he was always on the periphery of the society (the frontier), momentarily useful, and then discarded. As for himself, he did not desire integration. At the climax of his adventures he rode away.

Or he did as Abraham Lincoln did—boarded a train. In the stories told, as well as in the reality of Western life, the cowboys (like their cattle—and the Cavalry) very quickly began to board trains. So did the outlaws. The last great living heroes of the Wild West were train robbers like Jesse James. (In

1948, Frank Dalton died in Texas, a man who was both a survivor of the Cavalry column which arrived at the Little Bighorn too late to rescue Custer and the uncle of the Dalton Gang of train robbers.) The heroic good-guy cowboys often became railroad detectives. And gradually, in popular literature, some became bank detectives and Pinkertons. They moved into industry and into the cities. The private-eye detective, who began to appear in popular stories in the 1920's, had many of the characteristics of the cowboy—he was a loner, he carried a gun, he was an employee, he sought to protect and preserve the law and society, and he rejected society in the end—but his work was in an urban world, and his enemies were not representatives, or denizens, of a natural wilderness.

NEW HEROES IN NEW PLACES

Lincoln, too, had found success in a city. (Ironically, the assassin's bullet had been fired in a theater, the epitome—for many Americans—of the traditional evil temptations of the city.) The city rapidly became, for post-Civil War America, the symbol and the reality of modern industrial life. And the most popular of the tellers of tales of modern American life—Horatio Alger—told stories of boys who made it big in the city.

Alger did not write about cowboys, frontiersmen, pioneers, or towering heroes like Custer and Lincoln. Americans young and old were telling, hearing, and reading stories of all those heroes at the same time that millions of them were reading Alger's. Alger's heroes were obviously American, fierce democrats, independent, eager to work hard, educate themselves, and make their way to success. Their stories did not seem to contradict the traditional ones of yeomen and pioneers, or the newer stories of cowboys and soldiers; indeed, they seemed to reinforce them. Yet it was Alger above all the other storytellers who openly accepted the urban and industrial world, and who helped create a mythology which would sustain Americans, with all their myths and beliefs, in that world.

One of Alger's novels, *Struggling Upward: or Luke Larkin's Luck,* opens in a small town named Groveton in wintertime. It begins with an ice-skating race for the boys in the local school. The prize for the winner is "a Waterbury watch, of neat pattern."

The leading contenders in that race are:

> first, in his own estimation . . . Randolph Duncan, son of Prince Duncan, president of the Groveton Bank, and a prominent town official. Prince Duncan was . . . a rich man, and lived in a style quite beyond that of his neighbors. Randolph was his only son, a boy of sixteen, and felt that in social position and blue blood he was without a peer in the village. He was a tall, athletic boy, and disposed to act the part of a boss among the Groveton boys.

After Randolph Duncan "came a boy similar in age and physical strength, but in other respects, very different." He is "Luke Larkin, the son of a carpenter's widow, living on narrow means, and so compelled to exercise the strictest economy." Luke is the janitor of the school as well as a student.

> He had a pleasant expression, and a bright, resolute look, a warm heart, and a clear intellect, and was probably, in spite of his poverty, the most popular boy in Groveton. In this respect he was the opposite of Randolph Duncan, whose assumption of superiority and desire to "boss" the other boys prevented him from having any real friends.

Luke should have won the race, but he lost, because one of the other boys, a "toady" of Randolph's, tripped him. Randolph won, and so had two watches, a silver one and the new Waterbury.

Alger's novel was first published as a serial in *Golden Argosy* in 1886, in the magazine's "Way to Success" series. It was aimed at young people who lived in the new urban and industrial world, and it shifted—as did all of Alger's stories—the myths of American individualism and success from a rural to an urban setting. It seems unlikely that Alger's readers were aware of any change; they were Americans and they lived in the industrial world. Alger's settings simply made the stories more real.

The opening scene of *Luke Larkin's Luck* is a contest, in good American competitive spirit, in a typically American small town. The outcome of the contest is decided the way the outcome of successful American competition was always decided—on what you could "get away with."

The contestants are traditionally American: *democratic* good and evil. Alger defined the evil first, to make the contrast clearer. Every phrase and word used to describe Randolph Duncan was calculated to rub against the American grain. Duncan's very name smacks of British and Virginian aristocracy, and to make the point clearer, Randolph's father's name is Prince. He is described as a "bank president," a "prominent official," and a "rich man," expressions calculated to rouse distrust in "common" Americans who had acquired their democratic souls from the ideals of Andy Jackson's day.

Yet Prince Duncan's positions *could* have been earned; they could have been the results of American success. They are not necessarily descriptions of evil. The evil is made clear, for Duncan "lived in a style quite beyond that of his neighbors." There are other distasteful aristocratic connotations: "only son," "social position," "blue blood," "peer," and "boss." The wealth and achievement of the Duncan family were thoroughly tainted by anti-democratic behavior. It would naturally follow, in American belief, that the position they had achieved must have been gained by evil means. The story later makes it clear that such, indeed, was the case.

Luke Larkin's very name, in contrast to Randolph Duncan's, is common.

Luke's good democratic origins are clear: he is the "son of a carpenter's widow," "living on narrow means," exercising "strict economy," a janitor who worked at sweeping and making fires. The position, duties, and economies of a poor man of the people are vivid. So are the virtues which accompany them: "pleasant expression," "bright, resolute look," "warm heart," and "clear intellect."

While Luke is poor, poverty itself is not a virtue. It is "in spite of his poverty" that Luke has already achieved one important aspect of success: he is "the most popular boy" in town.

After the race, Luke congratulates Randolph on winning the watch, and admits that he envied him that watch.

"Oh well," Randolph said, "You are a poor boy. It doesn't matter to you."

"I don't know about that Randolph," Luke replied. "Time is likely to be of as much importance to a poor boy as to a rich boy."

Time, as precisely measured and subdivided by watches and clocks, was a significant and visible part of the growing American industrial world, with its railroad schedules and its factories and offices that opened and closed, started and stopped, at certain specified minutes and hours. A watch for a farmer was a luxury; access to a clock or a watch in the industrial world was an absolute necessity.

As Alger's story makes its complicated progress, Luke is accused of a crime he did not commit. He is saved from conviction (in a court run by Randolph's father, who is the local judge as well as the local banker) by "a tall, dark complexioned stranger" who then takes Luke to New York City, buys him two suits and a silver watch "superior even to a Waterbury," and puts him on the path to fortune.

Through the stranger, Luke meets a Mr. Armstrong, from whom some bonds had been stolen. Armstrong is immediately taken with Luke: " 'A thoroughly good boy, and a smart boy too!' said Armstrong to himself. 'I must see if I can't give him a chance to rise. He seems absolutely reliable.' "

Armstrong sends Luke on a journey to the West. Luke has a series of adventures, with con men in Chicago and in gold-mining camps in the Black Hills. He eventually returns with evidence which convicts banker Duncan of stealing the bonds from Armstrong.

Duncan, in disgrace, is allowed to return the bonds, but his dishonesty and mismanagement have ruined him. He "saved a small sum out of the wreck of his fortune, and with his family, removed to the West." In the West, the Duncans "were obliged to adopt a very different style of living." Randolph becomes "an office boy at a salary of four dollars a week," and he is "no longer able to swagger and boast as he has done hitherto."

The conclusion of the story is success for Luke. The father of Luke's best friend becomes the new president of the Groveton Bank. Luke receives a reward, and Mr. Armstrong takes him "into his office" in New York City "at a liberal salary." And so, Alger wrote, closed "an eventful passage in the life of Luke Larkin." Luke had "struggled upward from a boyhood of privation and self-denial into a youth and manhood of prosperity and honor." There had been "some luck about it," Alger admitted, "but after all," he concluded, Luke was "indebted for most of his good fortune to his own good qualities."

Every character in the story of Luke Larkin is a town dweller. The leading paternal characters are affluent *city* businessmen. None of the characters is identifiably rural, and farmers are never mentioned. Alger's heroes live in towns and they are going to the city. They look to the cities for economic opportunity and success. Like Abraham Lincoln, Luke finds his honor and prosperity, along with a "place" in an office and a salary, in the city. Urban America supplies the keys and symbols of success in all of Alger's stories.

The West, the wilderness and the frontier, had long been *the place* where Americans sought opportunity and success. Not Alger's heroes. It was barely twenty-five years since Horace Greeley had made the advice "Go west, young man, and grow up with the country" popular, but Luke Larkin does not seek his fame and fortune in the West. The West, in Alger's stories, is where people go to "prove" themselves. The West is the wellspring of democracy, where those who have fallen, like the Duncans, can get another chance or where the arrogant, like Randolph, are taken down a peg. The Duncans needed to be recycled into genuine Americans. Alger sent them West. Alger's West is a place which produces democratic virtues and strengthens moral character, but it is not the scene of progress or the environment for economic success. Success and progress are to be found in the city. The older frontier heroes had gone West; Horatio Alger's heroes went to the city.

The good qualities which earn Luke Larkin success are those of the older American sturdy, democratic yeoman. Luke is hard-working, self-denying, competitive, friendly, and reliable. The environment of his heroism has changed. And something else has changed, too. Not for Luke the sweating struggle on his own land to win profit and independence for himself and his family. Nor is he an independent entrepreneur, building his business on a shoestring and hard work.

Luke Larkin, the city hero, is, like the cowboy, an employee. And the setting is institutional. He was hired by an individual, but, like the cowboy, he works for an organization. He was a school janitor, then he was bookkeeper in an office, and finally successful, he was employed in an office at a liberal salary.

Alger's heroes, undoubtedly like most of Alger's readers, work in an office, or for an organization, a corporation, or a factory. They work their way up on ladders of success in structured, modern businesses and industries. Alger's heroes do not rise to the top of the ladders of success. Rather, like Luke, they start low—off the ladder altogether—and end comfortably off. They do not go from rags to riches, but from self-denial to comfort. Far from being anachronistic in the modern, urban, industrial world, Alger's stories provide a mythical paradigm for the modern organization man. The Alger hero's aspirations and successes are those of the urban white-collar worker. More than fifty million Americans bought, and more read, the Alger stories.

Alger's were not the only success stories being told of new heroes in urban, industrial America. Aside from the many who told similar fictional tales of urban and industrial success, there were tales being told of *real* people—stories more fabulous, in their reality, than any of Alger's fables. The new industrial society created undreamed-of wealth in America, which was the background which lent reality to Alger's stories. That wealth was sometimes the property of men who had started poor and worked their way up; real men who really lived and worked and succeeded in America. Andrew Carnegie was one such man.

Carnegie had come to the United States as a poor immigrant boy. He worked himself up from sweeper to messenger boy to partner, and then to owner, operator, and organizer of a giant steel business. When the United States Steel Corporation was formed in 1901, Carnegie sold his business and retired from active business life. He was paid nearly four hundred million dollars for his steel interests, and his income thereafter was in the neighborhood of twenty-three million dollars a year.

Carnegie's success represented an impossible dream for most Americans. His income amounted to $63,000 a day, more than most wage earners could hope to earn if they worked for sixty years. He earned in an hour twice as much as the average clerical worker or government employee earned in a year—and four times as much as the average industrial worker. Carnegie was the impossible dream, but he was a real person. Luke Larkin's success was much more believable—as were the successes of most of Alger's heroes.

Readers could find confirming examples of people who rose higher, or achieved some degree of comfort or security, in their real world. So despite their fictional nature, Alger's stories were closer to the lives of the people than Carnegie's life was. It was impossible, for ordinary people in their own experience, either to confirm or to deny the reality of Carnegie's success.

Carnegie, the greatest of all self-made men, the rugged individualist *par excellence,* was a business organization man. He had not started the steel business, he had worked his way up in the steel business. Actually, he had worked his way up in another business and then jumped into steel. He spent all his early years as an employee.

Stories about Carnegie were probably as widely circulated as Alger's. There were newspaper and magazine articles about the great industrialist. Carnegie himself made lecture tours and wrote books on the "Road to Business Success." He told young listeners that it wasn't enough simply to do your job for your employer—if you did only that, you would stay in the same job forever. No, he said, "the rising man must do something exceptional. . . . HE MUST ATTRACT ATTENTION."

There was little difference between Carnegie's attracting attention and Luke Larkin's luck. Carnegie believed that a man could create some of his own luck, that he must push if he were to be a rising man. It was a world, as Carnegie saw it, in which one specialized. The advice not to put all your eggs in one basket was all wrong, according to Carnegie. "I tell you," he said, "put all your eggs in one basket, and then watch that basket!"

The complex overlapping of myth and reality in the stories told by men like Alger and in the stories told by and about men like Carnegie helped create a mythology of the American urban and industrial world. That mythology was made up of hundreds of stories, told again and again, which provided images, analogies, attitudes, and models which seemed to reconcile the contradictions between time-conscious, complexly organized industrial work and city life and the ideals and realities of the independence, democracy, and simple virtues of yeomen farmers and pioneers.

For nearly three hundred years, from the founding of the colony at Jamestown to the end of the nineteenth century, progress in America had meant bringing civilization into the wilderness, and Americans had tried to pattern themselves on the heroes of those years. But by the end of the nineteenth century, progress had moved to the cities; its cutting edge was made up of railroad networks and factory systems and great bureaucracies. Armies of employees were the mark of the new progress—not armies of horsemen, or cowboys, or frontiersmen, or pioneers; armies of employees peopled with heroes created by Horatio Alger, organized and led—not by Daniel Boone or Abraham Lincoln, or George Armstrong Custer, or indeed by the Founding Fathers—but by industrial organizers like Andrew Carnegie and John D. Rockefeller.

The new Americans believed themselves to be like the old: still pathfinders, still pioneers, still carrying civilization into some wilderness. But the old wilderness was dead. So were its heroes. As Frederick Jackson Turner and a whole school of American historians were pointing out, the frontier and the West and the wilderness were *history.* The independent, rural, agrarian American yeoman had conquered the wilderness, and the civilization he had brought to the wilderness had made his children urban, industrial, organizational employees.

5

Individualism Incorporated

In 1888, Edward Bellamy published one of the first American science-fiction novels. It was called *Looking Backward,* and it is the story of a young man who falls asleep in 1887 and awakes in the year 2000. As he grows accustomed to life at the beginning of the twenty-first century, he is told the history of the twentieth century. It is the history of the great corporations and what happened to them.

"The outcry against the concentration of capital was furious," one of his newfound friends tells him. "Men believed . . . that the great corporations were preparing . . . the yoke of a baser servitude than had ever been imposed on the race, servitude not to men but to soulless machines incapable of any motive but insatiable greed."

Americans of the twentieth century, in *Looking Backward,* had fought against the great corporations, but to no avail: "The fact that the desperate popular opposition to the consolidation of business in a few powerful hands had no effect to check it," the young man's friend tells him:

> . . . proves that there must have been a strong economical reason for it. The small capitalists . . . had in fact yielded the field to the great aggregations of capital, because they belonged to a day of small things and were totally incompetent to the demands of an age of steam and telegraphs and the gigantic scale of its enterprises. . . . Oppressive and intolerable as was the régime of the great consolidations of capital, even its victims, while they cursed it, were forced to admit the prodigious increase of efficiency which had been imparted to the national industries, the vast economies effected by concentration of management and unity of organization, and to confess that since the new system had taken the place of the old the wealth of the world had increased at a rate before undreamed of.

The imagery Bellamy used to describe his fictitious twentieth century was the dominant imagery of the late nineteenth century. Images of "great corporations," "soulless machines," "insatiable greed," "gigantic scale," "prodigious increase of efficiency," "vast economies," "concentration," and especially of "wealth . . . before undreamed of" had become common for Americans. They were reinforced on all sides by physical things—buildings, railroads, construction projects—on scales never before seen by human beings, as Walt Whitman sang in the "Song of the Exposition":

> Steam-power, the great express lines, gas, petroleum,
> These triumphs of our time, the Atlantic's delicate cable,
> The Pacific railroad, the Suez Canal, the Mont Cenis and
>   Gothard and Hoosac tunnels, the Brooklyn Bridge,
> This earth all spann'd with iron rails.

Americans had begun to create a new vision of the nation, out of the physical progress, the machines, the power, and the wealth which was being created; the model for that vision was the great big-business corporation.

The railroads, by the late nineteenth century, were among the largest corporations in America. They had also become the inspiration and the means for the achievement of the national destiny and for the achievement of individual success. The railroads, like the nation, expanded ever westward *and* internally, creating new freedom—new mobility—and new opportunities wherever they went. Swift rail transportation carrying goods and people, accompanied by even swifter communication, made it possible for individuals to dream of national economic power. The way to such wealth and power was through the corporation.

The corporation had become the major device for the accumulation and management of capital. As a legal device, it was freely available under minimal government regulation. It provided for the centralized control of assets under the direction of those who were, by inclination, training, experience, or the common consent of the investors, best qualified to lead; and it provided both limited liability and some control over management to its stockholders. It had become a free and democratic economic device, as Americans believed, similar to devices like homesteading, or voluntary fraternal organizations, in which free individuals could pool their resources, manage their own affairs, and work for a common goal. After the Civil War, it had become the most common device by which large-scale American business grew and was managed.

Both railroads and corporations partook of the imagery of the machine to Americans. Fascination with the machine, both as symbol and as the reality of the physical universe, was a general nineteenth-century phenomenon. The American professor Henry Adams, at the Great Exposition in Paris in 1900, "began to feel the forty-foot dynamos as a moral force, much as the early Christians felt the Cross":

> The planet itself seemed less impressive, in its old-fashioned, deliberate, annual or daily revolution, than this huge wheel, revolving within arm's-length at some vertiginous speed, and barely murmuring. . . . Before the end, one began to pray to it; inherited instinct taught the natural expression of man before silent and infinite force. Among the thousand symbols of ultimate energy, the dynamo was not so human as some, but it was the most expressive.

Machines were railroads. They were great factories in which row after row of machines were served by organized workers. They were sources of energy, used in place of absent laborers or to replace less efficient and impressive natural sources—wind, water, and animals. They represented speed, great force, and the production of vast quantities of goods. The whole nation, it seemed, was gradually filling with people, food, and machines, providing vast resources of energy and power for the creation of more machines, more factories, more goods, and more services than had ever before been available.

Despite the great outpouring of wealth the machines brought, individual Americans still sought to pursue their own happiness. The traditional myths of the individual seemed still to apply.

"I take it that it is best for all to leave each man free to acquire property as fast as he can," Abraham Lincoln had said. "Some will get wealthy." Lincoln had gone on to say that he didn't believe "in a law to prevent a man from getting rich," but he did believe that "the humblest man" should have "an equal chance to get rich with everybody else."

It was with the values Lincoln expressed, out of the world in which Lincoln had grown up and lived his adult life, that Americans had come to the world of cities, machines, railroads, and corporations. Lincoln's "ambition was a little engine that knew no rest," his law partner Herndon wrote. Such ambition was no contradiction, as Americans perceived it, to a belief in the equal chance of the "humblest man." The individual was obliged to seize upon whatever resources or opportunities were open. Laws and governments were not supposed to stand in the way. Individuals were expected to exploit opportunities for their own economic advantage; they were to get rich, if they could.

That was success, the hoped-for outcome of the pursuit of happiness. An economic success served the whole society. It created wealth and jobs and more opportunities for others to pursue happiness. "The prudent, penniless beginner in the world labors for wages awhile, saves a surplus with which to buy tools or land for himself, then labors on his own account another while, and at length hires another new beginner to help him." That was Lincoln's parable of the ambitious American pursuing success: it is an image of individualism most Americans continue to hold. By the beginning of the twentieth century, Americans had become accustomed to the application of that image to the great corporation.

CORPORATE MYTHS AND REALITIES

Four sets of existing mythologies—of individualism, of voluntary cooperation, of mechanization, and of organization—were used, appealed to, and combined to create the mythology of the American big-business corporation. The powerful myths of individualism, with their emphasis on independence, the pursuit of happiness, the acquisition of property and wealth, and on success, became the most important part of corporate mythology. But the American emphasis on voluntary cooperation for the greater good of the community and the nation was also transformed into a part of corporate mythology. So was the vision of the power of machines, as expressed by Henry Adams and as intimately known by millions of American factory workers. And the possibilities inherent in organized, regimented masses of human beings—which Americans had first learned of in the Civil War—also became part of the myths of corporate employment and corporate growth in the years after that war.

The process of the transformation and combination of those existing mythologies went on *while* corporations were formed and re-formed, structured, expanded, and restructured. There were Americans who were aware of the process of mythmaking and myth-changing, but most did not see that the images they applied to justifying and explaining corporate growth and the corporate dominance of twentieth-century America were—by the very process of applying them to corporations—being transformed.

The aim of each of the new big businesses and their leaders was to create a national organization which could predict and control, from raw material to customer, the production and distribution of a particular line of goods with the greatest possible profit. The dream was not only of wealth but of control. It was an imperial dream. It depended upon the maximum efficient use of a vast transportation system, the centralized control of a carefully organized bureaucracy, and a widespread system of intelligence gathering and communication. One of the most skillful of the new corporate businessmen was the man who organized oil, John D. Rockefeller. "To know every detail of the oil trade, to be able to reach at any moment its remotest point, to control even its weakest factor," Ida Tarbell, the great historian of Standard Oil, wrote, "this was John D. Rockefeller's ideal of doing business." She continued:

> It seemed to be an intellectual necessity for him to be able to direct the course of any particular gallon of oil from the moment it gushed from the earth until

it went into the lamp of a housewife. There must be nothing—*nothing* in his great machine he did not know to be working right.

Control was achieved, first, by owning and directing the operation of all parts of the process necessary for a particular business. That meant either buying up companies already engaged in a part of the business or creating corporate divisions with specialized operations. The national marketing system of every big corporation was staffed by employees. The products of a big-business corporation were almost never sold by commission agents—as had been the normal practice in earlier industries. Employees were more controllable. When the whole of a manufacturing process was brought under central, corporate control, production was usually concentrated in fewer, larger plants, supervised by a bureaucracy of specialists. Specialized departments for purchasing, for engineering, for traffic flow, and for accounting were created. All departments and processes were controlled by a central office.

"The closest supervision of the Central Office is necessary," a Report of the Federal Commissioner of Corporations on the Beef Industry said, in 1905:

> . . . to enforce the exercise of skill and sound judgment on the part of the agents who buy the stock, and the agents who sell the meat. With this object, the branches of the Selling and Accounting Department . . . are organized in the most extensive and thorough manner. The Central Office is in constant telegraphic correspondence with the distributing houses, with a view to adjusting the supply of meat and the price as nearly as possible to the demand.

Efficient accounting procedures were also essential to the control of a national industrial corporation. Enormous fixed overhead costs demanded volume sales in large markets, accompanied by careful regulation of the flow of goods and money. An accounting department provided the necessary accurate and steady flow of information on costs, sales, purchasing, manufacturing, transportation, and marketing. Accounting also enabled the careful structuring of offices and functions, the creation of tables of organization with the theoretically clear lines of authority and responsibility essential to the control and operation of a large bureaucracy.

But it was the Central Office—"in constant telegraphic correspondence" with all parts of the organization—in which the effort to control was focused. The Standard Oil Company, according to Ida Tarbell, was "as perfectly centralised as the Catholic Church or the Napoleonic government." The image of what later generations would call totalitarian government—which for nineteenth-century Americans was best exemplified by the Catholic Church or by either of the Napoleons—constantly recurs in descriptions of the new big businesses. That image provided the closest approximation of the machine which could be found in human institutions. It implied absolute control of the whole structure by a single person; it implied an elaborately structured bureaucracy, filled with subordinates who were entirely loyal and obedient to the wishes of the leader; and it implied inexorable operations on a worldwide scale.

Standard Oil's corporate machine was tightly centralized, and it operated on Carnegie's adage: "Put all your eggs in one basket, and then watch that basket!" The Standard Oil Trust, which was formed in 1882, had nine trustees, of whom Rockefeller was the leader. The trustees, Ida Tarbell wrote:

> . . . have always acted exactly as if they were nine partners in a business, and the only persons concerned in it. They met daily, giving their whole time to the management and development of the concern. . . . Anything in the oil world might come under their ken, from a smoking wick in Oshkosh to the competition of Russian oil in China.

Standard Oil was, by the end of the nineteenth century, the largest producer and seller of petroleum products in the world. It controlled more than 80 percent of the American market, and it exported millions of barrels of petroleum products. The nine partners of the trust made all the decisions about the business, based on information sifted "for their eyes" by committees:

> There was a Crude Committee which considered the subject of crude oil . . . a Manufacturing Committee which studied the making of refined, the utilization of waste, the development of new products; a Marketing Committee. . . . Before each of these committees was laid daily all the information to be found on earth concerning its particular field. . . . These committees not only knew all about their own business, they knew all about everybody else's.

The trustees used all the information, and "nobody ever used information more profitably." Rockefeller, "a marvelous genius in organization," had "devised a machine," according to Tarbell, "whose thinking was felt from the seat of power in New York City to the humblest pipe-line patrol on Oil Creek." All the scattered operations of the company were controlled by Rockefeller "with absolute precision." This "thinking machine," the corporation, became much admired by Americans for its efficiency and precision and power—and that admiration stuck to those machines long after the robber barons, like Rockefeller, who had created them—and personified them—were dead.

CORPORATE INDIVIDUALISM AND COOPERATION

By the twentieth century Americans were caught up by these great corporate dynamos. Corporations had become visions of a steadily increasing flow of goods; visions of efficiency in their machine-like production, in their use of vast sums of money, vast quantities of energy, and the labor of thousands of human beings; visions of great pyramids of power and wealth and material goods, tightly controlled, efficiently operating, and productive beyond the dreams of most ordinary people. The corporations were individual imagination and daring made into giant machines. "Industry," to most Americans, came to mean all those visions of big business: it meant efficiency; it meant vast and complex organization; it meant tight central control. The corporation became a myth: the productive super machine, created by individual genius, controlled from a faceless center but directed with intelligence, reaching everywhere, and producing a never-ending stream of ever-cheaper, ever-better, ever-more goods.

It was also an octopus whose evil tentacles reached everywhere, grasped everything there was to take, crushed and devoured the weak and the innocent. It was mindless and anonymous, and yet all-seeing. It became symbolized by Wall Street. "Trust" became synonymous with "privilege" and "monopoly." Yet as is often the case with mythical monsters, even as it was distrusted, it was admired. "But this huge bulk, blackened by commercial sin," Tarbell wrote of Standard Oil, "has always been strong in all the great business qualities—in energy, in intelligence, in dauntlessness." Big business "has always been rich in youth as well as greed, in brains as well as unscrupulousness." And if big business "played its great game with contemptuous indifference to fair play, and to nice legal points of view," it was still possible for Americans to admire it because "it has played . . . with consummate ability, daring and address." The great multinational corporations of today, the "Seven Sisters" oil companies for example, are no less distrusted *and* admired by Americans.

Admiration for the great mythical corporation grew because Americans assumed that at the center of the octopus was the single eye, the single controlling brain—the greedy and ambitious, hard-working and independent, single American individual. In the mythology of corporations, every giant corporation has been *created* by a single individual—from Rockefeller to J. P. Morgan to Henry Ford to Henry Kaiser to Howard Hughes. That myth lives still. The great corporation becomes, in the logic of the myth, the living, *immortal* extension of all the characteristics and dynamics which belonged to the individual who created it. A corporation is, in this American mythical perception, *a single individual,* able to act on a national, even on a worldwide scale, vastly powerful, ruthless, efficient, greedy, and ambitious. The individual is living metaphor for the corporation; and, in the peculiar way of myths, the corporation has become a metaphor for the individual.

The creators of these vast corporate organizations have taken on the qualities of towering national heroes in American myth. They have become like

Washington or Jackson or General Grant. John D. Rockefeller, for instance, was said to have had "a sense of the big and vital factors" in business,

> . . . and a daring in laying hold of them which was very like military genius. He saw strategic points like Napoleon, and he swooped on them with the suddenness of a Napoleon. . . . His courage was steady—and his faith in his ideas unwavering.

The controlling individual, the individual possessed of vast power, able to make far-reaching decisions which were inexorably carried out by a machine-like organization; the individual of unimaginable wealth and success—that is the image which dominates American perception of the corporation. It is precisely the overlapping and confusion of the mythology of the corporation with the traditional mythology of the individual—the incorporation of individualism—which continues to explain and justify great corporations to Americans. Throughout the twentieth century, Americans have feared for the independence—and the very survival—of the individual in the face of the onslaught of corporate bigness and its bureaucratic anonymity. The tension generated by the identification of individualism with corporations, by the admiration *and* fear of corporate efficiency, power, wealth, and size, is exceedingly strong in American society today—but the myths of corporate individualism, of individualism incorporated, remain the explanations and continue to supply the logic Americans use to justify corporations.

Those who criticized the initial growth of corporate big business were, in the words of some businessmen, "moss-backs left behind in the march of progress." They were people who came from, or lived in, "scrubby little towns," not in the great industrial cities. The same argument is still used. There were and are few who would deny that the rise of big business represented progress: the great corporations produced more steel, more oil, more sewing machines, more automobiles, more of everything, than had ever been produced in the world before. That was progress, and few Americans indeed wanted to stop progress. Furthermore, the myths were that corporations were voluntary associations of large numbers of individuals working cooperatively to produce more and more, better and better. No American would want to stop such activity.

The modern corporation was a fact not a theory, George W. Perkins (a young partner in the J. P. Morgan banking company who had helped form International Harvester among other corporate giants) told an audience of Columbia University students in 1908. The corporation was simply "another name for organization," Perkins said, and the principle of organization was universal:

> . . . in the very beginning of things, the universe was organized—and all that man has done in society, in the Church, in business, and all that he ever can do in the centuries to come, can never bring to pass so complete a form of organization, so vast a trust, so centralized a form of control, as passes before our eyes in each twenty-four hours of our lives as we contemplate that all-including system of perfect organization called the Universe. It does not require a very vivid imagination to picture the waste, the destruction, the chaos that would follow if there were not perfect organization, perfect co-operation, perfect regulation, perfect control in the affairs of the universe.

Any American businessman in the first decade of the twentieth century would rightly assume his audience would transfer such imagery from the universe to big business.

"And so, under conditions which, in the mechanical development of the world, came on as naturally as day follows night, the great corporation came into existence." Progress, for a man like Perkins, was automatic. And the corporation was progress's most recent, most highly evolved, outcome. The logic of the argument that the corporation was an inevitable part of American progress remains generally unchallenged today.

The corporation was not merely inevitable, however; it was also *efficient.* "The most useful achievement of the great corporation," according to Perkins, "has been the saving of waste." Corporations brought together "the best brains, the best genius, the best energy" and coordinated them "in work for a common end." The result was waste prevented, by-products utilized, production made economical, expenses saved, and service made "better and more uniform." Common work and uniform service could not come from independent individuals operating separately. The corporation eliminated the wastefulness of individual work:

> Nothing develops man like contact with other men. A dozen men working apart and for separate ends do not develop the facility, the ideas, the general effectiveness that will become the qualities of a dozen men working together in one cause.

The vision of cooperative work in the corporation is also a vision of regimentation. Both are contained in the myths, in the same way and with the same kind of logic that waste and efficiency are both believed to be part of corporate behavior today.

The great corporations not only made it possible for individuals to work in cooperative harmony; they also, according to corporate spokesmen like Perkins, increased the number and availability of the opportunities for individual Americans to rise in the world:

> The larger the corporation, the more certain is the office boy to ultimately reach a foremost place if he is made of the right stuff, if he keeps everlastingly

> at it, and if he is determined to become master of each position he occupies.... Everything is giving way and must give way to the one supreme test of fitness.

Success did not come by chance. It was "an opportunity that has been lassoed and organized," by an employee or a cowboy or an office boy who was determined to rise in a bureaucratic table of organization. The corporations had *organized* the pursuit of happiness for Americans so that rising to success has come to mean promotion through the ranks of specialized, structured bureaucracies. The old mythic vision of the individual pursuit of happiness has remained, but the real world which gives form to that pursuit is corporate.

THE NEW MYTHOLOGY OF INDIVIDUALISM

The old-fashioned ways of individualism were wasteful and inefficient, "wholly self-seeking and often ruinous," according to corporate leaders like Perkins. The great corporations did away with "the old method of destructive competition" which, corporate leaders insisted, was characteristic of American individualism, and replaced it with "constructive and uplifting" rivalry between individuals who were employed "within the limits of the same organization."

The men, like George Perkins, Andrew Carnegie, John D. Rockefeller, and Henry Ford, who contributed so much to the creation of the mythology of corporations deliberately tried to distinguish between old-fashioned individualism and modern, up-to-date corporations. While they borrowed many of the traditional epithets and slogans which characterized individualism in the traditional myths and applied them to the corporations, they also tried in a variety of ways to put down individualism, to convince Americans that it was old hat, out of date, reactionary, and ultimately dangerous to American progress. They created a sharp distinction, for example, between the organized cooperation which they believed was characteristic of the big business corporation, and the destructive competition which they emphasized as the prime characteristic of American independent individualism. As a result, ruthless competition has become, for twentieth-century Americans, an inseparable part of their vision of traditional individualism.

Economic competition had, indeed, been part of the mythology of American individualism, but a minor part. It became important, and widely discussed, only with the growth of big business and corporations. Daniel Boone may have competed with other backwoodsmen to find the Cumberland Gap or Lincoln may have gone into competition with other ferrymen across Anderson Creek, but that competition was not a vital part of the myths of either of those heroes of individualism. Competition had not been important in the mythology of the frontier—although settlers did compete with the Indians, that competition was rarely expressed in the stories as economic competition or as individual competition—and it was not important in the traditional myths of farming or pioneering. Economic competition between individuals was accepted as a normal part—sometimes unpleasant, if greed went too far—of American entrepreneurial activity, but it was never the central focus of the myths of individualism. Some competition was believed to be socially important and of service to the community: Lincoln competed with Douglas for a Senate seat (and lost!). But significantly, the Lincoln myths almost completely ignore the competition of Lincoln's successful campaigns for the Presidency.

The free and competitive marketplace, which Thomas Jefferson used metaphorically in his first inaugural address—

> . . . every difference of opinion is not a difference of principle. We have called by different names brethren of the same principle. We are all Republicans; we are all Federalists. If there be any among us who wish to dissolve this Union, or to change its republican form, let them stand undisturbed as monuments of the safety with which error of opinion may be tolerated, where reason is left free to combat it.

—left an image, as Jefferson no doubt intended, of a free-standing, independent (even if wrongheaded) individual. But that individual was not importantly improved by competition. Indeed, there seemed little value in the competition among "brethren of the same principle." But it did exist.

The competition which became highly visible to Americans during the last third of the nineteenth century was not competition between individuals but rather the vicious, cutthroat, often overtly violent competition between growing corporations. Railroads, oil pipelines, huge steel companies, petroleum companies—all these and many more were openly in competition with each other, violently attempting each other's destruction (and sometimes succeeding). It was such competition, corporate leaders told Americans, which was characteristic of the old days of individualism. Corporations were devoted to abolishing such competition, they said, to the greater benefit of Americans. It was such competition which twentieth-century Americans came to believe *had been* characteristic of traditional American individualism, and still made Americans violent, bent on destroying all who competed with them.

The new corporate mythology thus revised the way Americans perceived their past by its insistence that competition among independent American individuals had been the *only* control on rampant greed and ambition. Most

Americans accept that today. The logic of the new myths, then, implied that competition had proven an inadequate control: American society, as the end of the nineteenth century neared, had suffered virtual chaos. In place of the proven inadequacy of competition, the new myths offered corporate organization and cooperation, structured regimentation of individuals under the control of specialists and qualified corporate leaders, carefully regulated economic activity to maximize efficiency, production, and wealth. The robber barons, in this new mythology, represented both the epitome of competitive individualism and the solution to the failure of competition. The new corporate vision appealed to the older myths of community service and voluntary cooperation at the same time as it revised individualism and provided an attractive explanation of the rise and ultimate benefit of corporate big business to a rapidly urbanizing, industrializing America.

Even those—and there were many—who did not believe that the great corporations really represented organized cooperation or any high ideals of community activity accepted the greater part of the new corporate mythology. Americans of all sorts, for example, came to believe that individual competition as the central regulator of and control on ambitious economic activity (by individuals or by corporations) was a desirable state to bring back, to restore to American life. In other words, even the critics accepted the revision. The impetus for American trustbusting throughout the twentieth century is based on the assumption that the competition which is postulated by corporate mythology can be restored in order to control corporate activity. On the other hand, the many Americans who argued—and still argue—for regulation of corporate activity in the public interest by agencies of government are arguing for the enforcement of corporate organization and cooperation, the regimentation of activity under the control of specialists and qualified leaders, a carefully regulated economic activity intended to maximize efficiency, production, and wealth. They are, in short, using the logic of the corporate mythology, just as the trustbusters do.

William K. Vanderbilt, the heir of Commodore Vanderbilt and the head of the New York Central Railroad, made the most famous and succinct statement of the individualistic ideal as it was incorporated into corporate myth. Vanderbilt was asked by a reporter for the *Chicago Daily News* in 1882 if he did not run his trains "for the public benefit." His immediate reply made him immortal: "The public be damned," he said.

Vanderbilt went on to explain:

> What does the public care for the railroads except to get as much out of them . . . as possible? I don't take any stock in this silly nonsense about working for anybody's good but our own, because we are not. When we make a move we do it because it is our interest to do so, not because we expect to do somebody else some good. Of course we like to do everything possible for the benefit of

humanity in general, but when we do, we first see that we are benefiting ourselves. Railroads are not run on sentiment, but on business principles, and to pay.

Few Americans have ever applauded Vanderbilt's bald opening statement. "The public be damned" has long been cited as the blatantly undemocratic statement of a robber baron. But the rest of his remarks are perceived today, as they have been for a century, as the principles of standard American individualism applicable indiscriminately to multinational corporations and to any American "on the make." That is a clear measure of the success with which corporate mythology has absorbed and revised, transformed and incorporated, the traditional myths of American individualism.

In the creation of the mythology of the corporations, the same comforting words and formulas which had been applied to the old myths of individualism were used. "Opportunity," "freedom," "community service," "cooperation," and "success" have remained central to the American view of the real world, but they are now images and ideals applied to corporations as well as to individuals. Corporations have legally become "persons"—beneficiaries, in American law, of all the rights and privileges which belong to individual human beings. The process of incorporating individualism makes a metaphor binding in law. Today American individuals can make themselves into corporations.

Corporations dominate the American economy. The large-scale, integrated corporate enterprise has become the indicator of economic health, growth, progress, and productivity for all. Individual, small-scale, non-expanding entrepreneurs still exist in great numbers as independent operators of farms, stores, manufacturing and service businesses. Their continued existence reinforces the American belief in the myths of traditional individualism (and of traditional capitalism), but economic and political policy, local and national, as well as the predominant perceptions of economic and political reality are shaped by the great corporations and the myths surrounding them.

Corporations have become the predominant American models of efficient government, of the integration of people and human activity (and thus of the accomplishment of *e pluribus unum*), and of success. They have so successfully taken to themselves the metaphor of the individual that most Americans visualize them as massive individuals, the apotheosis in scale and activity of the mythic expectations of individuals. They were, after all, created by genius-heroes. They produce wealth in greater quantity and diversity than has ever been imagined. They do the *work* of the entire nation, perhaps of the world. They *serve* American needs and desires.

"The time was ripe for it. It had to come," John D. Rockefeller said to a United States Senate Committee. "The day of combination is here to stay." He was asserting, in his own defense and in the defense of corporations generally, what most present-day Americans accept as a description of reality: the inevitable development of the big-business corporation. There have been few Americans who agree with Rockefeller's conclusion that "individualism has gone, never to return." But the myths of individualism, so central and important to specifically American ideals and reality, have come to include, and to be metaphorically incorporated into, those corporations which Rockefeller clearly envisaged as the opponents and destroyers of individualism.

NEW WORLDS TO INCORPORATE

"The captains of industry who have driven the railway systems across this continent, who have built up our commerce, who have developed our manufactures, have on the whole done great good to our people," Theodore Roosevelt, the first twentieth-century President, announced to Congress in 1901. "Without them," he said, "the material development of which we are so justly proud could never have taken place." Roosevelt's was the ultimate justification of the rise and dominance of corporations. The progress of America, as Americans have come to accept it in the twentieth century, depends on the ever-increasing production and use of energy, wealth, and goods. The giant American corporations, with their innumerable machines, their great factories, and their organized armies of employees, are the prime movers of that progress.

It would not do, Theodore Roosevelt said, unduly to hamper "the strong and forceful men upon whom the success of business operations inevitably rests." The identification of corporate operations with "strong and forceful" individuals has produced, in twentieth-century America, a powerful ambivalence and tension in American belief and policy and actions in regard to corporations.

That ambivalence was noticed by Roosevelt, and part of its basis pointed out: "The industrial changes which have so enormously increased the productive power of mankind," he said, had also changed the general patterns of the distribution of wealth in America. Like many modern Americans, Roosevelt was caught between the perception that something was wrong with the distribution of the massively increasing wealth of the United States and the equally powerful idea that the modern corporation, which had created the unequal distribution, had created the wealth.

If the corporation was the only modern and progressive manifestation of American individualism, then what were Americans to do about corporate behavior without damaging essential individualism? The tension built into the corporate mythology has not abated in the more than three-quarters of a century since an American President noticed the problem. The ambivalence remains.

Roosevelt's solution of the problem, his demonstration (not consciously, of course) of the logic of the myth, was to tell stories of the corporations and of their importance. "The same business conditions which have produced the great aggregations of corporate and individual wealth" in America, he said, have also made "them very potent factors in international . . . competition." The biggest corporations, "managed by the ablest men," were, Roosevelt said, leaders "in the strife for commercial supremacy among the nations of the world." The corporations were leading America on an errand into the wilderness of world competition for markets and resources. "America has only just begun to assume that commanding position in the international business world which we believe will more and more be hers," Roosevelt said, and it was therefore unthinkable that the corporations be restricted or hampered.

The President certainly echoed the sentiments of corporate leaders. Standard Oil, John D. Rockefeller had told the Industrial Commission in 1899:

> . . . has spared no expenses in forcing its products into the markets of the world among people civilized and uncivilized. It has had faith in American oil, and has brought together millions of money for the purpose of making it what it is, and holding its markets against the competition of Russia and all the many countries which are producers of oil and competitors against American oil.

Only by "such an industrial combination" as Standard Oil, or other giant corporations, could America utilize "the bounty which its land pours forth, and . . . furnish the world with the best and cheapest light ever known." (The petroleum business was then almost entirely based on the sale of kerosene for lighting and heat.) The great corporations like Standard, Rockefeller said, were pioneers. Like the pioneers, their work was of incalculable value to the nation. Corporations were carrying out America's mission in the world: their price was the incorporation of American individualism. They were now the pioneers.

"It is a great thing," Theodore Roosevelt had told a St. Louis audience in 1900:

> . . . to belong to a prosperous country, a country rich in mines, in factory, in farm, ranches and railroads . . . and woe to the country when a generation rises which . . . shrinks from doing the rough work of the world. . . . The man who counts is . . . the man who goes out into the world to struggle and stumble and get up again, and go on and try, and be beaten and try again, to face

> difficulties, and out of difficulties, trampling them under foot, to make his way to splendid ultimate triumph. So it is with the nation. . . . Thrice happy is the nation that has a great and glorious history, a history of glorious achievement for itself and the races of mankind. . . . Think of the peoples of Europe stumbling upward through the Dark Ages, doing much work in a wrong way, sometimes falling back, but ever coming forward again, forward, forward, until our great civilization, as we know it now, was developed at last out of the struggles and failures and victories of millions of men who dared to do the world's work.

The vision of doing "the world's work" is the ultimate appeal in the myths of American corporations. Americans still believe the world needs American technology, American know-how, American organization, American productivity—the work of American corporations. The vision of doing the world's work is a vision of millions of people creating wealth, advancing progress, serving their communities and civilization itself. The independent American pioneering individual had become a great corporation, pursuing its happiness in the markets and resources and available power in the world, serving its community by its work, its productivity, its goods, its outpouring of wealth and its constant raising of the "American standard of living," and fulfilling the mission of America by its willingness to do the world's work of bringing civilization to every corner of the country and every corner of the earth. And, too, it provided the ladder to success for Horatio Alger's heroes, promising affluence and security. Individualism was incorporated.

But was it also betrayed? Most Americans today believe corporations to be vast anonymous bureaucracies, grinding down the weak and innocent, regimenting and controlling the poor and the ambitious alike; powerful, independent, greedy, ambitious, intelligent living bodies. But corporations are, most Americans would agree, the embodiments of "good old American rugged individualism" carried to its logical conclusion. That is also the myth. Corporations are individualized.

6

The Engine of Progress

FOR THE PAST half century or more, increasing numbers of Americans have measured individual worth—their own and others'—by the goods and services they are able to consume. That "consuming" attitude is widely popularized in the media and in novels like *Scruples.* More and more, individual work has come to be perceived as no more than the means to get the wherewithal for consumption. Working to produce is no longer believed to be the purpose of individual life. Americans have given up the work ethic. Production has been given over to the corporation, while the American individual has become a consumer.

The incorporation of individualism has provided a mythical logic which makes it legitimate for productive work to be done by corporations. The individual worker in a giant big business, whether blue or white collar, is part of a large bureaucracy, a cog in a machine, who is less and less visibly productive of works, of finished products. In the modern urban world, community and home and work place are separated; few Americans any longer have the satisfying reinforcement of neighbors seeing them be productive. Individual work is rarely seen to produce *things;* more and more, all it produces is money.

Money is an intermediary, not an end product. In modern America, individual work makes money. That money is *used* in order to *consume* the goods and services (in order to acquire the products) the individual desires. And those products, those goods and services, are the result of corporate enterprise, not individual work. The individual American consumes. And American society has become, so we believe, a consumer society.

The consumer society believes that ever-increasing consumption is the individual pursuit of happiness. It is "the promise of American life." Consumption is the fulfillment of the American dream in this modern transformation of the mythology of American individualism. America's growth and destiny depends, in this myth, on increasing individual consumption. Economic, business, and government leaders of the nation are driven to find ways to increase consumption, because an affluent society is the destiny of

American democracy, the mission of American individualism as it has come to be defined in this post-industrial world.

Status, worth, and success are now judged by the quality and quantity of goods and services consumed. Economic and social mobility are based on consumption. Increasing consumption, individually and collectively, is a sign that wealth is more widely available, that society is increasingly democratic. The poverty level is continually redefined, and the list of the necessities of life—which *must* be provided for all in such a democratic society—has been enlarged from the basic food, shelter, and clothing to include other basics of the consumer society: money, electricity, transportation, telephones, leisure, and access to mass media. The American standard of living means ever-increasing consumption.

Although individuals are part of a consumer society, Americans have not entirely given up belief in individual work and productivity, nor are they entirely convinced that unmitigated consumption is a good thing. The logic of productive individualism continues to have force. But a variety of transformations, both of American belief and of the realities of urban, industrial life, through the course of the twentieth century, have produced an identifiably American mythology of the individual as consumer, and of America as a consumer society.

The giving of productive work to the corporation was one such transformation. Most Americans now simply assume the production of goods and services is automatic, a natural part of American life.

Cheap household consumer electricity, automobiles, and small, electricity- or internal-combustion-powered motors brought another such transformation. Automobiles have become essential to individual mobility, and motors have become vital to the individual American's control over work and the environment. These real products have become part of the American mythology of the consumer.

The experience of deprivation—felt by almost all Americans during the Great Depression of the 1930's and during the world war that followed—in combination with the model of economic success which World War II provided for Americans—produced yet further transformations in the mythology of Americans. Consumption—of almost any sort—has become the fundamental American measure of affluence, applicable equally to individuals, to nations, and to the world.

All these changes have combined in contemporary American life to produce the logic (and the mythology) of the individual American as consumer.

THE MACHINES OF MODERN INDEPENDENCE

The pursuit of happiness is at the core of the mythology of the individual. The introduction of electricity and of automobiles took place in the context of that mythology. The response to these modern technologies was not an economic response based on some rational assessment of class or self-interest. Rather, the response was based on a relatively swift (compared to other industrial societies) and now nearly universal American perception that electric power and the automobile made individuals more independent and more able to pursue their own happiness effectively. Americans generally believe that American *mores* and beliefs were transformed by these technologies, and so they were. But the *existence* and the *power* of the myths of individualism also *shaped the technologies.* Those myths swiftly gave electrical energy and the automobile a place in American society (and in the mythology of the consumer) which they have acquired only recently in other industrial societies.

Electrical power available in the home brought a fundamental change to life. Strictly speaking, electricity is not a human necessity. It does not *have* to be used in order to provide food, shelter, clothing, warmth, or even light. Many thought it a luxury when it first became available—and some "back to nature" enthusiasts try to survive without it today. But twentieth-century Americans took to it as ancient man took to fire. It has become a necessity in the urban and industrial world.

By 1917, the production of electricity for individual consumers in America exceeded the production for industrial use. By the 1960's, 90 percent of the electricity produced was for consumer, as differentiated from industrial, use, and that proportion has continued since. Only in America did the consumer become, so early and so overwhelmingly, the primary user of electrical power in an industrialized nation.

Electrical current, widely distributed, put at the disposal of Americans an energy source unlike any ever before available to an individual. Electrical energy could do work on a scale small enough that an individual could control and utilize it in a confined space. Other forms of energy—animal, wood, coal—had long been used, and newer forms—steam, petroleum, internal combustion, atomic—put greater sources of power at the disposal of humanity in general. But alternating electrical current and the motors it energized did work that hitherto only humans could do, did it at the flick of a switch, and did it in individual homes. It appealed to Americans. It gave individual Americans *independence:* independence from work itself, as well as independence from certain kinds of work.

The innumerable uses of electricity, the spin-off from the light bulb, helped create American consumerism. The small electric motor brought home refrigeration—which was followed by freezers, home air conditioning, forced hot-air or hot-water furnaces, oil heat (dependent upon electric pressure pumps), humidifiers, and dehumidifiers. It brought washing machines—followed by electric wringers, spinners, and drying machines which, whatever their heat source, required the ubiquitous electric motor.

It brought electric ironing devices. It brought electric vacuum cleaners and sewing machines.

It was electricity that enabled public life to enter the home through radio and television. It was electricity which brought the cultural revolution that came with the electric phonograph—and later the electric guitar and the electric organ. It brought, too, an ever-increasing variety of small electric gadgets of varying utility. Electricity did not replace all the older forms of heat sources, but once available, it swiftly became an easy alternative to other forms of heat for cooking, for hot water, and for toast, waffles, and popcorn. Even modern solar-heating plants depend on electric pumps to circulate the heat captured from the sun.

Industries aimed specifically at the electricity consumer developed to service and exploit the possibilities created by the individual possession of electrical energy. The appliance manufacturers and the electrical-utilities industry use ever-larger proportions of the natural resources of the United States—metals and minerals, plastics, coal, oil, hydroenergy, and petrochemicals—and the industrial resources—machine tools, manufacturing capacity, heavy machinery (like dynamos and turbines), skilled and unskilled workers, professionals of all sorts—in order to provide for the needs and demands of society. The modern American economy has developed, then, as a reflection of the imperatives of the mythology of individualism.

Electric energy has provided the American with a sense of *independence,* a sense of *control,* a sense of individual work and worth, in his or her own home: a reinforcement of the logic which has become, as generations of Americans have come to take electric power for granted, quite unconscious, but nevertheless powerful.

Automobile production was aimed at the individual consumer from the beginning, and the development of mass-production techniques, along with Henry Ford's desire to provide all Americans with wheels, assured the swift focus of automobile makers on the largest number of American consumers. By 1916, more than a million automobiles were sold in America each year. By the 1970's, there was a car for every other man, woman, and child.

The effect of the automobile on Americans was so swift that the process was nearly invisible. There was a generation without the automobile, a generation that saw its early development, production, and spread; the next generation was born into a world of cars. The "horse and buggy" era became a laughable anachronism even to people who were born and brought up in it.

As more and more Americans used cars, their vision of the past changed. They began to assume that in the old days everybody owned a horse—an analogy to their own relationship to the automobile. Of course that wasn't true. Horses were expensive. Horseback riding unconnected with work was something only the well-to-do could afford. The ordinary American—like the ordinary human being—in the days before the automobile walked. Railroads and streetcars had changed that pattern somewhat; they had added to the physical mobility of Americans, but the vast majority of ordinary Americans continued to own and operate no means of transportation other than their feet. The automobile changed that.

A motorcar required little more storage space than a horse; and when stored, its demands and requirements were at the sole discretion of its owner. An automobile did not die, run away, become violent or sick or complain if constant maintenance and feeding were not forthcoming. It did not move unless the owner chose to move it. A car could even be stored along curbs, at the roadside, in yards or alleys or other convenient spaces. Cars did work humans couldn't do, moved at speeds feet could not achieve, and had endurance beyond the limits of the finest animals. Little wonder that Americans began to assume that in days gone by a cowboy could park his horse, fight off the bandits, robbers, or Indians, and then leap on his trusty steed and thunder off in pursuit of retreating enemies or of the sunset with a hearty "heigh-ho." Park it, leave it, leap in, start 'er up, and off you go.

The automobile, like electricity, put at the disposal of the individual (at relatively low cost and great convenience) an energy source (and user of energy) and a variety of power never before available. It provided rapid transportation combined with freedom from exertion, from daily routines of care and feeding, with a minimum of maintenance and concern. It offered relative ease, convenience, and control. In a nation which believed physical movement to be a symbol of social mobility, economic rise, and human freedom, the prospects for the individual with an automobile were dazzling.

The automobile turned heavy industry to the service of the consumer. Steel, rubber, petroleum, machine tools, heavy machinery, and heavy construction—all became focused on the automobile industry. Car manufacturers became the center of the economy and of industrial effort, a vast consumer of resources, capital, labor, sales efforts, advertising, research, skills, and time. Today the largest American corporations with the greatest capital, the greatest income, and the greatest number of employees are either the petroleum companies that provide automotive energy or the car manufacturers.

Other modern industrial nations, in the process of modeling their economies on the American since World War II, have put increasing emphasis on the automobile; but in no other nation are there so many automobiles, and in no other nation is the automobile perceived (except by American observers) to be so important to individual and national life. Historians have argued that the automobile changed American morals and *mores*. Almost all believe that it has created the modern American landscape and the physical patterns of urban and suburban life. It has shaped the economies of almost all Americans as well as the economy of the nation. Why? Because it has become *the way* to be free and independent; *the way* for Americans to move under their own control, and thus to demonstrate (both to themselves and to the world) their independence, their power, their freedom.

It is almost impossible for Americans today to conceive of individual freedom, of independence or happiness, without some means of motor-driven transportation—the car primarily, or the motorcycle, truck, van, boat, snowmobile, beach buggy, or private airplane. The sign for many contemporary American adolescents of their independence and adulthood is their own "wheels," and a powerful rite of passage into adulthood is the driving test required for a driver's license.

Americans who live in central cities today often do not own wheels, whatever their income. They are, in a sense understood by them and by other Americans, "deprived," a state which makes them palpably less free and independent. There is little evidence that any significant number of Americans believe that mass-transportation systems of any kind will relieve such deprivation, because the logic is that mass systems cannot give individual freedom.

Americans consider a multitude of other machines necessary and important. With those machines, Americans can, *individually,* plow, mow, rake, heat, cool, have music, cook, wash, preserve foods, open cans, dry clothes, style hair, paint, type, have pictures, talk to others at great distances or nearby, cut down trees, trim hedges, plow snow—and demonstrate to themselves and to others their control over their environment. Independence, freedom, and autonomy come in great part, we believe, from the possession of machines and from their use by individuals. In recent years, for example, women have been in some part liberated (as Americans believe) by the machines they use. Machines have freed them, both from work and from subservience.

THE CULTURE OF DEPRIVATION

In the period following World War I, the transformation of American mythology from emphasis on the productive worker with a full dinner pail to the consumer with a high standard of living became both self-conscious and obvious. Neither advertising as a business nor aggressive salesmanship were inventions of the 1920's, but in combination the two became primary agents in the burgeoning of American consumption from the twenties on.

Advertising in the expanding mass media began to provide the mass markets of consumers necessary to the economic growth and continuing survival of the great industries. Advertising men and women could, it was discovered, "scare up" consumers, and, quite possibly, keep them scared—and buying. Bruce Barton, the twenties' most eminent advertising man and author, made clear what economic leaders in the consumer world had come to recognize: "We speak of the law of 'supply and demand,' " he wrote, "but the words have got turned around. With anything which is not a basic necessity the supply always precedes the demand."

With increasingly conscious effort, advertising people began to create demand. Barton wrote a popular best seller, a life of Jesus called *The Man Nobody Knows,* in which he explained how to create demand. Jesus was portrayed in the book as a great salesman. Christians were the consumers of the religion Jesus produced. Christianity, Barton wrote, had "conquered not because there was any *demand* for another religion but because Jesus knew how, and taught his followers how, to catch the attention of the indifferent, and translate a great spiritual conception into terms of practical self-concern." The slogans, campaigns, symbols, and myths of modern advertising were efforts to translate the products of big business into individual "practical self-concern" for Americans: "Blondes have more fun"—"More pain-reliever faster"—"More for less." The secret to the creation of demand was to make the potential consumer feel deprived.

The possibilities for advertising in the broadcast media (radio, newspapers, magazines) were increasingly realized. Advertisers and ad men made extensive use of slogans, repetition, and deliberate mythmaking. They learned to use the subtle, direct appeal to the individual by playing on guilt, embarrassment, social aspirations, social pressures, and sex. Whatever could be found to create a sense of being deprived, a sense of want, would help the consumer translate indifference into "terms of practical self-concern."

The stock-market crash of 1929 and the Great Depression that brought unemployment, poverty, and real deprivation to millions throughout the 1930's convinced many that while America had developed a massive industrial system capable of producing goods and services for virtually infinite consumption, it had failed to provide adequate distribution of those goods and services. If there was no money available to the consumer, there would be no consumption. More and more people began to argue that consumption was necessary to the economy. Ex-President Calvin Coolidge urged Americans to consume more in order to get business going again. That was "absolutely going against all the laws we have been brought up to," humorist Will Rogers wrote. "Imagine telling the working man to spend, that if he doesn't put his money into circulation why he won't have a job. . . . [It's] hard to tell what to believe nowadays."

Governor Gifford Pinchot of Pennsylvania, whose state was hard hit by unemployment and depression, told a Senate committee that President Herbert Hoover's proposal that individuals give more to community chests and other voluntary organizations so they could provide relief to the starving and the unemployed would only take money "out of consumption."

"The money for this emergency," Pinchot said, "ought to be taken in such a way as to cut down consumption the least possible, and that means taking it from the people who do not expend their whole income for consumption but spend it mainly for investment."

Pinchot was convinced, as were many others, that investment and production were not as necessary as consumption was to make the American economy work. The experience of the Depression made vivid that it was essential to the operation of the whole economy that the "little fellows" have money to spend. How they got it might have to take second place to the necessity of their getting *and* spending it.

Franklin D. Roosevelt, both as campaigner and as President for twelve years (1933–1945), led the public transformation of the mythology of the producing individual into the new world of the consumer. "A mere builder of more industrial plants, a creator of more railroad systems, an organizer of more corporations, is as likely to be a danger as a help," Roosevelt said to the Commonwealth Club in San Francisco during his 1932 campaign. "Our task now is not discovery or exploitation of natural resources, or necessarily producing more goods." The day of the producer, Roosevelt believed, had reached its peak. What faced America was "the soberer, less dramatic business of administering resources and plants already in hand, of seeking to reestablish foreign markets for our surplus production, of meeting the problem of underconsumption, of adjusting production to consumption, of distributing wealth and products more equitably, of adapting existing economic organizations to the service of the people."

Roosevelt made clear that he believed "the day of the great promoters or the financial Titan, to whom we granted anything if only he would build, or develop, is over." The watchword of Roosevelt's New Deal was to "prime the pump" of consumer spending.

"What we want, really," Rexford Tugwell, one of Roosevelt's close New Deal advisers, wrote in *The Battle for Democracy* in 1935, "is to provide the opportunity for every individual and every group to work and to be able to consume the product of others' work. This involves a creation of buying power which is coordinate with the creation of goods."

Almost all the important programs of the New Deal and the legislation sponsored or accepted by Roosevelt were aimed at the adjustment of production to consumption, and at the increased employment and payment of consumers. Most Americans became convinced, out of the real disaster and actual deprivation of the Depression, that individual hard work, individual productivity and progress, were no insurance against the disastrous effects of impersonal economic forces in a modern, industrial, urban society.

The mythology of the independent individual as producer was, it seemed to many, proven by the Depression to have been myth: it was at best a rationalization, or perhaps an anachronism; at worst, it was a cynical effort by economic leaders, industrialists, capitalists, bosses, to exploit gullible Americans; but it was no explanation of reality. The explanation lay, for most, in the words of President Roosevelt and, for many others, in the implications of the actions of federal and state governments, that the duty and responsibility of the individual to the society was to consume, as rapidly as possible, all the goods and services the society produced. If the individual consumed, the economy would prosper, production would continue, jobs would be plentiful. Without consumption, deprivation would continue.

Most Americans came to believe that the Depression had been the result not of individual or collective inability or unwillingness to produce goods and services but, rather, of the failure of the economic system to provide for adequate levels of consumption. Future depressions could be prevented only if the whole structure of American society, including the economy and the rapidly expanding bureaucracy of government, provided the basic needs of the consumer.

The experience of World War II convinced those who might still have doubted or had misgivings about the efficacy of consumption as the fundamental dynamo of the economic system. The war revitalized the productive capacity of the country, a capacity few Americans had doubted. The war "proved" America could produce whatever it needed in undreamed-of quantities. The war also produced full employment, increasing wage levels, and the consumption of goods and services to a degree few had believed possible. It was true that the consumption was not individual: the individual consumer was still deprived of goods and services by the war effort; but the enormous waste of wartime consumption was an impressive economic example to deprived Americans.

The fear that there would be an economic collapse after World War II like the one which had followed World War I combined with "after the war is over" dreams of glory to drive Americans to continue the patterns of economic success the war had established. The military demands of war had consumed on a vast scale. Products had been made, even theoretically durable goods like ships and vehicles and motors, to be used up, replaced, and used up again. Goods were packaged, in immense amounts of metal and paper in ingenious designs, for easy distribution and the use of individual consumers. Throwaway implements of a wide variety were designed and used, because it was cheaper to distribute them around the globe for one-time use than it was to provide for the collection, cleaning, maintenance, and redistribution of more durable goods. Everything produced was constantly and rapidly redesigned for greater convenience, higher performance, more complex tasks, so that items just being put into production were, so far as design was concerned, already obsolete and scheduled for replacement. Some called it "planned waste," others saw it as "technological advance," but many hoped that an economic equivalent of wartime consumption could be found so that the deprivation Americans had suffered for so long could finally be brought to an end.

CONSUMER DEPENDENCE AND INDEPENDENCE

The fifteen-year-long *felt* deprivation of the Depression and war years had been accompanied by the growth of a far-reaching sense of dependence. Many believed depression and then war had created (others thought merely *demonstrated*) widespread dependence on the federal government for individual and collective security among Americans. The government was believed to be responsible for jobs, for relief from starvation or exposure. More and more Americans looked to the government for general economic as well as individual well-being. The leadership and charisma of Franklin D. Roosevelt had created this dependence, some believed; and for many, Roosevelt was the symbol of hope amid the fears and deprivations of depression and war. After his death in 1945, just before the end of World War II, Franklin D. Roosevelt became—for at least the next quarter century and perhaps longer—the mythic American symbol of the *necessary* connection between the Great Depression and World War II. And connected to that symbolism by the logic of Roosevelt's myth are the images of Roosevelt the creator of the big government that cared for the little guy and of Roosevelt the creator of the consumer society.

Belief in the dependence of individual Americans on the government did not cease with the war. Rather, it has increased steadily in American life. It has been accompanied by a fluctuating but nevertheless far-reaching sense of dependence on the great industrial corporations—dependence for the production of goods, dependence for the energy required for individual (as well as national) survival, dependence for money and jobs, dependence for economic security. That sense of dependence has been made increasingly clear in recent years by the Great Blackout of the Northeast, by the oil crises of 1973 and 1979— in regard to energy—and by the efforts to bail out great corporations like Lockheed and Chrysler—in order to preserve the flow of goods, services, and jobs.

The obvious reality of dependence in the contemporary American world is justified in American belief, is explained to the satisfaction of Americans, is made a logical component of American *independent* individualism, by two lesson of the Depression and the war—the result of deprivation. Eliminate deprivation and independence results. The modern vision of America as an affluent society is based on such logic. So is the welfare system. On the other hand, many Americans believe the symbols of independence to be the substance. Thus, owning one's own place, serving oneself, being able to move freely, possessing individual control over one's immediate surroundings (owning and operating machines, automobiles)—all represent independence. And where the symbols are—so goes the mythic logic—there must also be the substance.

For a majority of Americans, the decade or so after 1945 brought a gradual release from deprivation. John Kenneth Galbraith, a Harvard economist, wrote a book about America, *The Affluent Society* (1958). Individual affluence along with individual security (in income, health, and economic growth) in the 1950's and 1960's brought a renewed sense of individual independence. Younger Americans used their affluence to assert independence of parents, of teachers and educational institutions, of government, of authority and "the establishment." Many "opted out," and "did their own thing"—in conscious protest of dependence upon parents, corporate enterprise, and government. They sought, as did many others, to bring about the end of deprivation for those who were not affected by the growing general affluence. Independence, all Americans came to believe, required an end to deprivation.

The reality as well as the most visible symbols of the consumer society—automobiles and highways, single-family dwellings in mass developments, and supermarket-shopping malls—are also part of the imagery and logic of the mythology of individual independence.

The automobile and the highway provide individual freedom and mobility. They give each person control over his or her own movement, over his or her own fate. They are a continuing source of folklore and folk heroes—in automobiles, in motorcycles, in eighteen-wheelers—of defiance of authority, of the community of independence—on the CB's and the bumper stickers—of self-help. Automobiles are the focus of American economic social community, and individual life. They *are* independence; and they *are* consumerism.

Single-family homes—in suburbs or cities, in estates or developments, in condominiums and cooperatives, in garden apartments and mobile-home parks—are the substance of American independence. A person's home is his or her own castle. The sturdy yeoman lives on his own land. Owning your own home gives you a place—visible to the whole community, the whole society. And—purchased with credit, filled with machines and appliances which the homeowner consumes—it is a dual symbol of independence and consumption.

Supermarkets and shopping centers are the cornucopias of wealth and productivity. They make visible the variety of goods and services available, the masses of people who are consuming, and the changeable techniques of consumption. Their presence indicates to most Americans that the society is affluent and democratic (everyone participates!). Most supermarkets and shopping centers are "self-service," which is independent individualism. They are, therefore, clearly evidence and explanations of American independence and consumption.

"Our favorite people and our favorite stories became so not by any inherent virtue," Joan Didion wrote in *Slouching Towards Bethlehem,* "but because they illustrate something deep in the grain, something unadmitted." She was writing about Howard Hughes, a hero of consuming Americans, because he was a successful, independent loner—the epitome of the power of the affluent consumer. "That we have made a hero of Howard Hughes," she continued,

> . . . tells us something interesting about ourselves, something only dimly remembered, tells us that the secret point of money and power in America is neither the things that money can buy nor power for power's sake (Americans are uneasy with their possessions, guilty about power, all of which is difficult for Europeans to perceive because they are themselves so truly materialistic, so versed in the uses of power), but absolute personal freedom, mobility, privacy. It is the instinct which drove America to the Pacific, all through the nineteenth century, the desire to be able to find a restaurant open in case you want a sandwich, to be a free agent, live by one's own rules.

In an industrial society devoted to the production of goods for individual consumers to use, Americans believe the purpose of those goods, the reason for consumption, to be the acquisition of "absolute personal freedom, mobility, privacy." Progress is measured by the degree of individual independence available. And in contemporary America, the consumer is the engine of progress.

7

Players, Models, Actors

As work and its products have ceased to define the individual's place in society, as Americans have come to perceive themselves as part of a machine world and dependent on machines, and as we have become consumers rather than producers, we have tried to find new and satisfying roles for ourselves, new models for the individual. The search modern Americans are conducting is not entirely rational or conscious; we are seeking heroes and heroines, mythical figures, who can show us how to continue to be Americans—frontiersmen, pioneers; successful, independent; pathfinders, idealists, innocents—in the modern, scientific, urban, industrial, bureaucratic, and anonymous, consuming world we have made for ourselves.

There are many sophisticated Americans who argue that we no longer have heroes or heroines; that we use up the images and the substance of our heroic figures and throw them away. And yet there seem to be heroic *types,* even in our media-conditioned, consuming society, which are repeated again and again in different actors, in different models, but in the same roles—Babe Ruth and Henry Aaron, Knute Rockne and Casey Stengel, William S. Hart, Gary Cooper, and Clint Eastwood, Franklin D. Roosevelt and John F. Kennedy. It is also the case that many of the heroes Americans create for themselves today bear remarkable resemblances to traditional heroic types: Martin Luther King, Jr., to Abraham Lincoln, starship and *Star Trek* and *Star Wars* heroes to pioneers, backwoodsmen, and Indian fighters, "new" frontiersmen to "old" frontiersmen, astronauts to Columbus and the Pilgrims.

Americans are looking for models and for roles. They are expecting their modern tellers of tales to speak of heroes and heroines whose lives, whose deeds, whose mythical overcoming of obstacles will explain and justify the continued existence of individual Americans in this mechanical, automated, televised, often depressing and sometimes terrifying world.

THE HERO AND HIS MACHINE

"What's this guy got that I ain't got?" is the opening line of a poem written by I. J. Kapstein about Charles A. Lindbergh for a poetry contest. "Lucky Lindy," the "Lone Eagle," was the outstanding American hero of the late 1920's and early 1930's. The man and his flight across the Atlantic, in the words of a contemporary writer, "fired the imagination of mankind." Schoolchildren all over America decided they wanted to be like Lindbergh. Lindbergh had what other modern Americans wanted: the qualities of traditional American heroes and the universal notice and approval of the present, modern world.

> What's this guy got that I ain't got?
> Why the hell am I here shipping out dry goods,
> while this guy ships himself over the Atlantic,
> and gets a big hand from all the big-timers
> with all them French broads
> falling all over themselves
> trying to kiss him? . . .
> He's in the same class with Steve Brodie
> jumping off Brooklyn Bridge,
> or like the guy that went over Niagara Falls in a barrel,—
> nervy guys but daffy as hell.
> . . . not that I'm knocking him,
> but there's plenty like him in Bellevue.
>
> Yeh, I'd give my right arm
> to do what this guy Lindbergh did.

Lindbergh the hero seemed to make old-fashioned American individualism, which had been personified in frontiersmen and cowboys, compatible with industrial America. The story of the "Lone Eagle" made it possible for Americans to believe that the complex machinery of impersonal industrial society was at the disposal of, and dependent on, the virtues of the lonely, independent, free American. Lindbergh was an unknown, Midwestern farm boy, of virtuous parentage, self-educated. ("What's this guy got that I ain't got?") He had trained himself to fly, and to fly well. He was a loner, the stuff of which pioneers were made. Like popular cowboy heroes, he was young, handsome, modest, and reticent—a type which would be re-created in all its monosyllabic glory by Gary Cooper in the movies of the 1930's and 1940's.

The frontier sought by Americans in the twentieth century is no longer the frontier of settlement; their ambition is no longer to carve out agrarian empires from the wilderness. The "new frontier"—which was what President John F. Kennedy called it—is to be found in the modern urban and industrial world. It was explored and tamed by invention, by production, by men with machines, like Edison and Ford and Lindbergh. The new frontier is to be found in the unexplored and uninhabitable extremities of the earth, and discovered and learned about (the "frontiers of knowledge") by men like Peary and Byrd; or it was to be found in testing the limits of human endurance and courage, by jumping off the Brooklyn Bridge, going over Niagara Falls in a barrel or orbiting the earth record numbers of times. "Frontier," "wilderness," "pioneering" have become metaphors in a new world of complex machinery and hard-driven "teams" of human beings; a world in which it has become possible for a man inside a complicated spacesuit machine to step out of a sophisticated space capsule, on the surface of the moon, and be heard by millions of people on earth to say: "One small step for man, one giant step for mankind." Men had ridden their machines—as *part* of those machines—a quarter of a million miles to the moon and back again.

Lindbergh's frontier was a combination of new frontiers: it was a test of human endurance, an exploitation of industrial genius, and a pushing of the limits to set a new record. His frontier was the wilderness of the air. He was "the Icarus of the twentieth century," according to *The New York Times,* "not himself an inventor of his own wings, but a son of that omnipotent Daedalus whose ingenuity has created the modern world." As he said, his flight to Paris "represented American industry." The crowds at Le Bourget Aerodrome in Paris sought not only to touch Lindy but to preserve a piece of his machine.

Lindbergh could not have flown the Atlantic—or at all—without his machine; just as Neil Armstrong could not have gotten to the moon without the thousands of machines in the space program. The old homesteader, the "forty-niner" could—and often did—go West without a Conestoga. Lindbergh's wings were *The Spirit of St. Louis;* without them he was no pioneer at all, and he could not seek a frontier. As John William Ward, the most perceptive interpreter of Lindbergh's flight, pointed out in *American Quarterly* in 1958, the heroic myth of Lindbergh contained "a new and open world with the self-sufficient individual at its center"; it contained "escape from institutions, from the forms of society, and from limitations put upon the free individual"; and it contained as well the complex institutions of industrial society, "an acceptance of the discipline of the machine, and the achievement of the individual within a context of which he was only a part." The telling of the Lindbergh story effortlessly combined all these contradictory elements; the implicit message of the story was that the contradictions were resolved by the logic of their being connected in the story. Lindbergh, the self-reliant American individual, pioneered, but only in a complex machine produced by the engineering and mechanical skills of a team of hard-working experts funded by "progressive" businessmen. Man and machine and industrial organization were one. They were complementary, in perfect balance. None could survive, function, or achieve without the others. The Lindbergh myth triumphantly celebrated the inseparability of the individual and industrial society. The acceptance of Lindbergh as a national hero indicated that there are roles available for Americans—the spiritual if not physical descendants of the frontiersmen, the pioneers, and the cowboys—in the modern world of airplanes, automobiles, vast industries, and sprawling cities.

THE MODERN HEROINE AND HER ROLES

In the course of the 1930's and 1940's, the images of American heroes and heroines portrayed by the movies—one of the most vivid and powerful modern tellers of tales—showed new values and new patterns for masculine and feminine roles. Movie protagonists were often gangsters, bold, aggressive, alienated, and alone, who—despite underlying kind hearts—were physically brutal toward their women. Such heroes, however, lost in the end. While their characters were clearly more important than the fact that they were killed or imprisoned at the end of the stories, those inevitable endings underlined the fundamental social undesirability of their behavior.

Other heroes were more traditional; they too were alienated, lonesome cowboy types, but they placed a high value on strong, proper "little women." Although aggressive men, they gave up their lives of violence in order to settle down with such a woman, or they regretfully rejected the little woman because of their own moral inadequacies and rode off alone into the sunset.

The theme of the rejection of the girl who was too good for the hero, because of his criminality, was frequently balanced by the theme of the hero of humble origins who, because of his shining character and morality, won the girl who was too good for him because of her high social position. American democratic ideals and the ideal of equality were clearly, in such movies, applicable to the relationships between men and women.

The new heroes of urban life—journalists, doctors, lawyers, and other professionals, sports and entertainment figures, young businessmen, and even industrial workers—more and more became the subjects of the stories. These men were usually aggressive and strong, but they were also part of a complicated world, subject to bosses or employers and to the demands of teamwork and organizational loyalty. Their moral and masculine integrity was often at stake in the plots.

There were frequently heroines in the movies of the thirties and forties who were "strong-minded, quick-witted, even aggressive." They were central to most movie stories. "The activity of women in American movies," critic Michael Wood wrote in *America in the Movies,*

> . . . is frequently unhappy and unsuccessful, and often desperate. But it is there, all over the place. Wherever you turn, the blame's on Mame. What's more, the activity of women is virtually the only intelligent activity in the movies, because men never have time to think.

Very often, the strong, intelligent heroine gave in to the male, but it was clear from all these movies that the questions of sexual equality and the roles of men and women in public and in private were openly debatable questions. "Despite the fact that Bette Davis, Rosalind Russell, and Katharine Hepburn regularly gave in to men on screen . . . ," Lois Banner wrote in *Women in Modern America,* "their ultimate surrender seems almost irrelevant to the triumph of their character."

The "age-old battle of the sexes" portrayed in movies in the thirties and forties, like the series made by Katharine Hepburn and Spencer Tracy, was in fact a new battle in American mythology, a battle between partners who were intellectual and moral equals, both strong, both aggressive. The resolution of their conflict, couched (very nearly literally) in a formula of ultimate feminine subjection to the male, remained acceptable to much of American society. But, very like the "crime doesn't pay" ending to gangster movies, the pattern of the plot situation and the important characteristics of the hero and the heroine cast the efficacy, the mythical logic, of the formula into doubt. The strong, confident command of a star like Mae West, who answered the question "Haven't you met a man who could make you happy?" with "Sure, lots of times," was not acceptable to many, but the existence of her movies in combination with the other, more formulaic ones emphasized the search for a new way to perceive sex roles in American society.

The obvious changes in the economic, political, and social roles of women in the twentieth century brought defensive reactions from both men and women. Traditional roles are not easily given up, and the realities of mythology are often easier to reinforce than to change. The erosion of the sanctity of the home, for example (that is, the blurring of the separation of private and public life), brought a heightened defense of the prime symbol of the home, mother. The gradual loss of a clear distinction between masculine and feminine spheres of influence brought heightened concern about masculinity and femininity, and increased efforts to defend the spheres that remained and extend their sway.

"Mom," in the sense that Philip Wylie defined her in *A Generation of Vipers* (1942), or as Philip Roth portrayed her in *Portnoy's Complaint* (1967), as a possessive, consuming virago, determined to castrate her sons and assert in all possible physical and psychic ways the superiority of woman and the dirty ineffectuality of men, was a twentieth-century defensive creation both on the part of women who were such moms and on the part of men who perceived all women that way. That role of "mom" defended, now *in extremis,* the rights of wives and mothers to predominance in child-rearing, education, and home life, at a time when the public world had deeply penetrated the home. Patterns of nursing, toilet training, and pre-school as well as school education were being challenged and changed, and the active participation of women in the economy in non-agrarian ways could no longer be ignored or written off as a temporary phenomenon. Mom assembled her apple pie and apron strings, her pedestal and sexlessness, her place in the home, and her control of education, added a high degree of seductiveness for good measure, retired occasionally to the coffee klatch or the beauty parlor, ran up the flag, made Mother's Day a national holiday, declared war on all that was male, made the very idea of male activities contemptible, and tried to build herself into an impregnable (!) institution.

Men, too, in various professions to varying degrees, responded to direct and indirect pressure from women by ghettoizing themselves and marking some professions—architecture, engineering—or some specialties within professions "for men only." The transportation industry—railway men of all sorts, commercial pilots, truck drivers, taxi drivers (although there was some slippage here during World War II and after), and gas-station operators—was for men. Professional sports were set aside for men—except for some which were "lady-like," such as tennis, golf, riding, and swimming. Around sports, transportation, and the manipulation of machinery, men attempted to build the macho counterpart to "mom." This, too, was to be a bastion, defensive in its nature, which detested all things feminine, put a premium on the little woman or the "piece of ass," declared the Big World to be a Man's World, hid behind the mysteries of mechanics and the intricacies of the "game," retired occasionally to the local bar, or more recently with the beer can to the television set, spent longer and longer hours at work, and at the same time insisted that the little woman was part of the business team, tried to be a buddy to his kids, was seductive to his daughters, and fought off all feminine efforts to erode his prerogatives.

The logic which supported the myths of woman's role in American society started from two premises: first, that the woman in an American sturdy independent yeoman family had a central economic role without which the family could not operate in society—the woman, like the man, was *productive,* visibly, of works which were essential; second, that the consequence of sexual intercourse was pregnancy and the production of a child, and that a woman could not avoid that consequence—a man could take preventative measures *and* a man did not become pregnant, so was able to walk away from the consequences of sex.

The advent of industrialism began the erosion of the first premise. In a full-fledged industrial, urban society, the vital producing economic unit became the factory or the corporation, and both men and women could be cogs in the machines. Money could be earned by any independent American individual regardless of sex. As industrial society developed in America, women became increasingly important consumers. The logic of the consumer society has put increasing emphasis on the independence and equality of women and has made it obvious that useful, productive women are women who earn money—and ordinarily money is earned in the society by working outside the home. The percentage of women wage earners in America has steadily increased since World War II. The "revolution in female employment," as William Chafe called it in *The American Woman,* was "spearheaded by the same middle-class wives and mothers who allegedly had found new contentment in domesticity" during the 1950's. By 1970, 60 percent of all "non-farm wives in families with incomes over $10,000" were employed, working to earn money in public life. The premise that there was socially valuable work in the home, specifically for women, which was also economically necessary, had evaporated with the advent of industries, versatile machines, and the necessity for money in the consumer society.

The 1950's introduced "the pill," a birth-control device exclusively under the control of women which enabled them to choose when to have babies. The pill meant that a most powerful sanction which men could apply to women, the necessity to have babies, was removed. And so was an underlying myth: that women, because they *had* to have babies, were somehow weaker than men, as well as inferior to them. *They* could not control motherhood; only men could—until the pill. The gaining of such important control over one's fate was clearly, in the logic of American individualism, a sign of independence and equality. For women as a class of individuals, the pill offered the possibility of a kind and quality of independence they had never possessed.

The elaborate Victorian myth of female weakness, according to Elizabeth Janeway in *Man's World, Woman's Place,* declared "that women must be protected because they bear and raise children:

> They need time to do this, and they need a special place, woman's place, where the contentious world does not intrude. . . . If women are protected by being given a special place, they should stay there and not try to have it both ways, be free at one time and protected at another. In order to convince them of this, it is argued that child-bearing and -rearing are the central themes of woman's role, the overriding purpose of her life for which she is naturally gifted. . . . She should look on the role of mother as her highest duty and her greatest fulfillment, and if she doesn't, sanctions will be applied. . . . Now the

myth of female weakness is being challenged by the fact that sex for women is no longer necessarily connected with child-bearing.

The mythology of female weakness is crumbling under the changes in modern America and the onslaughts of modern feminists. But there is still "mom," the consuming virago, the tower of strength. Women are powerful, too, in the traditional myths—powerful in their sexual productivity. The myths of female weakness were used to counterbalance that power. The counterbalance is disappearing, and as a result "men fear that they may find themselves not equal but dominated," Elizabeth Janeway wrote.

> Female sexuality has always made demands on men, but now the demands are felt as increased. "Can I satisfy her?" a man asks himself. Now he can no longer answer that it doesn't matter . . . because she is the weaker vessel, constrained by woman's role as bearer of children to stay in her place and submit. . . . Now if he can't satisfy her, *she* may pick up and move on. No longer can he forbid her to do this. . . . She will have a child only if she chooses to do so. Therefore she will stay only if she chooses to do so. Therefore she must be satisfied.

The "battle of the sexes" is a modern American phenomenon, the result of the transformation of the myths of the roles of each sex in our urban, industrial society. Those roles are being redefined within the context of the ideals of individual independence as Americans perceive the reality of independence in the contemporary consumer world. New heroes and heroines are now in the boots of John Smith and the moccasins of Pocahontas, in the shoes of John and Priscilla Alden, in the boots of Buffalo Bill and Annie Oakley, as well as in the polished shoes of Spencer Tracy and Katharine Hepburn. The heroines, like the heroes, are seeking identifiably American roles for American individuals among the machines, bureaucracies, cities, and power Americans have created.

MACHINES AND MYTHS AND REALITIES

Modern American heroes and heroines, roles and role models, are always and clearly part of a mechanical, industrial, consumer world because the tellers of tales are visibly machines which can be turned on or turned off by individuals in their own homes. Of course there have been mechanical media since the invention of the printing press, but only radio and television (which has come for many Americans to include the movies) are individually operable machines available to nearly everyone. Those machines reinforce daily the connection between modern heroes and heroines, modern roles, and machines.

Much of modern storytelling, as well as most descriptions of those realities which are beyond the immediate experience of any individual or community, is done through the medium of television. The way most Americans come to know their heroes and heroines is by watching television. And it is the way many come to know the realities of war, of diplomacy, of politics, of climate, and of events taking place elsewhere in the world. But the mechanical means by which the stories are told gives them an unreal quality, even when the stories and the people are real. The reality of events occurring in a machine which can be turned off at will is difficult to determine. At the same time, modern mechanical media tell stories of unreal, made-up people—heroes and heroines who are played by actors—but present them and dramatize them in exactly the same way as they do stories of real people. The difference between play and reality, between mythical and real person, between an actor who plays a part or a role in a made-up drama (which might well be a drama about real people) and an actor in a real role in a news broadcast—the difference between metaphor and reality, image and reality, is all but lost in the modern telling of a tale.

The metaphor of "roles," of "playing a part," is widespread in American myth and language. It is not simply the clear metaphor that "all the world's a stage, and all the men and women merely players"; it is more complex and much less conscious. We Americans believe that men and women have many different roles to play in their life. Some of the roles are deliberately created images (like the mask worn by an actor in the ancient Classical world—which the Romans called a *persona*). Some of the roles we believe are "real"; they have to do with the work the individual does, the groups and communities to which an individual belongs. Here, too, the distinction between image and reality is blurred. Some of the roles we believe to be traditional or natural, arising out of the past, out of the family, out of the sex and physical nature of the individual. Each role is a part a person plays, but it is also a part of the real person. Americans believe it is incumbent on the individual to integrate those parts and so to be a whole person. The integrated personality like the integrated society (and the integrated company or process?) is an American ideal, a way of creating one out of many (*e pluribus unum*).

Access to the tellers of tales has always been essential to heroism. Access to the mass media is essential to the creation of contemporary heroism (whether the hero is fictional, like the heroine of *Scruples,* or "real," like Elvis Presley). Only through the media can anyone hope to become known enough to be widely acknowledged or approved by Americans—as anyone who wishes to be a star or to change society believes implicitly. But the contemporary media are also devoted to the promotion of consumption. Advertising sells goods and, it has been discovered, also sells candidates, heroes, Presidents, and pop stars. The distinction between the consumption of goods and the moral of a heroic story, between politics and athletic games, has been as much blurred as the distinction between fiction and reality.

The modern tellers of tales, like their ancient counterparts, concentrate on people. Stories about abstract ideas or physically remote events are often personified (to make them more real). News, advertising, commentary, nonfiction as well as fiction, are personified and dramatized in order to provide human meaning and human impact. Heroes and heroines, real ones, are essential to the image makers in modern American society. And it is particularly difficult to distinguish between the real persons and the images, between the myths being conveyed and the truth being told. Is Telly Savalas the American hero? or is it Kojak, the role Savalas plays? Or is it the policeman-detective, the part Kojak plays? Is Archie Bunker an actor, an average American, a part being played, a hero, or a reality? Was John Kennedy a politician, a hero, a martyr, an image? Was he real or was he something made up?

Many of today's heroes and heroines are actors of parts or players of games. The line between reality and myth is made indistinct by the very words, metaphors, and definitions used to describe what these real people do in the real world. Their work, for instance, is "playing"—in sports, the theater, on television, in the movies, in music. But, by older American standards, play is not work. Yet the play of these heroes and heroines is highly visible to us all; we watch, fascinated. They—by those old standards—do no work. They play. And they *consume.* We know a great deal about the large quantities of money they are paid (they are, after all, *employees*—every one of them), and about how they spend that money. They are consumers, employees, players: idealized role models. And the products of the machines that tell us our tales.

THE TYPES OF HEROES

Howard Hughes was a modern American hero. His "central mission," according to *Fortune* magazine, was "to preserve his power as the proprietor of the largest pool of industrial wealth still under the absolute control of a single individual." "Mission" and "power," "proprietor" and "wealth" are resonant, for Americans, with past associations that mean individualism. "Under the absolute control of a single individual" gives wealth and power, mission and proprietorship, the purpose, the direction, and the promise which is the inheritance of every American. That absolute control implies freedom and independence—the goals most valued by Americans: freedom to choose and construct one's own family, one's own community; freedom to "have" the sex of one's choice, whether one is male or female; freedom to "do one's thing"; freedom, in the words of a widely popular song, "to climb any mountain, cross any stream." Absolute control—"to be able to find a restaurant open in case you want a sandwich, to be a free agent, live by one's own rules"—is the predominant vision of individualism today. But do Americans believe that they can attain any realization of that vision? that their pursuit of happiness will result in individual freedom and independence?

Stories of frontiersmen, pioneers, outlaws, cowboys, and cavalrymen are still told. The Western still exists in novels and non-fiction, in movies and television shows. Contemporary Americans may be demythologizing the old Western heroes and heroines and rewriting the histories of the frontiers and of the Indians, but they are still fascinated by the realities and the myths of the settling of America.

New heroic types have grown in modern America, joining Horatio Alger's heroes. The robber baron, the detective, the gangster, the crusading reformer, the suffragette, the feminist, the business adventurer, the technical wizard, the wheeler-dealer, the doctor, the lawyer, the reporter—all have become modern heroes and heroines, mythologized in novels, in the movies, and on television. We have taken some modern Presidents, and a few other leading political figures, and made them into Founding Fathers by identifying them with the democracy, the high ideals, the history, and the aristocratic character of the demigods of America. And we have also put some distance between ourselves and our heroes and heroines by making heroes of foreigners (like the English spies James Bond and John le Carré's Smiley) or by creating heroes and heroines who live in some futuristic world (like those who populate *Star Trek* and *Starship Galactica*) or who are non-human machines (like R2-D2) or who are impossible beings (like Superman, Superwoman, the Bionic Man, and the Bionic Woman).

But the patterns of modern heroic life retain identifiably American characteristics. The heroes and heroines come from obscure, poor, humble, or deprived origins which affirm the democratic nature of American individuals. The modern Founding Fathers, like Theodore Roosevelt, Franklin Roosevelt, Eleanor Roosevelt, and John F. Kennedy, all had to struggle to overcome handicaps which in effect made them common people: Theodore Roosevelt was a weak child and nearsighted to the point of blindness; Franklin Roosevelt was crippled by polio; John Kennedy was severely wounded in World War II; and Eleanor Roosevelt was painfully shy, with an unfortunate voice and a sense of her own ugliness. In overcoming their handicaps, they proved themselves worthy Americans, independent of their aristocratic backgrounds.

Hard work, training, and education are still central to heroic American individuals, but there is a strong emphasis on technical and formal education and on competitive experience that was not part of the individualistic pattern for Americans that the *Encyclopædia Americana* prescribed in the early nineteenth century. Twentieth-century success requires expertise. The stories of sports heroes, actors and actresses, spies, doctors, journalists, or even political heroes, emphasize the long, arduous years of training and experience necessary in order to ascend the complex, specialized ladders of success in the modern world. Even the older hero myths are revised to include specialist training: modern Westerns often concentrate on the months of practice the cowboy hero must devote to shooting. The spy must spend much of his time on karate training; the baseball-football-basketball player must have his camps and his constant training; the Olympic swimmer must practice hours every day in the pool; the actor must learn technique, must constantly rehearse; the politician has to be on the move, meeting people, developing his strategies, his polls, his card files, his managers and advisers. Esoteric forms of physical exercise, of philosophies, of foreign languages, expertise in diverse and highly technical aspects of business, industry, science, communications, travel, and wine are all assumed to be within the purview of the modern hero or heroine. All are symbolic of the technical training Americans assume is necessary for individual survival and success in the modern world.

The contemporary hero or heroine is ordinarily employed by a large, impersonal, bureaucratic organization with a structured hierarchy: it can be a professional sports team, a real or fictional spy organization, a large-scale corporate enterprise, a television studio. The hero or heroine rarely has contact with the top, with the real bosses of such organizations. Like Alger's heroes, contemporary heroes are in direct contact with, take their orders, their strategies for success, from middle management—from section leaders, team managers, program producers, colonels, or coaches. Captain Kirk in the 1979 movie *Star Trek* had to take a reduction in rank from admiral in order to command the starship *Enterprise* and be the hero of the film.

The bureaucracies which employ contemporary heroes and heroines are perceived with ambivalence. On one hand, they are believed to be "good"—the management of a professional team is buying the best players and trying to produce the best team, the mission of the Strategic Air Command is "Peace," the effort of the great corporation is to provide goods to its customers and dividends to its stockholders, and the Galactic Council is attempting to extend civilization into the wilderness of the universe—or at least to preserve it on some presently unoccupied, remote planet. On the other hand, those same bureaucracies are perceived as "evil," oppressive of individuals and ideals alike, regimented, often totalitarian, mindless, and utterly heartless. The bureaucracies are called "companies" (whether they are corporations or the Central Intelligence Agency) or "families" (as in the Mafia or in the parlance of industries) or "teams," all terms which signal ambivalence. Much of the time and effort of the contemporary heroes or heroines is spent avoiding the bureaucracy, cutting red tape, deliberately trying to foul up the operations of the organizations employing them, or "goldbricking," simply avoiding whatever it is that bureaucracy requires. "Catch-22" (a phrase from the title of Joseph Heller's novel, meaning the aimless ridiculousness of modern bureaucracy) and the "Peter Principle" (that all persons in modern employment will rise to the level of their incompetence) have become descriptive of the conflict of modern individuals with modern bureaucracies.

The focus in modern stories is on individual success *despite* the bureaucracies. Success is measured by ingenuity, courage, expertise, physical prowess, and the employee's ability to snatch personal pleasure, reward, and a hedonistic life style out of the pressures of employment and employers. Large quantities of money, private pleasure and consumption, and public acknowledgment of the individual's abilities, personality, and luck are the rewards at least of the fictionalized heroes and heroines of modern life (see *Scruples*, for example). Movie and television stars, the heroes and heroines of best sellers (and their authors), sports heroes and heroines, rock stars, and jet setters are all believed to enjoy those rewards. Such heroic success is perceived by most to be the harbinger of progress: it exceeds the established; it makes records by breaking records; it pushes the accomplishments of humanity and of America further. The success of real heroes and heroines is a demonstration that America remains at "the cutting edge of progress." As heroes and heroines are expected to do more, for themselves and for America, in order to become heroic, so Americans expect they should get more—money, personal pleasure, and public acknowledgment and approval ("Yeh, I'd give my right arm / to do what this guy Lindbergh did").

All the role models, the heroes and heroines and the anti-heroes and anti-heroines, of contemporary America are focused on the private, independent individual. Individual "declarations of independence"—independence of family and parents, of establishment and society, of sex roles and sex practices, of ethnic identities and ethnic inequalities—are still the norm in America. The equality of the individual is still fiercely demanded, fiercely insisted upon. Liberty and democracy are maintained as the ultimate goals of the individual pursuit of happiness. The diverse modern roles are available to any American; they represent pieces, fragments, parts, of common experiences. Americans today can opt out, sell out, or settle down, all with the firm belief that they are behaving as true Americans. They can be employees *or* entrepreneurs and still know that they can live up to American heroes and heroines, participate in American dreams.

III

E PLURIBUS UNUM

1

Real Community

In 1967, Joan Didion wrote an essay called "Slouching Towards Bethlehem" about the flower children of the Haight-Ashbury district of San Francisco. "We were seeing something important," she wrote:

> We were seeing the desperate attempt of a handful of pathetically unequipped children to create a community in a social vacuum. Once we had seen these children, we could no longer overlook the vacuum, no longer pretend that society's atomization could be reversed. This was not a traditional generational rebellion. At some point between 1945 and 1967 we had somehow neglected to tell these children the rules of the game we happened to be playing. Maybe we had stopped believing in the rules ourselves, maybe we were having a failure of nerve about the game. Maybe there were just too few people around to do the telling. These were children who grew up cut loose from the web of cousins and great-aunts and family doctors and lifelong neighbors who had traditionally suggested and enforced the society's values. They are children who have moved around a lot. . . . They are less in rebellion against the society than ignorant of it, able only to feed back certain of its most publicized self-doubts.

From the beginning of colonization, from the first efforts of Englishmen to plant a settlement at Roanoke, certainly from the beginning of the settlements at Jamestown and Plymouth and Salem, handfuls of unequipped young people desperately tried to create communities—and there were few around to tell them the rules of the game. Some of them were indeed in rebellion against society, but many were ignorant of it. Over and over in the experience of American expansion, the process of migration, separation from the rules and the established community, and re-creation of community in a social vacuum took place—with more or less success. We preserve ghost towns to commemorate some of the failures and have built museums—like Williamsburg, Old Sturbridge, New Harmony—to commemorate the successes.

The necessity to create a community, in the midst of atomization, social vacuum, ignorance, self-doubt, and youth, is one of the most powerful, long-lasting, and painful of the imperatives of American myths. Individualism and community are bound together in agonizing symbiosis: the atomization which normally occurred in the process of migration, for example, brought with it the intense efforts by migrants to create some kind of community—in Haight-Ashbury as on slave ships, on the frontier as in the cities.

IMAGES OF WHOLENESS

Migrants very often came to America with a vision of community: a set of images and expectations based on the places from which they came. Those visions were transformed by their experiences in America into the somewhat different visions of their children and grandchildren. The early English settlers in Virginia and in Massachusetts had clear visions of communities as English rural villages—with cottages clustered together, with hedges and fences and stiles, with roads and bridges, with water mills and inns, and with a church—as well as powerful expectations of mutual interdependence, of a helping community, of religious cohesiveness, and of social and economic services provided by the community to educate the young, care for the sick and helpless, and provide for the poor. They did not find such communities. They found that they had to make them, and they found the task of creating these ideal communities confusing, painful, and frustrating.

Part of the vision of community which migrants invariably brought to America was land. Land, in the European context out of which American society grew, was the source of all wealth, the determinant of social place and position, the *sine qua non* for the existence of community. The vision required a particular piece of land, with determinable boundaries. It required, too, the working of land, by the community, in order to sustain itself and provide for its ultimate wealth and welfare. That a relationship to land was also part of the vision of individual status and worth in the society made the symbiosis between individual and community even more obvious.

Early communities were called "settlements" or "towns" or "plantations." All of them carried virtually identical visions and expectations, of physical shape and boundaries, of the working of specific land, and of the integrated cohesiveness of people. These communities were the fundamental units of economic activity and of political, religious, and social life in the colonies. The expectation was that they would survive and prosper—if they did—because they completely integrated these aspects of life into one undifferentiated whole. Such communities were importantly self-sufficient: the ideal was that they would contain human, spiritual, moral, and physical resources, and use them in a comprehensive way to create and sustain an identifiable, independent, whole entity.

As more people immigrated, bringing different visions, and as children were born and brought up in America, accepting as normal what their fathers and mothers perceived as great changes, the vision of community was transformed. The identity of religious, political, economic, and social institutions with the whole community of the town or plantation or settlement or colony gradually disappeared as the predominant norm, to be replaced in the course of the first two centuries of settlement by increasing individualism on the one hand and increasingly specialized community institutions on the other. The town, which had been the embodiment of the early New England Puritan vision of a wholly integrated community of "The Saints," became, by the time of the Revolution, a specific carrier of political and economic images only. The family farm inherited much of the imagery and mythology of working the land which had originally belonged to the town or plantation community. The church became exclusively religious (the transformation of the community meetinghouse in New England in the late eighteenth century into a sanctified church building was a physical symbol of the changing myths), and other institutions of the community, like the farm and the government, were more and more removed from assumptions of religious meaning and purpose. The plantation ultimately became the embodiment of a specifically Southern vision which postulated ownership and dominance of the community by a "master" family served by slaves—but it preserved something of the community vision of social, economic, political, and religious cohesion and self-sufficiency.

The development of industry, the growth of cities, and the separation of economic and political activities from religious activities in nineteenth-century America brought increasing numbers of communitarian experiments—most of them specifically religious. The rhetoric of post-Revolutionary America was focused on individual independence, but the effort to build a nation, and the constant efforts to create settlement communities of migrants, made individual service to society—voluntary social efforts to build community—imperative. America (especially quintessential, frontier America) became, in myth and folklore, a place of barn raisings and house raisings, of quilting bees and church socials, of barn dances and harvest suppers, of community efforts to build and support churches and schools. It also became a land of experimental religious communities (Oneida is one example, the Shaker communities and New Harmony yet others), which operated on the twin assumptions that the organized effort of all individuals had to be directed toward community service and that true community was based on uniformity of belief.

Many of these experiments failed because they did not encourage the desire of each individual to pursue his or her own happiness in the midst of pressure to serve the society. By attempting to suppress almost all individual ambition and individual reward in favor of the greater social good, these communities, in a general society which shouted the praises of the free individual, doomed themselves to a limited number of recruits and a constant drain of members and children into the larger society. American society generally provided *both* the promise of significant and necessary community efforts *and* the promise of individual reward.

The most successful and long-lasting of the religious communitarian experiments was the Mormon. It succeeded precisely because it provided a strong demand for social effort, a powerful, even coercive, community, *and* great incentives for individual social and economic efforts. The Mormons proved that it was possible for a community to survive the hazards of frontier life and prosper with a different set of rules than generally observed by frontier communities. And the prejudice and violence directed against the Mormons, particularly by people residing in their vicinity, demonstrated the power of the imperative for homogeneity which was part of the general mythology.

IMAGES OF HOMOGENEITY

For nearly three centuries, from the beginning of the seventeenth to the beginning of the twentieth, Americans devoted their energies to creating agrarian communities. Industrialization brought great cities, but there were few, whatever their backgrounds, who did not agree—at the beginning of the twentieth century—with William Jennings Bryan's thundering "Burn down your cities and leave our farms, and your cities will spring up again as if by magic; but destroy our farms and the grass will grow in the streets of every city in the country." The norms of American society were rural and agricultural. The myths which have given vivid images, controlling metaphors, and substance to what Americans believe community to be are the myths of rural, small-town, agrarian communities.

The images most Americans carried into the twentieth century—of small towns and their life—were not consciously anachronistic. Rural communities were full-scale participants in American progress. The visions of elm-lined streets, big front porches, white paint, and picket fences were able to transform themselves to accommodate automobiles in the streets, machines in the homes and the barns, "science" in the agriculture, corporations sprawled across the nation, and mobile, dynamic, progressive, improving individual Americans. But those same visions of rural community implied continuity, permanence, establishment, fixed values, and unchanging habits in a world otherwise in constant flux. For Americans who are bewildered, bruised, or defeated by the freedom and competition and loneliness of the modern world, the images of static rural community still offer refuge. At the same time, these images make the rural community a place of stagnation, hypocrisy, and mindless conservatism.

For most Americans, small-town imagery provides the background for free individualism. The small town is "society," that abstract collection of all Americans which most Americans believe to be fixed, immobile, and structured. Families, social classes, place, position, wealth, inheritance, fame, and status all belong to and come from society. "Society" connotes tradition; it resonates with echoes of the traditional class structure, the pyramidal vision of class which immigrants to the New World brought from the Old (and which the Revolution abolished). Society maintains absolute standards of morality and conduct, which it enforces on each individual (or tries to!). Society is "they" and "them," a constant source of demands, burdens, and limitations that threaten the freedom and energy of the individual. Society demands conformity. It is a homogeneous, almost faceless mass of people with the same values, the same standards of behavior, set in their ways, permanent, immovable. And for each American, this abstract society is made real, is given living images, by the vision of the rural small town, "the village where Ma and Pa do stay." Even when real mothers and fathers have long since departed from such villages, and "the web of cousins and great-aunts and family doctors and lifelong neighbors" has vanished.

The imagery of homogeneity, the almost monolithic view of society contained in the mythology of the rural small town, has served, and still serves, several important functions.

It is a foil for individualism: the belief in a stable and fixed society makes it possible to emphasize near-anarchic individualism without risking the destruction of the social fabric. It was and is "safe" for Americans to be individualists, and to maintain individualism almost without respite in their social intercourse, because they simultaneously believe in (although they did not and do not talk about it so much, and when they do, they speak almost entirely negatively) the fixed, homogeneous nature of their society. The tension between the belief in individual freedom and the belief in social conformity is one of the great generators of energy.

The imagery of homogeneity also serves as a constant demonstration of the democratic nature of American society. Society is no more or less than the collective expression of the will of the people; the people are sovereign; society, then, represents the will of the sovereign. That logic explains (and justifies) the often oppressive nature of society, and it also explains how such oppression can exist in a free country. But even when "they" are perceived to be oppressive, Americans tacitly recognize "their" values and desires to be the expressed will of the majority. By such logic, Americans continue to believe that the whole society is democratic. It is such logic which underlay the public discussion and identification of "the establishment" and "the silent majority" in the early 1970's.

Finally, the imagery of homogeneity provides a sense of secure, unchanging rootedness in a society of the uprooted. The stories of hometowns and parents and grandparents all imply that you *can* go home again. Such stories reflect the fantasy that everything at home is always there, unchanging, immortal; they are the dreams of refuge in a changing, mortal world. Yet included in such dreams is the nagging fear that the permanence and stability which one yearns for will destroy freedom, homogenize individualism, stay mobility, and stop progress. "You can't go home again" is the expression of the fear that home is always changing, never stable, all too mortal (and that the individual is, too), *and* it is a warning to the individual that society, the hometown, the cozy rural small-town community, can destroy all freedom. The logic helps to regenerate the uprooted in each generation of Americans.

IMAGES OF PROXIMITY

In the course of the settlement and expansion of America, communities, like individuals, moved. Towns grew and split, like one-celled forms of life, spreading across a continent (in contemporary slang, individual people now "split"). They split and spread, of course, because individuals seeking more freedom, more opportunity, more progress than any town offered moved away from them, gathered in groups, and formed yet other towns:

> O tonight we'll dance by the light of the moon,
> To the fiddler's best and only tune,
> What though we're covered all over with dust,
> It's better than staying back home to rust,
> We'll reach Salt Lake some day or bust.

And when Salt Lake, or California, or Michigan, or Kentucky *was* reached, new homes were made in which to stay and "rust," and from which others would move and seek some still newer, better goal, or "bust."

There was great ambivalence about those who stayed back "home to rust," as one of the interviews in John Baskin's *New Burlington* shows:

> The Smiths made conscious choices to get away from New Burlington because of its provincialism. Roy, Will, Les. They went to the cities. To the life they wanted. Those who stayed settled into such a life. Great boys. Fine boys. But *dull* boys. They were frightened to go out. Always pushing the wheelbarrow of responsibility. In Burlington, everyone had a place. Everyone was accepted. Outside, there was no place. Outside were things they didn't know about. But there were no mysterious corners in New Burlington. Even going in to Xenia, or Wilmington, scared them.

The community—the small town—may have been provincial, but there were "no mysterious corners" in it. It was filled with responsibility, but everyone had a place in it. "The villagers had their shames and disgraces," but "in spite of the hypocrisy, we were all very close." It was a permanent place in which people lived in close proximity, tied together by homes, family, and homogeneity of values.

Within the boundaries of the town, among the people who lived in close proximity, the fundamental logic of the assumption that there would be homogeneity of values rested on the assumption of religious conformity. From the first establishment of European communities in the New World, religious belief and membership in *the* church were assumed to be central to all social and individual life. America was a Christian society and Americans were Christians. The strong Protestant flavor of American Christianity existed at least in part because all New World history took place in the context of the Protestant Reformation. At any rate, Americans quickly differentiated themselves and their communities from the rest of the world, which was popish or pagan or heathen. Christian men wore boots and trousers and shirts, and their women wore dresses to cover their bodies. Christians tilled the earth and got their living therefrom. Christians lived in houses, worshipped in churches, read books and newspapers printed in a Christian alphabet, and spoke a proper Christian tongue. Real communities could only be made up of such people: so Americans believed long after specific Christian theologies ceased to impinge on belief, and "American" (for most) had become synonymous with "Christian."

Such homogeneity of values did not preclude individual pursuit of happiness. In the logic of American belief, it encouraged individual ambition. Tom Wolfe, in *The Right Stuff,* described astronaut John Glenn's origins in New Concord, Ohio, in the logic of homogeneity in American community:

> . . . New Concord was a sort of town, once common in America, whose peculiar origins have tended to disappear in the collective amnesia. . . . It began as a religious community. A hundred years ago any man in New Concord with ambitions that reached as high as feedstore proprietor or better joined the Presbyterian Church, and some of the awesome voltage of live Presbyterianism still existed. . . . There was no contradiction whatsoever between the Presbyterian faith and ambition, even soaring ambition. . . . A good Presbyterian demonstrated his *election* by the Lord and the heavenly hosts through his success in this life. In a way, Presbyterianism was tailor-made for people who intended to make it in this world, as well as on the Plains of Heaven.

The vision of both the earthbound small town and the heavenly community assumed like-mindedness among its members. That homogeneity has traditionally carried the specific implication of religious conformity, but the logic does not lose its force, or the myth its imperative, if the religious content is completely removed (as it often is by Americans). Homogeneity of values remains the ideal and dominates the imagery of the community.

The *real* community is a melting pot. It mixes disparate elements (different families, different classes, people from different nations and places) into a unity. It creates unity by providing individuals (regardless of race, creed, or national origin) with opportunities to move, to rise, to change, to progress, to succeed. The logic is that, by using the opportunities provided by the community, the individual will become one in basic values with all its other members. The essential democracy, classlessness, and homogeneity of American community is thus proved by the logic of the melting pot.

Americans assume that neighborliness comes from proximity (and vice versa). Americans are known as "friendly" all over the world (and in many parts of the world, that friendliness is not particularly welcomed). Much of the friendliness grows from the assumption that being near another person, physically near, as at the next table, in the next seat, next door, or on the same street, creates community. Such geographical proximity requires neighborliness, friendliness, and knowing something about the other person. Proximity makes community, and the process of inquiring about the life, work, and beliefs of another person in turn will begin the process of "melting," of creating the homogeneity which is the other requirement of community. Small-town America lives in such logic, and remains an operative part of the realities of contemporary Americans.

IMAGES OF REALITY

"Forty years ago, one of the most famous and widely admired men in America was William Allen White, editor-publisher of the Emporia (Kansas) *Gazette,*" according to an article by Kenneth S. Davis in a 1979 issue of *American Heritage.* "White epitomized," Davis wrote,

> . . . the smiling, neighborly, small-town, middle-class America—the America of Norman Rockwell's *Saturday Evening Post* covers—that as recently as 1940 was widely deemed the "real," the "permanent" America.

William Allen White had "very consciously and deliberately" made himself "the spokesman for the American country town of his day—the town of one thousand to thirty-thousand population," and he had written that in such country towns "we gain in contact with our neighbors. We know people by the score, by the hundred. . . . Our affairs become common with one another, our joys mutual, and even our sorrows are shared. . . . It all makes life pleasantly liveable."

The "urban masses," according to Davis, "have no living experience of the kind of community" William Allen White personified. But the contrast between the urban reality of today and the proximate, homogeneous small town of William Allen White's day is not so great as such an assertion implies. Almost a quarter of all Americans—fifty million of them—live in towns smaller than thirty thousand people. The continuing existence of small communities has contributed heavily to the continuing availability of the mythology and imagery of the rural small town. Many of the visual images of Norman Rockwell, as well as the literary images of writers like William Allen White, are indeed recognized by many Americans as anachronistic, as subjects for nostalgia, as images of a dead era; yet the same Americans at the same time still refer to ideals of community and still seek to create real communities using the logic such images have helped produce.

Urban Americans, consciously and unconsciously, still seek a "smiling, neighborly, small-town" in which to live and work. Some of them move to the suburbs, because suburbs look like communities: in satisfying ways, they match the images which the myths of community in America have produced. Some move to the country, by getting a place in the mountains, in Vermont, in some small town. Some create communes—very often on the land—in which individual independence and family life are consciously subordinated to community activity and community concern. Other Americans join or create religious communes which, while often not traditional, nevertheless emphasize traditional American mythological religious homogeneity and community service.

The Americans who live in real communities are independent individuals (sturdy yeomen) who work hard to sustain themselves and their families (on their own land in their own homes), who are self-educated and self-reliant, who volunteer to serve with others for the greater good of the community, who are friendly and neighborly, and who are part of a physically bounded, proximate, homogeneous group of like-thinking, like-acting people. That is the logic of the mythology of community. Americans are to be found today seeking to live in, create, improve, build, and preserve such communities, whether they are in great cities or in the countryside, in Paris or New York or Vietnam or Alaska, whatever their variety of American—black or Puerto Rican, Chicano or WASP, Jewish or Presbyterian, Catholic or Muslim. The predominant symbol, metaphor, and model for the logic of real community in America remains the rural agrarian small town.

2

The Fragmented Image

AMERICANS LIVE IN CITIES. Life in the modern city or in its suburbs is, for most, a sharp contrast to the ideal, to the myth of the peaceful, neighborly, unified, cooperative *real* community, the *American* small-town community.

A sense of community in people is generated by the acceptance of individuals in their wholeness, not in the specific, particularized roles individuals play. A sense of community, according to Robert Nisbet in *The Sociological Tradition,* is characterized by "personal intimacy, emotional depth, moral commitment, social cohesion, and continuity in time." It is "a fusion of feeling and thought, of tradition and commitment, of membership and volition." The sense of community "may be found in, or given expression by, locality, religion, nation, race, occupation or crusade." But in American cities, most of these lack any connection to a sense of the community of the city. Of Nisbet's list, only race has remained an important symbol of city community, and even that symbolizes only a fragment of the whole. For the majority of Americans who live in cities, the images and symbols of community are fragmented. There is little sense that individuals are accepted and included in their wholeness.

Urban Americans have inherited both the Jeffersonian vision of cities as places of subservience, venality, and dependence, and the rural vision of cities as places of sin, corruption, and decadence. But, as all mythological perceptions of reality contain opposites, so the inherited myths of cities make them places of glittering opportunity, of civilization and culture, of great wealth and magnificence:

> Thine alabaster cities gleam,
> Undimm'd by human tears!

Mythical American cities are also marked by individual mobility and freedom. The individual—the traditional, sturdy, independent individual—can make his mark in a bigger, more significant way in the city than anywhere else. All of Horatio Alger's heroes rose from poverty to comfort because of the opportunities offered by the city. The images of the independent individual making his mark, of the lucky hero rising from rags to riches, still live in American cities and in the perceptions of the people who grow up in them.

As more and more Americans came to live in cities (the 1920 census was the first to show a majority living in urban places), they were required by their own needs and by the existing mythology of community to explain their preference for them. Aside from appealing to the vision of the city as *the* place of opportunity, they began to attack the vision of the rural small town, which was the primary symbol of community. The attack was not on the mythology of community but rather on the model, the paradigm, the symbol of community.

Sinclair Lewis's best-selling novel *Main Street,* published in 1920, was by no means the first attack on small-town life, nor the last. *Main Street* widely popularized a vocabulary which urban Americans have used ever since to attack the myth of the rural community and to justify city life. In the novel, Lewis contrasted the isolation, smallness, and emptiness of the small town with the sprawl, human warmth, and bustling opportunities of the city.

When one of the characters in *Main Street* had walked through Gopher Prairie for "thirty-two minutes," Lewis wrote:

> She had completely covered the town, east and west, north and south; and she stood at the corner of Main Street and Washington Avenue and despaired.
>
> Main Street with its two-story brick shops, its story-and-a-half wooden residences, its muddy expanse from concrete walk to walk, its huddle of Fords and lumberwagons, was too small to absorb her. The broad, straight, unenticing gashes of the streets let in the grasping prairie on every side. She realized the vastness and emptiness of the land. . . . They were so small and weak, the little brown houses. They were shelters for sparrows, not homes for warm laughing people.
>
> . . . At best the trees resembled a thinned woodlot. There was no park to rest the eyes.
>
> . . . She wanted to run, fleeing from the encroaching prairie, demanding the security of a great city.

Gopher Prairie was not merely one small town; it symbolized, for Lewis and for many of his readers, "ten thousand towns from Albany to San Diego." "Main Street" and "Babbitt" (from Lewis's 1922 novel, *Babbitt*) connoted loneliness and desolation, small-minded bigotry and "boosterism," as the predominant characteristics of small towns and rural life.

Twentieth-century Americans, consciously and unconsciously following critics like Sinclair Lewis and H. L. Mencken, enthusiastically and indiscriminately laid siege to the myth of rural community. In the name of freedom, opportunity, and diversity, they decried the ideal of community service as mindless "boosterism," called the ideals of homogeneity and earning the approval of the community "conformity" or "babbitry," and believed the sturdy, independent yeoman to be a stupid hick, a quaint native, or an impoverished, unthinking drudge. The city more and more became the symbol of freedom, opportunity, and diversity as opposed to the rural community. Urban life was an escape from small-town America.

Despite the continuing attack on the rural small town, the desire for and the effort to find community in city life continued. For more than a century, urban Americans in large numbers have been moving to the suburbs in order to find the "real" communities they have lost or lack because they live in cities. They have not wanted to give up the advantages of cities—their diversity, their opportunities, their cultural riches and multitude of services, goods, and people—so they have stayed close to the cities, tied to them by trains and highways. They work in cities, and play in them, but they *live* (dwell, have their homes) in real communities close to nature, amid more genuine values. Suburbs were built to re-create the ideal community life of the small town. They emphasize, as Sam Bass Warner wrote in *Streetcar Suburbs,* "the pleasures of private family life, the security of a small community setting, and the enjoyments of an increased contact with nature." The city dweller found the proximate, homogeneous ideal rural community symbolized in the suburb by the uniformity of "the latest styles, the freshly painted houses, the neat streets, the well-kept lawns, and the new schools and parks." The suburbs—and, as the suburbs have grown, the exurbs—have kept the rural community myth alive and in an ambivalent tension with the attractions of the cities: "Main Street" has moved to the suburbs.

Many suburbs, since the 1950's, have become parts of cities or have become cities themselves. With automobiles, great highways, huge schools, vast parking lots and shopping centers, the myth of the rural community has been under siege in the suburbs. The tension between the attraction, of the vision of community and those of urban diversity is more obvious as the suburbs have become more obviously parts of cities. At the same time, the everlasting search for homogeneity in community life—homogeneity increasingly characterized by race or ethnicity since the 1960's—has continued to bring urban Americans to the suburbs.

Neither the attack on small-town life nor the effort to find community in suburbs has destroyed the persistent contrasts between the mythology of community on the one hand and the mythology of the city on the other. In 1973, Peter Schrag wrote in *The End of the American Future* that Americans believed that "the city was, all demography aside, the exception; the country and its ethic" remained the American norm. The vision of the rural community dominated urban America:

> . . . Every time you flew across the country or looked at the ads on television, the vision returned: Down there was the real America, on the wheat fields of Kansas, in the small crossroads towns with their helpful banker and their friendly Mutual of Omaha insurance agent, in the shopping centers where the farmers congregated on Saturday afternoon and the women came to have their hair set, in the new developments of Topeka or Quincy or Macon or Rapid City, neighborhoods clustered around cities of twenty thousand or seventy-five thousand where they manufactured trailers or hardboard or bricks or Thermopane windows . . . places where women ran washing machines and men bought tires and where things always went better with Coke.

The American "middle"—the middle class, middle America—was urban, but its perception of itself was rural.

Yet by the 1960's, "the census defined places like St. Joseph, Missouri, Saginaw, Michigan, Billings, Montana, Gadsden, Alabama, and York, Pennsylvania, as 'Standard Statistical Metropolitan Areas,' " according to Schrag, and it was beginning to be obvious that the reality of the distinctions between urban and rural life was disappearing. Radio, television, magazines, and newspapers, along with the concentrations of populations, made urban life physically visible to, and part of the lives of, all Americans.

Americans in the 1970's believed that every American was, in reality, "a small-town boy come home," and that the city, its life, and its attitudes "was something you put on, but Main Street was something you remained forever." They still maintained that there was a contrast between real, American life on the one hand, and city life on the other. But, while they knew they "were not the sinful people or the crime-besieged victims of urban rot that they imagined the residents of New York to be," at the same time they knew they were no longer "the honest yeomen of national myth." Many Americans believed, by the third quarter of the twentieth century, that they had "lost the country," and with it the values of real community life, because, as Peter Schrag put it, "they had chosen to live in a world for which they had no ethic."

Americans today distinguish between the people who live in cities, which is almost everyone, and the people who live in "really big cities," like New York, Los Angeles, and Chicago. America, the real America, has, as Peter Schrag wrote, come to be defined as not-New York. New York (or Los Angeles) has come to be the symbol of the corruption and decadence Americans have traditionally associated with cities. At the same time, common ordinary city life, as most Americans lead it, has come to be identified with the idealized tradition of the rural community. In this contemporary form of the myth, the big city is seen to be besieging the rest of America: with its urban problems and urban decay and violence, with its jungle-like atmosphere where people are afraid to be on the streets or in the parks, the big city is spreading like an evil blob over the rest of America. Many Americans, even those who live in the suburbs of the big cities, have come to believe that

> the big cities were hopeless—beyond repair or salvation—and the only reasonable policy was to diversify, to get the industry out of the big cities and back to the middle-sized towns. . . . The future lay in the past, and the big city was a mad aberration which was, at long last, coming to its unnatural end.

Thus it is still possible for people who dwell in all but the largest cities (and many of those, too) to retain the mythology of rural community—much transformed—as the logical explanation of their urban lives.

URBAN FREEDOM

The madness, the aberrant behavior of big-city residents which confirmed the utter lack of community in big cities in the belief of many urban Americans, was symbolized in the mid-1960's by the story—spread across the nation—of Catherine Genovese. The story was summarized later by historian E. Digby Baltzell:

> Coming home from a night job in the early hours of a March morning in 1964, a young lady, Catherine Genovese, was stabbed repeatedly and over an extended period of time. Thirty-eight fellow residents of Kew Gardens, a respectable New York City neighborhood, admitted to having witnessed at least part of the attack. None of them, however, went to her aid, nor did anyone call the police until after she was dead.

The reaction of most Americans (aside from horror) to the story was to conclude that there is no community in the big city, and that the circumstances of life there do not encourage the growth of community. Everyone in a city is a stranger, and strangers are part of no community. Catherine Genovese, crying out in the dark, was a stranger, and her neighborhood (almost a suburb in the midst of a city) was made up of people who were strangers to each other. Bystanders, residents of the neighborhood who heard or saw the attack, did not want to get involved; they were not "concerned" in the affair. They did not believe themselves to be part of a community which included strangers, violence, or cries in the dark.

Many city dwellers reject the idea that proximity makes one a neighbor, part of a community. They seek independence and freedom, and many find it in anonymity. Anonymity offers escape from the oppressive pressures of the neighborhood, the small town, the community—an escape which implies individual freedom. Many urban Americans seek lives in which no one knows them unless they choose to be known, and they know no one. The real pressures of city life, the numbers of people, the noise, the constant physical presence and contact, the demands for attention and concern which city crowding and city sounds signify, all encourage people to treat each other as strangers, to respect one another's anonymity. If one is surrounded by strangers, one can be free—to be one's self, to be anything one chooses, to be independent. Freedom thus can be found in the city—and one can recognize that freedom, know it to exist, because of the lack of community. The modern urban myths which combine anonymity and freedom place "far more emphasis on individual morality and personal ethics" than the traditional myths of small-town community.

The urban myth of individual freedom requires contrast with the mythology of the small town to make it meaningful to American city dwellers. The Sinclair Lewis version of the mindless, repressive community explains the desirability of urban anonymity. "I find myself," theologian Harvey Cox wrote in *The Secular City,* "in functional relationships with mechanics, salesmen, and bank clerks whom I never see in any other capacity." Cox's contacts with such people were frequent, although brief. He came to know their mannerisms and their names, but his relationship with them was segmented. They were not part of his community. But, Cox insisted, that did not make such relationships "mean." The relationships, he wrote, "are no less human or authentic merely because we both prefer to keep them anonymous." By contrast, the sociability of a rural community could "mask a murderous hostility." Urban anonymity, Cox concluded, "need not be heartless."

The freedom which city mythology sees in anonymity, however, is postulated on the ability of each city dweller to create a unique community and to maintain it by an elaborate network of relationships with other people. Individual freedom in America—even in the anonymous city—is invariably accompanied by the imperative for community.

DIFFERENTIATION AND MELTING POT

Perhaps one of the most ancient elements in the mythology of cities is the assumption that cities are divided into differing geographical locales, and that within those locales will be found proximate, homogeneous communities. There were "quarters" in ancient cities. There are neighborhoods, there are blocks, there are ghettos, there are suburbs in modern cities. And there are "houses," projects, developments, estates, buildings, streets, and turfs. Within each division or subdivision, there is the image and expectation of urban community. Where you live in a city is where you are expected to belong to a community. Here at last, then, is an element in the traditional American mythology of cities which specifically provides for *urban* community.

Immigrants and native Americans, coming to cities, have found it important and necessary to differentiate themselves from the others near them in their strange new surroundings. By trying to keep their differences, maintain their particular ways, and live together, they have defended their identities and created real cultural diversity in contradiction to the ideal of homogeneity. Native or foreign, they came to cities for opportunity; they did not, in any conscious way, intend to become urban. All of them gave up much in the way of social and personal ties, community connections, habits, customs, and even languages in order to come to the cities. Most did not intend to give up their cultures as well.

Gradually the efforts of migrants to create mini-communities and live together coincided with the process by which "different," "foreign" newcomers to the cities were pushed to live in certain places—by laws, covenants, income levels, real-estate practices, and active prejudices. The newcomers were segregated by established residents using the logic of the myth of community homogeneity. For many of the migrants to American cities, the processes of differentiation and segregation did not importantly differ. They viewed the urban world as one made up of many different, identifiable groups of people who ordinarily tried to avoid each other—especially in their living arrangements.

"The Protestants, for that was what she called native-born Americans, moved out as the immigrants moved in," William Alfred, the grandson of an Irish immigrant, wrote of his grandmother's experiences in Brooklyn. There were a few German and Scandinavian families left in the neighborhood, but "then from the backyard tenement houses on the other side of Court Street . . . the Irish began to move in." Later came the Italians, with whom the Irish lived in "uncertain amity." A local store "was run by the Wechslers, the only Jews in the neighborhood. They were beloved by Irish and Italians alike, because of their kindness to children, and because they had the only phone on the block, and would walk the block's length to call a person to it."

The "block" often was assumed to define the limits of a particular community, and the people in that community were assumed to be racially, nationally, ethnically alike. With such assumptions, it was easy for neighborhoods to become ghettos, with sharp delineations of boundaries and sanctions to preserve and enforce them. "The neighborhood had its boundaries," Jack Agueros wrote about his Puerto Rican boyhood in New York in the 1940's:

> Third Avenue and east, Italian. Fifth Avenue and west, black. South, there was a hill on 103rd Street known locally as Cooney's Hill. When you got to the top of the hill, something strange happened: America began, because from the hill south was where the "Americans" lived. . . .
>
> When, as a group of Puerto Rican kids, we decided to go swimming to Jef-

ferson Park Pool, we knew we risked a fight and a beating from the Italians. And when we went to La Milagrosa Church in Harlem, we knew we risked a fight and a beating from the blacks. But when we went over Cooney's Hill, we risked dirty looks, disapproving looks, and questions from the police . . . "Why don't you kids go back where you belong?"

"Stick to your own kind" was the plaintive cry of one Puerto Rican girl to another in the musical *West Side Story.* The image is strong and widespread in the urban world. "I'm glad I live right here," a machinist interviewed by Robert Coles in the 1960's said of his suburb in *The Middle Americans:*

> "Hell, I've nothing against them, Negro people. They should stick to their own, like we do. I'm Polish. I mean, I'm American. My family has been here for four generations; that's a lot. . . . We're just like other people in this country, but we have memories, Polish memories. . . . How *could* I forget? My wife won't let me. She says you have to stay with your own people. We don't have only Polish people living near us, but there are a lot. Mostly we see my family and my wife's family on the weekends, so there's no time to spend doing anything else. . . .
>
> "I don't know who's *really* an American."

The city is a segregator, in the myths and practices that characterize urban life. Different people clannishly stick together in neighborhoods and ghettos, hostile to outsiders and loath to give up their peculiar ways in order to become "real" Americans. They do it by choice, because they want to stick to their own kind, and they do it because they are forced to stay out of the communities that belong to others.

But at the same time there is an imperative in the myth which requires the whole city to be one community. The city as segregator clashes with that vision of community which requires that cities—like the nation, like all real communities—create "one out of many." Cities, in the myth, should be melting pots, homogenizers in which all who come are unified, Americanized, and culturally standardized. "The central idea of the melting-pot symbol is clearly the idea of unification," Henry Pratt Fairchild, an outspoken opponent of immigration, wrote in *The Melting-Pot Mistake* in 1926. The idea of American unity "needs no logical demonstration to command general acceptance," he continued. "Everyone realizes, almost intuitively, that in any community, particularly a democratic one, unity is one of the essentials of stability, order, and progress."

The melting-pot myth was reinforced through much of the twentieth century by the general conviction that cultural uniformity was in the process of being attained in American cities. Individuals in various ethnic groups made obvious efforts to "melt," to "pass," to adhere to some ideal image of

Americanness. Their behavior was evidence to most urban Americans that cultural diversity was disappearing, that the melting pot was working.

The evidence was everywhere in the urban experience. Immigrants refused to speak their native language. They moved from ghetto neighborhoods into American ones whenever they could. Foreign-language presses, newspapers, and fraternal organizations declined. Children went to American schools. They were taught in English and became Americanized. Black magazines carried ads for hair straighteners and skin lighteners. Jews had their noses "done." Immigrants changed their names—sometimes voluntarily. A Jewish immigrant, met at Ellis Island by relatives already in America, was asked, "What kind of a name is Klugermann? Take a good American name. Take Cohen." And Cohen he became. Others had their names changed for them by immigration officials who could not pronounce or spell foreign names. Jade Snow Wong, a Chinese-American, wrote of her father that

> . . . At the age of seventy plus, after years of attending night classes in citizenship, he became naturalized. He embraced this status wholeheartedly. One day when we were discussing plans for his birthday celebration, which was usually observed the tenth day of the fifth lunar month by the Chinese calendar, he announced, "Now that I have become a United States citizen, I am going to change my birthday. Henceforth, it will be on the Fourth of July."

Every urban American had some experience of immigrants or of migrants to the cities who gave up their obvious differences. These were, for each individual, proof that the melting pot was real and successful. If people did not immediately melt, it was merely a matter of time. A generation or two might have to pass before all would progress into a thoroughly melted state.

On the other hand, in the experiences of immigrants and their descendants and of black and white Americans who came to and stayed in cities, there was little evidence that American cities were unified. Most commonly, cities were fragmented, made up of diverse groups of people with their own identities, their own ways, and their own communities. Experience contradicted the vision of homogeneity and the melting pot.

In a book entitled *Beyond the Melting Pot,* first published in 1963, Nathan Glazer and Daniel Moynihan wrote about New York City:

> Ideally, if we are to describe one aspect of a city . . . we should begin by spreading out as a background something about the city as a whole. We should speak about its politics, its economic life, its culture, its social life, its history. But none of these aspects of the city can be adequately described or explained except by reference to its ethnic groups.

For Americans today, the ideal of the melting pot and the belief that it was working seem to be part of the past. The ideal still lives in the vision of a homogeneous community, but more and more Americans now agree with Glazer and Moynihan that it is not unity which explains urban life or makes its realities but rather the ethnic groups with all their differences. They are the realities of contemporary cities. But they are not the only realities.

FRAGMENTED COMMUNITIES

As is commonly the case in cities today, the machinist with "Polish memories" who had "nothing against Negro people" lived and worked in two separate communities in the same city. "We're buddies on the job," he said. "We do the same work. We drink our coffee together and sit there eating lunch. But you leave and you go home and you're back with your own people."

His work community and his home community were separated by space and time. Only he put the two together. Nothing at work, with his buddies, reinforced a feeling of being "with your own people," of sameness. Nothing in his experience at home, with "everything in your life," reinforced his sense of comradeship and neighborliness with his buddies at work.

There was no visible, palpable connection between the machinist's two communities. All human beings depend on the reinforcement which comes from external, physical, and geographical sensations and familiarities for a sense of wholeness and oneness in their lives (that sense which provides the drive for community). Without such reinforcement, it is extremely difficult to maintain a sense of identity. So powerful are the influences of external, physical, and geographical familiarities seen to be that some institutions, like the armed forces and large corporations, deliberately move their management employees from place to place periodically, in order to destroy the influence of those familiarities and replace them with institutional ones. The company and its ways, or the service, becomes the familiar setting which gives the individual a sense of belonging, a sense of community, loyalty, and individual integrity.

Modern urban Americans have available to them a series of communities, none of which is complete or whole—in the logic of community mythology—and none of which gives the individual a sense of integrity. In each, the individual plays a role which is only a part. There is a home community, which includes a family, or a couple, or only a single individual; it is the dwelling of the individual, and its geographical location is often expected to be *the* community to which a person belongs. There is a family community, which extends beyond home and immediate family, and which may be large or small, geographically compact or scattered. And there is a work community, which includes co-workers, bosses, subordinates, and sometimes extends to unions, professional groups, and recreational groups associated with work.

There are communities of an individual's group or people, which can be neighborhoods, ghettos, suburbs, churches, or fraternal organizations, but which can also be segmented. There are communities of the street or of the neighborhood. There are communities of the place where particular people hang out and get together, which may be institutionalized for a whole variety of purposes—religious, political, educational, economic, social, or for entertainment. And there have developed, in the last decade or two, publicly recognized communities of race and sex which encourage mutual recognition of shared experience: the blacks, the Chicanos, the sisterhood, the gays.

The only connections these partial communities have with one another are that they exist in a single large urban area and that they are tied together in the mind and experience of a single individual. The communities in which a single individual participates are often widely separated by people, by time, and by the complicated, three-dimensional spaces of the city. In the experience of any one person, the subway or the bus or the highway runs from home or the neighborhood stop to work and back again. Beyond those stops it may as well drop off the edge of the earth. Only thus does there come to be a single, whole-city community: that community is different for each individual and rarely reinforced by the experience or reflected feelings of others.

The logical implication of the myths which proclaim the diversity of city life and the freedom of the city individual is that each individual is responsible for the construction of his or her own community—out of the parts, the opportunities, and the people that are available. Each person tries to make *connections* and *contacts* with other people in the city. Modern cities are mechanized. The transport systems help make connections between one community and another possible. They involve each person in a kaleidoscopic experience of pressing humanity, voices, noise, movement, rapidly changing scenes, and shifting masses of people. For many city dwellers, and a majority of those who live in inner cities, the public transport systems emphasize, daily, the great size and diversity of the city and the fragmentation of its communities. At the same time, for millions of people they reinforce the sense of anonymity which both protects the individual's privacy and independence and contributes to alienation.

The automobile provides a very different sense of connections between communities in the city. Both taxis and private cars encapsulate the individual and screen out much of the sense of kaleidoscopic distance between communities. The private car is a barrier between the individual in it and people on the streets or in their cars. The private car gives each individual a sense of control over time, distance, the machine itself, and the humanity with which one must come in contact, and therefore a sense of control over urban community. It is also a physical symbol of individual autonomy and of individual freedom. It is a palpable connection, by its very presence, between one community and another in the individual's life. The car itself is both symbol and reinforcement of the sense of belonging to a particular place, because the individual sees the car in different places but, once inside it, is in the same place.

The car as a capsule, too, can protect the individual from the dangers of life among strangers. As Jane Jacobs pointed out, in *The Death and Life of Great American Cities,* one way to avoid violence in the city is to take refuge in an automobile:

> ... This is a technique practiced in the big wild-animal reservations of Africa. . . . It is also the technique practiced in Los Angeles. Surprised visitors to that city are forever recounting how the police of Beverly Hills stopped them, made them prove their reasons for being afoot, and warned them of the danger. This technique of public safety does not seem to work too effectively yet in Los Angeles . . . but . . . think what the crime figures might be if more people without metal shells were helpless upon the vast, blind-eyed reservation of Los Angeles.

Valid or not, the great majority of American city dwellers feel secure, in control, and connected to their various communities in their automobiles. Those who do not own cars lack (and feel the lack of) an important means to belong to communities *and* to maintain a sense of individual integrity, independence, and dignity in city life.

Connection and contact with other individuals in the city, the *sine qua non* for the individual creation of community, has found its most important symbol in the telephone. The phone permits instant contact regardless of space. It allows an individual in one of his communities—home, work, or other—to "tie himself" to someone in another community. It permits a person to be "reached" by others. The metaphors commonly used for telephonic communication emphasize the analogy to face-to-face communication, an important part of the vision of community. The telephone helps to preserve a sense of privacy and individual autonomy, if one is the caller, and at the same time admits of invasion of privacy and the imposition of community on the individual. Like the automobile, the telephone helps to connect widely separated communities and individuals, and it is also the means to obtain food, aid, comfort, and to avoid danger in the city.

The modern city is a conglomeration of millions of individually created and maintained communities, shifting and overlapping. But it is also a conglomeration of individuals who have *not* created communities, and of individuals who feel their communities to be partial, imperfect, badly fragmented. For those, the imperative of individual moral and ethical responsibility leads to a sense of inadequacy, of alienation and guilt; feelings which drive people to despair, escape, and violence.

Radio and television (the great modern mythmakers and tellers of tales) supply, for many who cannot create it themselves, a sense of urban community and of individual belonging. Media "communities" are fragmented by the very nature of their presentation. But because those imaginary communities appear in the individual home, they satisfy, in part at least, the expectation of proximate community. Media programming favors individuals—disc jockeys, news commentators—who communicate directly, so it seems, to the individual listening and watching; and it favors complex family situations—in soap operas and situation comedies—which give viewers a sense of knowing and being part of a continuous, familiar human community. Many programs directly appeal to nostalgia for the small-town community, which is in most cases not nostalgia for something once known but rather expectation generated by the myths of rural community. The success of radio talk shows and call-in participation shows—and the more recent spread of citizen-band radios in cars—emphasizes the important place the broadcast media possess, for urban America, in the fulfillment of the ideal of community. Radio and television programs also emphasize the communities which are available to urban Americans without individual responsibility to create them. Many programs are based on the family and on ethnic groups, communities to which individuals belong. They are also based on ready-made, urban symbols of acceptance, care, nurture, protection, and help—hospitals and the police—for which the individual is also not responsible. They provide an escape, in short, from the pressure of the responsibility to create community and individual integrity out of the fragments at hand in city life.

THE CITY AS ONE COMMUNITY

The search for one *whole* community in a city is generated by the myths of the small town, which imply that any definable municipality is one community. But in the growing mythology of urban community, the city is a mass of individuals, families, and community fragments, with all the goods, services, jobs, and opportunities which they generate, held together by streets and cars, transit lines, buildings, and telephones. The whole-city community is given the appearance of integration by a helping infrastructure which is both bureaucratized and informal. The normal American city dweller is able to see the city as a whole through two images. One is that of the mayor, elected by everyone, who supervises City Hall, with its bureaucracy, offices, taxes, licenses, schools, and workers. The other is that of the police, uniformed and visible, the outward signs of the presence of a whole-city community.

The uniform, the badge, the gun, and the "cruiser" are the symbols of authority of the police. Their presence throughout a city is often the only everyday sign that a city government exists and that there is some community which is the whole city.

But authority, particularly the uniformed authority of government, has—since the Revolution—been perceived as a challenge to individual freedom and autonomy. So Americans are ambivalent about the police. Authority must be obeyed, even deferred to, when it is confronted—but only then. The police officer, the "cop" in normal American English, is a threat and a deterrent to individual freedom; but the cop is also an aid and a comfort, a representative of the whole community when the individual needs help.

School texts often call the police "our community helpers," and, although it is an equally powerful, but informal, American tradition that children learn contempt for these helpers as authority figures, urban Americans do seek the help of the police. Cops are expected to be able to direct people through the maze of city spaces. They are expected to maintain peaceable, predictable movement throughout the city, just as they are expected to maintain peace—even among family members. Whenever "things get out of hand"—that is, whenever individuals lose control of a situation—the normal expectation is that the police will be called in.

The police are also expected to help people in trouble (another form of "things getting out of hand" for the individual). Women in labor, without transportation, call on the police to take them to hospitals. The police are summoned in many medical emergencies. In most cases when the police are perceived to be helpers, their authority is assumed to be benign and to represent the benefit of being part of a city community. Their presence, their use, and the awareness of them constantly renews belief in the community-of-the-whole-city which they symbolize.

But the police are also seen to be the primary enforcers of laws, rules, and regulations, and in this role the contempt of Americans for authority, the emphasis on individual rights and freedom, predominates. The police officer then represents the City, the Government, the Law as restrictive of individual autonomy and oppressive of individual freedom. The cop then becomes a "pig," the "fuzz," a representative of an alien force invading, perhaps destroying an individual's community or symbolizing the powerlessness of group communities. The law and order which the police are generally believed to be trying to preserve is often seen as an imposition on, and thus a violation of, the many communities of the city. The police themselves are seen as a community, and their law and order as an effort to destroy other communities, to negate the responsibility, freedom, and independence of the city dweller. They are then not symbols of the ideal community of the whole city but rather parts of the bureaucratic infrastructure, at best symbols of fragmentation, with their own jobs to do and their own roles to play.

The police are only the most visible element of the city government. The impetus for community unity and the vision of the local government as representative of that unity which are part of the mythology of rural community have gradually transferred, as the population has transferred, to the cities. For migrants to the city for more than a century, the boss and his machine have fulfilled the mythical expectations of unity, protection, service, and economic expansion which true community government produces. Since the 1930's, the number of bosses and machines has been reduced, but the vision—and the reality—of the good boss who, with his machine, got things done, reconciled the various interests and elements in the city community, ran an efficient government, and symbolized the desires and accomplishments of the whole-city community, has been transferred to mayors, the elected heads of city governments. Today, a city boss—and some still exist—is ordinarily also the mayor. More importantly, the mayor, even when he is not the boss of a classic political machine, is believed to be the boss of the city, the only person who can get things done, the outstanding symbol of the unity of the whole city.

Only the mayor, as most Americans believe, can hope to represent all the people of the community. The mayor in the city, as the President in the whole nation, is seen as the symbolic representative of the free, autonomous individual who can act effectively and who creates community. The symbol and the reality are believed to be the same.

For the mayor, too, as for the individual in the city, life is fragmented. There are many communities to serve, and a bewildering variety of experts and specialists, trained and departmentalized in single aspects of the great diversity of opportunities, services, technologies, and possibilities available in the modern city. That the unity of community which urban Americans have sought through their mayor-bosses—from Big Bill Thompson and James Michael Curley through La Guardia of New York to Daley of Chicago—is ephemeral has not destroyed the expectations which the mythology of urban community generates in every urban American. Mayors remain symbols of unity; and people continue to expect them to provide it.

The city government itself—its metaphor is "City Hall"—is not generally believed to be a symbol of the unity of the city or an indication that a whole-city community exists. The city government is fragmented, a departmentalized bureaucracy filled with experts and red tape, arcane rules and entrenched civil servants. It is powerful, far-reaching, generally inefficient, invisible, responsive to interests but not to the community. The general assumption of most urban Americans is reflected in the modern folk saying that "you can't fight City Hall" and in the folk wisdom that you should avoid City Hall unless you represent some organized interest which it can serve. The law-making body in modern city governments, the council or city legislature, is elected on the basis of districts in the city, the boundaries of which are established by population numbers, not by the boundaries of real communities; there is little sense among city dwellers that such representatives are part of or responsive to the communities in their districts.

In a brilliant essay on urban pressure politics in the 1960's, Tom Wolfe in *Radical Chic and Mau-Mauing the Flak Catchers* caricatured the perception of urban government possessed by most Americans. That government is a community unto itself, in the popular perception, and it serves only insiders:

> . . . There are those who may think that the bureaucrats and functionaries of City Hall are merely time servers, with no other lookout than filling out their forms, drawing their pay, keeping the boat from rocking and dreaming of their pension like the lid on an orderly life. But bureaucrats, especially in City Hall, have a hidden heart, a hidden well of joy, a low-dosage euphoria that courses through their bodies like thyroxin. . . . Because they have a secret: each, in his own way, is hooked into The Power. The Government is The Power, and they are the Government, and the symbol of the Government is the golden dome of City Hall, and the greatest glory of City Hall is the gold-and-marble lobby, gleaming and serene, cool and massive, studded with the glistening busts of bald-headed men now as anonymous as themselves but touched and blessed forever by The Power . . .
>
> . . . You stop and talk with your good buddy by the door to the Registrar's . . . both of you in your shirtsleeves but with your ties held down smoothly by a small-bar tie clip, rocking back on the heels of your Hush Puppies, talking with an insider's chuckles . . . while your eyes play over the lobby and all the hopeless wondering mendicants who wander in off the street, looking this way and that for some sign of where the Assessor's office is, or the Board of Supervisors', or the Tax Collector's, probably taking their first plunge into the endless intricate mysteries of The Power, which they no more understand than they could understand the comradely majesty of this place, this temple, this nave and crossing of the euphoria of The Power.

In the stories, images, folklore, and perceptions of City Hall, city government keeps alive the vision of the fragmentation of community in the city.

Individual wholeness and integrated community, and at the same time fragmentation and segregation, are the contradictory expectations which modern American urban myths attempt to overcome and to resolve. Concern for "self-fulfillment," ranging from extremes of hedonism to extremes of transcendentalism, has grown in modern life as a result of the responsibility those myths have placed on the individual for the creation of community. So, too, have alienation, anomie, and violence grown as many urban Americans have found themselves unable to create, by themselves, a sense of belonging, of neighborliness, of community.

Many Americans seek to revive the sense of community and individual worth they believe Americans felt in that mythical past when small towns were real and good and cities were dreamlike and wicked, by distinguishing themselves from big-city people. And the big-city people seek a similar sense of community, and distinguish themselves from others, by projecting evil onto other neighborhoods, other groups, or onto the "system," symbolized by City Hall and the police. More and more urban Americans seem to be seeking natural, pre-existent communities against which to measure their freedom and success; and which, if found, release the individual from the responsibility for creating and maintaining community. They have found such communities in families, institutions, suburbs, ghettos, streets, neighborhoods, and, above all, in ethnic groups. But the vision of the sprawling modern industrial city, filled with a multiplicity of people, of groups, and of communities—fragmented, and at the same time whole—continues to dominate our myths of urban community.

3

People, Endless, Streaming

IN THE MIDDLE of the nineteenth century, Walt Whitman wrote a poem entitled "Give Me the Splendid Silent Sun." It began with a pastoral vision of "juicy autumnal fruit," fields of "unmow'd grass," and "nights perfectly quiet as on high plateaus west of the Mississippi."

But the vision of the city obtruded in Whitman's poem as it had in the lives of many Americans. "Keep your splendid silent sun," Whitman sang in the second verse:

> Keep your woods O Nature, and the quiet places by the
>   woods,
> Keep your fields of clover and timothy, and your
>   cornfields and orchards . . .
> Give me faces and streets . . .
> Give me Broadway . . .
> Give me the shores and wharves heavy-fringed with
>   black ships!
> . . . The life of the theatre, bar-room, huge hotel,
>   for me!
> . . . People, endless, streaming, with strong voices,
>   passions, pageants,
>
> . . .
>
> Manhattan crowds, with their turbulent musical chorus!
> Manhattan faces and eyes forever for me.

Millions of people in an endless stream have moved in the more than a century and a quarter since Whitman wrote his poem. They left rural backgrounds, the "villages where Ma and Pa do stay," the "high plateaus west of the Mississippi," the countries of Europe and the Old World, Indian reservations, and the black towns and ghettos of the rural South in order to live in and find success in American cities. The great majority of Americans, as we have seen, now live in cities. And they still move.

For early rural migrants, being in a city was like being at a county fair twenty-four hours a day. There were so many people, so much happening, such noise and smells and confusion, so much to see and do, so many possibilities. The difference between the opportunities offered by the cities and those available in the countryside was immediately apparent to any migrant. In a city, one could do almost anything *except* till the soil—and there were a few who did that, in tiny gardens, on rooftops, in window boxes. The streets of the cities were not paved with gold; they were all too often paved with mud and dung, litter and broken glass. Yet they offered opportunities undreamed of on the farm. They even offered the possibility of earning enough money to buy a farm—or to go West—or to live in the country.

The proliferation of stories of urban opportunity, of success and rising, of the ease of individual social and economic mobility in cities was not slowed by the duller realities of hard work, drudgery, and poor living conditions—any more than the myths of American opportunity on the land were. Even the unskilled could find jobs to do in the cities—and money to earn. "The pay here is good, but the labor is hard," a nineteenth-century Alsatian blacksmith said of an American factory, and his assessment reflected the attitude of many. The opportunities were there, visible, on all sides. And "Lowell was a damn sight better than County Cork" to Irish immigrants, according to Stephan Thernstrom, an urban historian, whatever the miseries of life in Lowell, because they "knew from bitter experience what County Cork was like." The vision of brutal reality behind them, and of something better ahead of them in the city, has brought blacks to the cities, Puerto Ricans to the cities, Mexicans and Vietnamese and "boat people" to the cities, as it has brought white Americans and Europeans in their millions to the cities.

Many told themselves the city was but a way station toward the land, and for a few it was. But for most, cities became permanent residences. People acquired skills in urban living and working; their children grew up in cities; the opportunities remained in cities. The cities melted immigrants from abroad and Americans from all over into urban Americans. Few of them left city life. When they or their children did go West, it was to Western cities; when they moved to the country, it was to the suburbs.

MOVING ON

Movement is the magic which keeps expectations high in America. From the movement of the first colonists to the New World through the westward movement of Americans to the movement of people into the cities, movement itself has been the continuing proof—to Americans—of social and economic mobility (we call it "progress") of the individual, the society, and the nation. Movement fuels the belief in unlimited opportunity and ultimate success. Movement—physical, geographical movement—is the symbol of social and economic mobility. It is also the symbol of progress, of independence, and of individual freedom all wrapped up in one. In their movement to the cities, within the cities, from one city to another, from cities to suburbs and back, Americans new and old have tied themselves symbolically to their immigrant past, to their colonial past, to their westward-moving, frontier past. They endlessly repeat the ritual pattern of seeking opportunity and freedom through movement.

An English character in John Fowles's novel *Daniel Martin* said about Americans:

> And yet there's a sort of forwardness, an independence, a lack of servility. A hope . . . I begin to see it as a choice of how you pay the bill. . . . Here they do it by looking forward to a dream world, where everyone succeeds, everyone's rich and happy. Horrors like the supermarkets and the freeways and the smog and the sprawl are just incidents on the road there. The wagon-trail myth. Today's problems aren't problems, but proofs of tomorrow's new frontier. You drive on, at all costs.

Stephan Thernstrom has characterized nineteenth-century urban Americans as a "footloose," "restless" people. Some working-class neighborhoods in cities, he wrote, kept their general social and economic character over fairly long periods of time, but the same people did not stay in them. The neighborhoods remained the same, but the people constantly changed.

Many of the findings of recent historians and sociologists have confirmed perceptions Americans have long had about the cities they live in. "The bottom layer of the social order," Thernstrom wrote, was "a group of families who appear to have been permanent transients, buffeted about from place to place, never quite able to sink roots." They were "the people who were least successful and who had the greatest grievances," and they rarely stayed in the same place for very long. The people lowest on the economic scale in cities tended to move, to look for better opportunity elsewhere, in another neighborhood or in another city. There was no indication that such people actually found better opportunity; like modern agricultural migrants, they were rarely in one place long enough to change their economic status.

The bottom layer of city dwellers were not, however, the only ones who moved. In fact, it was very often only the older residents of a neighborhood, who had become established, who did *not* move—and even for them, movement was expected to mark their social and economic progress (move to a better neighborhood) as well as their progress through life (move on retirement, move in with the kids, move to a "home").

Many of those who are constantly on the move are invisible. They are very poor, they are here today and gone tomorrow, and they are very often simply written off (as tramps and hobos often were) as morally deficient persons outside the reality of the community and society. The very poor have, until the twentieth century, simply been assumed to be part of human experience: they existed. All societies have elaborated behavior patterns which allow individuals to ignore the poor. In America the myths of progress and democracy promised that poverty would disappear as America became more developed, more productive, and wealthier. Since the poor in American cities *did disappear*—or at least, almost any individual poor person disappeared—it was simple to assume that they had gone to find greener pastures.

The movement of poor people away from any neighborhood could be, was, and is taken by most Americans as evidence that there is plenty of opportunity for everyone, if not in one place, then in another. By constant movement in search of opportunity, the poor have confirmed—at least for others—the efficacy of movement and the existence of opportunity. They are simply restless Americans, of whom Walt Whitman sang in "Song of the Open Road":

> You but arrive at the city to which you are destin'd,
> you hardly settle yourself to satisfaction before
> you are call'd by an irresistible call to depart.

For poor Americans themselves, movement brings hope. Like everyone else, they believe there is opportunity available—somewhere. The Joad family, for example, in John Steinbeck's *The Grapes of Wrath,* and the Okies and Arkies and many others—devastated by the Dust Bowl and the Great Depression—went West in the 1930's looking for the opportunities they hoped, they knew, were out there. They participated in the myth that movement brings opportunity and, with it, success. Against the power of the myth, they have only their own experience of poverty and failure—and most do not want their experience to be the generalization (many of the most popular movies and entertainments during the Great Depression were focused on the lives of the rich and the successful). Because the poor have moved—or drifted—in search of opportunity, they rarely discover "a sense of common identity and common grievance" with others who are poor. Even today, where there is considerable available awareness of poverty and of its institutionalization, poor Americans find it difficult to perceive themselves as a special group of the deprived. While some have come to see themselves as deprived for ethnic reasons—the lines of color and race—few believe they are part of an American proletariat. Because they move, they continue to believe in their opportunities and in the possibility of success.

"Those who did stay in the city and make their way there did, in general, succeed in advancing themselves economically and socially," Thernstrom wrote of turn-of-the-century Americans. Over a generation or two of a family, the experience of American urban life has generally confirmed the belief that the cities provide mobility. There was some downward mobility in American urban society, but generally "few men born into the middle class fell from there" and "a good many born into the working class either escaped from it altogether or advanced themselves significantly within the class."

The increasing availability of jobs demanding skills in new technologies has meant that most of the established skilled workers have "moved rapidly into these new positions." Their children have typically found places in the skilled trades or in the "even more rapidly expanding white-collar occupations." Unskilled workers, who were at first the majority of the migrants to the cities, were able either to rise slowly in industrial occupations over a generation or two or to enter the lower levels of the white-collar world as clerks, salesmen, or small entrepreneurs. Those who were unable to rise in occupation or social status could still manage to acquire property, both real and personal, and "establish themselves as members of the stable working class, as opposed to the drifting lower class." Expanding opportunities for the acquisition of skills, ever greater numbers of positions for skilled workers and service workers, and an ever greater number of openings and opportunities in white-collar jobs have made the dream of mobility a reality for the majority of those who have moved to American cities over the past century.

The reality of mobility was for a majority, but by no means for all. While that reality has seemed miraculous when measured against the expectations and realities of all of humanity for hundreds, or thousands, of generations, it has nevertheless *not* been the lot of many of those who live in American cities. In his 1949 Pulitzer Prize play, *Death of a Salesman,* Arthur Miller described the family and the failure of a middle-class, urban, traveling salesman, Willy Loman. Willy *traveled,* he *moved,* and so did his sons—but *movement,* the symbol of social and economic mobility, did not in his case prove to be the reality:

> I don't say he's a great man. Willy Loman never made a lot of money. His name was never in the paper. He's not the finest character that ever lived. But he's a human being, and a terrible thing is happening to him. So attention must be paid. He's not to be allowed to fall into his grave like an old dog. Attention, attention must be finally paid to such a person.

Willy Loman and his failure were invisible to the world because they contradicted the logic of the myth of mobility. Willy was mobile, he traveled all the time: he could not have failed. Thus the logic. But he *had* failed; for all his movement, he was immobile socially and economically. Thus his wife's cry "Attention, attention must be finally paid . . ."

Even for that majority whose upward mobility has given convincing reality to the myth, the realization was not instantaneous. Only rarely did a person in a single lifetime rise significantly on the social and economic scale. The expectation of mobility (and the assumption that it was being achieved) was kept alive, however, by many models of mobility in the urban world. Hierarchies of success, established steps on social and economic ladders, were available, visible, understandable—and seemed logical—to people who lived in the cities. Skilled workers and foremen in factories show the workers around them the next step, the real—because visible—possibility of mobility. Street vendors and small shopkeepers demonstrate a route into the world of business. The Industrial Commission in 1901 reported that "a very large number of the people who work in the sewing trade for contractors"—people in sweatshops or "sweating" at home—"usually hope to become contractors themselves." Precinct and ward political work showed the newcomer and the political beginner the steps to political success. The police, who were highly visible, became a traditional avenue to social mobility for groups of newcomers to the city. Domestic service gave many training in how to rise in status by changing behavior, dress, and habits. So did public education. Store windows, newspapers, athletics, fraternal organizations, churches, dance halls, bars and saloons, even the passing parade of people in the city, made the dream of success seem more real by providing images of the next step up, as well as of ultimate goals.

There is little control of the growth of American cities, so neighborhoods tumble into neighborhoods, new building sprawls into farmland, and tenements push against houses of the middle class. There is opportunity to see how others live and to find avenues to desirable ways of life. As the cities have grown larger, there has been more and more "ghettoization" on economic as well as ethnic lines, but the reputations of neighborhoods—this one good, that one bad, another one clearly a step up—constantly emphasize the symbolism of moving as a sign of mobility.

Movement is not only symbolic in American cities; physical movement—or people, of vehicles (endless, streaming)—is the primary visual image most Americans carry of their cities and of city life. The city streets, the "sidewalks of New York," "on the street" is "where it's at." The movement, activity, and public life of the street is the center of the American perception of what a city is. The street provides a modicum of safety for all. It is a vital part of the education of all city dwellers—"street-wise" is a sobriquet which implies some success in urban life. The street provides opportunities for commerce, for recreation, for education, for entertainment, and for a sense of community in a confused and often alien world. City street life is rich and varied. Traffic through the streets provides a counterpoint to the activity and traffic *within* any street. The noise and activity of major traffic arteries and major commercial centers draws people to them, if for nothing more than a sense of participation.

MOVING OUT

As the density of the population in cities has grown, the demand for land for housing, buildings, services, factories, can be satisfied only by spreading farther and farther from the center. That spread came as soon as efficient transport systems were developed. In the post-Civil War era, the growth of American cities was accompanied by the development of railroads, street railroads, elevated railroads, trolley cars, subways, highways, cars, and buses—all parts of constantly expanding commuter transportation systems. With those systems suburbs became inseparable parts of modern American cities.

There is comfort to be found by Americans in the "omnipresent newness" of suburbs, as described by urban historian Sam Bass Warner:

> Whether a man lived in a lower middle class quarter of cheap three-deckers, or on a fashionable street of expensive singles, the latest styles, the freshly painted houses, the neat streets, the well-kept lawns, and the new schools and parks gave him a sense of confidence in the success of his society and a satisfaction at his participation in it.

Suburbs encouraged Americans to feel they were participating in the advantages of cities by moving—to the streetcar suburbs of the late nineteenth century, to the Levittowns of the 1940's, or to the condominium developments of the 1970's.

Suburbs made the myth of the rural community and its life real to many urban Americans. The openness of the suburbs, their variety, and their wide range of prices made it possible for city dwellers, even the poor, to continue to dream of owning a house and a piece of land in a *real* community. Suburbs represented the certainty for city dwellers that if they could but "earn enough money they too could possess the comforts and symbols of success."

To be a city person and live in a suburb—whether it is a working-class suburb reached by public street transportation or a suburb served by commuter train and highway—requires daily physical movement. That movement, for Americans, is the daily re-enactment of mobility. It is also a daily symbol of mobility in the right direction: to the land, to the wide-open spaces (the West, the frontier, nature, the wilderness), and to real community. The suburbs, because they symbolize in so many overlapping and subtle ways the strongest imperatives of our myths, make cities properly American, make them justifiable to those who believe real communities are rural and real Americans go West to the frontiers to pursue happiness and find liberty, independence, and democracy. Movement, a *sine qua non* of urban life, reinforces the logic and the imagery of those myths of mobility.

"The movement of Americans from the rural areas into the cities . . . has reversed itself," an article in the British weekly *The Economist* stated in September 1979. "People are now moving out of the cities at a faster rate than those moving in from the country are replacing them." While the article points out that 70 percent of the American population still lives "on the 1.5% of the land that is classified as urban," nevertheless the population of entirely rural counties in the United States is increasing at a rate much higher than the rate of population increase for the country as a whole. "The fastest growth in the countryside is occurring not in those districts immediately next to cities," the article continued, "but in remote counties that may not have been colonised since the mining and timber booms of the last century."

The effort of well-informed non-Americans (we generally call 'em foreigners) to understand this particular phenomenon in America is illuminating, because it becomes clear that the motivation of "Back to the Land" (the title of the article) is not obvious or very understandable to those who are not American:

> . . . Even when they move to places far away from the sight and sound of a city, many of the newcomers to the country do not sever their urban connections. . . .
>
> Well over 10% of the workforce in rural counties now commutes to a city. . . . In California the counties of Riverside and San Bernardino are taking in 1,000 people a week, most of whom work in Los Angeles. Many of them, to escape the smog and expense of the city, are settling in mobile homes in the desert 100 miles from the office.

There has been little change in the motivations and purposes of urban Americans in the more than a century since suburbs began to be built. The city remains the place of opportunity, the country the place to live, and the movement between city and country the visible sign of success.

"The main reason for moving to the country is not an economic one," *The Economist* article continues in some surprise. "Most people are coming into the country ["coming into the country" is an English, not an American, usage] not because they need to, but *because they want to.*"

> By far the most important reason given for moving, by those who move, is the nebulous "quality of life." . . . The most typical migrants . . . are retired couples who were born in the area or had a second house there; the second

> most important group is adults, again often natives of the state, with small children and high incomes. The desire to "go back home," often to an ideal that no longer exists, spans all ages. Even where there are fresh economic incentives to live in a rural community . . . the people who move in are likely to say it is because of their family ties to the place. It is for this reason, too, that blacks are heading south again or declining to move north.

"It would be a mistake," the *Economist* article says, "to suppose that America is becoming a rural society. What is happening, however, is that city and country are becoming increasingly intermingled."

The American logic that "real" community is at least symbolized by rural communities where one has family ties has long been continuously reaffirmed and reinforced by the Americans who have gone to live and work in the great cities—by their creation and use of suburbs, by their constant migration from one urban place to another, and above all by their constant movement. It is the movement, both as physical and geographical reality, and as symbol of independence and upward mobility, which has caused the intermingling of city and country which is the outstanding and peculiar characteristic of American cities and urban life.

4

The Rituals of Community

It looked extremely rocky for the Mudville nine that day,
The score stood four to six with but an inning left to play,
And so, when Cooney died at first, and Burrows did the same,
A pallor wreathed the features of the patrons of the game.
A straggling few got up to go, leaving there the rest,
With that hope which springs eternal within the human breast.
For they thought if only Casey could get a whack at that,
They'd put up even money with Casey at the bat.

Ritual is an abstract drama, an acting out—through generally accepted motions, positions, words, architecture, clothing, furnishings, and choreography—of social ideals, stories, myths, and mysteries which are significant to a particular society (the significance is a matter of the particular myths and ideals of that society). Because ritual generates strong emotions, it leaves its communicants ("actors," "players," and "spectators") with a very strong sense of the reality of its drama. Once a ritual is created and accepted, it will generate a mythology of its own—logical explanations, accretions of stories, proofs of the efficacy (i.e., the reality) of its drama—which in turn becomes part of the mystery, the significance, and the social reality of the ritual.

Ritual is ordinarily associated with religion and gods or God—just as myth is. But ritual need not be religious in the customary sense. It must be significant: a visible acting out of our beliefs and ideals which is at the same time real to us. The games of the ancient Greeks were rituals, but they were also religious. The games of modern Americans are rituals, although they are secular. They are significant dramas which Americans believe are an important part of the realities of their lives and their society. They *matter.*

BEFORE THE GAMES

But Flynn preceded Casey, and likewise so did Blake,
And the former was a pudding and the latter was a fake;

So on that stricken multitude a death-like silence sat,
For there seemed but little chance of Casey's getting to the bat.
But Flynn let drive a single to the wonderment of all,
And the much despised Blakey tore the cover off the ball,
And when the dust had lifted and they saw what had occurred,
There was Blakey safe on second, and Flynn a-hugging third.

In the beginning, the most important rituals of democratic community were those created by the Revolution and its writ: the complex, interrelated rituals of electoral politics and representative, legislative government. Electoral politics and parliamentary procedure, debate, and behavior were the spectator sports of the first century of American national life. The existence of the new nation depended upon the participation of large numbers in the rituals which gave the nation reality. Debating, electioneering, speechmaking, and voting rituals all developed masses of initiates and communicants. Debating clubs and societies, fraternal organizations and voluntary associations of all kinds, schools, courts, and the legislative bodies of governments at all levels of the society provided initiation into and participation in the mysteries and significance of the national rituals. The ideals being celebrated by the rituals were clear to all: the existence in America, and in every place in America, of democratic, classless equality in communities made up of hard-working, independent individuals. The rituals *really* created communities and reaffirmed their existence and importance. The belief that they do so continues to be an available American myth.

The electoral and legislative rituals were established early in the existence of the nation, and they were associated with the realities of agrarian frontiers, farms, and small communities. In the mills and factories of the industrializing nation of the later nineteenth and twentieth centuries, on the construction jobs, in the great corporations, in the noisy, crowded neighborhoods of growing cities, electoral and legislative rituals drew fewer and fewer communicants as the realities dramatized in the rituals seemed further and further from modern realities. The electoral rituals have not disappeared, but they have become—much as religious rituals had become early in nineteenth-century America—separated from individual and community life. In modern America, the realities those rituals dramatize and the ideals they reaffirm are a separate part of the general view of reality. They are set aside for special days and seasons; they are participated in by special people. They have ceased to involve a great majority of Americans as communicants. They carry, today, little emotional significance for many of the spectators.

Electoral ritual dramatized and reinforced belief in the logic of federalism. By the beginning of the twentieth century, many no longer believed that logic; and as more and more Americans in the course of the twentieth century have focused their political expectations on the government in

Washington, the mythology of federalism has fallen into disrepute and federalism's logic is perceived by most as fallacy. The electoral rituals which supported federalism, which gave it its life and reality, are no longer perceived by many to reflect any of the significant realities of people who live in industrial, urban, culturally diverse, ghettoized communities, and who do specialized work in compartmentalized surroundings. So they do not participate in those rituals.

THE GAME

> Then from the gladdened multitude went up a joyous yell,
> It bounded from the mountain top and rattled in the dell,
> It struck upon the hillside, and rebounded on the flat,
> For Casey, mighty Casey, was advancing to the bat.
> There was ease in Casey's manner as he stepped into his place,
> There was pride in Casey's bearing and a smile on Casey's face,
> And when responding to the cheers he lightly doffed his hat,
> No stranger in the crowd could doubt, 'twas Casey at the bat.

Spectator sports have become the most popular and the most involving of the public rituals of twentieth-century industrial, urban America. And the people who participate in the games are communicants, not merely spectators. The first team match baseball game was played in 1846, and by the end of the nineteenth century, baseball involved thousands of Americans in innumerable daily enactments of its ritual. Football rapidly gained popularity after the first intercollegiate game in 1869, while basketball, invented in 1891, was not widespread until well into the twentieth century. Baseball has remained the Game in modern America, and is still the American paradigm of team sports. Its initiates are participants, whether they play or watch; the ritual is so involving, so real, so significant, that it colors and affects and explains and organizes the lives of its participants and of their communities.

Local teams draw large numbers of enthusiasts. Sandlot teams, neighborhood teams, school teams, lodge teams, teams sponsored by local businesses, teams of workers, teams made up of ethnic or immigrant groups, all attract aspirants, players, managers, advisers, and spectators. The Little Leagues of modern life, with their intensive involvement of children and parents, continue a pattern of popular participation now more than a century old. The games and their teams are not only sources of activity and entertainment, their rituals provide opportunities for communication among townspeople who would not otherwise have had any relationships at all. The teams, and participation in the rituals, are avenues by which newcomers are included in communities; individuals can win social approval and make the contacts with people that bring social mobility and economic advancement.

It is very difficult for the uninitiated to understand what's going on in modern games. It is even more difficult, as in all rituals, for the uninitiated to understand what everybody's so excited about. The movements and behavior of players are choreographed and freighted with significance calculated to move the emotions of all the communicants. The activities of managers and coaches, of referees and umpires, and of spectators are all part of a ritual, almost of a liturgy.

The *meaning* of any ritual is, at least in part, mysterious even to its initiates. It is not easily available to rational explanation or understanding. Initiation into the ritual—which in the case of American games is extremely widespread—tends to lessen the ability of the initiate to observe the ritual with rationality. The mass appeal of American games—their requirement of large numbers of communicants—reinforces the ideal of democratic participation and democratic community in their initiates. The games are contests between teams, rituals of competition modeled on competition between two political parties; one wins and one loses, one is "in" and one is "out." Increasingly in the twentieth century, the rules governing the rituals of games have been changed to assure that one team *wins*—that there is clear victory rather than tied scores, thus reinforcing the American ideal of victory and success—what English author John Fowles has called "the old Puritan fallacy: life is either a destination, an arrived success, or not worth the cost." In what some believe is the organized violence ritualized in modern games, many find realities and truths about themselves, their communities, and the world they live in.

WORK

Ten thousand eyes were on him as he rubbed his hands with dirt,
Five thousand tongues applauded as he wiped them on his shirt,
And while the writhing pitcher ground the ball into his hip—
Defiance gleamed from Casey's eyes—and a sneer curled Casey's lip.
And now the leather-covered sphere came hurtling through the air,
And Casey stood a-watching it in haughty grandeur there;
Close by the sturdy batsman the ball unheeded sped—
"That hain't my style," said Casey—"Strike one," the Umpire said.

The public display of skill, hard work, training, and cooperation by the members of sports teams—baseball, football, and basketball—was and is a ritual replacement of the public display of skill and hard work which in earlier, agrarian American communities had been made by people working on their farms or as artisans. In those small, rural (real) communities, a person's work was visible, watched by the community, and its value was reflected by the value put on it by the whole community. Franklin's adage "work makes the man" was an expression of a vital (and in earlier times entirely visible to the community) relationship between an individual and work. But people who work in factories, stores, warehouses, offices, trucks, schools, garages, and private homes, who live in communities—even rural communities—of more than a few hundred people, are usually socially disconnected from their work; it is not seen by other members of their communities, they are not seen at their work (even by their families), and very often, only part of their daily comings and goings are visible to their neighbors.

The visibility of the work of sports teams makes it possible for members of their communities (or for the whole nation), in effect, to say to themselves that here are useful, working, virtuous people. The communicant-spectators can participate in the "community" of the team, and feel the power, still, of "work makes the man," at least for their sports heroes. In very large towns and cities, where few people can see any connection between an individual and his work, teams play a vital, often central, role in creating a sense of individuals operating within a community—as opposed to the common urban sense of masses of disparate and unconnected individuals (endless, streaming).

THE TEAM

From the bleachers black with people there rose a sullen roar,
Like the beating of the storm waves on a stern and distant shore,
"Kill him! kill the Umpire!" shouted someone from the stand—
And it's likely they'd have done it had not Casey raised his hand.
With a smile of Christian charity great Casey's visage shone,
He stilled the rising tumult and he bade the game go on;
He signalled to the pitcher and again the spheroid flew,
But Casey still ignored it and the Umpire said, "Strike two."

Team games have ritualized several of the essential qualities of industrial life and have also generated a terminology ("teamwork") and an imagery which dominate American perceptions of that life. When the games first spread in the nineteenth century, most Americans had understood a team to be a group of animals working together to do a particular job. While there was a degree of specialization in an animal team—there were "lead" animals, "near" and "far" animals, and "off" animals who performed in slightly different ways within the team—the underlying assumption was that all worked uniformly and together. The imagery has continued: on an American team, we all pull together.

In the sports teams and their rituals, each person has a specialized task *and* all team members work together at the same task. When a baseball team is at bat, each team member performs the same task, but when it is the other team's turn at bat, each team member on the field is a specialist—infielder, outfielder, catcher, pitcher. The game is a competition and it is the cumulative effect of the skills of each team member and of teamwork which brings success and victory. A pitcher cannot pitch a no-hit game backed by lousy fielding.

The visual effect, which is made up of various circular motions, swinging motions, and reciprocal motions, with a ball and a bat as well as "moving parts," possesses all the elements in the imagery of machinery. The ritual of the game idealizes the team as a human machine of specialized parts which work together to produce the ultimate product, success. Like machine parts, the individuals on a team all are interchangeable with others who possess like skills.

Teams flirt with being machine-like rather than being exact reproductions of machines—although the Cincinnati Reds in recent years have enjoyed the reputation of being "The Big Red Machine." The logic of the team-sport ritual brings the imagery of the machine and of humans organized into machine-teams together with ideals of heroism, individual work, and skill acquisition. The sports hero teaches himself the skills he needs—in his own back yard, in the sandlot, on the street, at the playground. He works hard at that job. And his heroism magnifies his idiosyncrasies, makes him more individualized in dress and behavior both on and off the team, even in his relationships with his teammates. It is in both the specialization and the uniformity of the team that baseball—and football and basketball—idealizes the life of Americans in industrial cities.

The games also celebrate the individual, but they make it visible, as well as emotionally and psychologically clear, that the individual cannot even play the game without the team, without the community. Babe Ruth, Reggie Jackson, Pete Rose, and many other sports heroes have been spectacularly idiosyncratic players and very successful (witness the money they earn!) individuals. Home runs, no-hitters, touchdown passes, and spectacular football runs all provide demonstrations of individual prowess. But the stages provided for this heroic individualism are teams, games, communicants, leagues, and communities. Casey pursues not simply his own individual happiness in the rituals of the game but the salvation of the Mudville nine and the joy of the entire Mudville community.

THE COMMUNITY

"Fraud!" yelled the maddened thousands, and the echo answered "Fraud."
But one scornful look from Casey and the audience was awed;
They saw his face grow stern and cold; they saw his muscles strain,

And they knew that Casey would not let that ball go by again.
The sneer is gone from Casey's lip; his teeth are clenched with hate,
He pounds with cruel violence his bat upon the plate;
And now the pitcher holds the ball, and now he lets it go,
And now the air is shattered by the force of Casey's blow.

The development and spread of team sports in America have parallels in other "modernizing" nations. Modern spectator-team-games are a phenomenon of the industrial world.

The games which Americans made their own—baseball, football, and basketball—have in common that they were, from their origins, available to all in American society. Only football (Americans call it "soccer") in Western Europe and hockey in Scandinavia and Canada were available to all classes in the societies in which they developed *as* they developed. One of the characteristics of American games is their essentially democratic quality. Even those who are poor, if they are good athletes, can expect to get college scholarships, high pay, and upward mobility from American games. Those games were, from their beginnings, visible proof that the communities (and the nation) in which they were played were democratic and classless.

American football has, so far, proven to be the least exportable of the American spectator sports. Baseball moved into Mexico, Cuba, and Japan, and basketball has been taken up by many Europeans, but American football has stayed inside the United States. Perhaps the reason lies in the emphasis in football on lines—which must be defended, which must be penetrated, which must be moved. Basketball uses some of the peculiarly American imagery and idealism of lines—there are foul lines (as there are in baseball) and court lines which must be crossed—but in football the entire game is built around the frontier, the line, the boundary. Football ritualizes the moving frontier, and the teamwork, cooperation, and individual heroism necessary to move that frontier; simultaneously, it also ritualizes the teamwork, cooperation, and individual heroism necessary to resist the moving frontier (football players are pioneers *and* Indians at the same time). Ultimate victory in the game comes from moving the frontier more than the others do, crossing the goal line more frequently. There is little in such a ritual to appeal to the ideals and sensitivities of people who are not Americans.

In general, American team-sport rituals aim at the creation and maintenance of the ideals of community in the midst of the fragmenting forces of urban life. In those rituals, work, individuals, teams, machines, and frontiers fall into place and make a community out of the many players and fans, managers and promoters. The teams themselves, and therefore in the logic of the rituals the games the teams play, have long been perceived to be major elements in the integration of society. They idealize the integration of ethnic groups into the community and the participation of others in the mainstream.

Participation in sports rituals, particularly in the big leagues, is taken as an indication by most that the individual player is a success, and the group to which the player belongs is fully part of the community, essentially an American and entitled to all that that means. Participation, even at local levels, is taken as a sign by all that there is equality among those who visibly participate.The teams and their games are a means of upward mobility, leading in some few cases to fame and fortune, but more importantly and more frequently leading simply out of the orphanage, out of the ghetto, out of poverty. *Playing the game* makes people American, makes them equal—even though they may seem different, unequal. The ritual of the games makes people *really* part of a community, part of America.

> Oh! somewhere in this favored land the sun is shining bright,
> The band is playing somewhere, and somewhere hearts are light.
> And somewhere men are laughing, and somewhere children shout;
> But there is no joy in Mudville—mighty Casey has "Struck Out."

5

Classless Equality and Urban Democracy

THE SOCIETY OF THE MIDDLE MASS

American society has become middle-class in the twentieth century.

The new middle class grew gradually and almost imperceptibly in the nineteenth century. It is an urban class. Its economic base is the complex structure of industrialism. It is not an entrepreneurial bourgeoisie, although it includes entrepreneurs. Nor is it made up of the peasants and petite bourgeoisie—farmers, merchants, planters—who dominated the agrarian society of early-nineteenth-century America, although they, too, are included. The strength of the new middle class lies in cities and industries and corporate bureaucracies. It is also filled with members of twentieth-century professions—engineers, scientists, managers, educators, social workers. Its members are, almost all of them, employees. Into it have moved the children and grandchildren of immigrants, as well as the migrants and their children from American small towns and farms. Its values are modeled on older, agrarian values, but it is thoroughly modern and urban.

Class labels and ideals are, as we perceive them, European and foreign. Words like "peasant," "bourgeoisie," and even "class" itself are not American words. They are labels which in general American belief do not and cannot describe Americans.

Americans are uncomfortable with the terminology of class, as they are uncomfortable with the vision of structure and boundaries, the fixed levels which social classes imply. "Upper class" means "upper crust"; it means "aristocracy" or "hereditary nobility"; it means snobbishness and "snootiness" and arrogance. It implies unearned preference—something un-American. "Lower class" or "working class," on the other hand, means a fixed, menial position in society, lacking in hope. Both "upper" and "lower class" imply a failure of equality. "Lower class" denies mobility. All concepts of class, in effect, draw lines between the good guys and the bad guys; they are challenges to Americans, like frontiers. Class lines deny the efficacy of individual effort. American society, as Americans perceive it, does not, or at least *ought* not, admit of the importance or the permanence of class lines. If it did, it would be denying the fundamental rights and the freedom of all Americans.

The essential vision of Marxism—of fixed classes with consciously fixed, conflicting interests, of revolution based on class warfare—has long been perceived by Americans not merely as contrary to American belief but as a direct threat to the reality of American society. The Marxist idea of fixed classes denies the validity of American belief in the continuing American Revolution.

The self-evident truths that people are equal and possessed of inalienable rights summarize generations of American social experience. It was evident (especially after Jefferson said it) that the class structure of traditional society did not exist in America. Measured by the standards of class, family, and social position, there was a certain rough equality among Americans in their efforts to tame the wilderness, build communities, and provide government, an equality enforced by what would later be characterized as the frontier experience. The idealism of the Revolution made that equality an imperative.

This imperative also reflected social homogeneity. If there was an American nation, it was made up of Americans. Americans were not-Europeans. Europeans, as Americans saw them, were characterized by class consciousness and class-conditioned behavior, different languages, deference to position and authority, assumptions of inequality, and the taint of popery. These characteristics had to be removed from any who wished to gain entrance into American society. As Americans perceive it, the tendency of American history is toward classlessness. The Revolution was fought to destroy privilege. American reform, since the Jacksonian era, has been motivated by the desire to perfect equality and democracy. The old deferential society was destroyed and replaced with a society of the common man. The Civil War destroyed slavery and, along with it, the class-structured society which had been built in the South upon the backs of the slaves. Modern reforms have extended the franchise and tried to destroy privilege wherever it has been found. Americans have, as a result of this perception, rejected Marxism and much of Marx's terminology.

In American myth, America *is* a classless society. If it can be shown not to be, then something is wrong and needs to be put right. Classlessness is the ideal *and* the permanent state of American society; anything else is an aberration. Classlessness is one of the most important American definitions of democracy. It is the ultimate guarantee of equality and freedom.

Most Americans will admit, if pressed, that they are in the middle class. Few Americans, indeed, will willingly say that they are in any other class.

The use of "middle class" by Americans is of the same order that "middle America" or "Middle West" is. It does not signify the self-contained, middle order of a structure with lower and upper orders—as it does for Europeans. Rather, it is much closer to the view the Chinese have traditionally had of the Middle Kingdom. For Americans, the "middle"—whether middle class, Middle West, or middle American—is a large, solid, geographical center of almost limitless extent. Around and beyond it are other, haphazardly arranged areas of varying, but entirely peripheral, importance.

The "middle" in America is the center—quite possibly of the universe. It is the consensus; it is the silent majority; it is the mainstream. All else is ephemeral, if not un-American. The middle dominates, and *ought to* dominate. Those in it are the inheritors of American tradition, American belief, and American progress.

Within the middle mass, distorting it and pulling it in various directions, are people who believe themselves to be leaders, the properly constituted elite. They are, to some degree, followed by others. Occasionally they can push the whole mass, amoeba-like, along. They are too varied, and too numerous, however, to be a unified nucleus. They are sometimes recognized as "the establishment."

There are two sets of people along the edges of the middle mass, outside yet firmly attached. One comprises people who are, in varying degrees, defined as "other." They aspire to full inclusion in the middle and simultaneously wish to maintain their separateness. The people in the middle share their ambivalence, but believe the outsiders will ultimately be included. Blacks, Indians, Orientals, Puerto Ricans, Chicanos, some other ethnic and immigrant groups, and the very poor are among these others.

The second set of people outside the middle are those who perceive themselves to be elite, and who are often perceived by those in the middle simply as extraordinary. They draw their sustenance and values from the middle, but they are thought to be beyond the pale by most in the middle, and they uniformly believe themselves to be beyond the middle. Many of them aspire to lead and some asssume they do. Their activities, their goals, and their expressed beliefs are often extreme variants of the aspirations of those in the middle. There is, on both sides, ambivalence about them and their position in American life. They include, among others, Society (with a capital *S*), the jet set, the "beautiful people," the counter-culture of recent years, many intellectuals, and most social and political radicals.

American fantasies of aristocracy—from the stories of George and Martha Washington to those of John and Jacqueline Kennedy—are characteristic of the growth of the middle mass. The imperative of equality and classlessness continues to generate ambivalence—and a vision of an upper class. Landed wealth or inherited wealth, higher education, particularly if it was obtained at distant or foreign places, large houses (Noah Webster defined a "mansion" as a private residence with more than four chimneys) which are well decorated, expensively furnished, and staffed with servants, travel abroad, the ability to produce a genealogy, relationships with other important families, the right to use a military or political title: these criteria, or a significant combination of them, if accompanied by military or political service beyond the immediate locality, came, over the years, to define "aristocracy" for most Americans. George Washington could lay claim to most of them and was perceived to be an American aristocrat. He cemented aristocracy to the ideal of public service to the new nation, and ambivalence about aristocracy thus became a permanent part of the mythology of equality.

The society of the middle mass is, by its own belief, the present realization (the "cutting edge," the most highly evolved state) of classlessness and equality in America. It is the American community writ large, a reflection of every real community in America. It is homogeneous and proximate; therefore, in the logic of the myth, classless, democratic, and equal.

Ironically, modern Americans believe that the greatest threat to equality and to the middle mass comes from the political life of the communities most Americans belong to—the cities. The middle mass is urban, but the ambivalence about city life which Americans sustain is nowhere more obvious than in their distrust of urban politics.

REVOLUTIONARY POLITICS

America is, and all Americans believe it to be, a body politic. Access to and use of government to secure the great ideals of the society are the epitome of membership and participation.

Political life and government provided proof, after the Revolution and the establishment of America's Holy Writ, of equality and democracy. Political life became the form and the symbol of individual independence and the pursuit of happiness, of the community, of the continuing Revolution, and of classlessness. It is to political life, and to accessible government, that Americans have turned—in all the generations since the Revolution—in their effort to free individuals from the restraints of fixed social and economic structures. In an increasingly conscious effort (the beginnings of which, in the early nineteenth century, historians used to call "the rise of the common man") Americans have continued the Revolution by re-forming American society and institutions by destroying the vestiges of traditional society and making government and politics accessible to all.

The conduct of the Revolution is the symbol, and the working model, for reform. The Revolutionary committees—of Safety and of Correspondence, for example—Revolutionary congresses, volunteers and minutemen, declarations and constitutions, are repeatedly reconstituted and used in the organization of political parties, the development of conventions, and the growth of clubs, associations, societies, and fraternities for political, social, cultural, religious, and economic purposes. The lesson of the Revolution was that to change and reform institutions it was necessary to mobilize, direct, organize, and institutionalize the efforts of numbers of individuals. Large-scale change can be effected only by large-scale effort.

The Holy Writ of the Revolution, the compacts and covenants and constitutions of governments in America, had made some political institutions formal. The public documents and the social compact are perceived to guarantee the democratic character of governments. However, because governments have authority to govern, Americans distrust them.

There is even more distrust of informal institutions—such as political parties and other groups intent on political, social, or economic action. In part, that distrust stems from the continuing effort to bring order and predictability out of wilderness life, an effort concerned with defining institutions by giving them constitutions, by-laws, and proper procedures. In part, it comes from the belief in individual freedom, and the effort to limit institutional power, authority, and other potentially tyrannical organizations. In part, it comes from a vision of "conspiracy" fostered by the Revolutionary experience and the long-told stories of the Revolution. Regular, informal gatherings of people, particularly when they were "exclusive," were perceived to be dangerous to the liberty and equality of ordinary Americans. Political life in an open society, the myths of equality imply, must in all ways be open to all. Politics has to serve as a paradigm of classlessness.

The governments which were long the models of what governments ought to do were those closest and most accessible—local governments. As the vision of real community is based on the rural small town, so the vision of real democratic government is based on the expectations of rural Americans of their local governments.

Rural American community government was traditionally expected to create and maintain a predictable set of legal relationships and economic ground rules. It was to provide law and order. Its most important task was to increase economic opportunities. The government was expected actively to help the community expand and grow, and its members to find economic comfort and success. It was also expected to vary its rules when necessary in order to benefit insiders seeking success within the community. Local government was—and still is—the American model for the provision of domestic welfare within its geopolitical and human orbit.

It was difficult for traditional, rural Americans to distinguish between the economic interests of the community and those of individuals, because of the belief that individual improvement ordinarily brought community improvement. In America, a politician who was both a member of the community and its representative found it easy to confuse his own and the community's interests. A political career was universally recognized as a way to rise in life, as a means to success, and success was almost always measured by economic well-being.

The evident ambivalence about politics and politicians came from the distrust of authority and government which the Revolution had made permanent. It came, too, from the questionable nature of the origin and maintenance of the influence and power of politicians. Any aspiring politician needed to be a recognized participant in a local network of news, gossip, opinion, and morality. Lawyers and newspaper editors, because of their connections with courts and papers, were traditionally believed to be the best-qualified men for public office. Doctors, and sometimes ministers and teachers, were often involved in local politics, because they, too, were at the center of important community networks. Lincoln's work in a local store, and his hanging around in it, was important to his political career. Politics was "dirty" precisely because the politician was seen to be a vital part of the informal networks of relationships that were centered in stores and barbershops, as well as livery stables, saloons, pool halls, and other disreputable (often unmentionable) "smoke-filled" places. The dirtiness of politics was confirmed because some politicians did indeed cheat and take bribes.

The "clean" side of politics, for most Americans, was that the political life of the rural town was the outstanding symbol of the whole life of the community. Politics was the free, democratic pursuit of the happiness of the community. Access to political life was of enormous importance, therefore, and symbolic—as nothing else in America was—of the essential equality of all of American society. Black Americans after the Civil War *required* constitutional guarantees of such access because they had been defined as unequal in slavery. Women required the same guarantees because they, too, had been defined as unequal. Politics reflected all the important concerns—social, economic, legal, and even moral—of the people of the community. National politics was, by extrapolation, then, symbolic of the life and health of the whole nation.

THE POLITICS OF URBAN COMMUNITY

Americans who have moved to cities, who live in cities, who govern cities, who participate in the political life of cities (the middle-mass Americans) model their expectations of city government on democratic rural local government. Because cities were large, the federal model was applied to them. The logic seems to have been that a city was—like the United

States—a larger entity than a real community, and it therefore required a government which combined the interests and efforts of several communities. Those communities in most cities were called "wards" and they were relatively autonomous, possessing governments responsible for services, streets, schools, police, utilities, and general community welfare.

There was a city-wide "federal" legislative body—board of aldermen, city council—made up of representatives from each ward, which legislated for the city (as Congress did for the nation) and which provided itself with an executive—a mayor—very often from among its own members. The responsibility of the city government was to provide for city-wide needs and also to balance the economic desires of the wards. It was a source of some patronage (but ordinarily the wards could provide more jobs) and of great economic gain through contracts for buildings, for services, and for utilities.

The wards were usually subdivided into precincts, and those subdivisions were centers of popular participation and of control over local affairs. Few wards in early cities were homogeneous, and the result was a structure of political interaction among social groups and participation and leadership that was similar to the classless political pattern in rural communities.

There were no models or patterns for the government of the huge industrialized cities of the late nineteenth century. For well over a century now, cities have been doubling in size every generation and new cities have been appearing by the hundreds every generation. Even in cities smaller than the great metropolises, political leaders and the body politic in every generation have found themselves confronted with problems of scale and diversity completely outside the experience of the generations which preceded them. The goal of urban politics, as well as rural, was to provide a stable and predictable social environment and increasing economic opportunity. The urgent need to provide an expanding range of vital services, and the complicated task of assuring social and economic stability in the midst of enormous growth has come, again and again, squarely into conflict with the vision of democratic community which grew out of an agrarian and rural background.

That vision postulated a homogeneous community of independent individuals who sought their own advantage and the greater good of the community through active participation in government. Political leaders were elected by the whole community from among socially, morally, and economically responsible people.

Since the end of the nineteenth century, many Americans have felt a loss of control over the political process as cities grew. Widespread participation in elections and some local autonomy have continued, but the neighborhoods, precincts, and wards of the cities have increasingly become segregated by income, ethnic background, and social class. At the same time, cities have expanded to include more localities, and local representation in city government has declined in favor of representatives-at-large. Segregation, compartmentalization, and specialization in individual lives and in the city experience have created a sense of loss. Politics has become professionalized, and its practice is left to those who are specialists willing to devote their working lives to it.

Urban politicians have long tried to be responsive to the desires of their constituents. The urgent need to get things done, the increasing necessity to provide services to diverse groups, and the intense desire of all for predictability, for stability, and for local and individual economic and social advantage have given urban politics its fragmented and chaotic character. But urban bosses and their political machines have often provided for those desires. "I think," one nineteenth-century immigrant, quoted by Oscar Handlin in *The Uprooted,* said, "that there's got to be in every ward a guy that any bloke can go to when he's in trouble and get help." The urban politician has tried to be that guy.

The political machines of cities, as Walter Lippmann pointed out, were real sovereignties, made up of real friendships, loyalties, and aspirations. They have held large numbers of people together, and fulfilled their desires with patronage, jobs, services, and community benefits of all sorts. These sovereignties have required less individual decision-making and individual participation, resulting in a lessening of the individual's use to the political process. The rural American vision of a democratic community promised more. At the same time, political machines adjusted that vision to the realities of city life: they "produced" for their followers' social and economic needs, however capriciously; they gave and provided loyalty, as a substitute for community. They have been symbols of power and economic success for many who were not very successful and who felt powerless in the confusion and great scale of city life.

But modern urban politics, like urban bosses and their machines, are based on class and ethnic communities in cities. They conflict directly, therefore, with the mythology of classless community, with the vision of the city as one community; they make the reality of American democracy and equality seem questionable. As a result, many Americans intuitively perceive city politics to be corrupting, utterly undemocratic, and, in the words of Lincoln Steffens, "the shame of the cities."

The stories of corruption have grown richer, more elaborate, and more important as Americans have become more urban. From the tales of "Boss Tweed" and his Tammany Hall ring in New York City in the 1840's, through Lincoln Steffens's muckraking accounts at the turn of the century, through the legends of "Honey Fitz" and James Michael Curley in Boston—spun into novels like Edward O'Connor's *The Last Hurrah*—to Mike

Royko's tales of the *Boss,* Mayor Richard Daley of Chicago, the logic of the mythology of urban politics is that the bosses and the machines *are* the blight and shame of urban life—not the cities themselves (as the Jeffersonian tradition would have us believe). Urban politics are un-American, in this logic, based on loyalties and ethnic ties imported from somewhere else, corrupt, and anti-democratic.

Twentieth-century city politics has threatened to introduce class politics, class divisions, and class warfare to American life, as many Americans perceive those politics. That threat has made it necessary to counteract the bosses, to reform the cities, and to defend the essential classlessness of America. Much of the history of urban politics in America for the past three-quarters of a century has been the effort to reform.

In the mythology of twentieth-century urban reform, the bosses could be defeated, first of all, by educating the ignorant—in the right moral standards, in the English language, in democracy and good citizenship. Once the ignorant were Americanized, the bosses could no longer prey on them, and they would no longer support the bosses.

The bosses, many believed, based their power on segregated localism in the cities, on class or income or ethnic groups. If urban local autonomy was destroyed and replaced with a rationally operated, centralized city government, and if the cities were expanded in order to include suburban populations—of people who retained the vision of the classless rural community with its homogeneous democracy and equality—then such reformed cities would make class conflict unnecessary because they would once again be cities based on one whole community operated by one government.

Bosses and corrupt politicians could be replaced by professionals who devoted their life to public service and who had the knowledge and training to provide for the cities' needs. Civil servants, their jobs won by careful training and impartial examinations, would replace political appointees in city governments, and professional managers would replace elected officials. The vision of an impartial bureaucracy of managers (a vision borrowed from the corporation) running city government and getting things done is an important part of modern myths of urban government (a part balanced by a nightmare vision of bureaucracy, regulations, and red tape making urban government ineffectual, indeed impossible).

The imperative underlying the myths of the reformed city has led many Americans to the assumption that melting into the middle mass, insisting on centralized government and good leadership are the most important requisites for the preservation and development of democratic, egalitarian community. The logic seems—as mythic logic often does—to fit the past. The stories of urban reform, of the benefits gained from centralized government, of the beneficial consolidation of government services, of the excellence of political professionalism, and of the essentially classless nature of the urban experience, are legion—and current—in American life.

But there are polarities contained in these myths, as in all others. The problem of urban life remains. The solutions which the logic of urban democracy implies seem continually to evaporate. Cities are ungovernable—so many Americans believe. There is no community in any city, merely a conglomeration of communities—so many believe. American society is riddled with class distinctions—so many believe.

The strength of the myths comes from the fact that they produce both poles while, by their logical sleight of hand, they seem to solve the problem posed by the contradiction they contain: America is a middle-class, classless society. American cities are communities made up of communities. The imperative and the ideal remain: American society and all American communities are, have been, ought to be, must be, democratic, as all Americans are, have been, ought to be, must be created equal and treated equally by each other.

IV

THE POWER AND THE GLORY

1

Power and Power Failure

FOR THREE-QUARTERS of a century and more, Americans have been fascinated with power: American power, corporate power, military power, scientific power. The American Presidency has become in that time the most powerful office on earth. America has become the most powerful nation on earth. Nuclear power, unleashed by America, has become the most awesome power on earth.

As the perception has grown in the twentieth century that individuals are less and less effective in influencing the world, Americans have concentrated on—pinned their hopes on—the power of knowledge and expertise to effect and change the world. In a society of enormous cities, lemming-like regimented human beings, and incomprehensible self-operating machines, the only thing which seems to keep alive the image of the sturdy independent American is the seductively real vision of power.

THE EXCITEMENT OF POWER

There is an innocent excitement about this fascination with power which, as Joan Didion pointed out in *Slouching Towards Bethlehem,* distinguishes Americans from Europeans: ". . . the secret point of money and power in America is neither the things that money can buy nor power for power's sake," she wrote, because "Americans are uneasy with their possessions, guilty about power, all of which is difficult for Europeans to perceive because they are themselves so truly materialistic, so versed in the uses of power." Both the innocence and the excitement are parts of one aspect of the modern American romance with power—the sometimes horrible consequences of playing with power are another—but they have characterized and provided a logic for the modern use of power which is characteristically American.

"The greatest single problem in *The Ten Commandments* (1956)," Cecil B. De Mille, the maker of epic-spectacular-Biblical films *par excellence,* wrote in his *Autobiography,* "was the Voice of God." It was also not easy, De Mille said, to direct scenes "in which 8,000 people take part at one time," or to build, equip, and people a city in a foreign country. De Mille liked to compare a movie producer "to a commanding general, who must see that all the units of his armies, with all their distinct functions in the coming battle, are ready to strike simultaneously on the target date." Power is military, power is god-like, power is moving and providing for thousands of human beings: for Americans, power is the ability to *do* things on a massive scale, bigger, and better, and more effectively than anybody else.

Americans early associated power and empire. The excitement of empire was particularly vivid at the end of the Spanish-American War in 1898, because it had become clear, at least to some, that that " splendid little war" had truly projected America to "the cutting edge of history." The giant of the New World would use her power for her own profit and for the benefit of mankind. In a famous campaign speech, Albert J. Beveridge of Indiana (who was elected to the U.S. Senate in 1898) expressed the excitement—and something of the innocence—of Americans who saw power as a way to change the world for the better (i.e., into the image of America):

> The commercial empire of the Republic! That is the greatest fact of the future. . . . This Nation is to be the sovereign factor in the peace of the world. . . . In the light of that golden future our chain of new-won stations rise like ocean sentinels from the night of waters—Porto Rico, a nobler Gibraltar; the Isthmian canal, a greater Suez; Hawaii, the Ladrones, the Philippines, commanding the Pacific! Ah! as our commerce spreads, the flag of liberty will circle the globe and the highways . . . of all mankind be guarded by the guns of the Republic. . . . We are enlisted in the cause of American supremacy, which will never end until American commerce has made the conquest of the world; until American citizenship has become the lord of civilization; and the stars and stripes the flag of flags throughout the world.

Although somewhat more sober, there is a distinct echo of Beveridge's excitement over American power in John F. Kennedy's words to an Arizona audience in 1961:

> Other countries look to their own interests. Only the United States has obligations which stretch ten thousand miles across the Pacific, and three or four thousand miles across the Atlantic, and thousands of miles to the south. Only the United States—and we are only 6 percent of the world's population—bears this kind of burden.

On Monday, August 6, 1945, the President of the United States announced the dropping of an atomic bomb "on Hiroshima, an important Japanese army base." The atomic bomb, President Truman said, "is a harnessing of the basic power of the universe."

On the same day, a story was released describing the first atomic explosion, on July 16, 1945, at Alamogordo, New Mexico:

> Mounted on a steel tower, a revolutionary weapon destined to change war as it has been known, or which may even be the instrumentality to end all wars, was set off with an impact which signalized man's entrance into a new physical world. Success was greater than the most ambitious estimates. A small amount of matter, the product of a chain of huge specially constructed industrial plants, was made to release the energy of the universe locked up within the atom from the beginning of time.

The excitement generated among Americans at the American achievement—as most perceived it—of such incredible power still exists. The vision of unlimited power was almost immediately associated with the successful conclusion of World War II, as well as with a vision of a future in which American power would continue unlimited and successful. President Truman, in his announcement of the atomic bomb, had said that "this discovery may open the way for an entirely new concept of force and power. The actual harnessing of atomic energy may in the future supply the power that now comes from coal, oil and the great dams." The vision of American power—whether it was in the form of practical energy or "the energy of the universe"—was practically unlimited.

William L. Laurence, the official historian of the Alamogordo explosion, wrote in grandiose terms which reflected the nature of American excitement over power:

> . . . On that moment hung eternity. Time stood still. Space contracted to a pinpoint. It was as though the earth had opened and the skies split. One felt as though he had been privileged to witness the Birth of the World—to be present at the moment of Creation when the Lord said: Let there be light.

There were few Americans in 1945 who would have agreed with J. Robert Oppenheimer's quotation from Hindu mythology (Oppenheimer was the wartime director of the government's atomic laboratory): "I am become Death, the destroyer of worlds."

MISGIVINGS

Ever since the earliest of the great American corporations began to grow—even with the spread of large mills and factories and extensive railroads across the land—there have been Americans who have had misgivings about modern industrial power. The discipline of the mills and factories made machines of human beings, stripping them of their freedom and individuality. Many have fought that discipline—some with their lives. Yet the men and women who worked in great mills have also often taken great pride in the productivity—in the sheer volume of output—of *their* factory. They have been fascinated by the power, admiring it, even when it oppressed them economically, socially, personally.

Many have fought the great corporations tooth and nail. The largest-scale organized violence in American history outside of war, and the closest Americans have come to continued class conflict, has been in the great battles fought—violent, bloody battles involving thousands of Americans—between 1877 and 1941 against the great corporations. Americans have warred against the corporations from the inside—as workers, organizers, and executives—and from the outside—as lawyers, legislators, organizers, and advocates. Antitrust laws, regulatory commissions, trustbusting, union organizing, striking, and collective bargaining, consumer advocacy and lobbying, and other efforts to reduce corporate power and limit corporate growth have actively existed in America for as long as large corporations have existed. All are based on a fundamental distrust of the power of corporations. Yet the opponents of corporations often model their behavior, their organizational structure, and their efforts to possess power in opposition to the corporations on the corporate models and processes. All admire the productivity of the corporations, and few have sought to limit that productivity.

Opponents of corporations are fascinated with the corporation's power, wealth, productivity, size and scale. They want to take control of that power, while they oppose the means by which the power was acquired or generated. The "Seven Sisters," the great multinational oil companies, are widely believed to be pernicious institutions. They are at the same time secretly admired. And both attitudes are for the same reasons: because they are believed to dominate the foreign policy of the United States, to be able to control the internal affairs and economies of many nations, to produce most of the world's petroleum products; and because they are believed to be inexorable networks of resource control and productivity determining the individual and household economies of most Americans as well as the economy of the entire nation.

In the excitement created by war and by the vision of American empire and world power, few Americans saw the irony in Rudyard Kipling's new poem, first published in *McClure's* magazine in January 1899, called "The White Man's Burden":

Take up the White Man's Burden—
Send forth the best ye breed—
Go bind your sons to exile
To serve your captives' need. . . .

Take up the White Man's burden—
  The savage wars of peace—
Fill full the mouth of Famine
  And bid the sickness cease. . . .

Take up the White Man's burden—
  Have done with childish days—
The lightly proffered laurel,
  The easy, ungrudged praise.
Comes now, to search your manhood
  Through all the thankless years,
Cold, edged with dear-bought wisdom,
  The judgment of your peers!

The poem was written by an Englishman, born in India and living in Vermont. It was a warning: Americans, by 1899, could not "call too loud on Freedom" or expect "the lightly proffered laurel, / The easy, ungrudged praise" of the past. If America was to be a great power on earth, having taken up "the white man's burden," she would be searchingly and coldly judged by her peers, the other great nations, and she would be judged as well by "the silent, sullen peoples" to whom she brought the "savage wars of peace."

Kipling's was not the only warning generated by the Spanish-American War about the dangers of wartime frenzy and the hazards of imperialism. Mark Twain asked, in an article in 1901, "Shall we go on conferring our Civilization upon the peoples that sit in darkness, or shall we give those poor things a rest?" "Would it not be prudent," he asked,

> . . . to get our Civilization-tools together, and see how much stock is left on hand in the way of Glass Beads and Theology, and Maxim Guns and Hymn Books, and Trade-Gin and Torches of Progress and Enlightenment (patent adjustable ones, good to fire villages with, upon occasion), and balance the books, and arrive at the profit and loss, so that we may intelligently decide whether to continue the business or sell out the property and start a new Civilization Scheme on the proceeds?
>
> Extending the Blessings of Civilization to our Brother who Sits in Darkness has been a good trade and has paid well, on the whole. . . . The Blessings-of-Civilization Trust, wisely and cautiously administered, is a Daisy. There is more money in it, more territory, more sovereignty and other kinds of emolument, than there is in any other game that is played.

Mark Twain said, however, that the people "who Sit in Darkness" had "begun to show alarm. They have become suspicious of the Blessings of Civilization." They had begun to examine those blessings:

> The Blessings of Civilization are all right, and a good commercial property; there could not be a better, in a dim light. In the right kind of a light, and at a proper distance, with the goods a little out of focus, they furnish this desirable exhibit to the Gentlemen who Sit in Darkness:
>
> LOVE, / LAW AND ORDER,
> JUSTICE, / LIBERTY,
> GENTLENESS, / EQUALITY,
> CHRISTIANITY, / HONORABLE DEALING,
> PROTECTION TO THE WEAK, / MERCY,
> TEMPERANCE, / EDUCATION,
>
> —and so on.
>
> There. Is it good? Sir, it is pie. It will bring into camp any idiot that sits in darkness anywhere.

But, he warned,

> Privately and confidentially, it is merely an outside cover, gay and pretty and attractive, displaying the special patterns of our Civilization which we reserve for Home Consumption, while *inside* the bale is the Actual Thing that the Customer Sitting in Darkness buys with his blood and tears and land and liberty. That Actual Thing is, indeed, Civilization, but it is only for Export.

Mark Twain's misgivings and Kipling's irony went almost unnoticed at the turn of the century. The excitements of war and empire and power were too great for many Americans to resist. Yet there were questions and doubts about wars, empire, power, and great corporations. Kipling's poem was accepted by most as a paean to empire—but the ironic phrase reminding all of the "savage wars of peace" was repeated every time the poem was read or recited. The questions and the doubts remained alive in all the myths of power. No one, years later, who had seen or read about an atomic explosion was unaware of "Death, the destroyer of worlds," even those who exulted in the great power of the Bomb.

Was all the power generated in modern American society—industrial power, scientific power, war power, governmental power—conducive to the ultimate freedom, independence, and happiness of the individual? Equality of free, independent individual human beings was the goal of society, the purpose of government, the reason for all forms of power: such was the basis of the logic of American myths. Power *had,* by the imperatives of fundamental American myths, to be reconciled with individual freedom, human equality, and the pursuit of individual happiness. For many Americans in the course of the twentieth century, it was reconciled. But there were contradictions, there were misgivings.

POWER FAILURES

On November 9, 1965, just after dark, the electrical power supply for most of the northeastern United States failed. Went out. The nation's largest city, New York, was blacked-out, along with its entire metropolitan area, as were the heavily populated states of Connecticut, Rhode Island, and Massachusetts, including the entire Boston metropolitan area.

The stories of individual struggles to survive in the dark are countless—in stalled elevators, on long flights of stairs, in subway tunnels, on bridges, in automobiles with no traffic or streetlights, in unheated, unlighted homes from which one could not depart or to which one could not go without unaccustomed, strenuous physical work. Michael Dukakis, the young politician who would ten years later be Governor of Massachusetts, ran miles across Boston that night to drive his pregnant wife to the hospital to have her baby. There are many stories of community service—people directing traffic, guiding stranded people from dangerous places, giving first aid, comforting the immobilized, arranging food and shelter and heat for those desperately in need. Stories of violence and looting. Stories of the frantic efforts of power companies to restore service. Stories of the sudden jump in birth rate nine months later—"they were at home in the dark with nothing else to do."

Unquestioned belief that unlimited use of electrical power was the right of all Americans and that electrical power somehow made individual Americans free and independent ended that night. The total dependence of modern, urban Americans on complicated, corporate-produced, government-regulated networks of power production and transmission over which the individual had no control and which most individuals did not understand became very clear to millions. Power did not, it seemed, make Americans free—it made them prisoners of machines, of grids, of corporations, of experts, and of governments, all of whom seemed unable to guarantee the service, the ease, the very energy which Americans had come to believe *power* implied. Power made Americans *dependent.* The "lessons," the loss of faith, were not immediately obvious to all, but they began with the Blackout—and became part of the myths of power now available to Americans: Americans were no longer independent nor did they have unlimited freedom to pursue happiness.

The 1973 oil embargo by the Organization of Petroleum Exporting Countries (OPEC), and the fluctuations in the availability of crude oil and the ever-rising prices that have followed, taught the same lesson. Gasoline—petroleum—was another form of *power,* which propelled automobiles, trucks, and airplanes, drove machines and heated homes, and—Americans fondly believed—had made each of us more free, more independent, more capable of achieving happiness and prosperity. But no longer. Oil made us dependent, not independent; put us at the mercy of Arabs, Muslims, Venezuelans, Nigerians, and other unpredictable, uncontrollable foreigners.

The automobile is the primary symbol of freedom and mobility. Electricity is the primary symbol of power. The American way to bring the power of the whole society to bear on an incorrigibly antisocial person, for example, is to use an electric chair (viewed by the rest of the world as the typically American method of execution). At the same time, electrical power, controlled by the individual at a flick of the switch, does work and provides entertainment, comfort, service to individual Americans on a scale and with an unobtrusive efficacy which makes Americans more comfortable, more affluent, generally better off than any other people on earth. Power plants provide vast quantities of electricity, power lines transmit it all over the country, power grids and networks distribute it to everyone—and *power* thus becomes, every day, an imperative, working, real part of the lives of modern Americans.

The "accident" at the Three Mile Island nuclear power plant in 1979, which allowed the escape of radioactive steam, has added to the haunting fear of power failure. The power which is knowledge, expertise, and what Americans admiringly call "high technology" can fail; that is a lesson of the Blackout and of Three Mile Island. The power which is America's bigness, her wealth, her "muscle," can also fail; that is a lesson of OPEC—and Vietnam.

Most Americans in the course of the twentieth century have come to believe that social, political, and economic problems can be solved by the application of sufficient power. Recent failures of power have introduced, as Judith Coburn wrote in a November 19, 1979, article in *New West* magazine, the possibility of "a law of uncertainty of life in a high technological society." Coburn arrived at such a conclusion because of problems related to the building of a nuclear power plant called Rancho Seco:

> It began with a question about a decimal point. . . . A decimal point clearly in the wrong place. A dumb little goof in arithmetic. The kind anybody could make in a checkbook. But to an engineer, "an order of magnitude," one that could throw off a whole set of calculations by a factor of 10. And this was not a checkbook, but a nuclear power plant.

After detailing the efforts of many scientists, engineers, and government officials to determine the effects of the misplaced decimal point, Coburn concluded with a question: Was it possible for an expert to be right—in this case, right about a serious danger—*and* "for no one to be able to prove it?" The question, the article, and the widespread interest in such problems imply that knowledge, expertise, and technology are uncertain, their very effectiveness incapable of proof—and therefore doubtful. If expert knowledge is questionable—as it has become for some Americans—then the logic of the modern American mythology of power leads to serious questions about the effectiveness of any kind of power.

The mythology of power makes connections among all the various ways in which the word "power" is used by Americans, and among all the images the word conjures up in American minds. "Power failure" is a blackout or a brownout, it is a failure in expertise, it is Three Mile Island; it is also Watergate. On a much larger scale, it is what Americans now call simply "Vietnam." It is the inability of a large and complex corporate-military-governmental power elite, backed by all the wealth and might of a modern superpower, the United States of America, to free fifty Americans from a building in Teheran.

"The genie we have raised to rule the earth," the vast industrial might of America and Americans that Stephen Vincent Benét sang of at the end of his epic *John Brown's Body,* the power of America, has in the logic of American belief twice saved democracy and the world from the evil perpetrators of world war. It has fought the "savage wars of peace" in order to rescue the innocent and bring civilization to "those who sit in darkness." It has also created a nation of unprecedented wealth, prosperity, and productivity, the major material benefits of which are available to all who are American. And yet American power has failed: failed to provide for the continuing independence and happiness of individuals, failed to realize the extent to which power limits freedom, and has therefore destroyed freedom while trying to create or enhance it; it has failed to bring the democratic, egalitarian, independent individual control—over environment, over nature, over fate, over circumstances—which it seemed to promise. The glory of American power has, in the imperatives of the myths Americans believe most strongly, carried from its inception the seeds of its own demise.

Are Americans now, like Aladdin, trying to entice the genie back into its lamp?

2

Science and Progress

SCIENCE, BASED ON the metaphor of evolution, tied to all the imagery and promise of progress, became by the beginning of the twentieth century a new American myth (shared with others in the Western world, to be sure, but here applied to American circumstances). Science was as sweeping and encompassing a mythology as Christianity had been for earlier generations. It was as universal, as evangelical, as full of the promise of ultimate truth, of absolute answers to ultimate questions. Science, as early Christianity had, swept across the whole of the Western world. And it was even reconcilable in American practice to the older mythology of religion. It rapidly developed its "ministers"—in all the scientists; its "churches"—in laboratories, hospitals, experiment stations, and universities; its evangelists, its popularizers, its sects, doctrines, dogmas, laws, and even heresies. It had its theoreticians and pure scientists, who were its monks and nuns and theologians, removed from the everyday world and devoted to the contemplation of the ultimate. It had its "secular clergy," which taught, developed technologies, invented apparatus and applications to practical and technical problems. It was not a church, but its museums, planetariums, and exhibitions provided places of ritual, reinforcement, contemplation, and exegesis of its tenets, accomplishments, and promises to a lay public.

SCIENCE AS LAW

The complex body of mythology which Americans—and many others in the world—call "science" is a modern variant of a much older myth of Western rationalism, the myth of finding law. Modern science began its evolution approximately contemporaneously with the European discovery, invasion, and settlement of the New World, and it has, therefore, been a part of American mythology from the very beginning. With science, new Western myths of time as a progression grew; new myths of "evidence" (or "data") as the objects and relationships of objects in the physical universe, as well as new myths of knowledge as the description, cataloguing, accumulation, and arrangement of observations and experiments, gradually developed. The process of growth was slow, and it took place in the midst of debates and battles among scholars, clerics, philosophers, and other educated people.

While science was always a part of American belief, in the latter part of the nineteenth century it merged with the American belief in progress. The combined myths of progress and science began to dominate the ways in which Americans saw themselves and their world. The two mythologies became one. And the occasion for their coming together was the impact, in America, of the work of an Englishman, Charles Darwin.

One of the most powerful, far-reaching, and long-lasting myths in all of Western culture is the myth of finding law. It is so powerful and deep-seated that all who participate in Western rationalism, certainly all Americans, believe that it is not myth at all but reality. The end and goal of all human reason, according to that myth, the basis of all rational thought and of all logic, is the discovery of law—not its creation, or development, but its discovery. Laws, like the Western Hemisphere before Columbus, exist. They operate, whether human beings know them or not. They are the basis of all that transpires in the universe.

These laws are not always self-evident, but they are truths. They are not, in American belief, merely passive statistical regularities, but are dominated by the analogy and the imagery of civil and criminal law: they control and regulate and even punish. They make certain things "necessary." Human beings can find those laws—as Columbus discovered America—by the use of reason, the collection of evidence, and by action based on reason and the evidence ("experimental" action). By thought, reason, and communication, human beings can make laws explicable to themselves, once they are discovered. Furthermore, laws are useful because life can be adjusted more closely to their operation once they have been found.

The processes by which laws have been found, explained, and made useful to human beings have varied (Americans would now say they have evolved, because evolution is one of the laws) since the ancient Greeks first made the myth explicit. In different times and places, "all sane men agree," the "Ideal," "God has revealed," "it is customary," "reason demonstrates," "the evidence proves," and "science has shown" have described the process of finding law. But the underlying myth, that there is law to be found in the universe which requires explication and which requires human obedience, is fundamental in Western culture.

The myth retains its power today. The tensions generated by regulating law versus primordial chaos, of logical regularities versus irrational behavior, or astrological explanations versus astrophysical evidence, still exist and are continuing causes of argument, debate, and tension in America, as in the West generally. Scientific law still finds itself in conflict with divine law. Evidence and revelation are perceived to be contradictory. Higher law and national laws are in frequent conflict. Reason and logic often contradict "the evidence of one's eyes." And $E = mc^2$ is still as much an article of faith as the postulates of medieval scholastics. Underlying all the debate and controversy is the firm conviction that the true laws exist and need only the proper techniques, the right evidence, the best logic, in order to be discovered. And as much as medieval peasants and knights believed themselves utterly subject to the laws of God, so Americans believe themselves subject to the laws of science.

The mythology of science grew after the Renaissance (itself a symbol and a slogan in that mythology). Science was the province, primarily, of philosophers, and it was devoted to the study of the physical universe. By the eighteenth century, however, the Enlightenment had added man and his part in the physical universe to scientific study. Man was also an object in the universe, and therefore classifiable and knowable.

At the beginning of the nineteenth century, there was little differentiation among the branches of natural philosophy—as the study of science was then called. The distinction between science and technology was unknown. The philosopher of optics, the astronomer, the discoverer of the Law of Gravity, the lens designer and lens grinder—Isaac Newton—were all one person. So was the kite flyer, moral philosopher, printer, scientific experimenter, stove designer, and diplomat—Benjamin Franklin. As more and more of the objects in the universe were classified, and each class of objects possessed its own "building blocks of knowledge," which had to be mastered in order to be added to, differentiation among the sciences gradually became "necessary." Each branch of science began to develop its own techniques and to limit the class of objects it was interested in, as the task of accumulating all the evidence and discovering all the laws became more elaborate and monumental.

DARWIN AND SCIENCE

For Americans, the most important step in the growth of the mythology of science, and in the spread of the imagery of science, was the publication, by an English naturalist, of an "abstract," as he called it, of work he had done over twenty-two years. Charles Darwin published *Origin of Species* in 1859, and announced to the world, as Americans popularly perceived it, that he had discovered the laws of evolution and of natural selection. The "elaborately constructed forms" of plant and animal species, Darwin wrote in his conclusion:

> . . . so different from each other, and dependent upon each other in so complex a manner, have all been produced by laws acting around us. These laws

> . . . being Growth with Reproduction; Inheritance . . . ; Variability . . . and as a consequence . . . Natural Selection. . . . Thus, from the war of nature, from famine and death, the most exalted object which we are capable of conceiving, namely, the production of the higher animals, directly follows. There is grandeur in this view of life . . . having been originally breathed by the Creator into a few forms or into one; and that, whilst this planet has gone cycling on according to the fixed law of gravity, from so simple a beginning endless forms most beautiful and most wonderful have been, and are being, evolved.

Darwin's work accomplished two things: it gave cogent, solid argument, along with carefully assembled evidence, for the idea of natural evolution; and it postulated natural selection as the prime mechanism by which evolution took place.

The book was not concerned with the problem of the ultimate origins of life—"having been originally breathed by the Creator into a few forms or into one"—but rather with the "transformations in process" in all life forms. That was a specific problem, about which many scientists had written, observed, and experimented for nearly a century before Darwin wrote. Darwin's book was a culmination of all that work. It demonstrated, relatively conclusively for scientists at least, that the transmutation of species had actually occurred. In demonstrating the truth of the theory of evolution—which had long been a subject of scientific discussion—Darwin compiled and synthesized scientific evidence, carefully assembled from geological data and from the studies of plants and animals which were already available, or which were being made by his contemporaries. He put that evidence into conclusive form, and drew upon his own observations—particularly from his voyage on the *Beagle,* starting in 1831. Darwin's genius undoubtedly gave him insight into the matter, but his work on evolution was not simply inspiration. It involved the combination of long traditions, years of his own research, quantities of material not original to him, ideas which were part of the tradition in which he was working, as well as his own ability to create a cogent synthesis. He was the brilliant "singer" of evolution—as Homer was the singer of Troy. He "discovered" the Law of Evolution, as most Americans saw it.

It was in Darwin's speculations on the mechanisms of evolution that he was theoretical, making hypotheses and some not-so-inspired guesses on the causes of the evolutionary process. He postulated "variability from the indirect and direct action of the conditions of life" (acquired characteristics from the action of the environment) and natural selection over long periods of time as the causes of the evolution of species. His theories were based on his own speculations and on a reading of Malthus's *An Essay on the Principle of Population.* He knew nothing of genetics—Gregor Mendel's pioneering work in that field would not be known to scientists before the end of the nineteenth century. Darwin based the theory of natural selection on the somatic differences between individuals in a species, and on the idea that the environment had something to do with the causes of those differences and with the preservation of the more favorable ones.

Darwin's theory of natural selection became a matter for much skepticism and heated debate among scientists and others for more than a half century. In the end, the mechanisms Darwin postulated for natural selection—the struggle for existence, the law of the jungle, and the survival of the fittest—proved scientifically insignificant. Organisms which reproduce more participate more in genetic transmission. As the economist Thorstein Veblen pointed out early in the twentieth century, it is more important to produce children and food, for evolution, than it is to emerge victorious from combat. The general idea of natural selection—that certain characteristics (wherever they came from) were favored or discouraged by environments, and that the possessors of favored characteristics produced more children and got more food—would be accepted by scientists, as was the law of evolution itself. But the *process* of selection which Darwin postulated was ultimately rejected.

The impact of Darwin's ideas in America was diverse. "A spirited conflict among opinions of every grade must ensue," Asa Gray, an eminent Harvard College naturalist, wrote in the first American review of *Origin of Species:*

> . . . which . . . may be likened to the conflict in nature among races in the struggle for life, which Mr. Darwin describes; through which the views most favored by the facts will be developed and tested by "Natural Selection," the weaker ones be destroyed in the process, and the strongest in the long run alone survive.

The idea of evolution came to be accepted among scientists and others. Evolution has become a working law of science. Natural selection, on the other hand, was rejected as scientific law. But the imagery of the law of the jungle has continued to be seductive. The logic of natural selection did and does appeal to the view scientists have of their own behavior—as Gray's use of it in his review shows. It also appeals to the American idea of practicality and to the ideal of progress. It has continued to be part of the generally accepted mythology of science, therefore, despite its rejection as a working idea for scientists.

MYTHOLOGIES IN CONFLICT

It was the application of the law of evolution, and the theories of natural selection and its mechanisms, to human beings and human society which made Darwin's ideas so exciting to Americans, so popular, and so controversial. The implications of evolution and the natural-selection process for human origins, human development, and the history of social and individual life were profound. Controversy over some of those implications had been raging, among intellectuals and the educated, since the Enlightenment, but it was Darwin's work which made the debates popular and which gave urgency to finding resolutions to the controversies.

The idea of evolution, which Darwin had discovered to be a law, flatly contradicted the Biblical story of creation. "Any fool," as Americans commonly said, "could see that." For nearly two millennia (longer for Jews), the book of Genesis had provided the answer to the fundamental human question of where did human beings come from? The Bible also provided the basis for answers to the questions of where was man going? what was his ultimate end?

Darwin's work, couched in the logic of science, a logic which, in bits and pieces, nineteenth-century Americans had found workable and acceptable, challenged (to put it mildly) the old answers, the old laws, the old logic. *Origin of Species* and *The Descent of Man* (1871) provided new, seemingly scientific answers to basic questions. The answers contradicted the Bible. Was it possible to accept Darwin and still believe in the Bible, in Christianity, in religion? Was it possible to continue to believe in those things which Americans considered fundamental to civilization and humanity and yet believe Darwin?

The controversy between religion and science which Darwinism generated seems unreal to most Americans today. The conflict between Galileo and the Church was viewed, no doubt, in much the same way by the generation or two who lived after Galileo recanted. Galileo, in that case, had been "proved" to be just another "science nut," in much the same way most Americans today think someone who disputes the reality of evolution is just another "religious nut"—someone to be ignored as manifestly wrong. And most Americans believe that Galileo was objectively right and religious fundamentalists are wrong; that there can be no significant conflict between systems of belief when one is the truth and the other mere belief.

The "truth" and the "real" answers to the problems posed by the conflict between science and religion were not so clear to Americans at the end of the nineteenth century. For most of them, reality was that God had created man in His own image, placed him in the Garden of Eden, and ejected him because Adam had eaten the forbidden fruit of the tree of the Knowledge of Good and Evil. Many Americans had reconciled Locke's and Rousseau's ideas of man in a "state of nature" with man in the Garden of Eden and believed that primitive men—like the Indians—represented man in that state of nature after ejection from the Garden. The Garden of Eden was as real to most as Olduvai Gorge is to modern paleontologists. The creation was a real process, in real time, in a real past—as evolution over eons of geological time is to us today. The "creation myth" (we call it "myth" now, because we "know" it to be allegorical or unreal) was reality for most Americans, and all the available evidence proved it. Darwin, and science with him, posed a challenge to accepted reality. It was only slowly that Americans were willing to become the descendants of apes. It was not an easy matter to give up the grandeur, even the fallen grandeur, of the Image of God in favor of some chattering anthropoid merrily swinging through the treetops.

Darwin's scientific laws did not challenge the general attitude toward the place of formal religion in American life. By the latter part of the nineteenth century, most Americans had accepted the complete separation of religion from the secular, practical affairs of everyday life—religion was for church, on Sunday. Science applied to practical affairs, to the real world, in a way many Americans felt religion did not. Darwin, science, and scientific method appealed to many who saw in science the philosophic (almost the religious) expression of American practicality and adaptability to the real world.

But Darwinism, and scientific law and method, did challenge the basis of the Christianity which was still generally and widely accepted as the fundamental explanation of the universe and of the quality of American life. That Christianity required a certain deism of all Americans, references to God in public speeches and on formal, specifically American occasions. It also explained America's mission, American progress, and the secular evangelism which most Americans believed to be part of their national Christianity.

In the American world which had come to expect the separation of religion from everyday life, the religious response to the challenge of evolution and science had to come from the religious vested interests: the churches (as institutions), the clergy, and the theological schools. These were, as Americans believed, the rightful defenders of Christianity and the creation myth. And Charles Hodge, of the Princeton Theological Seminary, in 1874 disposed of the question What is Darwinism? with a simple, straightforward rejection: "It is atheism." The religious leaders who continued to reject Darwin's ideas, arguments, and evidence created the basis for twentieth-century American fundamentalism.

The fundamentalist path was not, however, the one most religious leaders, or most Americans, took. It involved too sweeping a rejection of the natural, secular world and its natural separation from religion. Most theologians reconciled religion and science, the Bible and Darwin, by separating them—as most Americans willingly separated them in their lives. Professor James Woodrow (President Woodrow Wilson's uncle) was dismissed by the Presbyterian Seminary of Columbia, South Carolina, in 1884 for his effort to reconcile Darwin and the Bible. His reasoning was ultimately accepted; he was vindicated by his church, became president of the University of South Carolina, and head of the South Carolina synod.

Woodrow reconciled science and religion by clearly separating them. He quoted Calvin: "Moses does not speak with philosophical acuteness on occult mysteries. . . . He who would learn astronomy, and other recondite arts, let him go elsewhere." The Bible, Woodrow said, "does not teach science; and to take its language in a scientific sense is grossly to pervert its meaning." The words of the Bible were to be taken allegorically, when compared to the facts of science:

> I have found nothing in my study of the Holy Bible and of natural science that shakes my firm belief in the divine inspiration of every word of that Bible, and in the consequent absolute truth . . . of every expression which it contains. . . . This is a very different thing from saying that I have found everything in the Sacred Scriptures to be in harmony with natural science. . . . But to show . . . there is no contradiction, all that is needed is to show that a reasonable supposition of what the passage in question may mean does not contradict the proved truth in science.

To reconcile the "absolute truth" of the Bible to the "proved truth" of science required, then, a correct interpretation of the Bible.

If the details of the creation story were a spiritual parable, then the story remained true and at the same time did not contradict the physical facts of evolution. God as First Cause and Creator remained a matter of firm faith; science could not prove otherwise. "The contents and aims of the Scriptures and of natural science are so different that it is unreasonable to look for agreement or harmony," Woodrow wrote. The two were completely separable, and it was obvious that "terms are not and ought not to be used in the Bible in a scientific sense." Once the spiritual and the natural were held completely separate, then "all alleged contradictions of natural science by the Bible disappear."

Once theologians found it acceptable to separate religion and science, and to reinterpret the Bible as a spiritual document quite reconcilable with the natural truths of science, then it was possible to accept both science and Darwin without qualms. "Evolution . . . is found to be a strong and useful ally of Catholic Dogma," J. A. Zahm, a Catholic theologian, wrote in 1896. "For if Evolution be true, the existence of God and an original creation follow as necessary inferences."

If science, on its own terms, as Darwin himself had argued in the conclusions to his books, was both separable from, and compatible with, religion and the churches—by the arguments of ministers and churchmen—then science was acceptable to the great majority of Americans, who found little difficulty in practice separating their religious concerns from their everyday lives. For many, indeed, the disputes between science and religion had been "a long struggle between scientific truth and theological error." "The age of speculation has gone by," Lester Ward wrote in 1913, and "the age of investigation has begun." Many Americans were willing to welcome an age of science:

> Its aims are all utilitarian, and its principles humanitarian. It is neither dogmatic nor visionary, but liberal and exact. Taking nature as its only source of information, and the phenomena of the universe as the materials for its deductions, it seeks in the observations of their uniformities in the present, to trace all things back to their true origin in the past, and calculate their true destiny in the future.

The promise of the myth of science underlay the growth and spread of progressivism. That promise is that science would bring ultimate truth into everyday, secular, natural life—a promise religion had fulfilled in the dark past, but did no longer, for many Americans. Science would be "liberal and exact," humanitarian as well as utilitarian. It would and could, using only present, visible, palpable materials and observations, be able to describe the present, and tell the truth about both past and future, *and* solve our problems.

The logic of Darwinism was that it confirmed the separate and distinct place of religion in life, and reserved to it spiritual things, at a time when Americans were primarily concerned with problems they saw as physical, secular, economic, political, and scientific. Its relationship to religion, and the way it fit into American beliefs about the separation of religion from the rest of life, was not, however, the only, or indeed the strongest, appeal which science and evolution made.

EVOLUTION IS PROGRESS

For Americans, evolution provided scientific proof, taken from the evidence of the physical universe, of the purpose, mission, and meaning of America. Evolution was proof of progress—unceasing, inevitable progress. And America was and is, as all Americans believe, the living, national embodiment of progress.

The law of evolution, as Darwin stated it in *Origin of Species* and *The Descent of Man,* proved that all of life had been evolving over unnumbered eons of time into higher, more complex, and better forms. Human beings were the highest, most complex, and best forms—as well as the latest—which had evolved. They were the products of progress.

Species themselves evolved in this same progressive fashion. The human species, *Homo sapiens,* had, since it had become human, also been making progress. There was no distinction, for Americans or for Darwin, between the purely biological evolution of species, and what we, today, would call the social, political, and economic development of particular nations. Darwin's description of biological evolution was not understood merely as an *analogy* to be applied to the histories of races or nations. His description of evolution was, certainly for nineteenth- and most twentieth-century Americans, the straightforward, scientific description of the actual way in which races, peoples, and nations evolved.

When Darwin wrote *Origin of Species,* Americans already possessed a view of progress which specifically applied to American society and the American nation, and which Darwin's law of evolution validated. The American Revolution, in the traditional view of progress, had grown (evolved) out of the colonial experience of gradually increasing democracy and freedom. The Revolution had created a new nation—therefore more complex, higher, and better than other, existing nations. That nation was the culmination of human experience up to that point—the "last, best hope of the world."

The new nation had a destiny, a manifest mission in the human world: to bring the benefits of its higher evolution to the rest of humanity. America's mission to carry to the world the benefits of her superior beliefs and institutions—democracy, equality, individualism, capitalism, and classlessness—was, after Darwin, not merely a spiritual duty laid upon her by God, the Founding Fathers, and her own desire to serve mankind, but a duty laid upon her by the very nature of the physical universe.

As it was inevitable that America would make continual progress, so it was inevitable that America would "light the way." Others might, and did, make similar claims—certainly the British and the Germans in the Western world were loud in their assertions of evolutionary superiority—but it was clear to Americans that America was the apex and the epitome of human progress. In the twentieth century, after *their* revolution, the Russians would claim to be at the forefront of human progress—and their assertions, which had wide appeal, although based on different assumptions about social development, were particularly threatening to the assumptions of American superiority and progress. American reaction to all such rival claims was strong and intolerant. *America* was the most highly evolved of all nations, and her people the highest, and best, of all peoples. That was the predominant and insistent belief. Darwin had proved scientifically what Americans had long believed, that America was the cutting edge of the evolutionary process, the most progressive representative of all humanity. Progress, the American destiny, and science became mutually interacting, mutually dependent processes as the new mythology of Darwinism, evolution, and science spread in American life.

SCIENTIFIC PROGRESS

The social Darwinists first spread the mythology of science in America. They were particularly attracted to Darwin's idea of natural selection, and in the course of their popularizing science, they made the law of the jungle, the survival of the fittest, and inevitable progress part of the images and myths available to all Americans.

Social Darwinism made individualism a scientific precept. It transformed it into economic individualism, and made it not simply a right, nor yet merely a duty: with social Darwinism, individualism became an expression of the racial character of Americans, a natural law. Individualism, by itself, with no mitigating or controlling social service, became the highest duty and service an American could perform for his race, nation, and species. It was inevitable, according to the social Darwinists, that each individual would struggle to survive, and the survivors, by definition, were those who best served society and human progress. Science proved that rugged individualism was the only hope of American society.

Success—survival—was the measure of fitness. Success had long been, for Americans, a moral goal. The Puritans had brought with them, later Americans believed, the idea that success was a sign of God's Grace, a sign that the successful individual was one of the elect. That aura continues to cling to the vision of success. For the social Darwinists, success was a sign that the racial and moral character of the individual was of the highest. If successful Americans could no longer claim to be among God's elect, they could still claim to be among nature's select. It was the individual who triumphed over competition, who succeeded by hard work, careful self-training, an eye to the main chance, the luck to be in the right place at the right time, and who had the versatility to grasp opportunity. The jack-of-all-trades, sturdy, independent, free American could not have been improved upon, in the imagination of most Americans, as a fit survivor. Horatio Alger's heroes were such survivors, and there have been few American heroes or heroines since Alger whose success was not a result of natural selection.

One who did not survive was deficient, according to the social Darwinists, a racial and moral failure. "A drunkard in the gutter is just where he ought to be," American sociologist William Graham Sumner wrote. "Nature is working away at him to get him out of the way, just as she sets up her processes of dissolution to remove whatever is a failure in its line."

There was nothing in nature which required failure, so far as the social Darwinists were concerned. There was no original sin. All men and all societies were perfectible, given the inexorable progress of nature. It was a matter for each individual. "Let every man be sober, industrious, prudent, and wise," Sumner wrote, "and bring up his children to be so likewise, and poverty will be abolished in a few generations." Those who were not so wise would not survive.

Nature was, for the social Darwinist, both a juggernaut and a fixed, absolute environment. Nature could destroy; she *would* prevail. The humans who best adapted to the natural environment, who tampered least with nature's course, would survive and progress. All others would fail. The absolute natural environment presented standards—laws—by which all human activity, behavior, and character were measured and governed. Science was simply the process by which human beings found—discovered—the laws which governed their absolute, natural environment. Once the laws were discovered, then nature could become useful to the Americans—and American destiny could properly be fulfilled.

Science, as the social Darwinists argued and most Americans came to agree, investigates the inevitable forces in the world—including the inevitable forces which operate in human societies. It has practical utility, because "the rules of right social living" can be derived from the laws it discovers. And like all universal myths, science can tolerate no contradiction. It alone describes reality. That which contradicts science is by definition unreal. It is arbitrary, or, worse, poetic: the result of invention, imagination, authority, or tradition.

In 1895, a philosophy professor at Harvard attacked, quite unsuccessfully (if success is measured by acceptance in the society), the reality of science. Josiah Royce argued that the laws of science were myths, that they were no more objective than any other human interpretations of the universe. He argued that all science did was to describe facts. Scientific laws were no more than descriptions. They were in no sense necessary; they were not laws. Nature, he said, *"in order to be describable"* had to be viewed as subject to, determined by, or necessitated by laws. Science was based on tautology.

Royce also pointed out that the assumption of objective universality in the laws of science was defended, in the logic of the mythology of science, by the postulate that only those things which were describable were objective. "The endless indescribabilities of our existence" were viewed by scientists, he said, as "merely 'individual' or 'internal.' " They were subjective, and limited by the individual point of view. Science rejected that which it could not describe, and by describing, make laws for.

Science, Royce pointed out, "is an essentially social affair." It was the "subjective and human need for such laws" as science made, not any objective reality, which made science so important in modern life. The universal laws, upon which all the assumptions of science were based, were human myths, Royce argued. They were created, not by cosmic necessity, but by the human need for certainty and the human desire for explanations. They were, like the Common Law described by Oliver Wendell Holmes, Jr., the product of "the felt necessities of the time"; descriptive of human realities, not of some separate, universal, physical, and objective reality.

Royce was arguing that science is myth—an argument no American wanted to hear.

PROGRESSIVE SCIENCE

For most Americans, any attack on the validity of the laws of science is still an attack on reality itself. But there was no need to challenge science in order to do battle with social Darwinism. The social Darwinists and their central beliefs were attacked in the twentieth century by men like Charles Pierce, William James, and John Dewey, who called themselves "pragmatists" (the very label appealed to progressive, practical Americans).

The pragmatists, who provided a philosophical base for progressivism, accepted the mythologies of Darwin, of evolution, of science, and even some of the logic of natural selection. They rejected out of hand, however, the social Darwinist ideal of the law of the jungle by reviving the traditional American ideals of "civilizing the wilderness" and of the adaptability of the individual. Nature ("the jungle"), they argued, was no immutable juggernaut: the environment was not absolute. Environments changed and so did people. Change, the pragmatists argued, was the only absolute in human affairs. And the truth, according to William James in *Pragmatism,* was "whatever proves itself to be good in the way of belief, and good, too, for definite, assignable reasons."

Natural selection, the pragmatists argued, required that human beings use their knowledge of science and evolution to their own purposes. In order to survive, human beings must decide what goals and norms they want, on the basis of what seems most useful. Then, using science and scientific knowledge, they must develop institutions capable of guiding change in useful directions. "Darwinian logic," John Dewey wrote, shifted human interest:

> . . . from an ultimate goal of good to the direct increments of justice and happiness that intelligent administration of existent conditions may beget and that present carelessness or stupidity will destroy or forego.

The pragmatists integrated Darwinism, scientific thought, and scientific method into the structure of twentieth-century progressive myths. American practicality, which emphasized adaptation to circumstances, available materials, and opportunities, and which aimed at the achievement of immediate goals without much regard for long-term effects or abstract ideals was made formal philosophy and given formal logic and scientific method. If it seems good and it works, do it—became the pragmatist imperative underlying progressivism.

The scientific study of living human beings and of existing societies—what came to be known as "social science"—was for the pragmatists essential to "moral and political diagnosis and prognosis." Knowledge was generally useful, they believed, insofar as it could be a "lever for moving the present into a certain kind of future." The natural sciences were useful because their findings and theories could be applied to society, and used as a lever for the future through technology. The pragmatists formally tied science to technology and revived the American belief in the usefulness of science which had been encouraged by Benjamin Franklin and Thomas Jefferson. The mythology of science has grown so strong in this century that Americans expect scientific answers to all questions, scientific solutions to all problems: "This book is written," Carl Sagan wrote in the introduction to *Broca's Brain* (1979),

> . . . just before—at most, I believe, a few years or a few decades before—the answers to many of those vexing and awesome questions on origins and fates are pried loose from the cosmos. If we do not destroy ourselves, most of us will be around for the answers. . . . By far the most exciting, satisfying and exhilarating time to be alive is the time in which we pass from ignorance to knowledge on these fundamental issues; the age where we begin in wonder and end in understanding.

The social sciences were for the pragmatists, and have become for most Americans, among the more important sciences. Through those sciences—sociology, economics, anthropology, psychology, and political science—human institutions could be studied, quantified, changed, and even created in order to assure progress into a specific, determinable future. The careful organization of human affairs, the creation of efficiency in behavior and institutions, the proper use of power—all based on the findings, the data, and the techniques of these sciences—should bring, in progressive belief, ever more beneficial progress to humanity. Such sciences have finally freed humanity, as the pragmatists and most progressive Americans believe, from the irrelevancies of the past and of non-scientific thought: people need no longer be burdened with the weight of moral or material absolutes. The use throughout American society of social scientific data, laws, and findings—from opinion polls to economic models to military scenarios—is a measure of the widespread success of pragmatist ideas in a society in which we are all progressives. Belief in the truth and efficacy of science has become part of our reality.

The pragmatists could not have predicted the effect of their synthesis of Darwin, science, and progressive belief. Few people consciously give up or change the realities by which they live, and few Americans perceived that the effect of Darwin's work would be to change American realities. "Myth grows," Claude Lévi-Strauss wrote in *Structural Anthropology,* "until the intellectual impulse which has produced it is exhausted." Many years earlier, John Dewey summed up the effect of Darwinism in America in much the same terms:

> Old ideas give way slowly; for they are more than abstract logical forms and categories. They are habits, predispositions, deeply engrained attitudes of aversion and preference.... Intellectual progress usually occurs through sheer abandonment of questions ... an abandonment that results from their decreasing vitality and a change of urgent interest. We do not solve them: we get over them. Old questions are solved by disappearing, evaporating, while new questions corresponding to the changed attitude of endeavor and preference take their place. Doubtless the greatest dissolvent in contemporary thought of old questions, the greatest precipitant of new methods, new intentions, new problems, is the one effected by the scientific revolution that found its climax in the *Origin of Species.*

Out of the new questions Darwinists, social Darwinists, pragmatists, and progressives asked in twentieth-century America have come, among other things, the atomic bomb and the elimination of polio from American life. The sciences have been supremely useful to Americans. They have produced "miracle" drugs and the Pill. The social sciences have created Nielsen ratings and the Rand Corporation; from them came the evidence and arguments upon which the "separate is inherently unequal" decision of the Supreme Court in *Brown v. Board of Education* in 1954 was based. But also from those sciences have come the breeder reactor and the China Syndrome, behavior-mod and thought control, radioactive pollution and modern advertising techniques. And many doubts. Today, belief in science is a habit, a predisposition in American thought. Whether or how much it, too, might give way—if at all—is not clear.

3

We Are All Progressives

AT THE BEGINNING of the twentieth century, there were Americans who no longer believed that the American system gave everyone a fair chance or that everything would turn out all right. The myth of American progress was changing.

The first generation of twentieth-century Americans saw America in crisis, not from outside threats, but from internal upheaval. They witnessed and participated in widespread labor unrest, great strikes, and massive violence—the Haymarket massacre in 1886, the Homestead and Coeur d'Alene strikes in 1892, the Pullman strike in 1894, and Coxey's Army marching on Washington in the same year. They had lived through the panics and the great depression of the 1890's with its brutal violence and despairing unemployment. They had seen the passage of an antitrust law, and its ineffectuality in limiting corporate growth. They had witnessed the spectacle of J. P. Morgan & Company literally bailing out the nearly bankrupt United States Treasury. They had lived through, and some of them had fought in, John Hay's "splendid little war," the Spanish-American War of 1898, and found that a crusade *could* win an empire. They had witnessed the desperate efforts of the Populists to bring democratic and economic reform to the country. They had seen legislatures corrupted, and the United States Senate becoming "a millionaires' club." They had heard William Jennings Bryan thunder, "You shall not press down upon the brow of labor this crown of thorns. You shall not crucify mankind upon a cross of gold."

They had not seen an end of labor violence, strikes, and poverty when prosperity returned after depression. Immigrants poured into the country and lived in misery. The rich built palaces in the cities and in resorts, married into the aristocracy of Europe, collected works of art from all over the world, and made larger and larger corporations, undeterred by Theodore Roosevelt's trustbusting. Younger journalists followed Ida Tarbell into "muckraking" (Theodore Roosevelt gave it the name), and readers were horrified at the corruption and vice Lincoln Steffens revealed in *The Shame of the Cities,* appalled at the poverty and exploitation depicted in Upton Sinclair's *The Jungle* and Frank Norris's *The Octopus.*

Out of their own experiences of modern life, many of that first twentieth-century generation created what some historians like to call a *Weltanschauung,* a world view, a particular way of looking at, understanding, and explaining the world as it exists *and* as it ought to be. They created, those young Americans, the images and the stories, the metaphors and the logic of progressivism. Many of them called themselves and their fellows "progressive," or "progressives." Today, their beliefs and those which have evolved from them have been inherited by what is known (very often with a sneer) as "liberalism."

The term "progressive" was a label for a cluster of social, economic, and political attitudes based on the belief that the country was in a serious crisis. The crisis was caused by the maldistribution of America's great and increasing wealth: many had too little of the wealth they were helping to create, and a few had too much. The crisis was one of American ideals, testing whether the strong, traditional beliefs in democracy and equality could flourish amid the onslaught of industrialism. To meet the crisis, progressives believed it was necessary to reaffirm the principles and practices of democracy in modern urban, industrial America. And they believed it was essential to develop a leadership which was unselfishly devoted to "doing" for the entire country. Insurgents and progressives began to appear in local politics, in local social service, and in the professions after the depression of the 1890's. They, and their ideas, became nationally prominent and nationally focused in the years after McKinley was assassinated and young Theodore Roosevelt became President.

Each generation of progressives in the twentieth century, after the first, added its own experience of existing crisis—there were wars from the Philippine insurrection to Vietnam, depressions and recessions, strikes and riots over unions, race, rights, and the wars; there was poverty in contrast with affluence, from 1913 breadlines to 1980 welfare and unemployment lines; there was great prosperity evident in the life styles of the very rich; there was political and moral corruption wherever one looked; there were urgent efforts made to bring about political and social and economic reform—by legislators and governmental executives, by experts and professionals, by organized groups of reformers led by modern, liberal leaders; and there were constant thundered warnings from journalists, novelists, and all the tellers of tales of rapid change, uncontrollable damage, corruption, and decay. American leaders would warn of crisis in constant modern litany: from Warren Harding's "Not nostrums but normalcy" to Franklin Roosevelt's "The only thing we have to fear is fear itself," to John Kennedy's "Ask not what your country can do for you—ask what you can do for your country," to Jimmy Carter's "crisis of confidence." We have, in our common experience, all become progressives: modern American life *is* crisis.

For many progressives, and for almost all Americans looking back on the progressive era, Presidents Theodore Roosevelt (1901–9) and Woodrow Wilson (1913–21) were the focus of the growing mythology of progressivism. Theodore Roosevelt had changed the Presidency. He had, according to a history written by Woodrow Wilson (when president of Princeton University), brought to the Presidency both "certain formulated notions" and "a thoroughly aggressive disposition to urge them." Roosevelt had believed, according to Wilson's book, that there was "a large and, if properly led, dominant" group of Americans who were independent of the great wealth and the great poverty which industrialism had bred in modern America (the American middle). The President of the United States, Wilson wrote, was "the natural and responsible, because sole, representative" of that dominant American middle. It was up to the President to lead the country and the government. The advancement of the whole country could be brought about, however, only if the government was "informed and administered by experts." There needed to be a trained, expert elite—according to this progressive view—in order to provide the leadership required to bring "the correction of obvious evils" in America.

Theodore Roosevelt had "stirred the American conscience," according to Wilson. He had "impressed the American people with the necessity" for dealing with the crisis in society which was, according to Wilson, that "perhaps one tenth of the population controls nine tenths of the wealth." Americans, "with their traditions of democracy on the one hand and their traditions of individualism on the other," Wilson wrote, had been unable to correct that evil. Roosevelt had pointed out a progressive way to solve the problem: by presidential and expert leadership of the democratic middle mass. The logic of the "imperial Presidency" became, along with the belief in crisis, part of the mythology of progressivism which Roosevelt and Wilson helped to create.

THE PROMISE

Theodore Roosevelt left the Presidency in 1909 and went big-game hunting in Africa. In the course of his safari, he "whisked through dozens of books." Among them was a new one, by a young man named Herbert Croly, *The Promise of American Life.* It sold perhaps 7,500 copies, but it was read by many leading men and women. Its ideas were spread further when, in 1914, Croly joined Walter Weyl and Walter Lippmann to start *The New Republic.* Croly was its first editor.

The Promise of American Life both reflected and inspired progressivism.

"The faith of Americans in their own country is religious," Croly wrote. That faith was basic to progressivism. While progressives might distrust "much that is done in the name of our country by our fellow countrymen," Croly said, America itself, with "its democratic system, and its prosperous future," was "above suspicion." The operative elements in the progressive faith were democracy and progress.

Individual "economic independence and prosperity" had always been associated, in American experience and American belief, according to Croly, with free democratic institutions. Those institutions had guaranteed continuing abundance and prosperity. If prosperity should not be abundant or accessible, then Americans would have "grave reasons for suspecting that our institutions were not doing their duty." Democratic institutions had made America "the highest hope of an excellent worldly life that mankind has yet ventured."

Americans in the past had been too optimistic, Croly argued, and most progressives agreed. The traditional American faith that prosperity, liberty, and equality would come automatically could no longer be justified.

"One of the great laws of life is progress, and nowhere have the principles of this law been so strikingly illustrated as in the United States," President McKinley had said in 1898. "Right action follows right purpose," he said.

> . . . We may not at all times be able to divine the future; the way may not always seem clear; but if our aims are high and unselfish, somehow and in some way the right end will be reached. The genius of the nation, its freedom, its wisdom, its humanity, its courage, its justice favored by divine providence, will make it equal to every task and the master of every emergency.

Progressives saw, in the "innocence" and optimism of a man like President McKinley, a great danger to American life. There were many Americans, progressives pointed out, who no longer believed that the nation produced individual progress or that everything was working out for the best. Some, encouraged by agitators, even believed that it was the system itself which produced poverty and political and economic inequality. The progressives believed, as Croly put it, that "unless a great majority of Americans not only have, *but believe they have,* a fair chance, the better American future will be dangerously compromised."

There was, according to progressives, a crisis of confidence in American life. Some people no longer believed that America was the "last, best hope of the world," and that American institutions and practices would, automatically, bring a better life to more people. "Agitators"—and subversives—encouraged that loss of belief. Belief in America, the American way, and a better future had to be restored. And it was up to progressive leaders to restore it.

The crisis progressives believed existed, and devoted themselves to solving, was twofold. There was the real crisis caused by the maldistribution of wealth and the resulting corruption of democratic institutions and egalitarian practice. Wealth, prosperity, and the benefits of American life were no longer accessible to the majority. They had to be made accessible. That was the promise of American life the progressives undertook to fulfill. That continuing crisis would bring uncounted numbers of progressives—among them Woodrow Wilson, Herbert Hoover, Franklin Roosevelt, Dwight Eisenhower, John Kennedy, and Jimmy Carter—to positions of leadership.

And there was the crisis of belief. Progressives were willing to give up traditional optimism, because it smacked of innocence, romance, and unreality. But they wanted to restore the belief in a better American future by leading Americans to face realities and change them through progressive reform. "The old sense of a glorious national destiny," Herbert Croly wrote, was to be transformed into a "sense of serious national purpose" which would be carefully planned, skillfully organized, and achieved through the efforts of high-minded, determined leaders.

The reform of American life and institutions and beliefs became, in progressive mythology, "a cause for which the good American must fight. . . . Like all sacred causes," Croly wrote, progressive reform of America "must be propagated by the Word and by that right arm of the Word, which is the Sword." The progressives undertook to lead a militant crusade for the fulfillment of the national purpose.

The imperative to find and define a national purpose and pursue it—in place of the "optimistic" assumption of an American mission and destiny—has become part of our active progressivism. In the late 1950's, President Eisenhower established a Commission on National Goals, which published its report in 1960—*Goals for Americans.* The goals recommended were to create a stronger Presidency, develop more creativity and excellence among Americans, and renew America's moral and spiritual strength in order to pursue America's global mission. These goals bore, as John Jeffries pointed out in *American Quarterly* in 1978, "often striking" resemblances to the purposes and efforts of the later administrations of John F. Kennedy and Lyndon Johnson. ". . . The more imperial presidency, the diplomacy of confrontation and crisis, the hyperbolic rhetoric of activism and mission, the 'politics of expectation,' [and] the belief in America's rectitude, power, and global mission" which characterized the leadership of the United States in the 1960's—as it has through much of the twentieth century—is part of the myth and logic developed by progressives for modern America. We are, in our self-conscious quest for national purpose, all progressives.

PRAGMATIC CRUSADERS

Progressives at the beginning of the century were excited by the prospect of being crusaders for reform. They had been brought up on stories and visions of the glorious cause of the Civil War. "In our youth our hearts were touched with fire," Oliver Wendell Holmes, Jr., a veteran of the Civil War, said of his own generation. "To fight out a war," he said, "you must believe something and want something with all your might." But "more than that," Holmes said, "you must be willing to commit yourself to a course . . . without being able to foresee exactly where you will come out. All that is required of you is that you should go somewhither as hard as ever you can. The rest belongs to fate."

But it was not enough, for the generation of progressives, to be fatalistic. For them, the Civil War had had a purpose: to preserve the Union and to destroy slavery. Their crusade would have a purpose as well.

Herbert Croly had warned that in giving up the assumption of "an automatic fulfillment of our national destiny," progressives were abandoning "more of the traditional American point of view" than they realized. They were giving up belief in the fundamental goodness of human beings, and in the ultimate rightness of the people. Those basic democratic beliefs, in the progressive view, were produced by eighteenth-century naïveté and nineteenth-century romanticism. Progressives saw themselves as pragmatists and realists who did not believe human beings were fundamentally good, or that individuals served society by pursuing their own happiness, or that the people would achieve anything without devoted, knowledgeable leaders.

Progressives had given up belief in traditional American individualism because they believed it resulted in "a morally and socially undesirable distribution of wealth." They lost faith in the goodness of the employee who "must attract attention," just as they lost faith in the system which encouraged dominant leaders to say—and believe—"the public be damned." They believed—as many still believe—that American individualism meant corporations and vast machines, bosses and robber barons, vested interests, special interests, and, above all, self-interest. They believed it to be *economic* individualism.

Wherever they looked, progressives found evidence that no individual or group could be trusted to carry out democratic ideals. In 1913 Charles A. Beard, a leading progressive historian, published *An Economic Interpretation of the Constitution,* in which he argued—quite effectively for the first generation of progressive Americans, at least—that the Founding Fathers had written the Constitution primarily to protect their own wealth and their own speculations in government bonds and notes. The progressives were willing to agree with John D. Rockefeller that "individualism has gone, never to return," although the individualism they meant was the sort that Rockefeller himself represented.

Progressives are, even today, willing to learn from "the devil himself" if they believe the lessons taught will help them lead the nation to the proper goals. The creation of the great wealth of America, they believe, is the result of the concentration of capital and the tight control of its use; it is the result of long-term planning, expert management, studied efficiency, and organized discipline of large numbers of people; it is the result of constant projection into larger and larger spheres of operation, and of dedicated and determined leadership.

If these methods create wealth, then surely similar methods are necessary to distribute that wealth equitably. The progressives could assure continued progress, along with continued democracy, by organizing, concentrating their forces, disciplining their followers, and providing expert, efficient management through their own dedicated and determined leadership. In the name of all the people, they would take control—of governments, eventually of corporations, and make them the instruments of progress.

The perceived threat of class warfare, of riots in the streets, gave urgency to the progressive desire for reform. "The good we secure for ourselves is precarious and uncertain," Jane Addams (the founder of Hull-House in Chicago) said, "until it is secured for all of us and incorporated into our common life." Her work in settlement houses and in political action, throughout her life, was devoted to making "the blessings which we associate with the life of refinement and cultivation" universal in American society, so that those blessings would be permanent.

"In the interest of the working man himself," Theodore Roosevelt said,"we need to set our faces like flint against mob violence just as against corporate greed."

The images of revolution and violence were not exclusive to the militant Roosevelt. "Don't you know," Woodrow Wilson observed,

> . . . that some man with eloquent tongue, without conscience, who did not care for the nation, could put this whole country into a flame? Don't you know that this country from one end to the other believes that something is wrong? What an opportunity it would be for some man without conscience to spring up and say: "This is the way. Follow me!"—and lead in paths of destruction!

The vision of violence, which for all progressive Americans is closely associated with socialism, Marxism, and European revolutions, made an imperative of economic reform. America could not wait for a European-style revolution. It had to change and so avert revolution. It had to change in a way which would make equality an *economic* reality, and thus prove the classlessness of American society.

The progressive vision of economic equality—a vision which dominates the twentieth-century American development of a consumer society—was based on the searing experiences of young Americans eager to maintain traditional American ideals amid the horrors of the modern urban, industrial, impersonal exploitation of human beings. "What could the fed say to the unfed?" Walter Weyl asked in a 1915 *New Republic* article about a meeting between reformer "experts" and a group of unemployed men. But Weyl was struck by the fact that

> . . . these unemployed men, being Americans, possessed more self-assurance than Englishmen or Germans in like case would have possessed. These wanderers, despised even by pickpockets, held the stubborn conviction that after all they were human beings and citizens, equal to the others in all respects except the accident of money.

Of course the poor unemployed "were not equal, if that word means anything," Weyl admitted. "They had not the health, the vigor, the firm intellectual grasp" which the well-fed experts had. Everyone "tried desperately to be equal," Weyl reported, "it was the least we could do." But the effort was unsuccessful. "It was not possible even for the short space of three hours to keep down the barrier. . . . The unemployed were addressed as 'you fellows,' 'friends,' 'boys,' but the title 'gentlemen' which is in vogue in almost every section was not used."

The progressive crusading vision was kept alive by vivid images of the "unfed" throughout the twentieth century. The continuing reality of economic deprivation in the midst of wealth, production, and mountains of goods reinforced the progressive lack of faith in human goodness and the desire to make American society economically equitable. For all their anti-Marxism, progressives believed and still believe in Marx's fundamental economic determinism—as cause and solution of social problems.

EDUCATED, EXPERT, EXECUTIVE LEADERS

Progressives are convinced that if American society is ever to become really democratic and remain true to the American dream, it requires a trained, elite leadership. Herbert Croly wrote that "only a comparatively small minority are capable at any one time of exercising political, economic, and civil liberties in an able, efficient, or thoroughly worthy manner." That minority, as Senator Robert La Follette of Wisconsin, an early progressive leader, put it, had to have "a proper attitude toward public affairs." Progress could be led only by loyal, properly trained, competent Americans. Leadership of the national democracy had to go to the few who were able, efficient, and worthy (not to the wealthy, the well-born, or the upper class). Those few would have to take control of the national government and through it take official national action to resolve the crises in American life.

Progressives believed that universal public education was the essential requirement for democracy, mobility, equality, and the expert leadership necessary for any modern society. Universal public education would raise general expectations of life and improve people's abilities as well as their visions of the higher life. John Dewey, who became the leading progressive educational philosopher of this century, wrote that

> each one of our schools [must become] an embryonic community life. . . . When the school introduces and trains each child of society into membership within such a little community, saturating him with the spirit of service, and providing him with the instruments of effective self-direction, we shall have the deepest and best guarantee of a larger society which is worthy, lovely, and harmonious.

Herbert Croly had argued that the whole nation should become a school, with "wise masters" exercising effective authority over properly disciplined pupils. For eight decades of the twentieth century, progressives have tried to extend public education (by making high school and college part of universal education, by extending the school day and the school year, by establishing vocational education, by providing access to all levels of education for all) and to make schools and schooling a universal experience. That a common experience of spending twelve to sixteen years in educational institutions has indeed guaranteed a society "which is worthy, lovely, and harmonious" is not yet clear.

"It is the particular business of the exceptional individual to impose himself on the public," progressives believed. The leaders of a progressive America would be trained in a public-education system which reached everyone without regard to origin, wealth, or status. The best qualified, best trained, and most exceptional of those men and women would lead. They would be an elite, daring, active, responsive to "the impulse beating at the very source of our lives urging us to aid in the race progress." The progressive elite would encourage and inspire those who were weak and less fortunate, and they would devote themselves to the improvement of "average human conditions."

To accomplish its great goals, progressive leadership had to close ranks, and do battle with the enemies of improvement, progress, and democracy. The progressive elite throughout the twentieth century has seen itself as disinterested and competent, trained, scientific, and efficient—"formed for constructive leadership." "There may not be many of us," one early progressive wrote to another (Gifford Pinchot to Hiram Johnson), "but we are a mighty high-grade lot."

Progressives had to do battle, however, with already established elites. The "establishment" in the progressive view is entrenched, powerful, corrupt, hereditary, and utterly unscrupulous in its efforts to achieve its own selfish ends and maintain itself in power. "A very small coterie of men" dominated American politics, according to Senator La Follette. President Woodrow Wilson was frustrated in his efforts to govern in the public interest by "a little group of willful men" in the Senate. Franklin D. Roosevelt believed that "economic royalists" controlled America, and in 1936 that "never before in all our history have these forces been so united against one candidate." The sociologist C. Wright Mills published a book in 1956 entitled *The Power Elite,* which further developed the progressive idea of the establishment and which documented its behavior. In 1976, Jimmy Carter successfully campaigned for the Presidency as an outsider—dedicated, moral, democratic, unselfishly motivated—fighting against the established power and influence of wealthy, corrupt, selfish insiders in Washington. Political perceptions and expectations today are conditioned by the progressive myth of the dedicated democratic leader or leadership group versus the corrupt, established, elitist old guard.

The aim of progressive leaders was to control the institutions which could guide modern life. The progressives, Harold Ickes (a Chicago lawyer who became Franklin Roosevelt's Secretary of the Interior) told Theodore Roosevelt in 1912: ". . . don't want to compromise with the old guard; they want to throw them out; they don't want to divide control; they want to take control."

"If corporations and governments have indeed gone on a joy ride," Walter Lippmann wrote in his *Preface to Politics,* "the business of reform is not to set up fences, Sherman Acts, and injunctions into which they can bump, but to take the wheel and to steer."

The progressive view is that leaders should take over, not destroy or overthrow, social, economic, and political institutions. If a political party, for example, became corrupt or unrepresentative, Senator La Follette argued that it was "abject folly" to destroy it—rather, the proper leaders should take it over and reform it. "Our work is a work of restoration," President Woodrow Wilson said at his first inauguration. "We shall deal with our economic system as it is and as it may be modified, not as it might be if we had a clean sheet of paper to write upon."

The ideal of the "takeover" combines the progressive vision of the proper leadership with the progressive perception that there *is* good in the organizations which have helped create the wealth, productivity, and institutions of modern America. The ideal progressive leader was a veritable "boss" who could construct and control a political machine capable of producing votes and distributing patronage efficiently—based on democratic ideals. The pioneer progressives in national politics—Robert La Follette, Hiram Johnson, and William Borah—created long-lived political machines (there is still a

La Follette active in Wisconsin state politics). So have later progressives—the Kennedys, for example (see Theodore White's description of the Kennedy machine in *The Making of the President, 1960*), and the Browns of California. Progressives are, of course, the sworn enemies of the bosses who dominate establishments as well as machines. But the techniques of organization and control which are characteristic of bosses are, in the progressive view, extremely efficient instruments for public good in the hands of proper leaders: witness Franklin Roosevelt's use of Frank Hague of New Jersey and James Michael Curley of Massachusetts, or John Kennedy's and Hubert Humphrey's and Jimmy Carter's use of Richard Daley of Chicago, or Kennedy's use of John Bailey of Connecticut. The image of the efficiency of political machines continues to be as fascinating to progressive Americans as the image of the efficiency of corporations. The progressive aim is to replace bad leaders with good ones, and to take control of those efficient institutions in order to bring about the better American future.

THE POLITICS OF PROGRESS

Early progressives focused much of their energy on politics and government, and their successors continue to. Only government, they believe, is based entirely on the principles of democracy. Only government can, in the progressive view, take "action which removes the many existing obstacles which prevent effective organization and cooperation." Only government can act for the whole community, establish stable and predictable economic and social relationships, and seek the economic advantage of the whole community. Only the federal government is sufficiently large to be able to control large, nationally organized corporations. Only government can grant "Magna Chartas" to deprived Americans, to enable them to organize and cooperate on a national scale. And finally, only governments have sufficient power to provide, as Senator George Norris put it in his *Autobiography*, "those services which cannot be effectively conducted by voluntary organization" and which are "of such vital importance to the entire nation that they should not be left to the hazard of private enterprise." Progressive Americans look to government, specifically to a properly led federal government, to resolve the crises of modern life, to provide for equality, and to maintain the progress, the wealth, and the power of America.

Progressives sought, and continue to seek, to modify the political systems in order to make governments more responsive to the mass of Americans, and in order to put those governments under the leadership and control of trained, expert, properly motivated men and women. They continue to encourage the growth of civil service so that merit replaces the spoils system. (Later progressives developed the social security system in order to have economic merit replace the patronage and services of political machines.) They seek to destroy the power of political machines and their bosses by emasculating party conventions and establishing primary elections and democratic caucuses. We still seek, as did the earlier progressives, to limit the power of state and federal legislatures through a great variety of devices: referenda, initiatives, limits on sessions, the expanded use of legislative commissions, the transfer of budgeting to the executive, and the general expansion of executive power. We also seek to destroy the cohesiveness and the power of urban political machines by at-large elections, expanded city limits, city-wide boards of education, professional city managers, local civil-service systems, and increased power for mayors elected in city-wide elections.

Progressive Americans have sought to expand the powers of larger governments and restrict those of smaller ones. Earlier progressives created more centralized government in the name of efficiency, democracy, and good leadership, and we continue their techniques and their aims—and the logic which justifies both.

The central progressive myth of American government is that legislatures are too corruptible and too amenable to the influence of special interests to be democratic. Legislatures should, in progressive belief, "represent all the people rather than any one class or section of the people," and until they can be made so representative they are neither efficient instruments of democratic government nor particularly trustworthy. The executive, on the other hand, is, in progressive belief, "the steward of public welfare." Modern experience has "conclusively proved," Herbert Croly wrote and progressives since have believed implicitly, that "executives, elected by the whole constituency, are much more representative of public opinion than are the delegates of petty districts." The idealized vision of the corporate executive, decisive, powerful, able to act in the best interests of the company—the epitome of independent individualism—is an overwhelming part of the progressive ideal of executive leadership in government. The President has come to be seen as the ideal policy maker, the controller, the organizer, for the whole government, and for the whole nation. Because he is a single, independent individual, the President has come to represent all of the American people—in modern American myth, in modern American reality—in a way no group of leaders could.

Progressive mythology is based on the assumption of crisis, and on rejection of the idea that crisis will resolve itself. For more than three-quarters of a century Americans have believed that there is, *right now,* a crisis. The reality of the continuing succession of crises requires, in progressive logic, a properly led crusade to establish the national goals, meet the crisis, overcome the dangers to society, and restore the nation to its high ideals. That crusade requires, first, a widespread, institutionalized effort to educate all Americans to the highest possible level. Second, it requires planned efforts to the end that governments become the prime guarantors of progress. Finally, the crusade must have leadership motivated by high democratic ideals and possessed of an unselfish spirit of public service. Only then can American power be properly realized, and the equality, democracy, and glory which that power promises be attained.

4

Nothing to Fear

ALTHOUGH THE "IMPERIAL PRESIDENCY" is a phrase only recently coined by Arthur M. Schlesinger, Jr., concern, admiration, hope, and consternation about the Presidency has been, for at least a quarter century, a major preoccupation of Americans. And the Presidency has been the focus of national political expectations since progressivism appeared at the beginning of the century.

The Presidency, as Americans understand it, is no myth. It represents reality, the ultimate in individual and national power. It is the incarnation of progressive leadership. The *person* in the office may be weak, ineffectual, lacking in power or ability—but not the office. To modern Americans, the Presidency is the most powerful office on earth, awe-inspiring, capable of moving and shaking (and destroying) the whole earth. It is in that perception, in those expectations of the office, in the logic of presidential power and the imperatives of presidential action, that the keys to the mythology of the modern Presidency lie. There is a contradiction which the myths of the modern Presidency resolve: how, in a democratic nation of generally egalitarian people, with a constituted government which is the agent of the people and not the sovereign, can a single individual be so powerful? Is a single leader of a central government compatible with a democratic nation? "Yes!" is the answer most Americans believe is most logical. Therein is the myth of the modern Presidency.

TRADITION TRANSFORMED

Our perceptions of the Presidency are based on the progressive belief in the necessity of a powerful, national government. The traditional American mythology of government, however, postulated a federal system of rather strong, independent state and local governments with a federal government of limited, delegated power. Within that system, almost all governmental power was divided among three branches—executive, judicial, and legislative—of which the legislative was considered to be the most powerful and the most democratic. In the course of the twentieth century, we have transformed that tradition.

Americans tend to assume that the tripartite separation of powers established by the Constitution is natural and normal. So powerful is the tripartite federal myth that all discussion of governmental structure and power—whether of American or other governments, contemporary or past—takes place within its context. It is the most normative of American political myths.

Since the ratification of the Constitution the federal model was overwhelmingly the most powerful model of how disparate groups and other sovereignties were to be made into one community, one nation, which represented them all and which worked to integrate their interests into one. The republic, God bless her! was long the model and the paradigm for the creation and preservation of "one out of many," America's motto and goal as a nation. Americans believed, and that belief is by no means dead, that the Constitution and federalism were the blueprint for all proper government—of communities, of institutions, of states, and of cities. The ideals of representation (both of people and of bodies politic), of compromise, and of adjustment of interests were invariably associated with federalism, and the metaphor of the republic dominated political and communitarian thinking.

A representative legislature was the core of the model. The logic of the progressive attack on legislatures is that legislatures are by their federal nature corrupt; they are corrupt precisely because they are localistic and representative of bodies or groups of people (constituencies). The attack on legislatures, and on federalism, which the early progressives began, is now part of American nationalism. Legislatures, we believe, represent local constituencies and special-interest groups—not the people, and not national interests.

Federalism, its myths and its models, is being abandoned. In the old days, progressive Americans believe, America was rural and agricultural, a federal republic. Now it is urban and industrial, a great nation. Federalism has become corrupted and outdated, like the symbolic town of Gopher Prairie in *Main Street.* State legislatures, for example, basing their representation on the federal model, long favored agrarian and rural interests at the expense of the cities. But progress, in the 1960's, in the form of the Supreme Court, gave constitutional reality to the new mythology of nationalism by requiring, in its "one man one vote" decisions, that the federal model of representation be entirely abandoned and that state legislatures reapportion their representation. Today only numerically equal groups of people living next to each other can be represented in American governments. The logic of federalism has ceased to inform American political practice.

In its place Americans have put a unitary, national model based on a progressive interpretation of equality: each individual has a vote which entitles him or her to representation in government, rights before the law, and a proportion of the community's or the nation's advantages equal to those of every other individual. No groups can be represented except those composed of equal numbers of proximate voters. The mythology of federalism continues in the rituals of election of officials and representative bodies at all levels of government, but the logic of the newer nationalist mythology is that these officials and bodies do not exercise any sovereignty or control except that which is dispensed to them by the national government (like "revenue sharing"). Finally, in the logic of our nationalist myths, the President—the executive branch—is the focus and the symbol, the effective wielder of power, and the individual responsible for the effective management of the nation, its people, and its government. The President is the *only* representative of all the people.

The stories of Abraham Lincoln in the Presidency are the basis for the progressive faith in the presidential, executive office. Lincoln, the humble man of the people, who represented all that was good, decent, and desirable, had used the power of the President (as Commander-in-Chief) for the noblest of ends: the preservation of the unity of the nation and the emancipation of Americans from bondage. The mixture of humble man of the people, mighty commander, great emancipator, and moral leader of a hesitant, divided, and doubting nation was at the core of progressive expectations of the President. Those characteristics have become, in our century, the basis for judging presidential greatness, and they have become the basis for justifying and explaining the American expectation of presidential leadership.

FOCUS ON THE PRESIDENT

The focus on the Presidency is part of our nationalism, our search for national unity and wholeness in a single person. All the logic and mythology of individualism—of independence, of the loner, of community service, of legitimate fame, of popularity and the approval of one's equals, and of the effectiveness of *one* sturdy, adaptive jack-of-all-trades set down in the midst of a savage, chaotic wilderness—has been taken up and applied, in the mythology of modern nationalism, to the whole nation through the symbolic and representative President of the United States.

There is a tradition among progressive historians that the United States became a significant world power in 1898, as a result of the Spanish-American War. The logic of the tradition is that we acquired territorial empire (beyond the coasts of North America), and we were set, by that war, on a course of power relationships, military and economic, which has characterized the nation ever since. While—as with most mythic logic—it can be shown that the tradition is inaccurate (America's expanding commercial and political empire was long established in 1898), nevertheless, the Spanish-American War symbolizes a reality. In the first place, the war and its outcome *did* establish the United States as a significant power in the considerations of the strongest governments of Europe. Second, the war, its execution, and its aftermath did focus American attention on the President of the United States (and certain of the powers which constitutionally belonged to the President) in a manner and with an intensity which had before been given only to Abraham Lincoln—the heroic, martyred leader of the greatest war Americans could conceive.

The presidential power to conduct foreign affairs, and the power of the President as Commander-in-Chief of the armed forces, were brought together by President William McKinley in 1898 and deliberately used by him, as President, to make the United States a world power. McKinley conjured up the image of the humble, popular Lincoln, revived Lincoln's uses of war powers, and established the image of presidential control and presidential decision-making for the United States as a world power on the world stage. By the use of his authority as Commander-in-Chief, McKinley acquired for the United States a territorial empire in the Caribbean and the Pacific. At the same time, the mass media spread stories of his humility, his popular origins, his prayers for guidance, and his ignorance of world geography. By his diplomatic and military direction, he "emancipated" the people of Cuba, Puerto Rico, and the Philippines from Spanish bondage, and made the United States their protector, defender, and educator, and the prime user of their land, their resources, and their markets. McKinley's Presidency is symbol—and reality as well—of the beginning of the modern American focus on the Presidency, and of the mythology of presidential power.

The mythology has not grown solely because of presidential foreign policy and military leadership. The ability of the mass media, of the great metropolitan newspapers and the large-circulation magazines to enter the homes, condition the responses, and provide a focus for individual Americans, was at the heart of Theodore Roosevelt's remark—after he had succeeded McKinley—that the Presidency was a "bully pulpit." The availability of the media to the President had become vividly clear in the Spanish-American War. While the press did not produce uniformity of opinion, it did concentrate on the war. And the national media began to focus on the President. Newspapers and magazines, and later movies, radio, and television, found the President, as a single person in a single office with national significance, highly attractive. The President was immediately identifiable—something few senators or congressmen were. He was a handy symbol, a personification of national ideals and desires, as well as of his own or his party's policies, programs, and ideals.

Presidents after McKinley used the mass media increasingly and with varying subtlety and skill to educate, to preach, to convince, and, most importantly, to set the limits and the content of discussion and debate over public issues and the course of public policy. Presidential access to the media, and the media's focus on the President, gave force and reality to the increasing progressive expectations of executive presidential leadership and policy making. One of the measures of presidential success has become the ability of a President to use the media to satisfy the popular expectations of presidential power, decisiveness, and ability to manage American crises. The techniques have differed—Woodrow Wilson required all press questions to be submitted in advance, in writing; Calvin Coolidge talked freely and easily at conferences with newspaper reporters (he even had a stenographer make a transcript of the conferences), but no reporter was ever allowed to quote him; Franklin Roosevelt developed the informal, "fireside," radio chat and the freewheeling press conference; Dwight Eisenhower made his answers to press questions so long, rambling, and confusing that he was almost impossible to quote—but nonetheless managed to convey his meaning; John F. Kennedy and Richard Nixon both staged their television appearances to offer carefully prepared images to the mass audience. The media success of a President has become part of the logic by which Americans judge Presidents and presidential power.

By the beginning of this century, most Americans accepted the idea that it was natural to focus on an individual leader in any collective, corporate activity. Almost all assumed that individual robber barons or captains of industry controlled, directed, and set policies for railroads, banks, and great industrial corporations; that individual editors or publishers controlled, directed, and set editorial policy for great newspapers; that every machine had its boss and every organized activity had its czar; and that those leaders were American individualism apotheosized. To be asked to accept the idea that the President did, or ought to, make and direct the policies of the United States government was not, in such a context, difficult even for the most convinced American democrat to accept. As Walter Lippmann wrote of Tammany in 1913, it was "typical of all real sovereignties"; it was "an accretion of power around a center of influence . . . a human grouping, a natural pyramid." And at the top was a single individual who ran the show. If, as the corporate myth held, there was to be an efficient organization of human effort, there had to be a single person in control who could get things done. What was true in large industrial organizations had to be true in national government, especially if that government was to control large national corporations. The logic of the progressive mythology became increasingly convincing.

The progressive focus on the President is also marked by his public visibility as campaigner, party leader, and prime mover in the formulation and execution of public policy. Taking a leaf from William Jennings Bryan, the Great Commoner who traveled thousands of miles campaigning for the Presidency in 1896 (and in 1900 and 1908), Presidents and presidential aspirants became "whistle-stopping" crusaders for office, for policies and programs—by rail (President Harry Truman was the last whistle-stopping campaigner in 1948) and later by plane (Franklin Roosevelt was the first). *Air Force One,* the presidential airplane, has become a modern symbol of the moving (mobile?), visible, active, powerful President.

Travel, with frequent stops and frequent speeches, has become part of the presidential role. It is being democratic, in contact with the people, and therefore more representative of the people than any congressman can be. It has become so much a part of the Presidency that not traveling draws attention to the President or the candidate. Warren Harding in his 1920 campaign signaled his kinship with the "martyred" President McKinley and the good old days by *not* traveling, by conducting an old-fashioned, and therefore safe, comfortable, and predictable "front porch" campaign. Herbert Hoover, Franklin Roosevelt, Dwight Eisenhower, Richard Nixon, and Jimmy Carter, at various times in their Presidencies, have refused to travel, and thereby emphasized the overwhelming importance of staying on the job and in the White House.

Congressmen and senators could, and did, travel back and forth to their states and districts, and some, recognized as party leaders or bosses, traveled farther afield. They always had. But only occasionally were such travels news, and very rarely were they national news. Crises of national importance were easier for the media to focus on, and more amenable to presidential action. The President could swiftly and publicly "knock a few heads together" in a genteel manner at the White House and solve a crisis, or settle a strike. Theodore Roosevelt did it, so it seemed, in the Coal Strike in 1904, and thereby set a pattern that Presidents since have followed and Americans have come to expect. The message of the myth is clear to all: Presidents can solve problems or crises (because they are powerful, decisive, active, mobile *individuals*—in good, American logic), and Congress can't.

CONTRAST WITH CONGRESS

For the first half of the twentieth century at least, Presidents and progressives fought to destroy the power of Congress to make American policy—and to destroy the power of the political parties controlled by senators and congressmen. The effort has been to give the President the power to legislate and to lead his political party. Congress, often backed by party leaders and party workers, fought back, in detail, over complicated matters of tariffs, taxes, appropriations, budgets, committees, rules, and conventions. The struggle between congressional power and presidential leadership has become part of the mythology of the Presidency: the best argument (the mythic logic) for presidential leadership is to tell a story of congressional inefficiency, bumbling, or corruption.

"The question of efficiency" is vital to a democracy, Professor Woodrow Wilson wrote in 1901. "We lack," he wrote, "above all things else, concentration, both in political leadership and in administrative organization." America had been governed, according to Wilson, by "mass meetings"; its policies, he sneered, were made "piece by piece" by congressional committees with no "single or consistent pattern of statesmanship." Wilson believed that no one but the President could supply the concentration, the "integration of the public business," the leadership necessary for efficient government. His argument, his logic, and his contempt for congressional committees, party caucuses, and "the private leadership of party managers" have all become part of the myths of the necessity of presidential power.

Congress—and the legislatures of the states—participated in spreading the progressive vision of legislative inefficiency and presidential efficiency. In 1910, for example, the House of Representatives, in a battle led by progressive insurgents, broke the centralized, concentrated power of the Speaker to control all committee assignments, chairmanships, and legislation. The Speaker was believed to be a czar, a boss (the Speaker at the time was "Uncle Joe" Cannon of Illinois) who had no mandate from the people. By reducing those powers of the Speaker which, in the hands of an executive, progressives believed made for efficient leadership, the House progressives reduced the policy-making power of the House in favor of the President. Congress remained influential, but over time it became an influence which Presidents found necessary to manipulate: it no longer made policy. The President in 1910, William Howard Taft, himself no political progressive, had stepped in to solve the congressional crisis over the Speakership.

When Woodrow Wilson became President in 1913, he refused to function simply as a kind of latter-day Tribune of the People with a veto! Rather, Wilson believed he alone could properly express the will of the people in policies and legislation, just as it was he who bore the responsibility for educating the people—directly through his own person—to their own best interest. The presidential powers to direct foreign policy and war gave Wilson the greatest scope for his model of the Presidency, but he also actively assumed the role of domestic educator and policy maker.

Wilson's decision to enter World War I brought him into open conflict with Congress. The defeat of a bill to arm merchant ships—by a "little group of willful men" in the Senate—and the large number of senators and representatives who voted against the Declaration of War were signals that Congress intended to maintain a strong voice in the making of American policy. But the voice was increasingly becoming a negative one. In the face of wartime exigencies, Congress was left with the assertion of the veto.

Direct confrontation between President and Congress came at the end of the war. The battle over the making and ratification of the Treaty of Versailles, which lasted from the Armistice in November 1918 to its final defeat in the Senate in March 1920, was a shattering confrontation. Its lasting effect was to strengthen the Presidency at the expense of the Congress. It created a set of mythic images—of presidential idealism and leadership and responsibility in contrast to congressional shortsightedness, irresponsibility, and venality—which still exist for Americans. They still condition American perceptions of present reality.

Late in 1918, after the Armistice, President Wilson went to Paris to negotiate a peace treaty. He was the first President ever to leave the country while in office, and the first (and very nearly the only) President to negotiate an important treaty in person with the heads of other major governments. There was little question of where American (as well as world) public interest and expectation were focused. The Treaty of Versailles, which Wilson brought back to the United States in July 1919, included the creation of a League of Nations, which would, it was hoped, supervise the carrying out of the peace treaty, bring about world disarmament, and be the instrument for permanent world peace. Wilson conducted a public campaign to get the treaty accepted by the Senate (which must approve treaties) and by the people (who could influence the Senate). He collapsed, as the result of a series of strokes, in October 1919 while touring the country and was incapacitated for some months (although few people knew how badly). In November 1919, and again in March 1920, the Senate voted on the treaty, which failed to pass. As a result, the United States was not a party to the Treaty of Peace and did not become a member of the League of Nations.

One interpretation, one myth, of the Senate's rejection of the treaty, probably the most widespread, was that it was the result of isolationism in America, and that it caused the League of Nations to be an ineffective body for the maintenance of world peace. According to this interpretation, the Senate's rejection, by weakening the League, helped to bring on World War II.

So powerful has the myth of the President's ability to represent the true interests of America become since the treaty battle that few Americans would, even today, contend that rejection of the treaty was a wise, foresighted decision on the part of the U.S. Senate. Yet, the Versailles Treaty is widely believed, by analysts like J. M. Keynes, to have been an inadequate, shortsighted, and possibly vicious instrument which unleashed forces upon the world—German resentment, Allied guilt, cynicism about the rights of small or vanquished peoples—which prepared the way for World War II. In rejecting such a treaty, the Senate may well have tried to avoid participating in an impossible settlement—which is what some of the opponents of the treaty did argue. But to say that the Senate was right to reject the treaty would be to argue that the Senate was more capable of wise judgment and efficient policy making than the President. That argument is so contrary to the myth of presidential leadership that very few Americans have taken it seriously since the early 1920's.

By extension, if the treaty upon which the League of Nations was based was inadequate, there ought to be doubt that American membership in the League would have prevented World War II. There is no evidence to demonstrate that the United States could have prevented that war, but the logic of common American mythology is that we could have.

Domestically, the defeat of the treaty by the Senate represents, in popular belief, the defeat of a beleaguered and idealistic President struggling to do what was right for the American people and the world. He was defeated, according to this view, by arrogant, venal politicians led by Senator Henry Cabot Lodge of Massachusetts, whose desire was simply to beat Wilson, whom he was supposed to hate.

On the other hand, some believe that since Wilson was sick his judgment was impaired. According to this view, he single-mindedly sought ratification of the treaty without regard to its failings, because he had made it. He shattered the Democratic Party and brought about the defeat of the treaty by his own arrogance, his failure of political judgment, and his effort to beat Lodge. But despite such arguments, Wilson remains a "doom-fated hero." It was, distinguished historian Allan Nevins wrote in the introduction to Gene Smith's *When the Cheering Stopped: The Last Days of Woodrow Wilson,* "nothing less than a disaster for America, that, contending day and night for international peace, battling to exhaustion against ignorance, partisanship, and malice, he collapsed just when he seemed to be raising the nation to the height of his own vision." The nation failed the President. The President knew what was best, but the people did not follow him.

The Senate victory in the League of Nations fight was, of course, altogether Pyrrhic. While Presidents after Wilson were careful to consult the Senate when they wished to make treaties, they soon—starting with Franklin Roosevelt—devised ways to make agreements with other nations, and to conduct foreign policy, with a minimum of Senate consultation. Congress has retained a veto over presidential policy, but the initiative and the "vision," after Wilson, were acknowledged by all Americans to be the President's. Recent battles in the Senate over the Panama Canal and the Strategic Arms Limitation Treaties confirm the mythology of presidential power.

By the 1920's, even most congressmen participated in the expectations of presidential leadership. Starting with the creation of the Bureau of the Budget in 1921 in the name of nonpartisan efficiency in government, the Congress began to give its powers to the executive branch of government. Traditionally, Americans had learned—as had their Founding Fathers—that the power of the purse was the essential legislative power for a democracy. But with the establishment of the Bureau of the Budget, Congress placed its power of the purse in the hands of experts, bureaucrats, and the executive branch, reserving to itself only the power of ultimate appropriation of funds and of reaction to individual items. It made itself a negative voice rather than an equal partner in the budgeting process, and shifted to the President the power to suggest, recommend, establish priorities—not merely within but among agencies. Congressmen are still important to government agencies for their votes. But they go to agencies not as policy makers but as suppliants or as investigators; they are watchdogs or boondogglers; they are to be managed, flattered, and educated; they are "on the Hill," important but remote; they are, in the end, not the Boss, but rather, the Board of Directors.

Since the 1920's, as a result of the logic of presidential leadership, Congress has given the President many of the powers traditionally associated with representative government. The Congress, as other Americans do, believes the President to be *representative,* both symbol and actuality of American democracy. The 1964 Gulf of Tonkin resolution (which, in effect, gave the President the congressional power to initiate war) was passed because Congress did not consider itself adequately representative, efficient, knowledgeable, expert, or capable of judging American national interests in a crisis—and it believed, as do most Americans still, that a President is. There has been some erosion of the belief since Vietnam and President Johnson, Watergate and President Nixon. The 1979 standby gasoline rationing legislation proposal, for example, used the logic of presidential power and effectiveness, but with tight congressional strings attached. The Congress is a necessary contrast to the President in American myths about government. It is a balance, a check—but certainly not a symbol of the power and glory of democratic ideals in action. *That* symbol has become, and remains, the President.

PRESIDENTIAL COLOSSUS: FRANKLIN DELANO ROOSEVELT

"Have we found angels in the forms of kings" to govern us? Thomas Jefferson asked, with considerable sarcasm, at his inaugural. Few Americans consider Presidents angels, but the modern mythology of the Presidency has done away with the sarcasm. The Presidency remains good in American eyes, despite the failings, failures, and even the corruption of the men who occupy the office. Not even the beginning of impeachment proceedings and the resignation of President Nixon under fire seem to have damaged the Presidency. It still contains, in our belief, the possibility of making the man in the office, like Woodrow Wilson—"great in vision, generous love of humanity, devotion to justice, hopefulness, and eloquence" (in Allan Nevins's words). The mythic logic of the office generates the assumption that Presidents are high-minded and efficient men who educate Americans to their own best interests and who make the policies and—in the belief at least of younger Americans who write that "the President passed a law . . ."—the laws to carry out those interests.

Franklin D. Roosevelt became President of the United States on March 4, 1933. He was still President, in his fourth elected term, more than twelve years later, on April 12, 1945, when he died. No one had ever been President for so long, and shortly after Roosevelt died, the Constitution was changed so that no one could ever be again. He was the second President in the twentieth century, and the fourth since Andrew Jackson, to serve two full terms—only Grant, Cleveland, and Wilson had done so before him (and Eisenhower is the only one who has since).

In the mythic image of him, already developed while he was alive, and which has grown since his death, F.D.R. did "bestride the narrow world / Like a Colossus" (most people know he was a paraplegic, but few ever think of it). He was the focus of the nation's hopes and a comfort to its fears in the successive catastrophes of the Great Depression and the Second World War. For millions of us who were younger Americans in 1945, *the* President died—the only one we had ever known—and for all Americans thereafter (including all the Presidents), the Presidency was modeled on the image of "that man in the White House" who had told Americans in 1933 that "the only thing we have to fear is fear itself—nameless, unreasoning, unjustified terror."

In the crisis of the Depression, which spread slowly across America in the years after the stock market crash in 1929, the focus of Americans on the President and their expectations of him had grown. Herbert Hoover, President from 1929 to 1933, contributed to that by his clear and official assumption of responsibility for policies to get the country out of the Depression, and by his optimistic pronouncements to allay popular fears about the future. But Hoover insisted that there were limits to presidential action, indeed limits to the capabilities of the national government. He seemed to insist on a *federal* vision of the possibilities for action in the Depression, a vision which seemed old-fashioned to many Americans in the face of an all-too-terrifying crisis. Hoover and his beliefs about limits on presidential and governmental power and action were, as almost all Americans have since perceived it, swept aside in the 1932 election in favor of an imperial President leading an almost omnipotent government.

Franklin Roosevelt, as campaigner and as President, willingly became the focal point of the desire for national action. He made himself the "dealer" of a "new deal": the active leader of a government which promised to provide for the well-being of every American. He provided a humane idealism, a cheer and optimism Americans have since come to expect of Presidents, and he promised to put those ideals into action: "Every man has a right to life; and this means that he has also a right to make a comfortable living," Roosevelt said in his 1932 campaign. He went on to say:

> . . . We have no actual famine or dearth; our industrial and agricultural mechanism can produce enough and to spare. Our Government formal and informal, political and economic, owes to everyone an avenue to possess himself of a portion of that plenty sufficient for his needs, through his own work.

The President, Roosevelt implied, was responsible to direct the government into action.

"Under Roosevelt," historian William Leuchtenburg has written, "the White House became the focus of all government—the fountainhead of ideas, the initiator of action, the representative of the national interest." The Depression, and the national emergency which the Depression created, was part of the reason the Presidency became the focus. "There is a countrywide dumping of responsibility on the Federal Government," *New York Times* reporter Anne O'Hare McCormick wrote in 1933. "America today literally asks for orders." Americans were "demanding omnipotent gestures from government," and President Roosevelt proved willing to make such gestures. Never had there been, she said, "a President as powerful as Mr. Roosevelt." And the reason for that power was that "the people as a whole trust the discretion of the President more than they trust Congress."

Roosevelt and his Administration, as we have seen, espoused the consumer society with its vision of the individual consumer as the dynamo of the economy. The New Deal commitment to consumption, to full employment, and to Keynesian economic policies has become part of the pattern and model of the Presidency. Roosevelt also committed the Presidency to the initiation of all important legislation. The pattern of demonstrating action by the initiation of legislation has become part of our expectation of Presidents. The success or failure of a presidential legislative program is now a popular index of the power and effectiveness of a particular President.

The President's creation and elaboration of bureaucracy, the establishment of agencies, the appointment of officials, and the creation of orders and regulations for bureaucracy to follow are all symbols and real substance of his power. Roosevelt began his administration with the creation of a very large variety of "alphabet" agencies—AAA, NRA, CCC, PWA. He continued throughout his Presidency (as have all Presidents since) to create agencies which were charged with rectifying wrongs in the economic or social or political systems of America, or with regulating these systems in order to bring about more equitable distribution of the wealth of America. Presidential power, as Americans have come to believe since Roosevelt, is demonstrated by the extent and activities of these growing bureaucracies. The reality of the ability of the President to solve America's problems is, we believe, manifest in these agencies.

Franklin Roosevelt also initiated the growth of the Executive Office, which has become a highly visible symbol of presidential power. In 1939, Roosevelt, by his epoch-making Executive Order 8248, created an Executive Office staffed with six administrative assistants. He moved a number of agencies into the Executive Office, among them the Bureau of the Budget. In the years since, the Executive Office has acquired an elaborate staff of presidential advisers and assistants, as well as new and potent agencies like the National Security Council and the Council of Economic Advisers. By 1972, there were forty-eight presidential assistants in the Executive Office, and 5,395 persons on the Executive Office staff. The Presidency, as differentiated from the great executive departments, has become a "fourth branch" of the government, the most visible and still the most accessible to the mass media. As a result, it is perceived to be the most active, the most responsive, and the most responsible of the government branches.

Franklin Roosevelt has become the Paul Bunyan of American Presidents: a myth based on vividly remembered reality. He was, in his lifetime, a shrewd politician who wove, both consciously and unconsciously, the available strands of presidential power into a solid, lasting fabric. Since his death, the President is generally acknowledged to be program initiator, domestic policy maker, enunciator of ideals, problem solver, war leader, diplomatic policy maker, and symbol of America's belief in herself as the last, best hope of the world.

Roosevelt was not simply a Depression President; he was a war President as well. In him—in the myths of him which are inextricable from popular beliefs—depression and war, victory and recovery, world power and prosperity, war and success are combined; they are so mingled that Americans cannot separate them. The President and the war ended the Depression: that is the lesson of the Roosevelt contribution to the mythology of the President. The great good the war had brought to Americans, aside from destroying tyranny abroad, protecting the United States, and bringing America vast world power, was to build economic success and restore prosperity. The Roosevelt legacy was the legacy of victory in the world and success—material, economic success—at home. Such victory and success have become the American expectation from the exercise of presidential power.

INDIVIDUAL COMMUNITY LEADER

The modern President is expected to lead a party, and at the same time to be above partisan politics. The desire is for an activist President at the center of an active state, shaping the destiny of the world in war or peace, depression or prosperity, *and* effectively "putting us all together," creating a community. The President, on the model of the myths of Franklin Roosevelt, is expected to unify the American people in the face of the perpetual crisis of diversity and fragmentation.

As a political leader (actually, he had become the head of a minority party and he tried to put together a lasting majority), Franklin Roosevelt is widely believed to have made a coalition of a wide variety of interest groups, ethnic groups, and regional and local political parties, and in so doing joined President, government, and identifiable groups in a relationship which has continued to dominate politics and which all now consider normal national politics. Instead of building a vertically integrated party, on the corporate and the older political party models, with a national committee at its center, and a President or a candidate as its spokesman, Roosevelt made a coalition with himself as center, policy maker, and active leader. He created a conglomerate party which recognized the autonomy and independent desires of the many groups which composed it and in which the President functioned as a broker and strategist, allocating resources, reconciling differences, and attempting to provide something for the interests and desires of each group. By so doing, Roosevelt effectively focused party leadership in the President, because only an active person in the White House (or believed soon to be in) could work with groups that seemed irreconcilable. Only such a powerful leader could promise or deliver rewards and services to groups that did not intend to compromise their own internal needs. "There's one issue in this campaign," Franklin Roosevelt said to Raymond Moley in 1936. "It's myself, and people must be either for me or against me." The pattern Roosevelt set logically extended the national focus on the President from the arena of government to that of party politics, and it has become the pattern of all presidential politics since.

As Samuel Lubell, an acute political observer, pointed out in *The Saturday Evening Post* after Roosevelt was elected for the third time in 1940, Franklin Roosevelt was "the first President to owe his election in such great measure to the teeming cities." Roosevelt had won, Lubell said, because groups of voters, "groups as wholes," in the cities had supported him: "Roosevelt won by the vote of labor, unorganized as well as organized, plus that of the foreign born and their first and second generation descendants. And the Negro." More and more Americans had become urban. Ethnic groups and interest groups had become increasingly identified with city life.

And black Americans, as a group, had become *the* symbol of America's urban, ethnic, minority groups. They were easily identifiable and recognizable. And they, too, looked to the President for recognition, benefits, and opportunities—for integration, into a party, into a community, into the nation.

American hopes and aspirations in this century have concentrated on the President because many felt that, in sprawling cities and vast industries, the individual had little control over events. The Depression (and the memory of it) proved the individual's lack of control. The President, on the other hand, was a single individual, one whom everyone knew, and one who *was* still effective, in control. The belief in presidential power is a belief that there is at least in the White House one person who *can* control what happens.

The Great Depression had proved, to many Americans, that the individual was helpless against the forces of society. But black Americans being lynched, the "Scottsboro Boys" being convicted, blacks trying unsuccessfully to get decent educations, decent housing, decent jobs were further proof. The black experience confirmed earlier what many whites came to believe during the Depression: that without some kind of group solidarity, without access to the resources of government, and, most particularly, without responsive leadership from the President, the individual was—in urban industrial America—without adequate protection, at the mercy of uncontrollable forces.

The relationship between blacks and the Presidency has helped define both the myths of American minorities and the myths of presidential power. The relationship has been intimate since Franklin Roosevelt. For almost every President, there are symbolic associations which are believed to describe important steps toward party unity, national unity, and the achievement of equality: President Truman and armed forces desegregation in 1947 and the Civil Rights plank of the Democratic platform in 1948, Eisenhower and the *Brown v. Board of Education* decision against segregation and Little Rock, Kennedy and the March on Washington and Dr. Martin Luther King, Jr., Johnson and the Voting Rights Act as well as the War on Poverty, Nixon in his very denial of intimacy, and Carter in the appointment of Andrew Young and Donald McHenry as American ambassadors to the United Nations. The question of the rights and the equality of a definable *group* of people—not individual rights and individual equality—is the question black Americans have posed to political leaders and Presidents. The belief that the President can answer the question, and can, as a party leader as well as the national leader, provide for the rights and equality of many groups is part of the logic of the myths of presidential power.

The power of the myth of homogeneity in America is manifest in the widespread belief that the President can—and should—create an integrated community (in party, government, and nation) to which all can belong. Americans are able to accept the existence of a culturally diverse society composed of many minority groups because they believe they are governed by a state which is led and controlled by a dynamic, powerful, concerned, *unifying* President. "We will always be a nation of differences," President Jimmy Carter said in his fireside chat on February 3, 1977:

> —business and labor, blacks and whites, men and women, people of different regions and religions and different ethnic backgrounds—but with faith and confidence in each other our differences can be a source of personal fullness and national strength, rather than a cause of weakness and division.
>
> If we are a united nation, then I can be a good President.

5

Marching As to War

In 1964, in his first State of the Union address to Congress, President Lyndon Johnson said that "this administration today . . . declares unconditional war on poverty" in the United States. He followed that declaration with a message, sent to Congress on March 16, 1964, proposing a legislative program for "total victory" in the war on poverty.

President Johnson was appealing to the image of the power of America at war: In a war, every American works with every other American for the common national purpose. Americans are willing to be organized, eager to undergo discipline, willing to integrate the vast resources and productive abilities of the whole nation in order to bring victory in war, and, out of war, more freedom, more democracy, and a better world. The myths of war include a vision of everyone working, dedicated to the same goal, sharing privation and danger. American war is crisis being resolved. Even in 1979 and 1980, in the crises over the Americans held hostage in Iran and the Russian invasion of Afghanistan, Americans appealed to the imagery—and to the efficacy—of unity in war in their search for resolutions.

The modern American mythology of war, and its logic, is based on inherited images and attitudes from the Civil War and from the Revolutionary past. In the first place, "war is hell"—the phrase was General Sherman's. The Civil War was a bloody holocaust: more Americans were killed in its four years than have been killed in all of America's wars—from the Revolution through the war in Vietnam—put together. The Civil War destroyed, in its bloody violence, the terrible institution of slavery and the vision of a landed American aristocracy which was based on slavery.

War is always violent, bloody, and destructive. But American wars are fought for great and good ends, and they result in good for America. The Revolution created freedom, independence, and democracy. The Civil War resulted in the expansion of freedom, the destruction of slavery, the growth of industrial might and wealth, and the formation of a unified, powerful nation. Both were, therefore, necessary wars—and good wars.

The mythology of war has been elaborated and added to by twentieth-century experience and belief. In our time, World War II has become the archetypical "good" war, fought for good reasons, and resulting in massive, long-lasting benefits to America and Americans. But twentieth-century wars both before and since World War II have also shaped the mythical perceptions of war, its reasons, its benefits, and its dangers. Perhaps the most important recent change in the mythologies of war is that war is not for us, as it was for nearly all Americans who were not military professionals before World War II, a *special* phenomenon reserved for special times and circumstances in the national life. It is, today, part of everyday American existence.

Bundled together in the modern mythology of war are three elements which Americans believe are the logic of war. Those elements are the explanations of America's wars as well as the lessons we have learned from those wars. One element is the belief that war is an instrument of American progress. War brings unity, efficiency, prosperity, security, and victory. If fought with total commitment, war results in power, growth, prestige, and a fulfilling of our destiny in the world.

Another element is the belief that war is chaotic and destructive. It is a hellish thing which destroys American ideals and democracy, creates abhorrent militarism and imperialism, and perverts American independence and America's destiny in the world. It is totalitarian and regimenting, destructive of individualism in the name of unity. It is to be feared and avoided.

The third element in the American logic of war is the belief that war is a parenthetical experience. It is outside and removed from normal, peaceful, non-military, and democratic lives. It is an aberration, best avoided (but once started, best fought with total devotion by all to a swift, efficient conclusion, so that peace and democracy and independence can return). Harvard professor Russell Fifield argued in an article in *The Yale Review* in 1978 that "the long American experience in Indochina"—that is, the Vietnam War—"may be placed in the same category" as the American acquisition of the Philippines, which, Fifield said, was "an aberration." Such an argument closes the parenthesis on the most recent American war.

We believe that war is progressive, evil, and parenthetical—all at the same time. And we use images and stories which illustrate all three elements in our explanations and stories of war and its place in American life.

LEADERS AND REFORMERS

A sense of unified national purpose and an exciting feeling of American glory came out of the war against Spain in 1898. In less than half a year, the United States had destroyed the last vestiges of the decadent Spanish Empire in the New World. Cuba had been freed, and the poor peoples of the Philippines and Puerto Rico had been brought under the direct protection and guidance of the United States. The American Navy had defeated the armadas of Spain. There were new slogans of new American heroes: "Charge!" (up San Juan Hill), and "You may fire when ready." The Navy and the Army had shown all the world that it was America's destiny to be a great power.

The image of the Spanish-American War as a glorious, exciting national enterprise lived on in the person of Theodore Roosevelt. Roosevelt, the hero, along with the "Rough Riders," of San Juan Hill, became President in 1901. In a long and "savage war of peace," his administration "pacified" the Philippines. He "carried a big stick," began construction of the Panama Canal, revised the Monroe Doctrine to provide for direct United States intervention in the affairs of Latin American nations, demanded the "open door" in China, and became one of the two Presidents to be awarded the Nobel Prize for Peace (the other was World War I President Woodrow Wilson). He encouraged the enlargement and modernization of the American Navy and sent a "Great White Fleet" around the world to demonstrate American power. He embodied the excitement, the good, which war produced.

In Roosevelt's day, peace and progress in America came to be couched in the imagery of war. Disciplined "troops" of reformers do "battle," even today, for freedom, justice, and charity. "Crusades" are mounted for social justice and "armies" of workers or of the poor have become part of the "fighting spirit" of progressivism. When Theodore Roosevelt formed the Progressive Party in 1912, the entire body of the national convention of that party rose and sang the popular hymn: "Onward, Christian soldiers, marching as to war. . . ." And Theodore Roosevelt told the convention: "We stand at Armageddon, and we battle for the Lord." Even American political reform was warfare.

In August 1914, Europe went to war. Woodrow Wilson was President, and the American government at first took a position of neutrality. There was such a thing, President Wilson said, as being "too proud to fight." The United States would maintain her independence and her freedom from the entanglements of Europe and remain neutral.

But belief in the good which war could do proved more powerful than the ideal of American freedom from entanglement in the affairs of Europe. If America was to be powerful, a leader in "the peace of the world," then neutrality was inadequate. War could assure independence of American action by making the United States the undisputed leader of the world; it could assure freedom from military entanglement by letting "all mankind be guarded by the guns of the Republic." To enter the war would be, as many Americans came to believe, a fulfillment of the national destiny, an American crusade for freedom and democracy throughout the world.

"We are glad," Woodrow Wilson said on April 2, 1917, when he asked Congress to declare war, "to fight . . . for the ultimate peace of the world, and for the liberation of its peoples." Wilson believed that "the world must be made safe for democracy" and that America must enter the war to bring about peace and security.

Wilson's progressive faith in unselfish leadership was combined with belief in crusade: "We have no selfish ends to serve. We desire no conquest, no dominion," he said. America was at war as "one of the champions of the rights of mankind." For Wilson, and for the many Americans who took up Wilson's expression of the myth in 1917 and after, there was no contradiction between independence and world leadership, between freedom of action and freedom from entanglement, or between championship of the rights of mankind and a powerful, victorious America dominating the affairs of the world. They were the same.

Despite serious opposition from those who believed the war was not for American ends—"We will have joined Europe in the great catastrophe and taken America into entanglements that will not end with this war, but will live and bring their evil influences upon many generations yet unborn," Senator George Norris of Nebraska argued—and despite opposition from those who believed that the war was being "sold" to Americans by "the merchants of death," America went to war. President Wilson saw the war as an opportunity to unify the nation. He said he would "count upon . . . an America united in feeling, in purpose, in its vision of duty, of opportunity, and of service." The war could submerge the differences among Americans by giving all an overriding reason to serve the nation, and it would thus fulfill the progressive view that the common humanity which united people was finer and better than such things as race, nationality, and class, which kept them apart.

But the war generated a kind of hysteria in which unity itself became a crusade. "There are, in my opinion, some things worse for a nation than war," Senator Henry Cabot Lodge of Massachusetts said during the debates on the Declaration of War. "The division of our people into race groups," he said, "when we should have but one allegiance, one hope, and one tradition is far worse."

The war brought vicious campaigns against "hyphenated Americans," those "race groups." Irish-Americans, Polish-Americans, Italian-Americans, and most particularly German-Americans were publicly harassed and the process of the Americanization of immigrants was hysterically speeded up. German ceased to be taught in most schools, and in communities where German was spoken, strenuous efforts were made to replace it with English. Businesses owned by people with German names were often subject to boycott; others were often refused jobs. Sauerkaut became "victory cabbage."

The war became, for some Americans, a crusade against immigrants, a crusade which closed free immigration to the United States and made that closure permanent in 1924.

The other side of the coin of unity was loyalty, especially, in progressive mythology, loyalty to the federal government and acceptance of official national action. Loyalty meant that there could be no open opposition to the war, and none to the government and its leaders. Even the Republican Party and its leaders did not formally oppose the Wilson Administration's war effort. Loyalty was tested by one's willingness to accept discipline and to serve the country: to join the Army, buy war bonds, do war work. Disloyalty—defined as opposition to the war or the government—was subversion, it was sedition, it was treason.

The specter of class warfare and violence in the streets, which was part of the progressive vision of the crisis in American life, was made more real for many by the violence and hysteria of the war. The creation of a loyally unified, disciplined America seemed most particularly to require the suppression of Marxism, socialism, Communism, and all adherents of such "foreign" and disruptive beliefs. The revolution in Russia in November 1917, and the subsequent calls for world revolution by the Soviet leaders, served to increase American fears of class warfare and disloyalty. The fear continued long after the war, and the myth of American unity came to include the logic that warlike loyalty and unity required a violent rejection of Marxism and other foreign ideas.

The war was an opportunity to prove the efficacy of strong progressive leadership. In the name of emergency and efficiency, war gave broad power to the President to lead and to act decisively. In World War I, the United States government took over all the railroads and ran them. It took control of food supplies, allocating and rationing them. It established agencies to control and to plan industrial production and allocation of raw materials. It controlled American shipping. It greatly expanded the armed forces and conscripted Americans into them. The government established agencies for propaganda, to provide direct access to all the people, and it controlled all communication from overseas. The President, and the agencies of the federal government, were, in the interest of an efficient war effort, virtually dictatorial in all matters that were part of that effort. Wilson's efficient leadership and, of course, the "boys" who were sent "over there" brought the war to a successful end, as most Americans believed, on November 11, 1918.

MEMORIES OF WAR

Memories of World War I contributed to the growth of the modern myth of war as progressive, good, and fulfilling. The nation, in those memories (stories, tales, and histories) was unified, loyal, efficient, immensely productive, brilliantly and humanely led. It poured out giant armies with the best modern equipment to win a war started by others but which no one else could bring to successful conclusion. The New World had come to the rescue of the Old—"Lafayette, we are here!" General Pershing said as American troops landed in France—with ideals of freedom and democracy, equality and fairness. At the end of the war, President Wilson went to Europe; he was acknowledged as its savior by a grateful Old World and brought an American plan for permanent peace and cooperation among nations. The light of the New World, of America, the world's last, best hope, was, because of the war, brought to the rest of the world. America sought no territorial empire and no vengeance on the defeated—her ideals were not corrupted by the war.

At home, the war had brought prosperity, increased production, and booming employment. The efficiency of government direction and planning of the war effort, the fervent unity of the American people, the idealism of millions of Americans eager to serve their country, became part of the myth of the war to make the world safe for democracy. America had won the war, and according to the logic of the myth of war, World War I had therefore contributed to the progress, well-being, and rectitude of America and Americans.

The memory of wartime as a good time, as something which made people finer or better, was continually renewed in the years after World War I by the activities of veterans' organizations. The American Legion, founded at the end of the war, and other veterans' organizations devoted themselves—as the Grand Army of the Republic had in the years after the Civil War—to keeping alive the military imagery of war, and the vision of American wartime unity and loyalty. Veterans' groups organized parades and military ceremonies, Armistice Day rituals, the selling of poppies to benefit veterans, the sponsorship of citizenship awards and essay contests on patriotic themes, as well as political activity for veterans' benefits, Americanization programs, and loyalty. The veterans emphasized the goodness of war and the idea that those who had served in war were a group set apart and were owed benefits and services.

The implication of the activities of the veterans' organizations was that war in some way improved those who fought in it. The organizations sought to renew the feelings of unity, comradeship, mutual loyalty, and high purpose which many veterans brought home from war. In time, the organizations relied on nostalgia, a desire for simplicity of life and purpose which seemed unavailable in the normal peacetime world. In retrospect, a time when life was precious and at risk, when the relief of not being killed or of going on leave was an enormous and uncomplicated pleasure, and when a soldier only had to worry about a known enemy, seemed—to many veterans—to have been a golden time, the "best years of our lives." Such nostalgia could become, and did for some, a nostalgia for war. It contributed, in many communities and for much of the nation, to the continuing vision of war as a progressive good.

But the memory of war also showed it to be chaotic and destructive. European civilization had been ruined by the Great War; millions had been killed, and a generation of young men who might have shaped a better world was dead. Many young Americans, too, had died, and some of those who survived had become disillusioned with the world, a "lost" generation. The chaos of war had also loosed revolution in the world, bringing more bloodshed, anarchy, and destruction in its wake. At home, hysterical patriotism had brought violence, oppression, and the suppression of democratic ideals, of democratic practice in government, and of democratic tolerance in social life. Suppression of objection to the war and violence against immigrants and slackers during the war were followed by Red scares, mass arrests, deportations, and the rapid growth of terrorist organizations like the Ku Klux Klan. The memory of the evils brought by World War I reinforced the vision that war was a destroyer.

World War I also brought economic chaos and massive social dislocation. It disrupted the normal development of American industry and brought about the overexpansion of American agriculture, with disastrous results. The war was followed by widespread unemployment, industrial chaos, and agricultural depression. This economic upheaval led ultimately, in this version of the myth, to the collapse of the American—and of the world—economy and to the Great Depression.

In the memories of World War I, the war also destroyed the effectiveness of American ideals for the world, brought massive American disillusionment with the possibility of making the world a better place, and ultimately caused America to isolate herself. The actions of Allied leaders at Versailles, in this vision of war's evil, corrupted President Wilson (the spokesman for America's high ideals), destroyed the possibility of American leadership, imposed a regressive and destructive punishment on Germany, and ultimately led to another world war.

Finally, while war was both good and evil, it was also an aberration. When war ended, peace was automatic and life could get back to normal. While some did argue that the war must be used to improve the quality of life, still, as Warren Harding said in his campaign for the Presidency in 1920, what many wanted after the war was "not nostrums but normalcy" (thereby coining a word which Americans have used since to label the attitude that war was an aberration). Harding quite deliberately, but many others less consciously, created a vision of the good old days before the war when life was happy, progressive, and prosperous. The belief that Americans could and did return to normalcy after World War I still persists, reinforcing the logic of the parenthetical nature of war.

METAPHORICAL WAR

The Great Depression revived the mythology of war and brought sometimes striking uses of imagery associated with it. Both Presidents charged with fighting the Depression had worked in Wilson's war administration, and both drew on that experience quite explicitly during the Depression. Herbert Hoover's worldwide, as well as American, reputation had been made during World War I. Hoover had brought relief to stricken Belgium, directed the Food Administration, and supervised American relief to war-torn Europe after the Armistice. As President, his establishment of the Reconstruction Finance Corporation as a major instrument in his effort to stimulate recovery drew directly on his World War I experience—the RFC was a reincarnation of the War Finance Corporation—and the more generalized myth of war which required "reconstruction" as part of its benefits.

Franklin D. Roosevelt ended his inaugural address, in March 1933, with the statement that, if necessary, he would ask Congress for wartime powers "to wage a war against the emergency" of the Depression. He said he believed the American people wanted "discipline and direction under leadership," much as they did in war. Roosevelt's deliberate use of the image of war against the Depression emphasized the positive, progressive good which war could bring to America. The constant use of "emergency" in titles of legislation and of government agencies established to combat the Depression, the use of semimilitary parades and symbols ("the Blue Eagle") in the publicity campaigns in support of the National Recovery Administration, and the use of military officers throughout the Civilian Conservation Corps (as well as the military terminology in the name) sustained the image of a good war against the Depression in the early years of the New Deal.

The use of the metaphor of war, and of images out of the myths and stories of war, by modern Presidents to bring recovery from Depression or to solve other crises (modern crises have become, by definition, warlike), have given the mythology of war a strong internal, domestic application. The "war" against the Depression (like the later "War" on Poverty) would bring progress at home, whatever happened to the rest of the world—so Americans hoped.

The Depression also created considerable revulsion against real war. The investigations of a Senate committee under the leadership of Senator Gerald Nye of North Dakota into the causes of World War I, publicly reported in 1934, reinforced the image of war as evil and destructive. America's entry into World War I, according to the report, had been brought about through the efforts and propaganda, and because of the investments, of large worldwide corporations which profited enormously from the war. The "merchants of death" had encouraged the war, and only they had profited from the suffering and bloodshed and destruction. In a Depression, when many felt that the great and wealthy corporations had failed the American people, the idea that World War I was the result of the machinations of corporations appeared to explain much of the evil of war. Protest against the possibility of war abroad, by those who were warring against Depression at home, grew. (Ironically, an organization calling itself the Veterans of Future Wars appeared on some college campuses to fight for peace.) The Neutrality Acts, the refusal of many to support any moves to stop Germany's expansion or Japan's war against China, and the position of those who would defend "America First" in a world crisis all emphasized the attitude that wars fought abroad which were not clearly wars to defend America from attack could only result in the evil, destructive results of war. No good could come of them.

THE GOOD WAR

In 1939 and 1940, the New York World's Fair—with its widely publicized image of the Trylon and Perisphere—gave millions a glimpse of the "World of Tomorrow." Even after the fair closed, the displays of the future world which were sponsored by corporate giants like General Motors and General Electric went on the road, toured America, and gave many more Americans concrete images of a "real" world of the future filled with amazing machines—television sets, automatic stoves, dishwashers, automatic washing machines, to name a few—in smooth, silvery, shiny cities tied together with ribbons of great highways. Huge airplanes traveling at unheard-of speeds would move people about the country, perhaps around the world. The future, as portrayed by the fair, was bright and filled with promises of material things for a consuming society—*if*—and they were, as Americans said, "big ifs"—the Depression ended and the world was not destroyed in the war already raging in Asia when the fair opened and spreading across Europe when it closed. Those fantastic images of a shining, automatic material future became part of the vision of the good that could come from World War II.

For most Americans, World War II started on Sunday, December 7, 1941, when the Imperial Japanese Navy attacked and virtually destroyed the American fleet at Pearl Harbor. The United States had been attacked, and it became *necessary* to go to war. World War II was fought out of righteous anger, to defend America from attack, and to preserve American freedom and American society.

"Praise the Lord, and Pass the Ammunition" was a popular World War II song. "Doctor Win-the-War" took over from "Doctor New Deal," President Roosevelt said. The Depression disappeared. Full employment returned and production grew to unprecedented levels. The relief agencies which had proliferated during the Depression ceased to be needed. The American people were unified as they had never been, and all were once again working together toward a common goal: to win the war.

World War II was *total* war, as Americans believed war ought to be. And most Americans insisted that there be no inconclusive armistice at the end of it; the only possible end to such a war was the unconditional surrender of the enemies. The war was a crusade, against aggression, tyranny, oppression, Fascism, and totalitarianism. Victory in such a crusade had to be total, and to that end Americans were willing to commit themselves.

The memories of war generated by the American World War I experience, and now contained in the mythology of war, also conditioned American responses to World War II—both during the war itself and long afterward. Past war experiences thus became part of the myths and stories told in modern America about World War II. Americans were determined, for example, that the disastrous results of World War I would not be repeated after World War II. War was indeed destructive, but Americans wanted to ensure that the destruction was limited to the combat zones and to wartime. The mistakes recognized in the lessons of the past would not be repeated. This war would be kept inside its parentheses.

Planning for demobilization of people and of the economy was carefully undertaken, so that the economic chaos which followed World War I would not happen again. Planning began for the establishment of a United Nations organization at the end of the war that would avoid the weakness of the old League of Nations. The United States was determined to take its proper place as a world leader after the war, so that there would indeed be peace in the world.

The Second World War brought America resounding success—economic affluence, world leadership, scientific advancement, military victory—after fifteen or more very long years of deprivation and a sense of failure. The war ended, as Americans looking back on it perceived it, with the death of Franklin Roosevelt and the dropping of the atomic bomb. Roosevelt's death marked the end of an era, the era of Great Depression, New Deal, and world war; and it left Americans fearful of a world without the presidential colossus they looked to for leadership. That fear was made even more immediate by the unleashing of atomic power, a scientific force so strange that, while it symbolized all the awesome power of science and progress and good war, it was also perceived as a potential Frankenstein's monster, American-made.

The image of World War II as hell became much more vivid for those

Americans who had not fought in it in the period following the war, as movies, stories, and photographs of the destroyed cities and countries spread in America, as veterans who had seen and been in hell returned home, as prison camps were opened in Europe and the Far East, as the war crimes tribunals in Nürnberg and Tokyo brought to light appalling evidence of atrocities, and as the full horror of the German death camps became known and visible in America. The vision of hell in Hiroshima, of a city obliterated by the blast of one bomb, presented a peculiar contradiction not present in most of the other hellish images of war: the device which could turn a whole city, with all its people, into an inferno in seconds was the result of American know-how, American ability to do the impossible, American science, and American progress and productivity. This new epitome of the evil of war was an American invention. Americans were fascinated by the power of the bomb and its successors, but at the same time they feared its power in the wrong hands and, as the postwar literature, of which Stanley Kubrick's movie *Dr. Strangelove* was an outstanding example, shows, serious doubts grew that there were, even in America, any right hands for such a terrible and terrifying weapon. The bomb became for Americans the prime symbol of their ambivalence about war (which could bring both progress and destruction), about science (which could harness the forces of the universe and unleash them), and about power itself, which was terrifyingly beautiful to watch, awesomely furious and destructive, and ultimately able to shake, change, and destroy the world and humanity.

The memory of World War I, the myth of war, and the hopes of Americans in 1945 all emphasized the parenthetical nature of war. The war would end, and thereby prove that war was an aberration. *But,* if World War II proved to be an aberration, if it was indeed parenthetical to the normal life of the nation, then what would happen if the United States went back to normal?

The vision of normalcy for most Americans at the end of World War II was the Depression of the many years before the war. A return to the Depression was what most feared. The federal government and the President obviously feared it; so did labor leaders, business leaders, and everyone else. Nor did many want to return to the days of the twenties, before the Depression. The immense difficulty, the basis of much of the fear in evidence in postwar America, was that there was no acceptable vision of normalcy to go back to.

If World War II was to prove to be a good war, then the progress, the full employment, the potential prosperity the war had produced had to be permanent. The end of the war should bring, Americans believed and hoped—not least because of the lasting images of the New York World's Fair and the government and business advertising during the war which promised a better material future "after the war is over," "when the lights go on again all over the world"—a continuation of the national economic success and well-being brought about by the war, without its destructiveness and horror. The aim of the war had been to create freedom from fear and freedom from want throughout the world (along with freedom of speech and freedom of religion—the Four Freedoms), and Americans were eager to confirm the successful accomplishment of those aims at home.

WAR AND PEACE

Fear of a return to normalcy produced in Americans a vision of war as the only available model or pattern for economic success and productivity. The decades since 1945 have seen a transformation of the American mythology of war as a result. The vision of normalcy faded, and with it the implication that there was a stable, secure, peaceful, prosperous world to which the nation could return after the aberration of war. Instead of normalcy, what Americans have sought for themselves individually, and for the nation, is stability and security in a world they no longer believe to be fundamentally stable or secure. Consciously and unconsciously, they have sought and created an economic and moral equivalent of war.

The cessation of warfare did not automatically bring peace in an unstable, insecure, abnormal world. Instead, it brought the necessity to create peace, to crusade for it—the necessity to seek security and stability aggressively, and the necessity to defend constantly what one has against the nameless forces of chaos. Peace became a crisis, an emergency that grew out of the fears of Americans. And crises could be met successfully only by crusades, by being at war. The myth of war, with all its analogies, its aggressive and heroic metaphors, its visions of loyalty and victory, its promises of defense and security, its focus on an enemy, its image of supreme effort and efficiency, its appeal of "the game well played" and of sacrifice, and its implications of national unity, national prosperity, and national success, has become the most important model for American behavior since World War II.

The transformation of the myth and its growth into a major concern of Americans was not rationally accomplished, nor was it planned. Much of the acceptance of it came from the war itself, and from the carry-over of wartime and war-related activities into the postwar years. Deconversion and demobilization, with the accompanying government activities, maintained the wartime sense of crisis. The plans, made in 1943, to provide an economic and educational base for veterans, embodied in the G.I. Bill of Rights—with the continuations and revivals of the G.I Bill in the 1950's and 1960's—established a long-term pattern for economic and educational benefits to be gained by Americans who served in war. The rights of young men (and some women) to a college education, a government-secured home mortgage, bonus and "readjustment" payments, were intended to be compensation for their having devoted "the best years of their lives" to the service of the nation in war, but those rights also provided ways to regulate the economy (by keeping millions of young men off the labor market), to subsidize the expansion of higher education and the construction industry, and to provide direct subsidies to individuals. Those rights were, as all Americans knew, the direct result of war and a lasting good to the nation. In this, as in many other instances, it has become progressively more difficult to distinguish between war and the economic benefits to be derived from war. In the mythic logic, they are the same.

The terminology of warfare has changed. In 1947, a Defense Department was substituted for the War (and Navy) Department. The Defense establishment, at its smallest much larger than any peacetime military establishment the United States had ever possessed, provides not for waging war—a temporary occupation, for which small cadres had been maintained in normal times—but rather for the permanent defensive posture of the United States, with large military forces permanently scattered around the globe. The name change was symbolic of the development of a permanent state of what Americans had, before World War II's end, known simply as "war."

The Cold War became, over the years since Americans have perceived it to exist (roughly since 1947), both the rational justification for, and the symbol of, the continuance of war after the end of World War II. It was not precisely the "moral equivalent of war" which many Americans sought in the immediate postwar years. The Cold War produced fear, both in America and elsewhere, and, at least in Korea and Vietnam, it was also massively destructive and hellish. But it was, in many respects, a moral equivalent to war; it seemed to require the total commitment associated with good wars, it provided a possibility for efficient and productive leadership, it focused American fears and gave them outlet, it provided an opportunity for continued wartime economic progress, and it made it possible to maintain a crusade for freedom and progress in the world.

The Cold War and its logic became part of the transformed mythology of war. Central to belief in the Cold War was the perception which had flourished since 1917 that Communism, embodied in the Soviet Union, was a threat to American success and existence in the world. In World War II, the U.S.S.R. had become a direct competitor for world leadership, and its Communism was bent on the destruction of the U.S.A., and its liberty and democracy. Such a threat, combined with the military might and the power of the Soviet Union, generated a crisis in American life which re-created the emergency of World War II. The possibility of finding security in a world in which Communism, a revolutionary ideology devoted to the overthrow of all political, social, and economic systems which were not of its own making, backed by the great power and potential of the Soviet Union, was present, seemed slight to the many Americans who had long distrusted both Communists and foreigners like the Russians. Americans came to believe that the new crisis could be met only by doing those things which war required: unifying the people, giving the government power for efficient leadership, building an adequate war machine and military establishment, and recreating the economic patterns of production and development which had been so successful in winning World War II—and in eliminating the Depression.

The lessons of the past—particularly of the years between the two world wars—taught many Americans that narrow nationalism, along with appeasement of aggression and expansion—in Manchuria, Ethiopia, Spain, China, Austria, Czechoslovakia—had caused World War II. The Cold War would provide an equivalent to war in order to prevent such aggression and expansion: the Soviet Union and Communism would be "contained."

The Soviet Union had, for example, drawn a line across Europe, an "Iron Curtain," as Winston Churchill called it in 1947. Every American knew such a line to be a defiance, a dare. Lines were drawn in other countries, and the American government began to speak of "defense perimeters." Frontier mythology dictated that there had to be preparation for war. The lines had to be defended. The enemy had to be contained. In the old days, militia had been trained and frontiersmen and pioneers had been armed and ready. In a modern world, defense required modern armies, which meant American or American-directed armies. The logic of a large military establishment, of NATO armies, and of military assistance to countries all over the world was inescapable.

In 1949, the Soviet Union set off its first atomic bomb. What sense of security the sole possession of the bomb had given to Americans disappeared. "Proof" of the aggressive intent of Communism came in the same year, when the Chinese Communists gained control of China and the Nationalist Chinese government fled to Taiwan. As most Americans perceived the situation, the Communists had both the bomb and China. The country's very existence was in danger. It was even possible that it had been Americans who lost China—some, particularly in the State Department, were so accused—and also gave the bomb to the Russians. Fear of atomic holocaust and ultimate defeat confirmed for most Americans the reasons for and the necessity of Cold War as an equivalent of the "good" war—World War II—in which the United States was neither severely damaged nor defeated.

Belief in Cold War gradually suppressed the vision of the destructive element in war. Fallout-shelter programs and discussions of survival rates led many to conclude that the United States would survive even atomic war, and that the reality of the emergency and the good produced by the Cold War outweighed the disadvantages. Steadily increasing defense spending, which started with the beginning of the Korean War in 1950 and has not yet stopped, brought increased employment, higher wages, growing prosperity, and business expansion. Corporate conglomerates and multinationals grew and spread. Aid to other countries opened greater markets for American products and capital. The "affluent society" grew and confirmed for more and more Americans that national economic success and war were connected.

The pattern became obvious. Defense industries and defense spending brought improved local economies. Millions of jobs were created. Government decisions to reduce defense programs or close military bases brought, to individuals and communities, the vision of depression, unemployment, and economic collapse. Political leaders responded to such visions and became, in effect, lobbyists for the continuation and expansion of defense budgets.

Defense and national security reasons for unusual economic or military action by the federal government came to be seen as overriding—as they had been in World War II. In the interests of defense or security, political traditions, economic ideas, and even constitutional limitations could be broken. Many, for example, remembered the projects of the Works Progress Administration during the Depression years as "made" work—provided by the government as a temporary measure only because people needed jobs and pay—which had no intrinsic value or importance. The hundreds of thousands of jobs, however, which have been provided by federal government funding of massive projects to produce soon-obsolescent military goods since the beginning of the 1950's are considered necessary, valuable, and intrinsically worthwhile work because they are believed to be vital for security or defense. Such jobs have come to be perceived as a normal and necessary part of the maintenance of affluence.

Defense and security became justification for the permanent establishment and expansion of the welfare state. The federal highway-construction program, launched in the mid-1950's, and costing billions of dollars by the mid-1970's, was established under the National Defense Highway Act of 1955. Defense was seen by most to be an excuse to provide federal government funding and control of the construction of new highways—something which political tradition and the Constitution had denied the government in the past. The National Defense Education Act established large-scale educational funding by the federal government, a variation of the G.I. Bill. Jobs, education, a healthy economy, and increasing statism became inextricably connected with the mythology of the good war, through the Cold War and its ancillaries, defense and security.

WAR AS POWER FAILURE

In June 1950, under a resolution of the United Nations Security Council and a decision of President Truman, American military forces entered into a war to push back Korean Communist forces, which had invaded South Korea. War was not declared. It was officially a United Nations "police action" commanded by Americans, with a majority of the non-Korean military forces provided by the United States. Russia was the "real enemy" in Korea, as most Americans believed (the North Koreans and the Chinese were "Russia's puppets"). Victory was the object; and total unity and dedication to winning the war was generally expected.

Winning the Korean War proved very difficult for Americans to define, and there was great controversy as a result. Total victory proved impossible, because the military objectives of the war were kept limited: America could not defeat the Russians or the Chinese in Korea, and the vision of atomic holocaust prevented most from playing with the idea of extending the limit of the war. It proved difficult, too, for many to understand how the Korean War was in their interest, or in defense of America—particularly since American troops there were fighting for the United Nations. It proved impossible to maintain unity about the Korean War, and impossible to convince the Americans fighting there that they were fighting for America. Ending the war became an important issue in the 1952 presidential campaign, and an armistice brought an end to the fighting in 1954.

The cease-fire did not end the Cold War. It did add to the Cold War myths the image of "limited" hot wars—"brushfire wars"—which might have to be fought, occasionally, to contain the enemy. The Cold War, however, continued—and the fear of atomic war was, if anything, increased by the American conviction that hot wars, if they were not total (and therefore atomic), were unsatisfactory and incapable of bringing victories. At the same time, the idea that hot wars would be limited reinforced the implication that the destructiveness and hell of the Cold War was limited. That, in turn, made more believable the emphasis on the Cold War as good, progressive, and constructive. So strong and entrenched had the association of government, defense spending, war, and economic prosperity become by 1961 that President (former General) Eisenhower warned the nation, in his farewell address, of the dangers inherent in the growing "industrial-military complex."

The war in Vietnam began, for Americans, as another limited manifestation of the Cold War. The Gulf of Tonkin incident in 1964, however, created belief in an unwarranted attack on Americans, and thereafter the war escalated rapidly. At first, most Americans viewed Vietnam as another Korea. Once again, it brought increased prosperity at home through the accustomed rise in defense spending. But, as in Korea, the imperative for total commitment grew more obviously contradictory to the nature of the warfare. And because the government of the United States was involved in more than warfare in Vietnam—it was committed to the building of a nation in South Vietnam—the objectives of the war became increasingly difficult to understand. "In going to Vietnam," Frances FitzGerald wrote in *Fire in the Lake:*

> . . . the United States was entering a country where the victory of one of the great world ideologies occasionally depended on the price of tea in a certain village or the outcome of a football game. For the Americans in Vietnam it would be difficult to make this leap of perspective, difficult to understand that while they saw themselves as building world order, many Vietnamese saw them merely as the producers of garbage from which they could build houses.

By the mid-1960's, the Vietnam War was being televised in the United States. The horror and holocaust, the actual hell of war, which Americans had come to disregard—except for vague fears of the bomb—in the affluence and success of Cold War, were literally brought home to many. The demands of total war—the draft, the increases in direct military costs, the debates over defoliation, tactical atomic weapons, and pacification, the strident demands from Presidents and other leaders for unity of speech and action and purpose—became more obviously contradictory to the horrors, the supposed limits, and the destroyed jungles of a tiny country halfway round the world. The demands of total war seemed, increasingly, spurious for a war in such a small, remote place.

The logic of total Cold War became "mythical" for the first time. In the face of the actualities of the war being fought—visible through television, reported in the newspapers, or told by returning soldiers—the idea that the Vietnam War was part of an important total global war became difficult to maintain. Americans began to see the story as illogical, unreal: a myth. The war was, in the title of Bernard Fall's book, *Hell in a Very Small Place.* It did not require, many Americans came to believe, total commitment from Americans. Quite possibly, it did not require commitment at all. Was America *required* by her destiny to hold back the "red hordes"? police the world? *make* nations?

Following a pattern renewed in the Korean War (thousands of Americans had done it, on both sides, in the Civil War), young Americans began to dodge the draft. Some left the country in order not to participate in the Vietnam War, and others faced imprisonment for refusing to be conscripted. Students organized and demonstrated against the war, in universities, on the streets, in rallies, at political conventions. By the late 1960's, many were convinced that the war was being fought for domestic, American reasons—

to increase defense spending to bolster political, military, or industrial establishments, to support the power of the federal government and the ability of the President to direct the economic and political destinies of the people of the United States. It had become difficult to believe that the war in Vietnam was being fought to defend the United States or to preserve American leadership in the world, or to contain the forces of Communism. Some Americans even began to doubt the "force" of Communism. It *was* clear that the war was killing and corrupting thousands of young men; it was draining billions of dollars out of the United States; it was creating increasingly violent political and social disaffection; it was corrupting and possibly destroying educational institutions and with them the young Americans who were supposed to be on the cutting edge of history and progress. Finally, the war was destroying the land, the forests, the fields, the homes, and the people of a small country. So great was the outcry that President Johnson decided not to run for re-election because he was too much associated with the origins and escalation of the war.

"Vietnam Vietnam Vietnam," Michael Herr wrote, "we've all been there." The grotesque images of the protests against the war—of the war's violence to Vietnam, the Vietnamese, and Americans, of the domestic violence at the 1968 Democratic National Convention and at Kent State University—have already faded for many Americans. The stories, plays, and movies of Vietnam, its war and its veterans, have begun to "purge our doubts and guilts and heal the suppressed divisions of the war years." As Michael Herr predicted, the word "Vietnam," so much repeated by Americans, has begun to lose "all its old loads of pain, pleasure, horror, guilt, nostalgia." Yet the war and the protests against it revived the vivid images of the hellish destructive chaos of war which had once been part of American mythology. Americans began to see war, once again, as damaging to their ideals and potentially destructive of the fabric of society.

By 1973, the United States had withdrawn its forces from Vietnam. Many Americans then argued, and still do, that the country's involvement in Vietnam was unique: "In no other war did the American government so underestimate the will and determination of the enemy," Russell Fifield wrote in 1978, "and so over-estimate the long-term staying power of the public to believe in the justice of the conflict." American withdrawal from the war was also unique, Fifield asserted.

> History records no other comparable example where a great power in the midst of a protracted and expensive war voluntarily reversed its course and ended its participation in the conflict.

A great many Americans since 1973 have tried to behave as if life was back to normal once the war was out of the way. But normalcy had become the Cold War for America in the years since World War II. And the reaffirmation of the destructiveness of war and of its parenthetical quality which grew out of the Vietnam War does not appear to have removed the belief in the progress and good which can be brought to America and to the world by "marching as to war."

On February 3, 1977, the new President of the United States, Jimmy Carter, deliberately evoked the image of Franklin Roosevelt—the symbol of the ultimate good, national economic success to be gotten from war—by televising a "fireside chat" to the nation (a comforting name Roosevelt had invented, which Carter's staff and TV stage managers revived). The chat was about the energy crisis, the economic crisis, and unemployment. Carter concluded with this explicit evocation of the good war:

> We have come through a very difficult period in our nation's history. But for almost ten years we have not had a sense of common national interest.
>
> We have lost faith in joint efforts and mutual sacrifices. Because of the divisions in our country many of us cannot remember a time when we really felt united.
>
> But I remember another difficult time in our nation's history when we felt a different spirit.
>
> During World War II, we faced a terrible crisis—but the challenge of fighting against fascism drew us together.
>
> Those of us old enough to remember know that they were dark and frightening times, but many of our memories are of people ready to help each other for the common good.
>
> I believe we are ready for that same spirit again.

There were, by the late 1970's, many Americans who disagreed, who felt that war, especially American war, was power failure.

REPRISE

MYTHS AND AMERICANS

BERNARD DE VOTO, one of the more passionate and enthusiastic historians of American exploration and the American West, wrote a letter to Catherine Drinker Bowen, a fellow historian and a biographer, which Bowen quoted in an essay on De Voto she wrote for *The Atlantic Monthly* in 1960. Bowen had been criticized for being too romantic about American history, and De Voto wrote to comfort her:

> Sure you're romantic about American history. . . . It is the most romantic of all histories. It began in myth and has developed through centuries of fairy stories. Whatever the time is in America it is always, at every moment, the mad and wayward hour when the prince is finding the little foot that alone fits into the slipper of glass. It is a little hard to know what romantic means to those who use the word umbrageously. But if the mad, impossible voyage of Columbus or Cartier or La Salle or Coronado or John Ledyard is not romantic, if the stars did not dance in the sky when our Constitutional Convention met, if Atlantis has any landscape stranger or the other side of the moon any lights or colors or shapes more unearthly than the customary homespun of Lincoln and the morning coat of Jackson, well, I don't know what romance is. Ours is a story mad with the impossible, it is by chaos out of dream, it began as dream and it has continued as dream down to the last headlines you read in a newspaper. And of our dream there are two things above all others to be said, that only madmen could have dreamed them or would have dared to—and that we have shown a considerable faculty for making them come true.

"Depend upon it," Max Müller wrote in *Introduction to the Science of Religion* in 1873, "there is mythology now as there was in the time of Homer, only we do not perceive it, because we ourselves live in the very shadow of it, and because we all shrink from the full meridian light of truth." Myths, and the non-rational processes of thought of which myths are the medium, are part of the human condition. We do not escape that condition—or the mythologies that go with it.

American myths are relatively new to human history. They are no less powerful and tenacious because they are only ten or fifteen generations old. And perhaps because American history is relatively brief, few Americans have tried to separate themselves and their realities from their myths in order to describe and understand those myths. Quite rationally and consciously, most Americans try to make themselves into the images they know their fellow countrymen prefer—in order to win elections, sell goods, get jobs, or simply to be able to get along with others. More importantly (because more pervasively), we receive and accept without any rational awareness or conscious analysis many of the images, attitudes, behavior patterns, symbols, heroes, stories, metaphors, analogies, and explanations—the myths, in short—which are available and which make us and our world logical, understandable, and American.

Myths are by their nature vague. They are difficult to define because they are so many things simultaneously, as G. S. Kirk pointed out. They elude rational analysis because they are being told as they are being analyzed. They are the available images which pervade the culture of every nation, every group, every family, and every individual. They are received from parents, teachers, peers, bosses, siblings, children, ministers, politicians, salespeople, grandparents, storytellers; from books, magazines, newspapers, radios, television, movies; from war heroes and sports heroes, from artists and musicians and actors, from charlatans and criminals; even from cities and towns, highways and houses, buildings and factories and airports. Not even the most aloof or the most determinedly impartial observer can escape their influence.

Myths are the mechanism by which people believe contradictory things simultaneously; they are also the mechanism by which those contradictions are (as people believe) resolved—or at least held in a tension which is not uncomfortable to the believers. Myths are not in themselves good or evil. They are the means by which the non-rational elements in all human thought and action are effectively combined with the rational; the means by which visions and ideals are combined with reality.

Myths *are*. They are part of all individual human experience, and of all collective human experience. The identification of particular myths, the rational analysis of their contradictions and paradoxes, will not make them go away. Just as the analysis of dreams does not make an individual stop dreaming, or indeed deprive him of the affect of a particular dream, so the urge to make myths and the power of particular myths are not destroyed by understanding. The demonstration of the visionary quality of ideals does not destroy the human desire to hope or human striving after ideals; so the analysis of myths does not stop a people from believing that their myths are descriptions of reality, nor does it change the desire to realize the ideals and visions embedded in the myths.

* * *

The American nation is a product of the eighteenth-century Enlightenment, and as many of us are aware, some of the greatest ideals and many of our public institutions were given form by men and women of the Enlightenment. "We hold these Truths to be self-evident . . ." is an expression of the great faith and hope of Americans still conditioned by the mythology of the Enlightenment.

The formulation of much of American pessimism and despair also comes from the Enlightenment. Edward Gibbon's *Decline and Fall of the Roman Empire* gave Americans a phrase and a complex set of images—a mythology—which describes the outcome of the most extensive, wealthiest, most progressive, best educated, most scientific, most powerful nation the earth had ever seen: Decline and Fall. American perceptions of empire have decline and fall built in. Decline and fall are both the outcome of and the alternative to empire. Which puts Americans in a fine pickle today. Is the inevitable result of imperial power decline and fall? Does imperial power always corrupt imperially?

"Boom or bust" has, since the days of early-nineteenth-century Western frontiers and the great trails of migration to the Far West, been one of the most vivid formulations of American alternatives, similar to the "win or lose" formulation first ritualized in the American political structure and now a vital part of American games. "Boom" means, as all "boomers" (and most "boosters") know, that things must get better, and bigger, and more productive, and richer. Booming means getting there. It means growth, movement, increase—it means an explosion! a big bang! like the atomic bomb or the formation of the universe. Or a sonic boom. "Bust" of course means the opposite (but not a passive opposite. Bust is just as explosive as boom!). "Kansas or Bust," "Pike's Peak or Bust," "California or Bust" meant that either you got there, or the wagon fell apart, the oxen died, you stopped moving, and you died. Bust means everything falls apart. Now! "Boom or Bust" is the American Way—and the Big Bang is part of it.

Ours is a New World, and we are a new people, innocent—innocents. In every generation, there are and will be discoverers, explorers, pathfinders who break new trails to newer, better futures. Our myth of the New World still gives us the terrible innocence of discovery and the assumption that wherever we blaze our trails is "unstoried, artless, unenhanced" until we arrive.

We are young, vigorous, unique; "on the cutting edge of history." Since we are new, what is young, or vigorous, or unique is good to us *prima facie.* It is confirmation that we are good, as a new people, a new world. All people, everywhere, value youth in some way, but America is the "fountain of youth"—at least for Americans.

As a New World, many Americans believe their country to be the last, best hope of the world, a place of youth, of new beginnings, of booming. Even those who believe that America is, in reality, no such place of hope or virtue believe it somehow *ought to be.* The imperative of the myth still operates powerfully in the "unbelievers," leading the harshest critics to the conclusion that the United States is the first, worst horror of the world—a total bust. If nothing else, America is unique—for its evil if not for its goodness.

We are revolutionaries, we Americans—although we abhor revolutions which are not made by our rules. Our vision of revolution is intertwined with images of cohesive communities, with metaphors of change, movement, growth, and expansion. Frontiersmen, pioneers, practical philosophers, and minutemen—young, restless, mobile men and women—are the revolutionaries, the people who re-form, revise, and re-create communities, new communities, independent communities. Independence "counts" for us. A dependent is an income-tax deduction—someone who is immature, handicapped, or failing; not someone equal or free; not someone independent or self-sufficient or autonomous. Our independence has made us unique; it has made us individually responsible for our own fate. Boom or bust is a personal imperative, part of independence, the drive behind the individual pursuit of success and happiness. And it is a national imperative.

"Reform" is the metaphor most Americans use to describe their revolutionary ideas and actions. "Change" is today an even more widespread term. It carries with it the American associations of young, good (right and proper, moral), reforming. Americans avoid the noun "reformation" because it has religious, Protestant connotations. For Americans, America *is* the Reformation. Americans *are,* by definition and origin and training, in American myths, both reformers and protestants. Protesters, with their imperative to confront evil and to define evil as that which is established, are American protestants seeking further reformation. Their desire to bring about change and their insistence that change is desirable, inevitable, and necessary are modern manifestations of the long-established American mythology of revolution, reform, and progress.

Change is movement, the explosive movement of boom or bust. And it is modern: "We live in an extraordinary age. These are times of stunning changes . . ." is Carl Sagan's (the opening lines of *Broca's Brain*) expression of an American truism. Americans change! Without change and movement, there is, by American definition, stagnation, decay, and death. *Americans* move! Therefore, Americans are young, free, good, changing, progressing, reforming, vital, alive, growing, rising. In contemporary American myth and symbol, homes are mobile, communities are mobile, the nation is mobile, and above all, the individual *is, must* be, *ought* to be, by right *can* be mobile.

"One small step for man, one giant step for mankind" is not only Neil

Armstrong's step onto the surface of the moon (the American representing mankind and fulfilling the American destiny). It is also precisely what Americans believe is accomplished by individual movement. It is—like all mythical statements—reality and symbol, expectation and metaphor, ideal and imperative combined. In Armstrong's image are a host of American images: the steps of the Pilgrims onto Plymouth Rock, the charge of the minutemen onto Concord Bridge, the signature of John Hancock on the Declaration, the trek of Lewis and Clark to the mouth of the Columbia, the proclamation of emancipation by Abraham Lincoln, Henry Ford's first flivver, Armistice Day in World War I, perhaps even the hellish brilliance of the fireball at Alamogordo. All are "steps," movement in pursuit of change, progress, revolution, independence, and happiness; and all—as we believe—in the service of, for the good of, humankind.

For Americans, the individual is the central actor, the source of all good, of all the boom, in the mythologies of being American. In our urban life, it is the responsibility of the individual to create community. Twentieth-century "imperial" cities have destroyed the communities Americans assumed to exist, and brought about (as might have been expected) the decline (and fall?) of big cities and urban life. The result has been an increase in emphasis on the privacy, the autonomy, and the effectiveness of the individual. But the moral implications of individual freedom and independence have long been part of American mythology: the bust always accompanies the boom. Individual responsibility and worth in America have for two centuries or more been accompanied by alienation, violence, crime, hedonism, the worship of youth, the denial of death, and the decline of religion.

The American nation today is frequently perceived as the individual writ large. To the nation belong the qualities, the virtues, and the ideals of the individual. Americans still tell tales of and believe in the unity, the great purposes, and the ultimate destiny of the American nation. Very often they are tales of organized, mass action; tales of war which embody nationalism and the vision of freedom. American wars are revolutions, the Civil War on a world scale. The end and purpose of those wars is freedom, the destruction of slavery (whatever its form), and the construction of individual and national independence. Wars, in American myth, are the expression of the belief that Americans can do anything they desire, can build nations or rebuild societies, can speed progress, bring freedom and democracy to the world, so long as they are united, organized, and willing to devote all their human and material resources to the end desired. America, imperial America, *is* "one giant step for mankind."

Americans frequently voice the fear that their world is falling apart. Certainly values and myths, beliefs and logics which we have held dear are being questioned by many. And the questions are serious. Are giant, multinational corporations a danger to American life? or the belief in the goodness of, and necessity for, such corporations? Is the fear of Great Depression a danger to American life? Is the consumer society good for us? hazardous to our health? Was Charles Lindbergh the last great American hero? Is that a good thing? What does American life really mean? Where are we going?

Did Americans begin to become widely aware of changes in their myths as a result of the Great Depression and World War II? Do our present doubts about America, its past and its future, grow out of that awareness? Have our fundamental American ideals become distorted by our modern pursuits? or by modern realities?

Is it the case that some pristine, ideal pursuit of happiness has become corrupted by the consumer society? Has America's errand into the wilderness been destroyed by the Vietnam War? Does the "imperial Presidency" make democracy no more than the distorted dream of an idealized past?

Is America running out of energy? power? Is our energetic use of power destroying us? Have we polluted ourselves and our country by it? Is our faith in science becoming another form of hazardous nuclear fallout—invisible, cumulative, deadly?

Is our belief that things are different now—change happens faster, disaster is more momentous, knowledge is more certain, corruption is more monumental—merely another myth, the product of our progressivism and not really different from the quaint, old-fashioned ideas of our grandparents (or theirs)? But if things really *are* different now, what is going to happen to *us?*

No one, historian, scientist, Marxist, theologian, or astrologer, can predict. The best one can do is extrapolate from the past, which is what all modern scientists, economists, members of the Club of Rome, ecologists, and industrialists do when they predict the future. So, for that matter, do writers of science fiction (and palm readers). And the past is, as Leslie Hartley said at the beginning of *The Go-Between,* "a foreign country. People behave differently there." It is prologue to the future, controlling future events, only if human beings, using some human logic, believe it to be.

All human beings are tied to the histories of their family, their people, and their nation. In the telling and hearing of those histories, or of stories believed parts of them, in the rituals and re-enactments of them, in the tracing of genealogies and the attachments to grandparents, many find a sense of belonging and a sense of place—the security which comes from knowing one's place in time. Many people, too, seek to know their histories in order to be released from the mistakes of the past or to break the cycle of endless repetitions of the patterns of the past. Yet knowledge of what we ordinarily call history, no matter how scientific, objective, and complete that knowledge may be, does not release an individual or a people from the images, the analogies and metaphors—the myths, in short—through which all history is viewed, and by which history is made useful, logical, and real to any of us.

The study of American myths will not make us any better able to predict the future. But it should enable us to know better who we are and what makes the reality of our present world. It will perhaps make it possible for us to see more clearly, and more rationally, exactly what drives us as a people. We can then, perhaps, put that knowledge to rational use.

Myths do change, as all of human life changes. But, despite the modern belief that even our change is different and more rapid than change used to be, the process of changing myths is slow and essentially conservative in nature. The impulses which created our myths are still with us, carried in the myths themselves. The bases we use today to decide what is a good story, who is a hero or heroine, what is a gripping metaphor or an obvious analogy—the logic of our mythologies is still, in short, identifiably American.

"Myth may teach man many things," Ernst Cassirer wrote in *The Myth of the State* (1946), "but it has no answer to the only question which . . . is really relevant: to the question of good and evil." The mythology of a people is essentially descriptive, not judgmental. Reason and rationality imply a search for a distinction between good and evil, and rational human beings apply those categories to their myths. The result is the perceived conflict between rational thought, which is judgmental, and mythic thought, which does not judge, which is innocent therefore—and amoral. American myths do not supply answers to questions of the good or evil in contemporary American life. The analysis of those myths, then, can only show the connections between present and past American myths, their content, their logic, and their imperatives for Americans now and in the past. We still interpret, understand, and judge our real world through the myths we possess. As the myths change, so will our assessments of reality.

"In any case," a young black student of mine said, "the past *hurts.*" One of the ways Americans try to avoid that pain is to insist that the present is very different from the past: we have lost our innocence—perhaps we have even lost our empire.

In the 1920's, Alfred P. Sloan set General Motors on the process of retooling to produce new models. Of course, the new models weren't very different from the old. Cars were cars, after all. They had to have an internal combustion engine (because God and Henry Ford had given them one) with enough horsepower to pull around the metal of the cars fast enough to induce people to buy them; they had to have four wheels to go round and round because, for modern progressive evolutionary Americans the fact that God had not given us wheels was no argument that He didn't want us to have them because, after all, He had given us Henry Ford—and to what other purpose? Besides, wheels made us Americans. So retooling didn't mean throwing out the cars, it only meant making them—well—different. More attractive. Maybe even better. If something better came up.

Retooling thereby became an important part of the modern American myths of change. But what sort of change?

Economists and high government officials have recently warned that we face a serious and permanent reduction in the American standard of living because of the developing shortage of petroleum. What kind of change is that? Do we stop consuming? What happens to the engine of progress if we do? Does a high standard of living have to mean everyone having two cars, burning up petroleum in cars and trucks, homes and buildings, trains and ships and airplanes at an exponentially increasing rate? Would it be a great bust if the GNP—or the great corporations—or the population—didn't *grow?*

Have we finally reached the Pacific? And if we have, is that The End? of us? of our nation? of the movie? of our great ideals? Must we now give up our madness? decide that no one's foot fits the glass slipper?

Is the reality we face merely the reality of getting used to a lower standard of living? (Merely?!) Or is that reality also composed of communities, of fiercely equal Americans helping each other, of independent Americans making individual decisions about how they will make do?

The prototypical American individual was a jack-of-all-trades who could turn his or her hand, or judgment, to making or deciding with whatever materials happened to be around whatever seemed necessary for survival or the common good. No Renaissance man—or woman—this American, but someone who could make do or make better a life in the wilderness.

In today's world of business and government and educational bureaucracies, composed of specialized departments, staffed with highly educated, specially trained experts with lifelong experience in their fields, is there any place for an American jack- or jill-of-all-trades? Or for the judgment and decisions of such a person?

And if Americans started to make do, make decisions, and use to best advantage whatever they had at hand—wood, sunlight, clay, coal, people, tools, machines—would America and our vision of her mission in the wilderness change? Or would we still be dreaming "madmen's dreams"?

Can we in reality (as in myth) lick anything? Can we conserve?—our energy? our resources? Can we create a civilized world in this new wilderness that does not need so much oil, energy, resources? And can we stay rich and growing while we do it?

I make no pretense of being able to answer such questions. But it is clear that American myths, with their logic, their ideals, their imperatives for thought and action, have changed in the past. Yet Americans used to be as mixed up in their thoughts, motives, beliefs, emotions—and as inconsistent in their behavior—as they are now. They could occasionally separate the good from the bad, but they didn't always do what they knew to be right. Americans often chose pleasure over rectitude, and even when they did choose the right, it didn't always produce the good. They were romantics, impossible dreamers, impossible doers. Their myths—like ours—were sometimes self-fulfilling prophecies. Sometimes they were blindfolds—like ours. Sometimes they were high ideals. Like ours?

Bibliography

THE SOURCES LISTED are those books which I know have influenced my interpretations or from which I have consciously taken ideas. Since this book touches many important topics in American history, and the literature on most of those topics is vast, I have made no effort to list representative works. The books are listed by topics, under the chapter headings in which they were first used. I have tried not to list any source more than once. Any book cited in the text is not included here.

Overture: Americans and Myths

MYTHS The best summary of modern thought about myths and their functions is G. S. Kirk, *Myth: Its Meaning and Functions in Ancient and Other Cultures* (Cambridge, England, and Berkeley, 1970), especially 252–70.

Ruth Benedict, *Patterns of Culture* (New York, 1934), *The Chrysanthemum and the Sword* (Cambridge, Mass., 1946); Bruno Bettelheim, *The Uses of Enchantment: The Meaning and Importance of Fairy Tales* (New York, 1976); Joseph Campbell, *The Hero with a Thousand Faces* (New York, 1949); Ernst Cassirer, *The Myth of the State* (New Haven, 1946), *The Philosophy of Symbolic Forms,* Vol. II, *Mythical Thinking* (1955); Erik H. Erikson, *Childhood and Society* (New York, 1950), *Young Man Luther: A Study in Psychoanalysis and History* (New York, 1958), *Identity and the Life Cycle: Selected Papers,* Vol. I, No. 1, *Psychological Issues* (1959); M. I. Finley, *The Ancient Economy* (Berkeley and Los Angeles, 1973); Joseph Fontenrose, *The Ritual Theory of Myth* (Berkeley, 1966); Henri Frankfort *et al., Before Philosophy: The Intellectual Adventure of Ancient Man* (Baltimore, 1973); Sigmund Freud, *Civilization and Its Discontents* (New York, 1961), *A General Introduction to Psychoanalysis* (New York, 1953), *The Interpretation of Dreams* (New York, 1923), *Moses and Monotheism* (New York, 1955), *Totem and Taboo* (New York, 1950); Carl G. Jung, *The Archetypes and the Collective Unconscious* (Princeton, 1959), *Man and His Symbols* (London, 1964), *Symbols of Transformation* (New York, 1956), *Two Essays on Analytical Psychology* (New York, 1956); Clyde K. M. Kluckhohn, *Mirror for Man: The Relation of Anthropology to Modern Life* (New York, 1949), "Myths and Rituals: A General Theory," *Harvard Theological Review,* XXXV (1942), 45–79; Edmund Leach, ed., *The Structural Study of*

Myth and Totemism (London, 1967); Albert B. Lord, *The Singer of Tales* (Cambridge, Mass., 1960); Claude Lévi-Strauss, *The Elementary Structures of Kinship* (London, 1969), *The Raw and the Cooked: Introduction to a Science of Mythology: I* (New York, 1969), *From Honey to Ashes: Introduction to a Science of Mythology: II* (New York, 1973), *The Savage Mind* (Chicago, 1966), *Structural Anthropology* (New York, 1963); Gilbert Murray, *The Rise of the Greek Epic* (New York, 1960); Henry A. Murray, ed., *Myth and Mythmaking* (Boston, 1960); Otto Rank, *The Myth of the Birth of the Hero and Other Writings* (New York, 1959).

FOREIGN OBSERVERS OF AMERICA. Sir Denis W. Brogan, *America in the Modern World* (New Brunswick, N.J., 1960), *The American Character* (New York, 1944), *Politics in America* (New York, 1969); James Bryce, Viscount Bryce, *The American Commonwealth* (New York, 1918); Lewis Chester, Godfrey Hodgson, Bruce Page, *An American Melodrama: The Presidential Campaign of 1968* (New York, 1969); Alistair Cooke, *America* (New York, 1973); Charles Dickens, *American Notes for General Circulation* (London, 1842), *The Life and Adventures of Martin Chuzzlewit* (London, 1844); Durrand Echeverria, *Mirage in the West: A History of the French Image of American Society to 1815* (1957); J.-J. Servan-Schreiber, *The American Challenge* (New York, 1968); Daniel Snowman, *America Since 1920* (New York, 1968); Alexis de Tocqueville, *Democracy in America* (New York, 1966); Frances Milton Trollope, *Domestic Manners of the Americans* (New York, 1949).

INTERPRETATIONS OF AMERICAN MYTHS. Bernard De Voto, *The Course of Empire* (Boston, 1952); Michael Kammen, *People of Paradox: An Inquiry Concerning the Origins of American Civilization* (New York, 1972); Leo Marx, *The Machine in the Garden: Technology and the Pastoral Ideal in America* (New York, 1964); Arthur K. Moore, *The Frontier Mind* (Lexington, Ky., 1957); Lewis Mumford, *The Myth of the Machine: The Pentagon of Power* (New York, 1970); Bruce A. Rosenberg, *Custer and the Epic of Defeat* (University Park, Pa., 1974); Henry Nash Smith, *Virgin Land: The American West as Symbol and Myth* (Cambridge, Mass., 1950); Richard Slotkin, *Regeneration Through Violence: The Mythology of the American Frontier, 1600–1860* (Middletown, Conn., 1973); Walter Prescott Webb, *The Great Plains* (Boston, 1931).

DEBUNKING. See Thomas J. Fleming, *One Small Candle: The Pilgrims' First Year in America* (New York, 1964), 204 ff., for an attempt to "correct" and debunk the story of the First Thanksgiving. Charles A. Beard is probably the most famous of the American historian "debunkers." See his *An Economic Interpretation of the Constitution of the United States* (New York, 1913) and *The Idea of National Interest* (New York, 1934). More recent efforts have been made by Thomas A. Bailey: see "The Mythmakers of American History," *Journal of American History,* LV (June 1968), 5–21, and his massive effort in a college textbook, *Probing America's Past: A Critical Examination of Major Myths and Misconceptions* (Lexington, Mass., 1973).

I MISSION AND DESTINY

1 Crusader, Fortress, Policeman, Peacemaker

NATIONALISM. George Dangerfield, *The Awakening of American Nationalism, 1815–1828* (New York, 1965); Karl W. Deutsch, *Nationalism and Its Alternatives* (New York, 1969); Carl Russell Fish, *The Development of American Nationality* (New York, 1929); Carlton J. H. Hayes, *Nationalism: A Religion* (New York, 1960); Hans Kohn, *American Nationalism: An Interpretive Essay* (New York, 1957), *The Idea of Nationalism: A Study in Its Origins and Background* (New York, 1967); David M. Potter, "The Historians' Use of Nationalism and *Vice Versa,*" *American Historical Review,* LXVII (1962), 924 ff.; Louis L. Snyder, *The New Nationalism* (Ithaca, N.Y., 1968); Michael Walzer, *The Revolution of the Saints: A Study in the Origins of Radical Politics* (Cambridge, Mass., 1965).

2 Banners on the Towers

NEW WORLD. Hugh Honour, *The New Golden Land: European Images of America from the Discoveries to the Present Time* (New York, 1976); Samuel Eliot Morison, *Admiral of the Ocean Sea: A Life of Christopher Columbus* (Boston, 1942), 2 vols.; Edmundo O'Gorman, *The Invention of America: An Inquiry into the Historical Nature of the New World and the Meaning of Its History* (Bloomington, Ind., 1961); J. H. Parry, *The Spanish Seaborne Empire* (London, 1966).

EARLY PEOPLE. Geoffrey Bibby, *The Testimony of the Spade* (New York, 1956); Louis A. Brennan, *No Stone Unturned: An Almanac of North American Prehistory* (New York, 1959); Grahame Clark and Stuart Piggott, *Prehistoric Societies* (New York, 1965); Peter Farb, *Man's Rise to Civilization: The Cultural Ascent of the Indians of North America* (New York, 2nd edn., 1978); Bertrand Flornoy, *The World of the Inca* (New York, 1958); Harold S. Gladwin, *Men Out of Asia* (New York, 1947); Thor Heyerdahl, *Kon-Tiki: Across the Pacific by Raft* (Chicago, 1950), *American Indians in the Pacific: The Theory Behind the Kon-Tiki Expedition* (London, 1952), *Aku-Aku: The Secret of Easter Island* (London, 1958); Frank C. Hibben, *Digging Up America* (New York, 1960); Jesse D. Jennings and Edward Norbeck, eds., *Prehistoric Man in the New World* (Chicago, 1963); Kenneth Macgowan and Joseph A. Hester, Jr., *Early Man in the New World* (New York, 1962); H. M. Wormington, *Ancient Man in North America* (Denver, 4th edn., 1957).

3 No Friends to Welcome Them

COLONIAL LIFE. Bernard Bailyn, *Education in the Forming of American Society* (New York, 1960); Wesley Frank Craven, *The Virginia Company of London,*

1606-1624 (Williamsburg, 1957); James Deetz, *In Small Things Forgotten* (New York, 1977); Alice Morse Earle, *Child Life in Colonial Days* (New York, 1899); Philip J. Greven, Jr., "Family Structure in Seventeenth-Century Andover, Massachusetts," *William and Mary Quarterly,* 3rd Series, XXIII (April 1966), 234–56; Oscar Handlin, "The Significance of the Seventeenth Century," *Seventeenth Century America: Essays in Colonial History,* James Morton Smith, ed (Chapel Hill, N.C., 1959); Peter Laslett, *The World We Have Lost* (New York, 1965); Edmund S. Morgan, *The Puritan Dilemma: The Story of John Winthrop* (Boston, 1958), *The Puritan Family* (New York, 1966); Wallace Notestein, *The English People on the Eve of Colonization, 1603-1630* (New York, 1954); Mark Van Doren, ed., *Samuel Sewall's Diary* (New York, 1927); Timothy L. Smith, "Congregation, State and Denomination: The Forming of the American Religious Structure," *William and Mary Quarterly,* 3rd Series, XXV (April 1968); Julia C. Spruill, *Women's Life and Work in the Southern Colonies* (Chapel Hill, N.C., 1938).

INDIAN ADJUSTMENT. Alfred W. Crosby, Jr., *The Colombian Exchange: Biological and Cultural Consequences of 1492* (Westport, Conn., 1972); Wilbur R. Jacobs, *Dispossessing the American Indian: Indians and Whites on the Colonial Frontier* (New York, 1972); Karen Ordahl Kupperman, *Settling with the Indians* (1980); Douglas Leach, *Flintlock and Tomahawk: New England in King Philip's War* (New York, 1966); Nancy Oestreich Lurie, "Indian Cultural Adjustment to European Civilization," *Seventeenth Century America: Essays in Colonial History,* James Morton Smith, ed. (Chapel Hill, N.C., 1959); Alden T. Vaughan, *New England Frontier: Puritans and Indians, 1620-1675* (Boston, 1965); Wilcomb F. Washburn, ed., *The Indian and the White Man* (Garden City, N.Y., 1964).

4 The Birth of the Nation

TEXTBOOKS. Morison and Commager's *The Growth of the American Republic* (New York, 5th edn., 1962), 2 vols., devotes 178 of over 1600 pages to the period before the Revolution. William A. Williams, *The Contours of American History* (Chicago, 1966), devotes about 100 of nearly 500 pages to pre-Revolutionary history. See Frances FitzGerald, *America Revised: History Schoolbooks in the Twentieth Century* (Boston, 1979).

REVOLUTION. Bernard Bailyn, *The Ideological Origins of the American Revolution* (Cambridge, Mass., 1967); Thomas C. Barrow, "The American Revolution as a Colonial War for Independence," *William and Mary Quarterly,* 3rd Series, XXV (1968), 452–64; Richard Buel, Jr., "Democracy and the American Revolution: A Frame of Reference," *ibid.,* XXI (1964), 165–90; Edwin G. Burrows and Michael Wallace, "The American Revolution: The Ideology and Psychology of National Liberation," *Perspectives in American History,* VI (1972), 167–306; Elisha P. Douglass, *Rebels and Democrats: The Struggle for Equal Political Rights and Majority Rule During the American Revolution* (Chapel Hill, N.C., 1955); Jack Greene, *A Reinterpretation of the American Revolution* (New York, 1967); J. Franklin

Jameson, *The American Revolution Considered As a Social Movement* (Princeton, 1926); Merrill Jensen, *The New Nation: A History of the United States During Confederation* (New York, 1950), "The Idea of a National Government during the American Revolution," *Political Science Quarterly,* LVIII (1943), 356–79; Irving Kristol *et al., America's Continuing Revolution* (New York, 1976); Jackson Turner Main, *The Social Structure of Revolutionary America* (Princeton, 1965), "Government by the People: The American Revolution and the Democratization of the Legislatures," *William and Mary Quarterly,* 3rd Series, XXIII (1966), 391–407; Edmund S. Morgan, *American Slavery, American Freedom: The Ordeal of Colonial Virginia* (New York, 1975); Allan Nevins, *The American States during and after the Revolution* (New York, 1924); Robert R. Palmer, *The Age of the Democratic Revolution: A Political History of Europe and America, 1760–1800* (Princeton, 1959); John Shy, *A People Numerous and Armed: Reflections on the Military Struggle for American Independence* (New York, 1976); Frederick B. Tolles, "The American Revolution Considered as a Social Movement: A Re-evaluation," *American Historical Review,* LX (1954), 1–12; Charles Warren, *The Making of the Constitution* (Cambridge, Mass., 1947); Gordon S. Wood, *The Creation of the American Republic, 1776–1787* (Chapel Hill, N.C., 1969).

FRANKLIN. Leonard W. Labaree *et al.,* eds. *The Autobiography of Benjamin Franklin* (New Haven, 1964); Carl Van Doren, *Benjamin Franklin* (New York, 1952); Carl Van Doren, ed., *Benjamin Franklin's Autobiographical Writings* (New York, 1945); Benjamin Franklin, *The Complete Poor Richard Almanacks,* Whitfield J. Bell, Jr., ed. (Barre, Mass., facsimile edition, 1970), 2 vols; Catherine Drinker Bowen, *The Most Dangerous Man in America: Scenes from the Life of Benjamin Franklin* (Boston, 1974).

WASHINGTON. The best one-volume biography of Washington is James T. Flexner's *Washington, the Indispensable Man* (Boston, 1974); but also see Marcus Cunliffe, *George Washington: Man and Monument* (Boston, 1958), Curtis Nettels, *George Washington and American Independence* (New York, 1951), and Bernhard Knollenberg, *Washington and the Revolution* (New York, 1940). There are two excellent modern, long biographies: James T. Flexner's *George Washington,* 4 vols. (Boston, 1965–72), and Douglas Southall Freeman's *George Washington, a Biography,* 7 vols. (New York, 1948–57), as well as Washington Irving's *Life of George Washington,* 5 vols. (New York, 1855–59). See also the lecture on Washington in Bernard Mayo, *Myths and Men: Patrick Henry, George Washington, Thomas Jefferson* (Athens, Ga., 1959).

JEFFERSON. Gilbert Chinard, *Thomas Jefferson, the Apostle of Americanism* (Boston, 1929); Fawn M. Brodie, *Thomas Jefferson, an Intimate History* (New York, 1974); Thomas J. Fleming, *The Man from Monticello: An Intimate Life of Thomas Jefferson* (New York, 1969); Henry Steele Commager, *Jefferson, Nationalism and the Enlightenment* (New York, 1975); Max Beloff, *Thomas Jefferson and American Democracy* (London, 1948); Daniel J. Boorstin, *The Lost World of*

Thomas Jefferson (New York, 1948); Merril D. Peterson, *The Jeffersonian Image in the American Mind* (New York, 1962), *Thomas Jefferson and the New Nation: A Biography* (New York, 1970); Erik H. Erikson, *The Dimension of a New Identity* (New York, 1974); Adrienne Koch, *Jefferson and Madison: The Great Collaboration* (New York, 1950); and Dumas Malone, *Jefferson and His Time,* 5 vols. (Boston, 1948–74).

JEFFERSON AND LIBERALISM. Vernon Louis Parrington, *Main Currents in American Thought: An Interpretation of American Literature from the Beginnings to 1920* (New York, 1930), I, 342–56; Louis Hartz, *The Liberal Tradition in America: An Interpretation of American Political Thought since the Revolution* (New York, 1955); Carl L. Becker, *The Declaration of Independence: A Study in the History of Political Ideas* (New York, 1933); Charles M. Wiltse, *The Jeffersonian Tradition in American Democracy* (Chapel Hill, N.C., 1935).

OTHER FOUNDING FATHERS. On Patrick Henry, see: Richard R. Beeman, *Patrick Henry: A Biography* (New York, 1974); Robert D. Meade, *Patrick Henry,* 2 vols. (Philadelphia 1957–69). On Samuel Adams, see: Ralph V. Harlow, *Samuel Adams, Promoter of the American Revolution: A Study in Psychology and Politics* (New York, 1923), and John C. Miller, *Sam Adams: Pioneer in Propaganda* (Boston, 1936). On Benedict Arnold, see: James T. Flexner, *The Traitor and the Spy: Benedict Arnold and John André* (New York, 1953), and Charles C. Sellers, *Benedict Arnold, the Proud Warrior* (New York, 1930). On John Adams, see: James T. Adams, *The Adams Family* (Boston, 1930); John Adams, *Diary and Autobiography,* L. H. Butterfield, ed., 4 vols. (Cambridge, Mass., 1961); Gilbert Chinard, *Honest John Adams* (Boston, 1933); Catherine Drinker Bowen, *John Adams and the American Revolution* (Boston, 1950); Page Smith, *John Adams* (Garden City, N.Y., 1962); and Peter Shaw, *The Character of John Adams* (Chapel Hill, N.C., 1975). On Lafayette, see: Louis Gottschalk, *Lafayette Comes to America* (Chicago, 1935), *Lafayette and the Close of the American Revolution* (Chicago, 1942); and Anne C. Loveland, *Emblem of Liberty: The Image of Lafayette in the American Mind* (Baton Rouge, 1971). On Madison, see: Irving Brant, *The Fourth President: A Life of James Madison* (Indianapolis, 1970), *James Madison,* 6 vols. (Indianapolis, 1941–61); Adrienne Koch, *Madison's "Advice to My Country"* (Princeton, 1966); and James M. Burns, *The Deadlock of Democracy: Four-Party Politics in America* (Englewood Cliffs, N.J., 1963).

HAMILTON. Louis M. Hacker, *Alexander Hamilton in the American Tradition* (Westport, Conn., 1975); John C. Miller, *Alexander Hamilton: Portrait in Paradox* (New York, 1969); Broadus Mitchell, *Alexander Hamilton,* 2 vols. (New York, 1957–62); Clinton L. Rossiter, *Alexander Hamilton and the Constitution* (New York, 1964); Claude G. Bowers, *Jefferson and Hamilton: The Struggle for Democracy in America* (Boston, 1925); Jonathan Daniels, *Ordeal of Ambition: Jefferson, Hamilton, Burr* (Garden City, N.Y., 1970).

5 *Nationalism Made Manifest*

NATIONALISM AND REGIONALISM. Ray A. Billington, *America's Frontier Heritage* (New York, 1966); Dan E. Clark, "Manifest Destiny and the Pacific," *Pacific Historical Review,* I (March 1932), 1–17; Amaury de Riencourt, *The American Empire* (New York, 1968); Timothy Dwight, *Travels in New-England and New York* (1821–22); Ruth Miller Elson, "American Schoolbooks and 'Culture' in the Nineteenth Century," *Mississippi Valley Historical Review,* XLVI, 3 (December 1959), 411–34; Timothy Flint, *Recollections of the Last Ten Years* (Boston, 1826); James H. Kettner, *The Development of American Citizenship, 1608–1870* (Chapel Hill, N.C., 1978); Henry F. May, *The Enlightenment in America* (New York, 1976); Howard W. Odum and H. E. Moore, *American Regionalism: A Cultural Historical Approach to National Integration* (New York, 1938); Frederick Jackson Turner, *The Significance of Sections in American History* (New York, 1932); Noah Webster, "Essay on the Necessity, Advantages and Practicability of Reforming the Mode of Spelling" in *Dissertations on the English Language* (Boston, 1789); Rush Welter, "The Frontier West as Image of American Society: Conservative Attitudes Before the Civil War," *Mississippi Valley Historical Review,* XLVI, 4 (March 1960), 593–614, *The Mind of America, 1820–1860* (New York, 1975).

JACKSON AND HIS AGE. Lee Benson, *The Concept of Jacksonian Democracy: New York as a Test Case* (Princeton, 1961); Alfred A. Cave, *Jacksonian Democracy and the Historians* (Gainesville, Fla., 1964); Carl R. Fish, *The Rise of the Common Man, 1830–1850* (New York, 1927); Frank Otto Gatell, ed., *Essays on Jacksonian America* (New York, 1970); Richard P. McCormick, "New Perspectives on Jacksonian Politics," *American Historical Review,* LXV (1960), 288–301; Marvin Meyers, *The Jacksonian Persuasion: Politics and Belief* (Stanford, 1957); Arthur M. Schlesinger, Jr., *The Age of Jackson* (Boston, 1945); Charles G. Sellers, Jr., *Jacksonian Democracy* (New York, 1958); Glyndon G. VanDeusen, *The Jacksonian Era, 1828–1848* (New York, 1959); John William Ward, *Andrew Jackson, Symbol for an Age* (New York, 1955).

THE SOUTH AND SLAVERY. John W. Blassingame, *The Slave Community: Plantation Life in the Antebellum South* (New York, 1972); Jesse T. Carpenter, *The South as a Conscious Minority, 1789–1861: A Study in Political Thought* (New York, 1930); Wilfred Carsel, "Slaveholders' Indictment of Northern Wage Slavery," *The Journal of Southern History,* VI (1940), 504 ff.; Wilbur J. Cash, *The Mind of the South* (New York, 1941); Avery O. Craven, *The Growth of Southern Nationalism, 1848–1861* (Baton Rouge, 1953); Clement Eaton, *The Growth of Southern Civilization, 1790–1860* (New York, 1961); Eugene D. Genovese, "The Slave South: An Interpretation," *Science and Society,* XXV (1961), 320–37, *The World the Slaveholders Made: Two Essays in Interpretation* (New York, 1969); Winthrop D. Jordan, *White over Black: American Attitudes Toward the Negro, 1550–1812* (Baltimore, 1969); Ralph E. McGill, *The South and the Southerner* (Boston, 1963); Eric L. McKitrick, ed., *Slavery Defended: The Views of the Old South* (Englewood Cliffs, N.J., 1963); Thomas V. Peterson, *Ham and Japheth:*

The Mythic World of Whites in the Antebellum South (Metuchen, N.J., 1978); Ulrich B. Phillips, *Life and Labor in the Old South* (Boston, 1929); Charles S. Sydnor, *The Development of Southern Sectionalism, 1819–1848* (Baton Rouge, 1948); William Robert Taylor, *Cavalier and Yankee: The Old South and American National Character* (New York, 1961); Earl E. Thorpe, *Eros and Freedom in Southern Life and Thought* (Durham, N.C., 1967); C. Vann Woodward, *The Burden of Southern History* (Baton Rouge, rev. ed., 1968).

6 *Frontiers and Other Dreams*

BLACKS AND RACISM. Gordon W. Allport, *The Nature of Prejudice* (Reading, Mass., 1954); *America's Race Problems: Addresses at . . . American Academy of Political and Social Science . . .* (New York, 1901) (New York, 1969); Frederick M. Binder, *The Color Problem in Early National America as Viewed by John Adams, Jefferson and Jackson* (The Hague, 1968); Harold Cruse, *Rebellion or Revolution?* (New York, 1968); David Brion Davis, *The Slave Power Conspiracy and the Paranoid Style* (Baton Rouge, 1969); W. E. B. Du Bois, *Black Reconstruction in America: An Essay Toward a History of the Part Which Black Folk Played in the Attempt to Reconstruct Democracy in America, 1860–1880* (New York, 1964), *The Souls of Black Folk: Essays and Sketches* (Chicago, 1903); Stanley Elkins, *Slavery: A Problem in American Institutional and Intellectual Life* (Chicago, 1959); E. Franklin Frazier, *On Race Relations: Selected Writings,* G. Franklin Edwards, ed. (Chicago, 1968); George M. Fredrickson, *The Black Image in the White Mind: The Debate on Afro-American Character and Destiny, 1817–1914* (New York, 1971); Eugene D. Genovese, *Roll, Jordan, Roll: The World the Slaves Made* (New York, 1976); Rhoda L. Goldstein, ed., *Black Life and Culture in the United States* (New York, 1971); Herbert G. Gutman, *The Black Family in Slavery and Freedom* (New York, 1976); John S. Haller, Jr., *Outcasts from Evolution: Scientific Attitudes of Racial Inferiority, 1859–1900* (Urbana, Ill., 1971); Joel Chandler Harris, *The Complete Tales of Uncle Remus,* Richard Chase, comp. (Boston, 1955); Nathan Irvin Huggins, *Slave and Citizen: The Life of Frederick Douglass* (Boston, 1980); Richard Kluger, *Simple Justice: The History of Brown v. Board of Education and Black America's Struggle for Equality* (New York, 1976); C. Eric Lincoln, "Color and Group Identity in the United States," in John Hope Franklin, ed., *Color and Race* (Boston, 1968), 249–63; August Meier, *Negro Thought in America, 1880–1915: Racial Ideologies in the Age of Booker T. Washington* (Ann Arbor, Mich., 1968); Ruth Miller and Paul J. Dolan, *Race Awareness: The Nightmare and the Vision* (New York, 1971); Wilson J. Moses, *The Golden Age of Black Nationalism, 1850–1925* (Hamden, Conn., 1978); Gunnar Myrdal, *An American Dilemma* (New York, 1944); Robert E. Park, *Race and Culture* (Glencoe, Ill., 1950); J. R. Pole, *The Pursuit of Equality in American History* (Berkeley, 1978); Hortense Powdermaker, *After Freedom: A Cultural Study in the Deep South* (New York, 1969); John Rawls, *A Theory of Justice* (Cambridge, Mass., 1971); Herbert J. Storing, "The School of Slavery: A Reconsideration of Booker T. Washington," *100 Years of Emancipation,* Robert A. Goldwin, ed. (Chicago, 1963); Booker T. Washington,

Up from Slavery (Boston, 1901); Forrest G. Wood, *Black Scare: The Racist Response to Emancipation and Reconstruction* (Berkeley, 1968); C. Vann Woodward, *The Strange Career of Jim Crow* (New York, 3rd rev. edn., 1974).

INDIANS. Ralph K. Andrist, *The Long Death: The Last Days of the Plains Indians* (New York, 1964); Dee Brown, *Bury My Heart at Wounded Knee: An Indian History of the American West* (New York, 1971); "Chief Joseph's Own Story," *North American Review* CXXVII (April 1879); Angie Debo, *A History of the Indians of the United States* (Norman, Okla., 1970); Edward P. Dozier, *The Pueblo Indians of North America* (New York, 1970); Harold E. Driver, *Indians of North America* (Chicago, 2nd rev. edn., 1969); Ralph H. Gabriel, *The Lure of the Frontier: A Story of Race Conflict* (New Haven, 1929); Robert V. Hine and Edwin R. Bingham, eds., *The Frontier Experience: Readings in the Trans-Mississippi West* (Belmont, Calif., 1963); E. Adamson Hoebel, *The Cheyennes: Indians of the Great Plains* (New York, 1960); Helen Hunt Jackson, *A Century of Dishonor: A Sketch of the United States Government's Dealings with Some of the Indian Tribes* (Boston, 1891); William H. Kelly, ed., *Indian Affairs and the Indian Reorganization Act* (Tucson, Ariz., 1954); Clyde Kluckhohn and Dorothea Leighton, *The Navaho* (Garden City, N.Y., 1962); Roy H. Pearce, *The Savages of America: A Study of the Indian and the Idea of Civilization* (Baltimore, rev. edn., 1965); Archibald G. Price, *White Settlers and Native Peoples: An Historical Study of Racial Contacts Between English-speaking Whites and Aboriginal Peoples in the United States, Canada, Australia, and New Zealand* (Cambridge, Eng., 1950); *Report of the Commissioner of Indian Affairs for the Year 1864* (Washington, 1865); "The Right to Remain Indian: The Failure of the Federal Government to Protect Indian Land and Water Rights." A Report to the U.S. Commission on Civil Rights by the All Indian Pueblo Council, Albuquerque, N.M., 1972; Henry R. Schoolcraft, *History of the Condition and Prospects of the Indian Tribes of the United States,* Vol. I (Philadelphia, 1851); Wilcomb E. Washburn, *The Indian in America* (New York, 1975).

7 *Transformation of the Wilderness*

Paul Brooks, *The Pursuit of Wilderness* (Boston, 1971); *Land: The Yearbook of Agriculture, 1958* (Washington, 1958); George Perkins Marsh, *Man and Nature,* David Lowenthal, ed. (Cambridge, Mass., 1965); Peter J. Schmitt, *Back to Nature: The Arcadian Myth in Urban America* (New York, 1969); Henry David Thoreau, *Walden: Or, Life in the Woods* (Boston, 1854), *The Annotated Walden,* Philip Van Doren Stern, ed. (New York, 1970).

II THE PURSUIT OF HAPPINESS

2 *Prototypes*

Sacvan Bercovitch, "The Typology of America's Mission," *American Quarterly,* XXV (1978), 135–55; Robert Beverley, *The History and Present State of Virginia*

(1705), Louis B. Wright, ed. (Chapel Hill, N.C., 1947); John Spencer Bassett, ed., *The Writings of Colonel William Byrd of Westover in Virginia Esquire* (New York, 1970); James Fenimore Cooper, *The Pioneers, or the Sources of the Susquehanna; A Descriptive Tale* (New York, 1823), *The Prairie: A Tale* (Philadelphia, 1827), *The Pathfinder; or, The Inland Sea* (Philadelphia, 1840); Gilbert C. Fite, "The Pioneer Farmer: A View over Three Centuries," *Agricultural History,* L (1976), 275–89; Pierre Marambaud, *William Byrd of Westover, 1674–1744* (Charlottesville, Va., 1971); Carl Sandburg, *Abraham Lincoln: The Prairie Years,* 2 vols. (New York, 1926), *Abe Lincoln Grows Up* (New York, 1928).

3 Independent Individualism

William H. Bridges, "Family Patterns and Social Values in America, 1825–1875," *American Quarterly,* XVII (1965), 3–11; Richard DeCharms and Gerald H. Moeller, "Values Expressed in American Children's Readers: 1800–1950," *Journal of Abnormal and Social Psychology,* LXIV (1962), 136–42; *Encyclopædia Americana,* A Popular Dictionary of Arts, Sciences, Literature, History, Politics and Biography, Brought Down to the Present Time; Including a Copious Collection of Original Articles in American Biography; on the Basis of the Seventh Edition of the German Conversations-Lexicon. Francis Lieber, ed., 13 vols. (Philadelphia, 1829–33); Oscar Handlin, *The Uprooted: The Epic Story of the Great Migrations That Made the American People* (New York, 1951); Robert A. Nisbet, "The Social Impact of the Revolution," in Irving Kristol *et al., America's Continuing Revolution* (Garden City, N.Y., 1976), 77–82; Richard L. Rapson, "The American Child as Seen by British Travelers, 1845–1935," *American Quarterly,* XVII (1965), 520–34; Bernard Wishy, *The Child and the Republic: The Dawn of Modern American Child Nurture* (Philadelphia, 1968).

4 The Employee

COWBOYS AND FRONTIERS. Ray A. Billington, *America's Frontier Heritage* (New York, 1966); E. Douglas Branch, *The Cowboy and His Interpreters* (New York, 1926); J. Frank Dobie, *The Longhorns* (Boston, 1941); Marshall W. Fishwick, "The Cowboy: America's Contribution to the World's Mythology," *Western Folklore,* XI (1952), 77–92; Joe B. Frantz and Julian Ernest Choate, Jr., *The American Cowboy: The Myth and the Reality* (Norman, Okla., 1955); Edwin S. Fussell, *Frontier: American Literature and the American West* (Princeton, 1965); Emanuel Hertz, ed., *The Hidden Lincoln: From the Letters and Papers of William H. Herndon* (New York, 1938); Stephen B. Oates, *With Malice Toward None: The Life of Abraham Lincoln* (New York, 1977); Phillip Ashton Rollins, *The Cowboy: His Characteristics, His Equipment, and His Part in the Development of the West* (New York, 1922); L. Steckmesser, *The Western Hero in History and Legend* (Norman, Okla., 1965); Frederick Jackson Turner, *The Frontier in American History* (New York, 1920).

Other Heroes. Horatio Alger, Jr., *Struggling Upward; or Luke Larkin's Luck,* a condensed version in Moses Rischin, ed., *The American Gospel of Success: Individualism and Beyond* (Chicago, 1965), 67–89; Andrew Carnegie, *Autobiography,* J. C. Van Dyke, ed. (Boston, 1920), *The Gospel of Wealth and Other Timely Essays* (1890), Edward C. Kirkland, ed. (Cambridge, Mass., 1962), "The Road to Business Success: A Talk to Young Men," from an address to students of the Curry Commercial College, Pittsburgh, June 23, 1885, in *Empire of Business* (New York, 1968); Rychard Fink, Introduction to Horatio Alger, Jr., *Ragged Dick and Mark, the Match Boy* (New York, 1962); Louis M. Hacker, *The World of Andrew Carnegie, 1865-1901* (Philadelphia, 1968); Howard Haycraft, ed., *The Art of the Mystery Story: A Collection of Critical Essays* (New York, 1946), *Murder for Pleasure: The Life and Times of the Detective Story* (New York, 1941).

5 *Individualism Incorporated*

Louis D. Brandeis, "Business—A Profession," Brown University Commencement Address, 1912, in *Pursuing the American Dream,* Kenneth S. Knodt, ed. (Englewood Cliffs, N.J., 1976), 135–38; Alfred D. Chandler, Jr., "The Beginnings of Big Business in American Industry," *Business History Review,* XXXIII (1959), 1–31, "The Railroads: Pioneers in Modern Corporate Management," *ibid.,* XXXIX (1965), 16–40, "The Railroads: Innovators in Modern Business Administration" (with Stephen Salsbury), *The Railroad and the Space Program: An Exploration in Historical Analogy,* Bruce Mazlish, ed. (Cambridge, Mass., 1965), 131–40, *The Railroads: The Nation's First Big Business* (New York, 1965); Thomas C. Cochran, *200 Years of American Business* (New York, 1977), *Business in American Life: A History* (New York, 1972); Joseph S. Davis, *Essays in the Earlier History of American Corporations,* 2 vols. (Cambridge, Mass., 1917); E. Merrick Dodd, Jr., *American Business Corporations until 1860* (Cambridge, Mass., 1954); Peter F. Drucker, *The Concept of the Corporation* (New York, 1946), *The New Society: The Anatomy of the Industrial Order* (New York, 1950); George H. Evans, Jr., *Business Incorporations in the United States, 1800-1943* (New York, 1948); Sidney Fine, *Laissez-Faire and the General-Welfare State: A Study of Conflict in American Thought, 1865-1901* (Ann Arbor, Mich., 1956); Albert Fishlow, *American Railroads and the Transformation of the Ante-Bellum Economy* (Cambridge, Mass., 1965); Robert W. Fogel, *Railroads and American Economic Growth: Essays in Econometric History* (Baltimore, 1964); Louis Galambos, *The Public Image of Big Business in America, 1880-1940: A Quantitative Study in Social Change* (Baltimore, 1975); Oscar and Mary Handlin, *Commonwealth, a Study of the Role of Government in the American Economy: Massachusetts, 1774-1861* (New York, 1947), "Origins of the American Business Corporation," *Journal of Economic History,* V (1945), 1–23; James Willard Hurst, *The Legitimacy of the Business Corporation in the Law of the United States, 1780-1970* (Charlottesville, Va., 1970); Robert G. McCloskey, *American Conservatism in the Age of Enterprise: A Study of William Graham Sumner, Stephen J. Field, and Andrew Carnegie* (Cambridge, Mass., 1951); Arthur S. Miller, *The Supreme Court and American Capitalism* (New York, 1968); Allan Nevins, *John D.*

Rockefeller: The Heroic Age of American Enterprise, 2 vols. (New York, 1941); George W. Perkins, *The Modern Corporation* (New York, 1908); Stephen Salsbury, *The State, the Investor, and the Railroad: The Boston and Albany, 1825–1867* (Cambridge, Mass., 1967); Anthony Sampson, *The Seven Sisters: The Great Oil Companies and the World They Shaped* (New York, 1975); John F. Stover, *The Life and Decline of the American Railroad* (New York, 1970); Ida M. Tarbell, *The History of the Standard Oil Company,* David M. Chalmers, ed. (New York, briefer version, 1966); George R. Taylor, *The Transportation Revolution, 1815–1860* (New York, 1962); U.S. Industrial Commission, *Preliminary Report on Trusts and Industrial Combinations,* 56 Cong. 1 Sess., Docu. 476 (30 December 1899).

6 The Engine of Progress

CONSUMER SOCIETY. The Editors of *Fortune, The Changing American Market* (Garden City, N.Y., 1955); John K. Galbraith, *The New Industrial State* (New York, 1968); Morrell Heald, "Business Thought in the Twenties: Social Responsibility," *American Quarterly,* XIII (1961), 126–39; Dallas D. Johnson, *Consume! The Monetary Radical's Defense of Capitalism* (New York, 1940); Eric Larrabee, "The Doctrine of Mass Production," in *American Perspectives: The National Self-Image in the Twentieth Century,* Robert E. Spiller and Eic Larrabee, eds. (Cambridge, Mass, 1961), *The Self-Conscious Society* (Garden City, N.Y., 1960); Gardiner C. Means, *The Corporate Revolution in America: Economic Reality vs. Economic Theory* (New York, 1962); James W. Prothro, *The Dollar Decade: Business Ideas in the 1920's* (Baton Rouge, 1954); David Riesman, *Abundance for What? and Other Essays* (Garden City, N.Y., 1964); W. W. Rostow, *The Process of Economic Growth* (Oxford, 2nd edn., 1960).

MACHINES. Arthur A. Bright, Jr., *The Electric-Lamp Industry* (New York, 1949); C. C. Chesney and C. F. Scott, "Early History of the AC System in America," *Journal of the American Institute of Electrical Engineering,* LIII (1934), 726 ff.; Charles E. Edwards, *The Dynamics of the United States Automobile Industry* (Columbia, S.C., 1965); James J. Flink, *The Car Culture* (Cambridge, Mass., 1975); John W. Hammond, *Men and Volts: The Story of General Electric* (New York, 1941); Samuel Insull, *Central Station Electric Service* (Chicago, 1915), *Public Utilities in Modern Life* (Chicago, 1924); Matthew Josephson, *Edison: A Biography* (New York, 1959); Forrest MacDonald, *Insull* (Chicago, 1962); Harold C. Passer, *The Electrical Manufacturers, 1875–1900* (Cambridge, Mass., 1953); John B. Rae, *The Road and the Car in American Life* (Cambridge, Mass., 1971).

ADVERTISING. Joseph M. Appel, *Growing Up with Advertising* (New York, 1940); Harry Lewis Bird, *This Fascinating Advertising Business* (Indianapolis, 1947); F. A. Burt, *American Advertising Agencies: An Inquiry into Their Origins, Growth, Functions and Future* (New York, 1940); Stuart Ewen, *The Captains of Consciousness: Advertising and the Social Roots of the Consumer Culture* (New

York, 1976); L. L. Varda, *Hidden Myth: Structure and Symbolism in Advertising* (New York, 1975).

DEPRIVATION. Roger W. Babson, *The Folly of Instalment Buying* (New York, 1938); Harold Barger, *Outlay and Income in the United States, 1921–1938* (New York, 1942); M. Ada Beney, *Wages, Hours, and Unemployment in the United States, 1914–1936* (New York, 1936); Paul H. Conkin, *FDR and the Origins of the Welfare State* (New York, 1967); Carl N. Degler, "The Ordeal of Herbert Hoover," *The Yale Review,* LII (1963); Paul H. Douglas, *Real Wages in the United States, 1890–1926* (Cambridge, Mass., 1930); John K. Galbraith, *The Great Crash* (Boston, 1955); Julian Goldman, *Prosperity and Consumer Credit* (New York, 1930); Seymour E. Harris, ed., *The New Economics: Keynes' Influence on Theory and Public Policy* (New York, 1947); Fred Henderson, *Capitalism and the Consumer* (London, 1936); Robert F. Himmelberg, ed., *The Great Depression and American Capitalism* (Boston, 1968); *The Memoirs of Herbert Hoover: The Great Depression, 1929–1941* (New York, 1952); Francis T. Juster, *Household Capital Formation and Financing, 1897–1962* (New York, 1966); Maurice Leven, Harold G. Moulton, and Clark Warburton, *America's Capacity to Consume* (Washington, 1934); Irving S. Michelman, *Consumer Finance: A Case History in American Business* (New York, 1966); National Industrial Conference Board, *Wages in the United States, 1914–1930* (New York, 1931); Murray N. Rothbard, *America's Great Depression* (Princeton, 1963); E. R. A. Seligman, *The Economics of Installment Selling: A Study in Consumers' Credit, with Special Reference to the Automobile* (New York, 1927); Robert Sobel, *The Great Bull Market: Wall Street in the 1920's* (New York, 1968); Rexford G. Tugwell, *The Battle for Democracy* (New York, 1935); Studs Terkel, *Hard Times: An Oral History of the Great Depression* (New York, 1970); Herbert Stein, *The Fiscal Revolution in America* (Chicago, 1969).

AFFLUENCE. Jules Abels, *The Welfare State: A Mortgage on America's Future* (New York, 1951); American Management Association, *The Power of Packaging* (New York, 1961); Stephen K. Bailey, *Congress Makes a Law: The Story Behind the Employment Act of 1946* (New York, 1950); Raymond A. Bauer, Ithiel de Sola Pool, and Lewis A. Dexter, *American Business and Public Policy: The Politics of Foreign Trade* (Chicago, 2nd edn., 1963); May Bender, *Package Design and Social Change* (New York, 1975); Otto Butz, *The Unsilent Generation* (New York, 1958); Gerhard Colm, ed., *The Employment Act: Past and Future* (New York, 1956); Council of Economic Advisors, *The Impact of Foreign Aid upon the Domestic Economy* (Washington, 1948); Edward S. Flash, Jr., *Economic Advice and Presidential Leadership* (New York, 1968); John K. Galbraith, *The Affluent Society* (Boston, 2nd rev. edn., 1969), "How Keynes Came to America," in *A Contemporary Guide of Economics, Peace, and Laughter,* Andrea D. Williams, ed. (Boston, 1971); Sheldon Glueck, ed., *The Welfare State and the National Welfare: A Symposium on Some of the Threatening Tendencies of Our Times* (Cambridge, Mass., 1952); Robert A. Gordon, *The Goal of Full Employment* (New York, 1967), *Prosperity and Unemployment: A Conference,* ed. with Margaret S. Gordon (New York, 1966); Leonard S. Guss, *Packaging Is Marketing* (New York, 1967);

Alvin H. Hansen, *America's Role in the World Economy* (New York, 1945); Gabriel Kolko, *Main Currents in Modern American History* (New York, 1976); Robert Lekachman, *The Age of Keynes* (New York, 1966); Arthur D. Little, Inc., *The Role of Packaging in the U.S. Economy: A Report to the American Foundation for Management Research, Inc.* (Cambridge, Mass., 1966); Raymond F. Mikesell, *The Economics of Foreign Aid* (Chicago, 1968); Edwin G. Nourse, *The 1950's Come First* (New York, 1951); Vance Packard, *The Status Seekers: An Exploration of Class Behavior in America and the Hidden Barriers That Affect You, Your Community, Your Future* (New York, 1959); Walt W. Rostow, *The United States in the World Arena: An Essay in Recent History* (New York, 1960); Ben B. Seligman, *Permanent Poverty: An American Syndrome* (Chicago, 1968); Paul F. Smith, *Consumer Credit Costs, 1949–1959* (Princeton, 1964); Arthur Smithies, "The Effect Abroad of American Private Enterprise," *Annals of the American Academy of Political and Social Sciences,* CCCLXVI (1966), 51 ff.; Harold G. Vatter, *The U.S. Economy in the 1950's: An Economic History* (New York, 1963).

7 *Players, Models, Actors*

HEROES. Donald L. Bartlett and James B. Steele, *Empire: The Life, Legend, and Madness of Howard Hughes* (New York, 1979); James A. Bishop, *The Days of Martin Luther King, Jr.* (New York, 1971); Lerone Burnett, *What Manner of Man: A Biography of Martin Luther King, Jr.* (Chicago, 1968); James M. Burns, *John Kennedy: A Political Profile* (New York, 1960); John G. Cawelti, *The Six-Gun Mystique* (Bowling Green, Ohio, 1971); Robert W. Creamer, *Babe: The Legend Comes to Life and Times of George Herman Ruth, the Best-Known and Best-Remembered of America's Sporting Gods* (New York, 1974); Alex Haley, *Roots* (Garden City, N.Y., 1976); Jim Harmon, *The Great Radio Heroes* (Garden City, N.Y., 1967); Robert Jewett and John Shelton Lawrence, *The American Monomyth* (Garden City, N.Y., 1977); William B. Manchester, *Portrait of a President: John F. Kennedy in Profile* (Boston, 1967); J. Nachbar, ed., *Focus on the Western* (Englewood Cliffs, N.J., 1974); Mordecai Richler, "James Bond Unmasked," *Mass Culture Revisited,* Bernard Rosenberg and David M. White, eds. (New York, 1971), 341–55; Jackie Robinson, as told to Alfred Duckett, *I Never Had It Made* (New York, 1972); Joan Rockwell, "Normative Attitudes of Spies in Fiction," *Mass Culture Revisited,* 325–40; Bill Roeder, *Jackie Robinson* (New York, 1950); William Ruehlmann, *Saint with a Gun: The Unlawful American Private Eye* (New York, 1974); John W. Ward, "The Meaning of Lindbergh's Flight," *American Quarterly,* X (1958), 3–16; Dixon Wecter, *The Hero in America: A Chronicle of Hero-Worship* (Ann Arbor, Mich., 1963); W. A. Wilbur, *The Western Hero: A Study in Myth and American Values* (Menlo Park, Calif., 1973); Tom Wolfe, *The Right Stuff* (New York, 1979).

MEDIA. Kenneth G. Bartlett, "The Social Impact of the Radio," *Annals of the American Academy of Political and Social Sciences,* CCL (1947), 89–97; Thomas

E. Coffin, "Television's Impact on Society," *The American Psychologist,* X (1955), 630–41; Herbert J. Gans, *Popular Culture and High Culture: An Analysis and Evaluation of Taste* (New York, 1974); George Gerbner and Larry Gross, *Trends in Network Drama and Viewer Conception of Social Reality, 1967–1973* (Philadelphia, 1974); Joe McGuinniss, *The Selling of the President, 1968* (New York, 1969); H. Marshall McLuhan, *The Mechanical Bride: Folklore of Industrial Man* (New York, 1957); H. L. Marx, ed., *Television and Radio in American Life* (New York, 1953); Horace Newcomb, *TV: The Most Popular Art* (Garden City, N.Y., 1974); Vance O. Packard, *The Hidden Persuaders* (New York, 1957); Bernard Rosenberg and David M. White, eds., *Mass Culture: The Popular Arts in America* (Glencoe, Ill., 1957); Tony Schwartz, *The Responsive Chord* (Garden City, N.Y., 1973); Charles A. Siepmann, *Radio, Television, and Society* (New York, 1950).

ROLES. Michael P. Banton, *Roles: An Introduction to the Study of Social Relations* (New York, 1965); Erik H. Erikson, *Childhood and Society* (New York, 1950); Angus Campbell, Phillip E. Converse, and Willard L. Rodgers, *The Quality of American Life: Perceptions, Evaluations, and Satisfactions* (New York, 1976); William Glasser, *The Identity Society* (New York, rev. edn., 1975); Talcott Parsons *et al., Family, Socialization, and Interaction Process* (Glencoe, Ill., 1955); Helen Perlman, *Persona: Social Role and Personality* (Chicago, 1968); David Riesman *et al., The Lonely Crowd: A Study of the Changing American Character* (New Haven, 1950).

HEROINES. Marian Anderson, *My Lord, What a Morning: An Autobiography* (New York, 1956); Elizabeth Baker, *Technology and Woman's Work* (New York, 1964); Lois W. Banner, *Women in Modern America: A Brief History* (New York, 1974); Louis D. Brandeis and Josephine Goldmark, *Women in Industry* (New York, 1969); Helen Campbell, *Prisoners of Poverty: Women Wage-Workers, Their Trades and Their Lives* (Boston, 1887); William H. Chafe, *The American Woman: Her Changing Social, Economic and Political Roles, 1920–1970* (New York, 1972), *Women and Equality: Changing Patterns in American Culture* (New York, 1977); Clarence Day, *Life with Father* (New York, 1935); Carl N. Degler, "The Woman in America," *Daedalus,* XCII (1964), 653–70; Betty Friedan, *The Feminine Mystique* (New York, 1963); Molly Haskell, *From Reverence to Rape: The Treatment of Women in the Movies* (New York, 1974); Elizabeth Janeway, *Man's World, Woman's Place: A Study in Social Mythology* (New York, 1971); Russell B. Nye, *The Unembarrassed Muse: The Popular Arts in America* (New York, 1970); Herbert W. Richardson, *Nun, Witch, and Playmate: The Americanization of Sex* (New York, 1971); Marjorie Rosen, *Popcorn Venus: Women, Movies and the American Dream* (New York, 1973); William Scoresby, *American Factories and Their Female Operatives . . .* (1845) (New York, reprint, 1968); Robert W. Smuts, *Women and Work in America* (New York, 1971); Barbara Welter, "The Cult of True Womanhood, 1820–1860," *American Quarterly,* XVIII (1966), 151–74, *The Woman Question in American History* (Hinsdale, Ill., 1973); Michael Wood, *America in the Movies: Or, "Santa Maria, It Had Slipped My Mind"* (New York, 1975).

III E PLURIBUS UNUM

1 Real Community

RURAL COMMUNITY. Lewis Atherton, *Main Street on the Middle Border* (Bloomington, Ind., 1954); John Baskin, *New Burlington: The Life and Death of an American Village* (New York, 1976); Albert Blumenthal, *Small-Town Stuff* (Chicago, 1932); William Jennings Bryan, *The First Battle* (Chicago, 1896); La Wanda F. Cox, "The American Agricultural Wage Earner, 1865–1900: The Emergence of a Modern Labor Problem" *Agricultural History,* XXII (1948), 95–114; Kenneth S. Davis, "The Sage of Emporia," *American Heritage* (October/November 1979), 81 ff.; Joan Didion, *Slouching Towards Bethlehem* (New York, 1968); Don Harrison Doyle, *The Social Order of a Frontier Community: Jacksonville, Illinois, 1825–70* (Urbana, 1978); Gilbert C. Fite, "Daydreams and Nightmares: The Late Nineteenth-Century Agricultural Frontiers," *Agricultural History,* XL (1966), 285–93; Hamlin Garland, *A Son of the Middle Border,* Henry M. Christman, ed. (New York, 1962); Ray Ginger, *The Age of Excess: The United States from 1877 to 1914* (New York, 2nd edn., 1975); Margaret J. Hagood, *Mothers of the South: Portraiture of the White Tenant Farm Woman* (Chapel Hill, N.C., 1939); Richard Hofstadter, *The Age of Reform: From Bryan to F.D.R.* (New York, 1955), *Social Darwinism in American Thought* (Boston, rev. edn., 1955); *The Memoirs of Herbert Hoover: Years of Adventure, 1874–1920* (New York, 1951); Paul E. Johnson, *A Shopkeeper's Millennium: Society and Revivals in Rochester, New York, 1815–1837* (New York, 1978); Ellis R. Kirkpatrick, *The Farmer's Standard of Living* (New York, 1971); Richard Lyle Power, *Planting Corn Belt Culture: The Impress of the Upland Southerner and Yankee in the Old Northwest* (Indianapolis, 1953); Earl H. Rovit, "The American Concept of Home," *American Scholar,* XXIX (1960), 521–30; Theodore Saloutos, "The Agricultural Problem and Nineteenth-Century Industrialism," *Agricultural History,* XXII (1948), 156–74; W. J. Spillman, "Farming as an Occupation for City-Bred Men," *Yearbook of the United States Department of Agriculture, 1909* (Washington, 1910); Lincoln Steffens, *The Autobiography of Lincoln Steffens* (New York, 1931); *Report of the Country Life Commission,* U.S. Senate, 60 Cong. 2 Sess., Docu. 705 (Washington, 1909).

RELIGIOUS COMMUNITY. Leonard J. Arrington, Feramorz Y. Fox, Dean L. May, *Building the City of God: Community and Cooperation Among the Mormons* (Salt Lake City, 1976); Leonard J. Arrington and Davis Bitton, *The Mormon Experience: A History of the Latter-Day Saints* (New York, 1979); Katherine Burton, *Paradise Planters: The Story of Brook Farm* (New York, 1939); Maren L. Carden, *Oneida: Utopian Community to Modern Corporation* (Baltimore, 1969); Edith R. Curtis, *A Season in Utopia: The Story of Brook Farm* (New York, 1961); David Brion Davis, "Some Themes of Counter-Subversion: An Analysis of Anti-Masonic, Anti-Catholic, and Anti-Mormon Literature," *Mississippi Valley Historical Review,* XLVII (1960), 205–24; Mark Holloway, *Heavens on Earth: Utopian Communities in America, 1680–1880* (New York, 1951); George B. Lockwood, *The New Harmony Movement* (New York, 1905); Nelson Lowry, *The Mormon Village: A Pattern and Technique of Land Settlement* (Salt Lake City, 1952); William J.

McNiff, *Heaven on Earth: A Planned Mormon Society* (Philadelphia, 1972); Wallace Stegner, *Mormon Country* (New York, 1942); William E. Wilson, *The Angel and the Serpent: The Story of New Harmony* (Bloomington, Ind., 1964).

2 *The Fragmented Image*

MODERN CITIES. H. Wentworth Eldredge, ed., *Taming Megalopolis,* Vol. I, *What Is and What Could Be* (New York, 1967); Lewis Mumford, *The City in History: Its Origins, Its Transformations, and Its Prospects* (New York, 1961), *The Culture of Cities* (New York, 1938).

BECOMING URBAN. E. Digby Baltzell, ed., *The Search for Community in Modern America* (New York, 1968); Harvey Cox, *The Secular City: Secularization and Urbanization in Theological Perspective* (New York, rev. edn., 1966); Don S. Kirschner, *City and Country: Rural Responses to Urbanization in the 1920's* (Westport, Conn., 1970); Richard R. Lingeman, "Home Town, U.S.A.: In the Footsteps of Four Novelists," *The New York Times,* January 29, 1978; Henry L. Mencken, *The American Credo, a Contribution Toward the Interpretation of the National Mind,* with George Jean Nathan (New York, 1920); James M. Ratcliffe, ed., *The Good Samaritan and the Law* (Garden City, N.Y., 1966); Abraham M. Rosenthal, *Thirty-eight Witnesses* (New York, 1964); Maurice R. Stein, Arthur J. Vidich, and David M. White, eds., *Identity and Anxiety: Survival of the Person in Mass Society* (New York, 1960); Roger Starr, *The Urban Choices: The City and Its Critics* (Baltimore, 1967); Melvin M. Webber, "Order in Diversity: Community without Propinquity," *Cities and Space: The Future Use of Urban Land,* Lowdon Wingo, Jr., ed. (Baltimore, 1963).

SUBURBS AND METROPOLISES. Wendell Bell and Marion D. Boat, "Urban Neighborhoods and Informal Social Relations," *American Journal of Sociology,* LXII (1957), 391–98; William M. Dobriner, *Class in Suburbia* (Englewood Cliffs, N.J., 1963), *The Suburban Community* (New York, 1958); Daniel J. Elazar, *Cities of the Prairie: The Metropolitan Frontier and American Politics* (New York, 1970); Sylvia Fleis Fava, "Suburbanism as a Way of Life," *American Sociological Review,* XXI (1956), 34–37; Peter Schrag, *The End of the American Future* (New York, 1973); John R. Seely, R. Alexander Sim, and E. W. Loosley, *Crestwood Heights: The Culture of Suburbia* (New York, 1956); Sam Bass Warner, Jr., *Streetcar Suburbs: The Process of Growth in Boston, 1870–1900* (New York, 1969).

MELTING POT. Robert Coles and Jon Erikson, *The Middle Americans: Proud and Uncertain* (Boston, 1971); Stanley Feldstein and Lawrence Costello, eds., *The Ordeal of Assimilation: A Documentary History of the White Working Class* (Garden City, N.Y., 1974); Nathan Glazer and Daniel Patrick Moynihan, *Beyond the Melting Pot: The Negroes, Puerto Ricans, Jews, Italians, and Irish of New York City* (Cambridge, Mass., 2nd edn., 1970); Louis H. Masotti and Jeffrey K. Hadden, ed., *The Urbanization of the Suburbs,* Vol. 7, *Urban Affairs Annual Review* (Beverly

Hills, Calif., 1973); Henry J. Schmandt and Warner Bloomberg, Jr., eds., *The Quality of Urban Life,* Vol. 3, *Urban Affairs Annual Review* (Beverly Hills, Calif., 1969).

FRAGMENTS. Erik Barnouw, *Tube of Plenty: The Evolution of American Television* (New York, 1975); John Dollard, *Caste and Class in a Southern Town* (Garden City, N.Y., 3rd edn., 1957); William Y. Elliott, ed., *Television's Impact on American Culture* (East Lansing, Mich., 1956); Herbert J. Gans, *The Urban Villagers: Group and Class in the Life of Italian Americans* (New York, 1962); Jane Jacobs, *The Death and Life of Great American Cities* (New York, 1961); Kenneth Keniston, *The Uncommitted: Alienated Youth in American Society* (New York, 1965); Max Lerner, "The Negro American and His City: Person in Place in Culture," *Daedalus* (1968), 1390–1408; Ithiel de Sola Pool, ed., *The Social Impact of the Telephone* (Cambridge, Mass., 1977); Robert Presthus, *The Organization Society: An Analysis and a Theory* (New York, 1962); Maurice R. Stein, *The Eclipse of Community* (Princeton, 1960); Robert Stein, *Media Power: Who Is Shaping Your Picture of the World?* (Boston, 1972); Gerald D. Suttles, *The Social Construction of Communities* (Chicago, 1972); Arthur J. Vidich and Joseph Bensman, *Small Town in Mass Society: Class, Power and Religion in a Rural Community* (Princeton, 1958); William H. Whyte, Jr., *The Organization Man* (New York, 1956); Raymond Williams, *Television: Technology and Cultural Form* (New York, 1975); Eli Zaretsky, *Capitalism, the Family, and Personal Life* (New York, 1976).

ONE CITY. Michael P. Banton, *The Policeman in the Community* (New York, 1964); Alexander B. Callow, Jr., ed., *The City Boss in America: An Interpretive Reader* (New York, 1976); David H. Gilston and Lawrence Podell, *The Practical Patrolman* (Springfield, Ill., 1970); H. F. Gosnell, *Machine Politics: Chicago Model* (Chicago, 1937); Scott Greer, *Governing the Metropolis* (New York, 1962); Harlan Hahn, ed., *Police in Urban Society* (Beverly Hills, Calif., 1971); Floyd Hunter, *Community Power Structure: A Study of Decision Makers* (Chapel Hill, N.C., 1953); Peter A. Lupsha, "The Politics of Urban Change," *Current History* (December 1968); Blake McKelvey, *The Emergence of Metropolitan America, 1915–1966* (New Brunswick, N.J., 1968); William K. Muir, *Police: Steetcorner Politicians* (Chicago, 1977); Edwin O'Connor, *The Last Hurrah* (Boston, 1956); Jonathan Rubinstein, *City Police* (New York, 1973); Mike Royko, *Boss: Richard J. Daley of Chicago* (New York, 1971); Bruce M. Stave, *The New Deal and the Last Hurrah: Pittsburgh Machine Politics* (Pittsburgh, Pa., 1970), *Urban Bosses, Machines, and Progressive Reformers* (Lexington, Mass., 1972); James Q. Wilson, *Varieties of Police Behavior: The Management of Law and Order in Eight Communities* (Cambridge, Mass., 1968); Tom Wolfe, *Radical Chic and Mau-Mauing the Flak Catchers* (New York, 1970).

3 People, Endless, Streaming

Jane Addams, *The Spirit of Youth and the City Streets* (New York, 1909); G. W. Curtis, "Editor's Easy Chair," *Harper's New Monthly Magazine,* XXIV (February

1862), 409; Charles N. Glaab and A. Theodore Brown, *A History of Urban America* (New York, 1967); *Reports of the United States Industrial Commission on Immigration and on Education* (Washington, 1909), XV; Jacob Riis, *How the Other Half Lives: Studies Among the Tenements of New York* (New York, 1890); Fred A. Shannon, "A Post Mortem on the Labor-Safety-Valve Theory," *Agricultural History,* XIX (1954), 31–37; Stephan Thernstrom, *Poverty and Progress: Social Mobility in a Nineteenth Century City* (Cambridge, Mass., 1964), "Urbanization, Migration, and Social Mobility in Late Nineteenth Century America," *Towards a New Past: Dissenting Essays in American History,* Barton J. Bernstein, ed. (New York, 1968); Urban Land Institute, *Growth and Change in Rural America* (Washington, 1979).

4 *The Rituals of Community*

Robert H. Boyle, *Sport: Mirror of American Life* (Boston, 1963); Paul Gardner, *Nice Guys Finish Last: Sport and American Life* (New York, 1975); Allen Guttmann, *From Ritual to Record: The Nature of Modern Sports* (New York, 1978), "Who's on First? or, Books on the History of American Sports," *Journal of American History,* LXVI (1979), 348–54; David Halberstam, "Baseball and the National Mythology," *Harper's* (September 1970); Neil D. Isaacs, *Jock Culture U.S.A.* (New York, 1978); Jerry Isenberg, *How Many Miles to Camelot? The All-American Sport Myth* (New York, 1972); Roger Kahn, *The Boys of Summer* (New York, 1973); Howard L. Nixon II, *Sport and Social Organization* (Indianapolis, 1976); Michael Novak, *The Joy of Sports: End Zones, Bases, Baskets, Balls, and the Consecration of the American Spirit* (New York, 1976); David Riesman and Reuel Denney, "Football in America: A Study in Culture Diffusion," *American Quarterly* (1951), 309–19; Harold Seymour, *Baseball: The Early Years* (New York, 1960); Leverett T. Smith, *The American Dream and the National Game* (Bowling Green, Ohio, 1975); David Q. Voigt, *American Baseball,* Vol. I, *From Gentlemen's Sport to the Commissioner System* (Norman, Okla., 1966), *America Through Baseball* (Chicago, 1976).

5 *Classless Equality and Urban Democracy*

Robert S. Allen, ed., *Our Fair City* (New York, 1947); Edward C. Banfield and James Q. Wilson, *City Politics* (Cambridge, Mass., 1963); Robert L. Bish and Vincent Ostrom, *Understanding Urban Government: Metropolitan Reform Reconsidered* (Washington, 1973); Blaine A. Brownell and Warren E. Stickle, eds., *Bosses and Reformers: Urban Politics in America, 1880–1920* (Boston, 1973); Lyle W. Dorsett, *Franklin D. Roosevelt and the City Bosses* (Port Washington, N.Y., 1977); John P. East, *Council-Manager Government: The Political Thought of Its Founder Richard S. Childs* (Chapel Hill, N.C., 1965); Norman I. and Susan S. Fainstein, *Urban Political Movements: The Search for Power by Minority Groups in American Cities* (Englewood Cliffs, N.J., 1974); John J. Hamilton *The Dethronement of the City Boss* (New York, 1910); Samuel P. Hays, "The Politics of Reform in Municipal Government in the Progressive Era," *Pacific Northwest Quarterly,* LV (1964), 157–69, "The Social Analysis of American Political History, 1880–1920," *Political Science Quarterly,* LXXX (1965), 373–94; Walter Lippmann, *A Preface to Politics* (Ann Arbor, Mich., 1962); Blake McKelvey, *The Urbanization of America, 1860–1915* (New Brunswick, N.J., 1963); Samuel P. Orth, *The Boss and the Machine: A Chronicle of the Politicians and Party Organization* (New Haven, 1921); Clifford W. Patton, *The Battle for Municipal Reform: Mobilization and Attack, 1875–1900* (College Park, Md., 1969); Lincoln Steffens, *The Shame of the Cities* (New York, 1957); Frank M. Stewart, *A Half Century of Municipal Reform: The History of the National Municipal League* (Berkeley, 1950); Harold A. Stone, Don K. Price, and Kathryn H. Stone, *City Manager Government in the United States: A Review after Twenty-five Years* (Chicago, 1940); M. R. Werner, *Tammany Hall* (Garden City, N.Y., 1928); Douglas Yates, *The Ungovernable City: The Politics of Urban Problems and Policy Making* (Cambridge, Mass., 1977); Harold Zink, *City Bosses in the United States: A Study of Twenty Municipal Bosses* (New York, 1968).

IV THE POWER AND THE GLORY

1 Power and Power Failure

Michael Amrine, *Great Decision* (New York, 1959); Wilson Clark, *Energy for Survival: The Alternative to Extinction* (Garden City, N.Y., 1975); Judith Coburn, "How Safe Is Rancho Seco?" *New West* (November 19, 1979); Barry Commoner, *The Poverty of Power: Energy and the Economic Crisis* (New York, 1976); *Congressional Quarterly, Energy Crisis in America* (Washington, 1973); G. William Domhoff, *The Powers That Be: Processes of Ruling Class Domination in America* (New York, 1978); Paul R. and Anne H. Ehrlich, *The End of Affluence: A Blueprint for Your Future* (New York, 1974); Suzanne I. Keller, *Beyond the Ruling Class: Strategic Elites in Modern Society* (New York, 1963); Flora Lewis, *One of Our H-Bombs Is Missing* (New York, 1967); Enrique Hank Lopez, *The Harvard Mystique: The Power Syndrome That Affects Our Lives from Sesame Street to the White House* (New York, 1979); Los Alamos Scientific Laboratory Public Relations Office, *Los Alamos: Beginning of an Era 1943–1945* (Southwest Parks, Ariz., n.d.); Bruce Miroff, *Pragmatic Illusions: The Presidential Politics of John F. Kennedy* (New York, 1976); Gifford Pinchot, *The Power Monopoly: Its Make-up and Its Menace* (Milford, Pa., 1928); Lawrence Rocks and Richard P. Runyon, *The Energy Crisis* (New York, 1972); William M. White, *Power, Production, Prosperity* (New York, 1946).

2 Science and Progress

John R. Betts, "Darwinism, Evolution, and American Catholic Thought," *Catholic Historical Review,* XLIV (1959), 161–85; Paul F. Boller, Jr., *American Thought in Transition: The Impact of Evolutionary Naturalism, 1865–1900* (Chicago, 1969); Paul A. Carter, *The Spiritual Crisis of the Gilded Age* (De Kalb, Ill., 1971); William A. Clebsch, *American Religious Thought: A History* (Chicago, 1973); Hamilton Cravens, *The Triumph of Evolution: American Scientists and the Heredity-Environment Controversy, 1900–1941* (Philadelphia, 1978); Theodosius Dobzhansky, "Mendelism, Darwinism, and Evolutionism," *Proceedings of the American Philosophical Society,* CIX (1965), 205–15; John C. Greene, *Darwin and the Modern World View* (New York, 1963), *The Death of Adam: Evolution and Its Impact on Western Thought* (Ames, Ia., 1959); Richard Hofstadter, *Social Darwinism in American Thought* (Boston, rev. edn., 1955); Oliver Wendell Holmes, Jr., *The Common Law* (Boston, 1881); Winthrop S. Hudson, *Religion in America: An Historical Account of the Development of American Religious Life* (New York, 2nd edn., 1973); A. G. Keller and M. R. Davie, eds., *Essays of William Graham Sumner* (Hamden, Conn., 1934); Thomas R. Malthus, *An Essay on the Principle of Population . . .* (George Town, First American, from Third London Edition, 1809); Perry Miller, *The Life of the Mind in America: From the Revolution to the Civil War* (New York, 1965); Roy F. Nichols, *Religion and American Democracy* (Baton Rouge, 1959); Carl Sagan, *Broca's Brain: Reflections on the Romance of Science* (New York, 1979); Arthur M. Schlesinger, "A Critical Period in American Religion, 1875–1900," *Proceedings of the Massachusetts Historical Society,* XXIV (1933), 523–48; Elwyn A. Smith, *Religious Liberty in the United States: The Development of Church-State Thought Since the Revolutionary Era* (Philadelphia, 1972); Edmund W. Sinnott, *Meetinghouse and Church in Early New England* (New York, 1963); Herbert Spencer, *The Principles of Sociology,* 3 vols. (New York, 1880–97); Cushing Strout, ed., *Intellectual History in America: From Darwin to Niebuhr* (New York, 1968); Stephen Toulmin and Jane Goodfield, *The Discovery of Time* (New York, 1965); R. J. Wilson, ed., *Darwinism and the American Intellectual: A Book of Readings* (Homewood, Ill., 1967); Morton White, *Social Thought in America: The Revolt Against Formalism* (Boston, 1957); Gertrude Himmelfarb, *Darwin and the Darwinian Revolution* (New York, 1968).

3 We Are All Progressives

Jane Addams, *Twenty Years at Hull-House* (New York, 1960); David M. Chalmers, *The Social and Political Ideas of the Muckrakers* (New York, 1964); Lawrence A. Cremin, *The Transformation of the School: Progressivism in American Education, 1876–1957* (New York, 1962); Herbert Croly, *The Promise of American Life* (Indianapolis, 1965); Louis Filler, *Appointment at Armageddon: Muckraking and Progressivism in the American Tradition* (Westport, Conn., 1976), *Crusaders for American Liberalism* (Yellow Springs, Ohio, new edn., 1961); Frank Freidel, *Franklin D. Roosevelt: The Apprenticeship* (Boston, 1952); Eric Goldman *Rendezvous with Destiny: A History of Modern American Reform* (New York, 1956); Samuel P. Hays, *The Response to Industrialism, 1885–1914* (Chicago, 1957); John W. Jeffries, "The 'Quest for National Purpose' of 1960," *American Quarterly,* XXX (1978), 451 ff.; Gabriel Kolko, *The Triumph of Conservatism: A Reinterpretation of American History, 1900–1916* (Glencoe, Ill., 1963); Robert M. La Follette, *La Follette's Autobiography: A Personal Narrative of Political Experiences* (Madison,

Wis., 1960); Christopher Lasch, *The Agony of the American Left* (New York, 1969), *The New Radicalism in America, 1889–1963: The Intellectual As a Social Type* (New York, 1965); Daniel Levine, *Varieties of Reform Thought* (Madison, Wis., 1964); Arthur S. Link, *Wilson: Campaigns for Progressivism and Peace, 1916–1917* (Princeton, 1965); Henry F. May, *The End of American Innocence: A Study of the First Years of Our Own Time, 1912–1917* (New York, 1959); George E. Mowry, *The Era of Theodore Roosevelt and the Birth of Modern America, 1900–1912* (New York, 1958); George W. Norris, *Fighting Liberal: The Autobiography of George W. Norris* (New York, 1961); William Preston, Jr., *Aliens and Dissenters: Federal Suppression of Radicals, 1903–1933* (Cambridge, Mass., 1963); *Goals for Americans,* Report of the Presidential Commission on National Goals (1960); David A. Shannon, *The Socialist Party of America: A History* (New York, 1955); Thorstein Veblen, *The Theory of the Leisure Class* (New York, 1953); Dixon Wecter, *The Saga of American Society: A Record of Social Aspiration, 1607–1937* (New York, 1937); James Weinstein, *The Decline of Socialism in America, 1912–1925* (New York, 1967); Burton K. Wheeler, with Paul F. Healy, *Yankee from the West* (Garden City, N.Y., 1962); Robert H. Wiebe, *The Search for Order, 1877–1920* (New York, 1967); Woodrow Wilson, *Division and Reunion, 1829–1909,* Edwar) S. Corwin, ed. (New York, rev. edn., 1912).

4 Nothing to Fear

PRESIDENCY. James M. Burns, *The Deadlock of Democracy: Four-Party Politics in America* (Englewood Cliffs, N.J., 1963), *Presidential Government: The Crucible of Leadership* (Boston, 1966); E. S. Corwin, *The President: Office and Power* (New York, 1957); David Donald, *Lincoln Reconsidered* (New York, 1961); John K. Galbraith, *American Capitalism: The Concept of Countervailing Power* (Cambridge, Mass., 1952); Peter Karsten, *Patriot-Heroes in England and America: Political Symbolism and Changing Values over Three Centuries* (Madison, Wis., 1978); Harold J. Laski, *The American Presidency: An Interpretation* (New York, 1940); Max Lerner, "The Broker State," *Ideas for the Ice Age* (New York, 1941); Richard E. Neustadt, *Presidential Power* (New York, 1960); Clinton Rossiter, *The American Presidency* (New York, 1956); Arthur M. Schlesinger, Jr., *The Imperial Presidency* (New York, 1974); James Weinstein, *The Corporate Ideal in the Liberal State: 1900–1918* (Boston, 1968).

COMMANDER-IN-CHIEF. Raoul Berger, *Executive Privilege: A Constitutional Myth* (Cambridge, Mass., 1974); Thomas Eagleton, *War and Presidential Power: A Chronicle of Congressional Surrender* (New York, 1974); David Healy, "McKinley as Commander-in-Chief," *Threshold to American Internationalism: Essays on the Foreign Policies of William McKinley,* Paolo E. Coletta, ed. (New York, 1970); Margaret Leech, *In the Days of McKinley* (New York, 1959); Gerald F. Linderman, *The Mirror of War: American Society and the Spanish-American War* (Ann Arbor, 1974); Seward W. Livermore, *Politics Is Adjourned: Woodrow Wilson and the War Congress, 1916–1918* (Middletown, Conn., 1966); Ernest R. May, *Imperial*

Democracy: The Emergence of America As a Great Power (New York, 1961), *The Ultimate Decision: The President as Commander-in-Chief* (New York, 1960), *The World War and American Isolation, 1914–1917* (Cambridge, Mass., 1963); Walter Millis, *The Road to War: America, 1914–1917* (Boston, 1935); H. Wayne Morgan, *America's Road to Empire: The War with Spain and Overseas Expansion* (New York, 1965); Charles C. Tansill, *America Goes to War* (Boston, 1938); Rexford G. Tugwell, *The Enlargement of the Presidency* (Garden City, N.Y., 1960).

MEDIA. Charles H. Brown, *The Correspondents' War: Journalists in the Spanish-American War* (New York, 1967); Hadley Cantrill and Gordon W. Allport, *The Psychology of Radio* (New York, 1935); William H. Harbaugh, *The Life and Times of Theodore Roosevelt* (New York, rev. edn., 1963); Robert MacNeil, *The People Machine: The Influence of Television on American Politics* (New York, 1968); Frank Luther Mott, *American Journalism, A History: 1690–1960* (New York, 1962); J. E. Pollard, *The Presidents and the Press* (New York, 1947); Francis Russell, *The Shadow of Blooming Grove: Warren G. Harding in His Times* (New York, 1968); Marcus M. Wilkerson, *Public Opinion and the Spanish-American War: A Study in War Propaganda* (New York, 1932).

CONGRESS. Blair Bolles, *Tyrant from Illinois: Uncle Joe Cannon's Experiment with Personal Power* (New York, 1951); Charles G. Dawes, *The First Year of the Budget of the United States* (New York, 1923); William R. Gwinn, *Uncle Joe Cannon, Archfoe of Insurgency: A History of the Rise and Fall of Cannonism* (New York, 1957); Kenneth W. Hechler, *Insurgency: Personalities and Politics of the Taft Era* (New York, 1940); V. O. Key, Jr., *Politics, Parties, and Pressure Groups* (New York, 3rd edn, 1956); Richard Lowitt, *George W. Norris: The Making of a Progressive, 1861–1912* (Syracuse, N.Y., 1963); Fritz M. Marx, "The Bureau of the Budget: Its Evolution and Present Role," *American Political Science Review*, XXXIX (1945), 658–84; Robert K. Murray, *The Harding Era: Warren G. Harding and His Administration* (Minneapolis, 1969); Russell B. Nye, *Midwestern Progressive Politics: A Historical Study of Its Origins and Development, 1870–1958* (East Lansing, Mich., 1959); Don K. Price, "General Dawes and Executive Staff Work," *Public Administration Review*, IX (1951), 167–72; Woodrow Wilson, "Democracy and Efficiency," *The Atlantic Monthly* (March 1901), 289–99.

FOREIGN POLICY. Selig Adler, *The Isolationist Impulse: Its Twentieth Century Reaction* (New York, 1957), *Uncertain Giant: 1921–1941: American Foreign Policy Between the Wars* (New York, 1965); Thomas A. Bailey, *Woodrow Wilson and the Great Betrayal* (Chicago, 1963); Raoul Berger, "The Presidential Monopoly of Foreign Relations," *Michigan Law Review* (November 1972), 35 ff.; Paul Birdsall, *Versailles Twenty Years Later* (New York, 1941); Edwin Borchard, "Shall the Executive Agreement Replace the Treaty?" *Yale Law Journal* (September 1944), 668 ff.; *Congressional Record*, 66 Cong. 1 Sess. (November 19, 1919), 8767–805; Manfred Jonas, *Isolationism in America, 1935–1941* (Ithaca, N.Y.,

1966); J. M. Keynes, *The Economic Consequences of the Peace* (New York, 1920); Lawrence Lafore, *The End of Glory: An Interpretation of the Origins of World War II* (Philadelphia, 1970); James O. Robertson, "The Progressives in National Republican Politics, 1916–1921," Unpubl. Ph.D. dissertation, Harvard University, 1964; Karl Schriftgeisser, *The Gentleman from Massachusetts: Henry Cabot Lodge* (Boston, 1944); Gene Smith, *When the Cheering Stopped: The Last Years of Woodrow Wilson* (New York, 1964); A. J. P. Taylor, *The Origins of the Second World War* (Greenwich, Conn., 1963); William Allen White, "The Dead Treaty," Emporia (Kansas) *Gazette,* March 20, 1920.

ROOSEVELT AND AFTER. David Burner, *The Politics of Provincialism: The Democratic Party in Transition, 1918-1932* (New York, 1968); James M. Burns, *Roosevelt: The Lion and the Fox* (New York, 1956); Carl N. Degler, "The Ordeal of Herbert Hoover," *Yale Review,* LII (1963), 563 ff.; Frank Freidel, *The New Deal and the American People* (Englewood Cliffs, N.J., 1964), *Franklin D. Roosevelt: The Ordeal* (Boston, 1954), *Franklin D. Roosevelt: The Triumph* (Boston, 1956); Leonard Kriegel, "Last Stop on the D Train: In the Land of the New Racists," *The American Scholar* (Spring 1970), 272–88; William E. Leuchtenburg, *Franklin D. Roosevelt and the New Deal, 1932-1940* (New York, 1963); Samuel Lubell, *The Future of American Politics* (Garden City, N.Y., 2nd edn., 1956); Eugene Lyons, *Herbert Hoover: A Biography* (Garden City, N.Y., 1964); August Meier and Elliott Rudwick, eds., *The Making of Black America: Essays in Negro Life and History,* Vol. II, *The Black Community in Modern America* (New York, 1969); Raymond Moley, *After Seven Years* (New York, 1939); Albert U. Romasco, *The Poverty of Abundance: Hoover, the Nation, the Depression* (New York, 1965); Arthur M. Schlesinger, Jr., *The Coming of the New Deal* (Boston, 1958), *The Politics of Upheaval* (Boston, 1960); Chuck Stone, *Black Political Power in America* (Indianapolis, 1968); John Tipple, *Crisis of the American Dream: A History of American Social Thought, 1920-1940* (New York, 1968); Joan Hoff Wilson, *Herbert Hoover: Forgotten Progressive* (Boston, 1975); James Q. Wilson, *Negro Politics: The Search for Leadership* (Glencoe, Ill., 1960).

5 Marching As to War

WORLD WAR I AND BEFORE. Howard K. Beale, *Theodore Roosevelt and the Rise of America to World Power* (Baltimore, 1956); Robert L. Beisner, *Twelve Against Empire: The Anti-Imperialists, 1898-1900* (New York, 1968); Benedict Crowell and Robert F. Wilson, *How America Went to War: An Account from Official Sources of the Nation's War Activities, 1917-1920,* 6 vols. (New Haven, 1921); Robert D. Cuff, *The War Industries Board: Business-Government Relations during World War I* (Baltimore, 1973); Foster Rhea Dulles, *The Imperial Years* (New York, 1966); Edward R. Ellis, *Echoes of Distant Thunder: Life in the United States, 1914-1918* (New York, 1975); Peter G. Filene, *Americans and the Soviet Experiment, 1917-1933* (Cambridge, Mass., 1967); Frank Freidel, *The Splendid Little War* (Boston, 1958); John Higham, *Strangers in the Land: Patterns of American Nativism, 1860-1925* (New York, 1973); Herbert Hoover, *The Ordeal of Woodrow*

Wilson (New York, 1958); William James, "The Moral Equivalent of War," *International Conciliation,* No. 27 (February 1910); Donald Johnson, *The Challenge to American Freedoms: World War I and the Rise of the American Civil Liberties Union* (Lexington, Ky., 1962); Harold D. Laswell, *Propaganda Technique in the World War* (New York, 1938); Meno Lovenstein, *American Opinion of Soviet Russia* (Washington, 1941); James R. Mock and Cedric Larson, *Words That Won the War: The Story of the Committee on Public Information, 1917-1919* (Princeton, 1939); H. C. Peterson and Gilbert C. Fite, *Opponents of War, 1917-1918* (Madison, Wis., 1957); Julius W. Pratt, *The Expansionists of 1898: The Acquisition of Hawaii and the Spanish Islands* (Baltimore, 1951); Harry N. Scheiber, *The Wilson Administration and Civil Liberties, 1917-1921* (Ithaca, N.Y., 1960); John M. Thompson, *Russia, Bolshevism, and the Versailles Peace* (Princeton, 1966); David F. Trask, ed., *World War I at Home: Readings on American Life, 1914-1920* (New York, 1970); William A. Williams, *The Roots of Modern American Empire: A Study of the Growth and Shaping of Social Consciousness in a Marketplace Society* (New York, 1969); Carl Wittke, *German-Americans and the World War* (Columbus, Ohio, 1936).

MEMORIES OF WAR. Roscoe Baker, *The American Legion and American Foreign Policy* (New York, 1954); Charles A. Beard, *American Foreign Policy in the Making, 1932-1940: A Study in Responsibilities* (New Haven, 1946); John M. Clark, *The Costs of the World War to the American People* (New Haven, 1931); Wayne Cole, *Senator Gerald P. Nye and American Foreign Relations* (Minneapolis, 1962); Stanley Cooperman, *World War I and the American Novel* (Baltimore, 1967); Dorothy Culp, *The American Legion: A Study in Pressure Politics* (Chicago, 1942); Roger Daniels, *The Bonus March: An Episode of the Great Depression* (Westport, Conn., 1971); Helmuth C. Englebrecht and Frank C. Hanighen, *Merchants of Death: A Study of the International Armaments Industry* (New York, 1934); D. F. Fleming, *The United States and the League of Nations, 1918-1920* (New York, 1932); Charles Hirschfeld, "The Transformation of American Life," in *World War I: A Turning Point in Modern History,* Jack J. Roth, ed. (New York, 1967); E. Jay Howenstein, Jr., *The Economics of Demobilization* (Washington, 1944); Hugh Johnson, *The Blue Eagle—From Egg to Earth* (Garden City, N.Y., 1935); Charles Johnson, "The Army, the Negro, and the Civilian Conservation Corps; 1933–1942," *Military Affairs,* XXXVI (1972), 82–88; Walter Johnson, *The Battle Against Isolation* (Chicago, 1944); Richard S. Jones, *A History of the American Legion* (Indianapolis, 1946); Paul A. C. Koistinen, "The 'Industrial-Military Complex' in Historical Perspective: The Inter-War Years," *Journal of American History,* LVI (1970), 819–39; William L. Langer and Sorell E. Gleason, *The Challenge to Isolation, 1937-1940* (New York, 1952), *The Undeclared War, 1940-1941* (New York, 1952); Joseph P. Lash, *The Campus Strikes Against War* (New York, 1935); Donald J. Lisio, *The President and Protest: Hoover, Conspiracy, and the Bonus Riot* (Columbia, Mo., 1974); Arno J. Mayer, *Politics and Diplomacy of Peacemaking: Containment and Counterrevolution at Versailles, 1918-1919* (New York, 1967); David Mervin, "Henry Cabot Lodge and the League of Nations," *Journal of American Studies,* IV (1971), 201–14; Rodney G. Minott, *Peerless Patri-*

ots: Organized Veterans and the Spirit of Americanism (Washington, 1962); Robert K. Murray, *Red Scare: A Study of National Hysteria, 1919-1920* (Minneapolis, 1955); Gerald D. Nash, "Experiments in Industrial Mobilization: WIB and NRA," *Mid-America,* XLV (1963), 157–74; Burl Noggle, *Into the Twenties: The United States from Armistice to Normalcy* (Urbana, Ill., 1974); Frederic L. Paxson, "The Great Demobilization," *American Historical Review,* XLIV (1939), 237–51; David R. B. Ross, *Preparing for Ulysses: Politics and Veterans During World War II* (New York, 1969); John Salmond, *The Civilian Conservation Corps, 1933-1942* (Durham, N.C., 1967); George Soule, *Prosperity Decade: From War to Depression, 1917-1929* (New York, 1947); Ralph Stone, *The Irreconcilables: The Fight Against the League of Nations* (Lexington, Ky., 1970); Stephen R. Ward, ed., *The War Generation: Veterans of the First World War* (Port Washington, N.Y., 1975); W. Lloyd Warner, *American Life: Dream and Reality* (Chicago, rev. edn., 1962); Dixon Wecter, *When Johnny Comes Marching Home* (Westport, Conn., 1970); John R. M. Wilson, "The Quaker and the Sword: Herbert Hoover's Relations with the Military," *Military Affairs,* XXXVIII (April 1974), 41–47; John E. Wiltz, *In Search of Peace: The Senate Munitions Inquiry, 1934-1936* (Baton Rouge, 1963); Lawrence S. Wittner, *Rebels Against War: The American Peace Movement, 1941-1960* (New York, 1969).

THE GOOD WAR. John Morton Blum, *V Was for Victory: Politics and American Culture During World War II* (New York, 1976); Jerome S. Bruner, *Mandate from the People* (New York, 1944); Bruce Catton, *The Warlords of Washington* (New York, 1948); Robert A. Divine, *Second Chance: The Triumph of Internationalism in America During World War II* (New York, 1967); John Hersey, *Hiroshima* (New York, 1946); Eliot Janeway, *The Struggle for Survival: A Chronicle of Economic Mobilization in World War II* (New Haven, 1951); I. L. Kandel, *The Impact of the War upon American Education* (Chapel Hill, N.C., 1948); Donald W. Nelson, *Arsenal of Democracy: The Story of American War Production* (New York, 1946); Gaddis Smith, *American Diplomacy During the Second World War* (New York, 1965).

SINCE THE GOOD WAR. Gar Alperovitz, *Atomic Diplomacy: Hiroshima and Potsdam* (New York, 1965); Richard J. Barnet, *Roots of War* (Baltimore, 1973); Barton J. Bernstein, "America in War and Peace: The Test of Liberalism" *Towards a New Past: Dissenting Essays in American History* (New York, 1968); Bernard Brodie, ed., *The Absolute Weapon: Atomic Power and World Order* (New York, 1946); Demetrios Caraley, *The Politics of Military Unification: A Study of Conflict and the Policy Process* (New York, 1966); J. Lawton Collins, *War in Peacetime: The History and Lessons of Korea* (Boston, 1969); *Congressional Quarterly, China and United States Far East Policy, 1945-1967* (Washington, 1967); Robert H. Connery, "Unification of the Armed Services—the First Year," *American Political Science Review,* XLIII (1949), 38–52; James E. Dougherty, *The Politics of the Atlantic Alliance* (New York, 1964); John Foster Dulles, *War or Peace?* (New York, 1950); Dwight D. Eisenhower, *Mandate for Change, 1953-1956* (New York, 1963), *Waging Peace, 1956-1961* (New York, 1965); Arthur A. Ekirch, Jr.,

The Civilian and the Military: A History of the American Antimilitarist Tradition (New York, 1956); Bernard Fall, *Hell in a Very Small Place: The Siege of Dien Bien Phu* (Philadelphia, 1967); Herbert Feis, *The Atomic Bomb and the End of World War II* (Princeton, 1966); T. K. Finletter, *Power and Policy: U.S. Foreign Policy and Military Power in the Hydrogen Age* (New York, 1954); John K. Gaddis, *The United States and the Origins of the Cold War, 1941–1947* (New York, 1972); Paul Y. Hammond, *Organizing for Defense: The American Military Establishment in the Twentieth Century* (Princeton, 1961); Robert J. Havighurst *et al., The American Veteran Back Home: A Study of Veteran Readjustment* (New York, 1951); Trumbull Higgins, *Korea and the Fall of MacArthur: A Précis in Limited War* (New York, 1960); Raul Hilburg, *The Destruction of the European Jews* (London, 1961); Samuel P. Huntington, *The Common Defense: Strategic Programs in National Politics* (New York, 1961); Herman Kahn, *On Thermonuclear War* (Princeton, 1960); George F. Kennan, *American Diplomacy, 1900–1950* (Chicago, 1951); William H. Kinter, *Forging a New Sword: A Study of the Department of Defense* (New York, 1958); Joyce and Gabriel Kolko, *The Limits of Power: The World and United States Foreign Policy, 1945–1954* (New York, 1972); Walter LaFeber, *America, Russia, and the Cold War* (New York, 1967); Seymour Melman, *Our Depleted Society* (New York, 1965); Robert E. Osgood, *Limited War: The Challenge to American Strategy* (Chicago, 1957), *NATO: The Entangling Alliance* (Chicago, 1962); Thomas G. Paterson, ed., *The Origins of the Cold War* (Lexington, Mass., 1970); Carroll W. Pursell, ed., *The Military-Industrial Complex* (New York, 1972); David Rees, *Korea: The Limited War* (New York, 1964); John W. Spanier, *The Truman-MacArthur Controversy and the Korean War* (Cambridge, Mass., 1969); Isidor F. Stone, *The Hidden History of the Korean War* (New York, 1969); Tsou Tang, *American Failure in China, 1941–1950* (Chicago, 1963); Raymond Vernon, *Sovereignty at Bay: The Multinational Spread of U.S. Enterprises* (New York, 1971); Leon Weaver, *The Civil Defense Debate: Differing Perceptions of a Persistent Issue in a National Security Policy* (East Lansing, Mich., 1967); Russell Weigley, *The American Way of War: A History of United States Military Strategy and Policy* (New York, 1973); Keith W. Olson, *The G.I. Bill, the Veterans, and the Colleges* (Lexington, Ky., 1974).

Index